CODICES BOETHIANI II

WARBURG INSTITUTE SURVEYS AND TEXTS

Edited by Charles Burnett, Jill Kraye and W. F. Ryan

XXVII

CODICES BOETHIANI

A CONSPECTUS OF MANUSCRIPTS OF THE WORKS OF BOETHIUS

II. AUSTRIA, BELGIUM, DENMARK, LUXEMBOURG, THE NETHERLANDS, SWEDEN, SWITZERLAND

EDITED BY
LESLEY SMITH
with the assistance of
Theodore Christchev, Richard Gameson, Anke Holdenried,
Fiona Robb, Teresa Webber and Joseph Ziegler

THE WARBURG INSTITUTE – NINO ARAGNO EDITORE

LONDON–TURIN 2001

ISBN 0 85481 121 4
ISSN 0266 1772

Designed by and computer set at the Warburg Institute
Printed by Henry Ling, The Dorset Press, Dorchester, Dorset

Contents

Acknowledgements

Once more it is a pleasure to recognize the generous assistance of many people. Gratitude is due to the librarians of each of the libraries whose collections are represented here. We owe special thanks to Dr Johannes Tomaschek (Admont), Dr Harold Waeber (Bern), Dr Joseph Leisibach (Fribourg), Fr Dr Gregor Lechner and Dr Michael Grünwald (Göttweig), Dr Frank Koren and Dr Sigrid Reinitzer (Graz), Fr Benedikt Baumgartner (Lambach), Dr Birgitte Lindholm (Lund), Dr Luc Deitz (Luxembourg), Dr Eva Irblich, Dr Katharina Hranitzky and Dr Andreas Fingernagel (ÖNB), Professor Peter Ochsenbein and Dr Karl Schmuki (St Gallen), Fr Benedikt Wagner (Seitenstetten), Dr Ragnhild Lundgren (Strängäs), Dr Marlis Stähli (Zürich), Dr Charlotte Ziegler (Zwettl). Advice and help were also given by Professor Dr Albert Derolez, Professor Jos Hermans, Dr Martin Kauffmann, Dr Anne Korteweg, Professor Henry Mayr-Harting, Professor Nigel Palmer, Professor Marina Passalacqua and Dr Martin Schøyen. Dr Jill Kraye and Professor Charles Burnett have given expert help with content as well as with publication. Our thanks go to them as well as to Professor Will Ryan of the Warburg Institute, and to the British Academy for support.

List of Plates

Abbreviations

1. BOETHIUS

Arith.	*De arithmetica*, ed. Friedlein, 1867.
Cat.	*Categories*, *AL*, i.1–2.
DCPhil.	*De consolatione philosophiae*, Loeb, 1973.
De Int.	*De interpretatione*, *AL*, ii.1.
Div.	*De divisione*, *PL*, 64:875–92.
Epitaph	*Epitaphs*, Teubner, 1871.
in Cat.	Commentary on *Categories*, *PL*, 64:159–294.
1 in Int.	First commentary on *De interpretatione*, Teubner, 1877.
2 in Int.	Second commentary on *De interpretatione*, Teubner, 1880.
1 in Isag.	First commentary on *Isagoge*, *CSEL*, 48.
2 in Isag.	Second commentary on *Isagoge*, *CSEL*, 48.
in Topica Cic.	Commentary on Cicero, *Topica*, *Ciceronis Opera*, ed. J. C. Orelli and J. G. Baiter, Zurich, 1833, V.i.269–388; reprinted in *PL*, 64:1039–174.
intr. Syll. Cat.	Introduction to the *Categorical syllogisms*, *PL*, 64:761–94.
Isag.	Porphyry, *Isagoge*, *AL*, i.6.
Mus.	*De musica*, Teubner, 1867.
Op. Sac.	*Opuscula sacra*, Loeb, 1973.
Post. Anal.	Aristotle, *Posterior analytics*, *AL*, iv.1–4; not Boethius.
Prior Anal.	Aristotle, *Prior analytics*, *AL*, iii.1–2.
Soph. Elench.	Aristotle, *De sophisticis elenchis*, *AL*, vi.1.
Syll. Cat.	*De syllogismis categoricis*, *PL*, 64:793–832.
Syll. Hyp.	*De syllogismis hypotheticis*, *PL*, 64:831–76.
Topica Aris.	Aristotle, *Topica*, *AL*, v.1.
Top. Diff.	*De differentiis topicis*, *PL*, 64:1173–1216, and Nikitas, pp. 1–92.
Vita	*Vita*, I–VIII.

2. SELECT BIBLIOGRAPHY

AL	*Aristoteles Latinus*, ed. G. Lacombe and L. Minio-Paluello, 3 vols, Rome, 1939; Cambridge, 1955; Bruges–Paris, 1961.
Alexandreis	*Walter of Châtillon, Alexandreis*, ed. M. L. Colker, Padua, 1978.
Anthologia Latina	*Anthologia Latina sive Poesis latinae supplementum*, ed. F. Buecheller and A. Riese, 3 vols, Leipzig, 1894–1926.
Avicenna	*Avicenna Latinus*, ed. S. van Riet and G. Verbeke, 9 vols, Louvain-la-Neuve, 1972–89.

Bergmann	R. Bergmann, *Verzeichnis der althochdeutschen und altsächsischen Glossenhandschriften*, Berlin/New York, 1973.
Bernhard	M. Bernhard, 'Glossen zur Arithmetik des Boethius', *Scire Litteras. Forschungen zum mittelalterlichen Geistesleben*, ed. S. Krämer and M. Bernhard, Munich, 1988, pp. 23–34.
Bernhard and Bower	M. Bernhard and C. M. Bower, *Glossa maior in institutionem musicam Boethii*, Munich, 3 vols, 1993–.
BHL	*Bibliotheca hagiographica latina antiquae et mediae aetatis*, Brussels, 1898–1901; Supplements 1911 and ed. H. Fros, 1986.
Bischoff, *M. S.*	B. Bischoff, *Mittelalterliche Studien*, 3 vols, Stuttgart, 1966–81.
Bishop, *English Caroline*	T. A. M. Bishop, *English Caroline Minuscule*, Oxford, 1971.
Bloomfield	M. W. Bloomfield *et al.*, *Incipits of Latin Works on the Virtues and Vices, 1100–1500 A.D. Including a Section of Incipits of Works on the* Pater Noster, The Medieval Academy of America, 88, Cambridge, Mass., 1979.
Bolton	D. K. Bolton, 'The Study of the *Consolation of Philosophy* in Anglo-Saxon England', *Archives d'histoire doctrinale et littéraire du moyen âge*, 44, 1977, pp. 33–78.
Bower	C. M. Bower, 'Boethius' *De institutione musica*: A Handlist of Manuscripts', *Scriptorium*, 42, 1988, pp. 205–51.
Bruckner	A. Bruckner, *Scriptoria Medii Aevi Helvetica*, 14 vols, Geneva, 1935–78.
Bubnov	N. Bubnov, *Gerberti postea Silvestri II papae opera mathematica*, Berlin, 1899.
Burnett, *Adelard*	*Adelard of Bath*, ed. C. Burnett, Warburg Institute Surveys and Texts, XIV, London, 1987.
Burnett, *Glosses*	*Glosses and Commentaries on Aristotelian Logical Texts: the Syriac, Arabic and Medieval Latin Traditions*, ed. C. Burnett, Warburg Institute Surveys and Texts, XXIII, London, 1993.

Bursill-Hall	G. L. Bursill-Hall, *A Census of Medieval Grammatical Manuscripts*, Grammatica speculativa. Sprachtheorie und Logik des Mittelalters, 4, Stuttgart and Bad Cannstatt, 1981.
Callmer-Nilsen	*Bibliotheken der nordischen Länder in Vergangenheit und Gegenwart*, ed. Ch. Callmer and T. Nilsen, Elemente des Buch- und Bibliothekswesen, 9, Wiesbaden, 1983.
Cappuyns, 'Boèce'	M. Cappuyns, 'Boèce', *Dictionnaire d'histoire et géographie ecclésiastique*, ix, Paris, 1937, pp. 358–61.
Cappuyns, 'Opuscula sacra'	M. Cappuyns, 'Le Plus Ancien Commentaire des 'Opuscula Sacra' et son origine', *Recherches de théologie ancienne et médiévale*, 3, 1931, pp. 237–72.
Chatelain	E. Chatelain, *Paléographie des classiques latins*, 2 vols, Paris, 1884–92 and 1894–1900.
Classen, *Gerhoch*	P. Classen, *Gerhoch von Reichersberg. Eine Biographie mit einem Anhang über die Quellen, ihre handschriftliche Überlieferung und ihre Chronologie*, Wiesbaden, 1960.
CMD-NL	G. I. Lieftinck, *Manuscrits datés conservés dans les Pays-Bas: Catalogue paléographique des manuscrits en écriture latine portant des indications de date*, 2 vols, Amsterdam, 1964; Leiden, 1988.
Colophons	Bénédictins du Bouveret, *Colophons de manuscrits occidentaux des origines au XVIe siècle*, 6 vols, Fribourg, 1965–82.
Conches	*Guillaume de Conches, Glosae super Platonem*, ed. E. A. Jeauneau, Paris, 1965.
Courcelle	P. Courcelle, *La Consolation de Philosophie dans la tradition littéraire*, Paris, 1967.
Courcelle II	P. Courcelle, 'Etude critique sur les commentaires de la "Consolation" de Boèce (IX–XV siècles)', *Archives d'histoire doctrinale et littéraire du moyen âge*, 14, 1939, pp. 5–140.
CPL	*Clavis patrum latinorum*, Steenbrugge, 1961.
de Coussemaker	E. de Coussemaker, *Scriptores de musica medii aevi*, 4 vols, Paris, 1864–76.

CTC	*Catalogus translationum et commentariorum: Mediaeval and Renaissance Latin Translations and Commentaries*, ed. P. O. Kristeller et al., 6 vols, Washington D.C., 1960–.
Delisle	L. Delisle, *Le Cabinet des manuscrits de la Bibliothèque Impériale* vol. I and *Nationale* vols II–IV, Paris, 1868–81.
Derolez-Victor	A. Derolez and B. Victor, *Corpus catalogorum Belgii, The Medieval Booklists of the Southern Low Countries*, 1. *Province of West Flanders*, 2nd edn, Brussels, 1997; 2. *Provinces of Liège, Luxemburg and Namur*, Brussels, 1994.
Dondaine-Shooner	H. F. Dondaine and H. V. Shooner, *Codices manuscripti operum Thomae de Aquino*, 3 vols in progress, Rome, 1967–.
Folkerts	M. Folkerts, *'Boethius' Geometrie II: Ein mathematisches Lehrbuch des Mittelalters*, Boethius, ix, Wiesbaden, 1970.
Folkerts II	M. Folkerts, 'Die Altercatio in der Geometrie I des Pseudo-Boethius. Ein Beitrag zur Geometrie im mittelalterlichen Quadrivium', *Fachprosa-Studien. Beiträge zur mittel-alterlichen Wissenschafts- und Geistesgeschichte*, ed. G. Keil, Berlin, 1982, pp. 84–115.
Gerbert, *Scriptores*	M. Gerbert, *Scriptores ecclesiastici de musica*, 3 vols, St Blasien, 1784.
Gibson	*Boethius: His Life, Thought and Influence*, ed. M. T. Gibson, Oxford, 1981.
Gibson, *Timaeus*	M. T. Gibson, 'The Study of the *Timaeus* in the Eleventh and Twelfth Centuries', *Pensamiento*, 25, 1969, pp. 183–94.
Glorieux, *Arts*	P. Glorieux, *La Faculté des arts et ses maîtres au XIIIe siècle*, Paris, 1971.
Glorieux, *Théologie*	P. Glorieux, *Répertoire des maîtres en théologie de Paris au XIIIe siècle*, Paris, 1933.
Goy	R. Goy, *Die Überlieferung der Werke Hugos von St Viktor*, Stuttgart, 1976.
Hain	L. Hain, *Repertorium bibliographicum, in quo libri omnes ab arte typographica inventa usque ad annum MD typis expresse ordine alphabetico vel simpliciter enumerantur*

	vel adcuratius recensentur, 4 vols, Stuttgart and Paris, 1826–38.
Häring, *Gilbert*	N. Häring, *The Commentaries on Boethius by Gilbert of Poitiers*, Toronto, 1966.
Häring	N. Häring, 'Handschriftliches zu den Werken Gilberts, Bischof von Poitiers (1142–54)', *Revue d'histoire des textes*, 8, 1978, pp. 133–94.
Hauréau	B. Hauréau, *Initia operum scriptorum latinorum medii potissimum aevi*, 8 vols, Turnhout, 1974.
Hedlund	M. Hedlund, *Katalog der datierten Handschriften in lateinischer Schrift vor 1600 in Schweden*, 2 vols, Stockholm, 1977–80.
Hervieux	L. Hervieux, *Les Fabulistes latins*, 5 vols, Paris, 1893–99.
Hoffmann	H. Hoffmann, *Buchkunst und Königtum im ottonischen und frühsalischen Reich*, 2 vols, Monumenta Germaniae Historica. Schriften, 30, Stuttgart, 1986.
Kaeppelli	Th. Kaeppelli and E. Pannela (vol. IV), *Scriptores Ordinis Praedicatorum medii aevi*, 4 vols, Romc, 1970–93.
Kottler	B. Kottler, 'The Vulgate Tradition of the *Consolatio Philosophiae* in the Fourteenth Century', *Mediaeval Studies*, 17, 1955, pp. 209–14.
Krämer	S. Krämer, *Handschriftenerbe des deutschen Mittelalters*, Mittelalterliche Bibliothekskataloge Deutschlands und der Schweiz, Ergänzungsband 1, 3 vols, Munich, 1989–90.
Kristeller	P. O. Kristeller, *Iter Italicum*, 6 vols, London–Leiden, 1963–97.
Die Kuenringer	*Die Kuenringer. Das Werden des Landes Niederösterreich*, exhibition catalogue, Vienna, 1981.
Lambert	B. Lambert, *Bibliotheca hieronymiana manuscripta*, 4 vols, Instrumenta Patristica, IV, Steenbrugge, 1969–72.
Lang	O. Lang, *Mittelalterliche Handschriften*, exhibition catalogue, Einsiedeln, 1992.
Lehmann	P. Lehmann, 'Skandinavische Reisefrüchte', *Nordisk tidskrift for bok- und bibliotheksvasen*, 24, 1937, and 25,

1938.

Leonardi — C. Leonardi, 'I Codici di Marziano Capella', *Aevum*, 34, 1960, pp. 1–99, 411–524 (nos 1–241).

Lieftinck-Gumbert — G. I. Lieftinck and J. P. Gumbert, *Manuscrits datés conservés dans les Pays-Bas: Catalogue paléographique des manuscrits en écriture latine portant des indications de date*, 2 vols, Amsterdam, 1964; Leiden, 1988.

Lohr — C. Lohr, 'Medieval Latin Aristotle Commentaries', *Traditio*, 23, 1967, pp. 313–413 (I); 24, 1968, pp. 149–245 (II); 26, 1970, pp. 135–216 (III); 27, 1971, pp. 251–351 (IV); 28, 1972, pp. 281–397 (V); 29, 1973, pp. 93–199 (VI); 30, 1974, pp. 119–45 (VII).

Lohr, *AH* — C. Lohr, *Aristotelica Helvetica. Catalogus codicum latinorum in bibliothecis Confederationis Helveticae asservatorum quibus versiones expositionesque Aristotelis continentur*, Scrinium Friburgense, 6, Fribourg, 1994.

Manitius — M. Manitius, *Geschichte der lateinischen Literatur des Mittelalters*, 3 vols, Munich, 1911–31.

Markowski — M. Markowski, *Repertorium commentariorum medii aevi in Aristotelem quae in bibliothecis Wiennae asservantur*, Wrocław, Warsaw, Cracow, Gdańsk and Łódź, 1985.

Masai-Wittek — F. Masai and M. Wittek, *Manuscrits datés conservés en Belgique*, vol. 1–, Brussels and Ghent, 1968–.

Masi — M. Masi, *Boethian Number Theory. A Translation of the* De Institutione Arithmetica, Amsterdam, 1983.

MBKÖ — *Mittelalterliche Bibliothekskataloge Österreichs*, ed. T. Gottlieb, A. Goldmann, G. Möser-Mersky, M. Mihaliuk and H. Paulhart, 5 vols, Vienna, 1915–71.

MBKDS — *Mittelalterliche Bibliothekskataloge Deutschlands und der Schweiz*, ed. P. Lehmann, P. Ruf and C. E. Ineichen-Eder, 4 vols, Munich, 1918–79.

Minnis, *Chaucer* — *Chaucer's Boèce and the Medieval Tradition of Boethius*, ed. A. J. Minnis, Cambridge, 1993.

Minnis — *The Medieval Boethius: Studies in the Vernacular Translations of the 'De consolatione philosophiae'*, ed. A. J. Minnis, Cambridge, 1987.

Munk Olsen	B. Munk Olsen, *L'Étude des auteurs classiques latins au XIe et XIIe siècles*, 3 vols, Paris, 1982–89.
Naumann	H. Naumann, 'Notkers Boethius. Untersuchungen über Quellen und Stil', *Quellen und Forschungen zur Sprach- und Culturgeschichte der Germanischen Völker*, 121, Strasbourg, 1913.
Nauta	*Guillelmi de Conchis. Glosae super Boetium*, ed. L. Nauta, Corpus Christianorum continuatio medievalis, 158, Turnhout, 1999.
Nikitas	D. M. Nikitas, *Boethius' 'De topicis differentiis' und die byzantinische Rezeption dieses Werkes*, Paris–Brussels, 1990; pp. 1–92 contain a complete critical edition of *Top. Diff.*
Obertello	L. Obertello, *Severino Boezio*, 2 vols, Genoa, 1974.
Passalacqua	M. Passalacqua, *I codici di Prisciano*, Rome, 1978.
Peiper	R. Peiper, *Anicii Manlii Severini Boetii Philosophiae Consolationis libri quinque*, Leipzig, 1871.
Pellegrin, 1954, 1955	E. Pellegrin, 'Manuscrits d'auteurs latins de l'époque classique conservés dans les bibliothèques publiques de Suède', *Bulletin de l'Institut de recherche et d'histoire des textes*, 3, 1954, pp. 7–32 and 4, 1955, pp. 7–33.
Pellegrin, 'Membra disiecta Floriacensia'	E. Pellegrin, 'Membra disiecta Floriacensia', *Miscellanea codicologica F. Masai Dicata*, ed. P. Cockshaw, M. Garand, and P. Jodogne, Ghent, 1979, pp. 83–103; repr. in E. Pellegrin, *Bibliothèques retrouvées. Manuscrits, bibliothèques et bibliophiles du Moyen Age et de la Renaissance*, Paris, 1988, pp. 159–210.
PL	J.-P. Migne, *Patrologiae Latinae cursus completus*, 221 vols, Paris, 1844–64.
Rand	E. K. Rand, 'Johannes Scottus. I. Der Kommentar des Johannes Scottus zu den Opuscula Sacra des Boethius. II. Der Kommentar des Remigius von Auxerre zu den Opuscula Sacra des Boethius', *Quellen und Untersuchungen zur lateinischen Philologie des Mittelalters*, I.2, ed. L. Traube, Munich, 1906.
RB	F. Stegmüller, *Repertorium biblicum medii aevi*, 11 vols, Madrid, 1950–80.

Reynolds — L. D. Reynolds, *Texts and Transmission: A Survey of the Latin Classics*, Oxford, 1983.

Rijk — L. M. de Rijk, 'On the Chronology of Boethius' Works on Logic', *Vivarium*, 2, 1964, pp. 1–49 (I) and 125–62 (II).

Saxl — F. Saxl, *Verzeichnis astrologischer und mythologischer illustrierter Handschriften des lateinischen Mittelalters*, II. *Die Handschriften der National-Bibliothek in Wien*, Sitzungsberichte der Heidelberger Akademie der Wissenschaften. Philosophisch-historische Klasse, 1925–6, Heidelberg, 1927.

Saxl and Meier — F. Saxl and H. Meier, *Verzeichnis astrologischer und mythologischer illustrierter Handschriften des lateinischen Mittelalters*, III. *Handschriften in englischen Bibliotheken*, 2 vols, London, 1953.

Scarpatetti — B. M. von Scarpatetti, *Katalog der datierten Handschriften in der Schweiz in lateinischer Schrift vom Anfang des Mittelalters bis 1550*, 3 vols, Zurich, 1977–91.

Schaller — D. Schaller and E. Könsgen, *Initia carminum latinorum seculo undecimo antiquiorum*, Göttingen, 1977.

Schenkl — H. Schenkl, *Bibliotheca Patrum latinorum Britannica*, Vienna, 1891–1908.

Schneyer — J. B. Schneyer, *Repertorium der lateinischen Sermones des Mittelalters für die Zeit von 1150–1350*, 11 vols, Münster-i.-Westphalia, 1973–90.

Senser — C. Senser, *Die Bibliotheken der Schweiz*, Elemente des Buch- und Bibliothekswesens, 13, Wiesbaden, 1991.

Silk, *Commentarius* — E. T. Silk, *Saeculi noni auctoris in Boetii Consolationem Philosophiae Commentarius*, Rome, 1935.

Silvestre — H. Silvestre, 'Le Commentaire inédit de Jean Scot Érigène au mètre IX du livre III du "De Consolatione Philosophiae" de Boèce', *Revue d'histoire ecclésiastique*, 47, 1952, pp. 44–122.

Stegmüller — F. Stegmüller, *Repertorium commentariorum in sententias Petri Lombardi*, 2 vols, Würzburg, 1947.

Steinmeyer-Sievers — Die althochdeutschen Glossen, ed. E. Steinmeyer and E.

Sievers, 5 vols, Berlin, 1879–1922.

Thorndike/Kibre — L. Thorndike and P. Kibre, *A Catalogue of Incipits of Mediaeval Scientific Writings in Latin*, revised edition, London, 1963.

Toneatto — L. Toneatto, *Codices artis mensoriae. I manoscritti degli antichi opuscoli d'agrimensura (V–XIX sec.)*, 3 vols, Spoleto, 1994–95.

Troncarelli, *Boethiana* — F. Troncarelli, *Boethiana Aetas*, Alessandria, 1987.

Troncarelli, 'Opuscula' — F. Troncarelli, 'Aristoteles Piscatorius. Note sulle opere teologiche di Boezio e sulla loro fortuna', *Scriptorium*, 42, 1988, pp. 3–19.

Troncarelli, *Tradizioni* — F. Troncarelli, *Tradizioni perdute: La 'Consolatio Philosophiae' nell' alto medioevo*, Padua, 1981.

Unterkircher — *Katalog der datierten Handschriften in lateinischer Schrift in Österreich*, ed. F. Unterkircher, 8 vols in progress, Vienna, 1969–.

Unterkircher, Fiedler, Stickler — F. Unterkircher, R. Fiedler, M. Stickler, *Die Bibliotheken Österreichs in Vergangenheit und Gegenwart*, Elemente des Buch- und Bibliothekswesen, 7, Wiesbaden, 1980.

Usener — H. Usener, *Anecdoton Holderi. Ein Beitrag zur Geschichte Roms in ostgotischer Zeit*, Bonn, 1877.

Verfasserlexikon — *Die deutsche Literatur des Mittelalters: Verfasserlexikon*, ed. W. Stammler and K. Langosch; re-edited K. Illing and C. Stöllinger-Löser, 10 vols in progress, Berlin–New York, 1978–.

Walther — H. Walther, *Initia carminum ac versuum medii aevi posterioris latinorum*, 2nd edition, Göttingen, 1969.

Weijers — O. Weijers, *Pseudo-Boèce, 'De disciplina scolarium'*, Leiden–Cologne, 1976.

Wickhoff — *Beschreibendes Verzeichnis der illuminierten Handschriften in Österreich*, ed. F. Wickhoff, 7 vols, Leipzig, 1905–17.

Winkler — E. Winkler, *Die Buchmalerei in Niederösterreich von 1150–1250*, Artes Austriae, 2, Vienna, 1923.

Wittig	J. S. Wittig, 'King Alfred's *Boethius* and its Latin Sources', *Anglo-Saxon England*, 11, 1983, pp. 157–98.
Xenia Bernardina	*Xenia Bernardina. Die Handschriften-Verzeichnisse der Cistercienser-Stifte*, 2 vols, Vienna, 1891.
Zinner	E. Zinner, *Verzeichnis der astronomischen Handschriften des deutschen Kulturgebietes*, Munich, 1925.

Introduction

i. THE CENSUS

Codices Boethiani is a conspectus of Boethius's works—including his commentaries on Porphyry and Aristotle, and his translations of Aristotelian logic—as these survive in manuscripts throughout the world. As in *Aristoteles Latinus*, the order is geographical, thus:

I Great Britain and the Republic of Ireland.
II Austria, Belgium, Denmark, Holland, Netherlands, Sweden, Switzerland
III Czech Republic, Slovakia, Hungary, Poland, Portugal, Russia, Slovenia, Spain; Australia, Japan, New Zealand, United States of America
IV Italy, Vatican City
V Germany
VI France
VII General index
(Volumes will not be published in this sequence and volume numbers may differ from those given in this list.)

We include fragments, as witnesses to manuscripts that once existed complete. We do not include excerpts and quotations, relevant though these are to the reception and knowledge of Boethius as an author. Neither do we include the wide vernacular tradition of the *De consolatione philosophiae*, even when it has a Latin component. Commentaries are noted only when they are accompanied by the *complete* text commented. For instance, some manuscripts of Nicholas Trivet do incorporate the complete *Consolation*; others (the majority) are continuous commentaries with lemmata. Individual works of Boethius exist in various printed editions, few of which satisfy all the canons of modern scholarship. Often a sound critical text has been established on a narrow manuscript base. A new edition of the Boethian corpus, thoughtfully executed, would tell us a great deal about the learning and literature of the sixth century and the latinity of the Middle Ages. *Codices Boethiani* will contribute to the identification of useful manuscripts. But any census has its underlying rationale. We are concerned not primarily with searching out the best manuscripts for an editor, but with the transmission and use of the works of Boethius. How are they deployed on the page? For whom, by whom? What company do they keep? The *Opuscula Sacra*, for example, drift away from the *Consolation of Philosophy* towards the theologians: Augustine and Hugh of St Victor. The *Consolation* itself has several forms: a Carolingian philosophical text, an element in a school primer, along with the *Disticha Catonis*; a Carthusian paper manuscript heavy with German and Latin apparatus; an illuminated 'coffee-table' volume for a wealthy patron in France or England. A few manuscripts defy classification. They are unusual in their conception, construction. physical appearance or provenance. In our descriptions we have tried to articulate the normal types of manuscript, so that these exceptions may be recognized more easily.

Each entry consists of six parts: (1) material, structure, measurements and script, (2) summary of contents, (3) annotation to the text, (4) illumination and initials, (5) provenance, (6) bibliography. Notabilia—e.g., fluency in Greek—and characterization of the manuscript, if any, follow (1). As to (3) the fundamental distinction is between a gloss provided by the original scribe and notes added by subsequent readers, in (4) we are more concerned with the role of the coloured initial in organizing the text than with localizing style or identifying artists. Where an original or early provenance (5) is clear, we have named the owner and / or quoted the *ex libris*. When in doubt, we have given the *ex libris* or remained silent. More recent owners are cited if they contribute to the history of a collection—e.g. Graevius at Cologne—or if they caught our attention. Eighteenth- to twentieth-century owners have often been omitted. The prudent reader will bear in mind that this volume of the conspectus covers seven countries, and although we have been able to return to manuscripts in major collections to check details, other descriptions are based on a single visit. Manuscripts for which we rely entirely catalogue descriptions are marked with an asterisk.

ii. THE TRIVIUM

The *logica vetus* (1–12)

The *logica vetus* was well characterized by A. van de Vyver, 'Les Etapes du développement philosophique du haut Moyen-Age', *Revue belge de philosophie et d'histoire*, 8, 1929, pp. 425–52. Boethius is a major author, translator and commentator, but not the only one; tenth- and eleventh-century collections would still include the relevant pages of Isidore and Martianus Capella. and those useful *ignoti*, Ps.-Apuleius and Ps.-Augustine. The 1930s saw the establishment of *Aristoleles Latinus*: first the census of manuscripts (*AL*) and then the editions (here AL i. 1–6, ii.l, iii. 1–2, v.l, vi.l). Boethius's translations of Aristotelian logic were disentangled and put on a sound textual footing by Lorenzo Minio-Paluello, whose work in the 1960s, and the image that he presented to younger scholars,[1] maintained *Aristoteles Latinus* as an active concern to the present day. The twelve Boethian texts in the *logica vetus* consist of translations (1, 4, 6 below), commentaries (2–3, 5, 7–8) and monographs (9–12).

[1] See the memoir by W. Kneale, *Proceedings of the British Academy*, 72, 1987, pp. 441–54; and for an exposition of Minio-Paluello's scholarly method his own *Opuscula: The Latin Aristotle*, Amsterdam, 1972.

1. Porphyry, *Isagoge,* 1 bk, trans. Boethius: ***Isag.***
inc. Cum sit necessarium, Chrisaorie; *expl.* sed sufficiant etiam haec ad discretionem eorum communitatisque traditionem.
Edition: L. Minio-Paluello, *AL,* i.6, Bruges etc., 1966.

2. Boethius, *First commentary on the 'Isagoge',* 2 bks: ***1 in Isag.***
Boethius's analysis of the translation of the *Isagoge* by Marius Victorinus.
inc. Hiemantis anni tempore in Aureliae montibus concesseramus; *expl.* diligentiore postea consideratione tractabitur.
Edition: S. Brandt, CSEL, 48, Vienna etc., 1906.

3. Boethius, *Second commentary on the 'Isagoge'*, 5 bks: ***2 in Isag***.
Boethius's analysis of his own translation of the Isagoge.
inc. Secundus hic arreptae expositionis labor nostrae seriem translationis expediet; *expl.* quinque rerum disputationem et ad Praedicamenta servanti.
Edition: S. Brandt, CSEL, 48, Vienna etc., 1906.

4. Aristotle, *Categoriae,* I bk, trans. Boethius: ***Cat.***
also called 'Praedicamenta'.
inc. Aequivoca dicuntur quorum nomen solum commune est; *expl.* qui autem solent dici paene omnes sunt annumerati [or, mixed recension] sed qui consueverunt dici paene omnes enumerati sunt.
Edition: L. Minio-Paluello, *AL,* i.1–2, Bruges etc., 1961.

5. Boethius, *Commentary on the 'Categoriae',* 4 books: ***in Cat.***
inc. Expeditis his quae ad praedicamenta Aristotelis Porphyrii institutione digesta sunt; *expl.* quod sub se aliquas partes speciesque contineat.
Edition: *PL,* 64: 159–294.

6. Aristotle, *De interpretatione,* I bk, trans. Boethius: ***De Int.***
Also called 'Peri hermenias'.
inc. Primum oportet constituere quid sit nomen et quid verbum; *expl.* simul autem eidem non contingit inesse contraria.
Edition: L. Minio-Paluello, *AL,* ii.l, Bruges etc., 1965.

7. Boethius, *First Commentary on the 'De interpretatione'* , 2 bks: ***1 in Int.***
inc. Magna quidem libri huius apud Peripateticam sectam probatur auctoritas; *expl.* tractatus edoceat secundae editionis series explicabit.
Edition: C. Meiser, Teubner, Leipzig, 1877.

8. Boethius, *Second Commentary on the 'De interpretatione',* 6 bks: ***2 in Int.***
inc. Alexander in commentariis suis hac se inpulsum causa pronuntiat sumpsisse

longissimum expositionis laborem; *expl.* et si non proderit obloquitur.
Edition: C. Meiser, Teubner, Leipzig, 1880.

9. Boethius, *Introductio in syllogismos categoricos,* 1 bk: ***Intr. Syll. Cat.***
Also called 'Antepraedicamenta'.
inc. Multa veteres philosophiae duces posteriorum studiis contulerunt; *expl.* easdem lector inveniet praetereundum videtur.
Edition: *PL,* 64:761–94.

10. Boethius, *De syllogismis categoricis,* 2 bks: ***Syll. Cat.***
inc. Multa Graeci veteres posteris suis in consultissimis reliquere tractatibus; *expl.* in rebus mendaciumque meditabitur.
Edition: *PL*, 64*:* 793–832.

11. Boethius, *De syllogismis hypotheticis,* 2 bks: ***Syll. Hyp.***
inc. Cum in omnibus philosophiae disciplinis ediscendis atque tractandis summum vitae positum solamen existimem; *expl.* hic operis longitudinem terminemus.
Edition: *PL,* 64: 831–76; L. Obertello, *A. M. Severino Boezio, De hypotheticis syllogismis. Testo critico, traduzione, introduzione e commento,* Brescia, 1969.

12. Boethius, *De divisione,* 1 bk: ***Div.***
inc. Quam magnos studiosis afferat fructus scientia dividendi; *expl.* introductionis brevitas patiebatur diligenter expressimus.
Edition: *PL*, 64: 875–92.

The ***logica nova*** (13–15,21)

Four 'new' translations of Aristotelian logic were current from the mid-twelfth century. The translation of the *Posterior Analytics* (21) is not thought to be by Boethius. We should remember that only on the discovery of the *Logica nova* could the familiar texts be seen as the corpus of *Logica vetus.*

13. Aristotle, *Sophistici Elenchi,* 1 bk, trans. Boethius: ***Soph. Elench.***
inc. De sophisticis autem elenchis et de his qui videntur quidem elenchi; *expl.* inventis autem multas habere grates.
Edition: B. G. Dod, *AL,* vi.1, Leiden etc., 1975.

14. Aristotle, *Priora Analytica,* 2 bks, trans. Boethius: ***Prior Anal.***
inc. Primum dicere circa quid et de quo est intentio (Florentine recension) [or] Primum dicere oportet circa quid et cuius est consideratio (Chartres recension); *expl.* si autem non, non erit unum unius signum.

Edition: L. Minio-Paluello, *AL,* i ii. 1–2, Bruges etc., 1962.

15. Aristotle, *Topica,* 8 bks, trans. Boethius: ***Topica Aris.***
inc. Propositum quidem negotii est methodum invenire a qua poterimus syllogizare de omni problemate ex probabilibus; *expl.* ad quas habundare difficile est continuo.
Edition: L. Minio-Paluello, *AL,* v.1 Brussels etc., 1969.

Rhetoric (16–18)

Cicero's *Topics* was a common constituent of Carolingian manuscripts of the *logica vetus,* and Boethius's commentary, though something of a rarity was certainly available by the 840s.[2] The *De differentiis topicis* did not come into regular use before the late tenth century.[3] From the thirteenth century bk IV often circulated on its own.

16. Boethius, *In Topica Ciceronis,* 6 bks: ***in Topica Cic.***
inc. Exhortatione tua, Patrici,[4] rhetorum peritissime, quae et praesentis honestate propositi et futurae aetatis utilitate coniuncta est; *expl.* fortuitarum concursio est.
Edition: *Ciceronis Opera,* ed. J. C. Orelli and J. G. Baiter, Zurich, 1833, V.i.269–388; reprinted in *PL,* 64: 1039–174.

17. Boethius, *De differentiis topicis,* 4 bks: ***Top. Diff.***
inc. Omnis ratio disserendi quam logicen Peripatetici veteres appellavere in duas distribuitur partes; *expl.* quos in Aristotelis Topica a nobis translata conscripsimus expeditum est.
Editions: *PL,* 64:1173–1216; critical text by D. Z. Nikitas, *Boetius, De topicis differentiis,* Corpus Philosophorum Medii Aevi: Philosophi Byzantini 5, Paris etc., 1990, pp. lxxviii and 1–92. See also trans. and commentary by E. Stump, Ithaca, NY, 1978.

Related Texts

18. Cicero, *Topica,* 1 bk.
inc. Maiores nos res scribere ingressos C. Trebati; *expl.* ornamenta quaedam voluimus non debita accedere.

[2] Lupus of Ferrières was angling for a papyrus (*sic*) manuscript of the *in Topica Cic.* c. 842/6: Letter 16 to the archbishop of Tours, ed. P. K. Marshall, Leipzig, 1984, pp. 23–4.

[3] Van de Vyver, pp. 443–6.

[4] Perhaps *quaestor palatii* in Italy 534–5: J. Martindale, *Prosopography of the Later Roman Empire,* Cambridge, 1980, ii.839–40.

Edition: A. S. Wilkins, 2nd edn, Oxford, 1935.

19. Ps.-Apuleius, *Peri Hermenias,* 1 bk.
inc. Studium sapientiae, quod philosophiam vocamus, plerisque videtur tres species seu partes habere; *expl.* praeterea eorum non potest numerus augeri.
Edition: P. Thomas, Teubner, Leipzig, 1908.

20. Ps.-Augustine, *Categoriae decem,* 1 bk.
inc. Cum omnis scientia disciplinaque artium diversarum non nisi oratione tractetur; *expl.* iam doctos aut indoctos manifestius erudire.
Edition: L. Minio-Paluello, *AL,* i.5, Bruges etc., 1961. The status of the *Categoriae decem* in the Carolingian era is well characterized by J. Marenbon, *From the Circle of Alcuin to the School of Auxerre: Logic, Theology and Philosophy in the Early Middle Ages,* Cambridge, 1981, pp. 16–18 *et passim.*

21. Marius Victorinus, *De definitionibus,* 1 bk.
inc. Dicendi ac disputandi prima semper oratio est, etiam dialecticis auctoribus et ipso M. Tullio saepius admonente; *expl.* satis esse duxi.
Edition: *PL,* 64: 891–910. Critical text by T. Stangl, *Tulliana et Mario-Victoriniana,* Munich, 1888, pp. 12–48; reprinted by P. Hadot, *Marius Victorinus: recherches sur sa vie et ses oeuvres,* Paris, 1971, pp. 329–65.

22. *Liber sex principiorum,* 1 bk.
inc. Forma vero est compositioni contingens, simplici et invariabili essentia consistens; *expl.* secundum naturam moveri ut ignis.
Edition: L. Minio-Paluello, *AL,* i. 7, Bruges etc., 1966.
A mid-twelfth-century text of unknown authorship, which was incorporated in the *logica vetus.* The erroneous attribution to 'Gilbertus Porretanus' is first made by Albert the Great c. 1250.[5]

23. Aristotle, *Posteriora Analytica,* 2 bks: *Post. Anal.*
inc. Omnis doctrina et omnis disciplina intellectiva ex preexistente fit cognitione; *expl.* hoc autem omne similiter se habet ad omnem rem.
Edition: L. Minio-Paluello and B. G. Dod, *AL,* iv. 1–4, Bruges etc., 1968.

24. Ps.-Boethius, *De disciplina scolarium,* 1 bk.
inc. Vestra novit intencio de scolarium disciplina compendiosum postulare tractatum; *expl.* ultima tamen alterius saporis inquinamenta permanebunt.
Edition: O. Weijers, *Pseudo-Boèce, 'De disciplina scolarium'*, Leiden etc., 1976.
An anonymous text, written c. 1230–40, probably in Paris.

[5] See L. Minio-Paluello, 'Magister Sex Principiorum', *Studi medievali,* 3 ser., 6, 1965, pp. 123–51; reprinted in Minio-Paluello, *Opuscula: The Latin Aristotle*, Amsterdam, 1972, pp. 536–64.

25. *De unitate et uno,* 1 bk.
inc. Unitas est qua unaquaeque res dicitur esse una; *expl.* et est id quod est.
A twelfth-century text, perhaps by Gundissalinus, that is often found with *Op. Sac.*
Edition: *PL,* 63: 1075–78; critical text by P. Correns, *Beiträge zur Geschichte der Philosophie des Mittelalters*, i.l, Münster-i.-W., 1891, pp. 1–56 (text at 3–11).

26. Ps.-Boethius, *De rhetorice cognatione*
inc. Quanta sibimet ars rhetorica cognatione.
PL, 64: 1217–22

27. Ps.-Boethius, *De locorum rhetoricorum distinctione*
inc. Persona est quae in iudicium vocatur.
PL, 64: 1221–4

iii. THE QUADRIVIUM

1. *De arithmetica,* 2 bks: ***Arith.***
inc. pref. In dandis accipiendisque muneribus; *expl.* censebitur auctor merito quam probator.
inc. text Inter omnes priscae auctoritatis viros; *expl.* huius descriptionis subter exemplar adiecimus.
Edition: G. Friedlein, Teubner, Leipzig, 1867; reprinted Frankfurt, 1966.

2. *De musica,* 5 bks, of which the fifth lacks caps xx–xxx: ***Mus.***
inc. Omnium quidem perceptio sensuum ita sponte ac naturaliter quibusdam viventibus adest; *expl.* ut in diatonicis generibus nusquam una.
Edition: G. Friedlein, Teubner, Leipzig, 1867; reprinted Frankfurt, 1966.

Related Texts

3. *Geometria*
Boethius's *Geometria* seems to have been a translation or a paraphrase of Euclid's *Elements* I–V, possibly even the entire text of Euclid.[6] Although it has not survived as an independent text, it may well have contributed to several anonymous treatises *De geometria* of the eighth to tenth centuries.[7]

[6] See Cassiodorus, *Variae* I.xlv.4, ed. A. J. Fridh and J. W. Halpom, CCSL, 96, Turnhout, 1973, p. 49: 'Euclidem translatum Romanae linguae idem uir magnificus Boetius edidit'; cf. Cassiodorus, *Institutiones* II. vi.3, ed. R. A. B. Mynors, Oxford, 1937, p. 152.
[7] Pingree, in Gibson, pp. 155–61.

4. Ps.-Boethius, *Geometria* I
inc. Geometria est disciplina magnitudinis immobilis, formarumque descriptio contemplativa; *expl.* variable.
Edition: Books I–II, *PL,* 63: 1352–64; I and II–IV excerpts, ed. C. Lachmann, *Gromatici veteres,* Berlin, 1848, pp. 377–92.

5. Ps.-Boethius, *Geometria* II
inc. Quia vero mi Patrici,[8] geometrum exercitissime, Euclidis de artis geometricae figuris obscure prolata te adhortante exponenda et lucidiore aditu expolienda suscepi; *expl.* Nos vero haec ad praesens dicta dixisse sufficiat.
Edition: M. Folkerts, *Boethius' Geometrie II: Ein mathematisches Lehrbuch des Mittelalters,* Wiesbaden, 1970.

iv. *OPUSCULA SACRA* I–V *Op. Sac.* I–V

The five *Opuscula Sacra,* long regarded as *dubia,* were conclusively accepted as genuine when Heinrich Usener published the Cassiodoran account of Boethius's family and writings, the *Ordo generis Cassiodororum* (1877).[9] Their first modern edition is Rudolph Peiper's Teubner of 1871.[10] We have used the Loeb edition, by H. F. Stewart and E. K. Rand (1918), revised by S. J. Tester (1973), citing the *Opuscula* by number I–V and the line number of the 1973 Loeb edition.

I *De trinitate – inc.* Investigatam diutissime; *expl.* vota supplebunt.

II *De trinitate ii – inc.* Quaero an pater et filius; *expl.* rationemque coniunge.

III *De hebdomadibus – inc.* Postulas ut ex hebdomadibus nostris; *expl.* aliud omnia bona.

IV *De fide catholica – inc.* Christianam fidem novi ac veteris testamenti; *expl.* laus perpetua creatoris.

V *Contra Eutychen – inc.* Anxie te quidem; *expl.* causa perscribit.

[8] *Pace* Folkerts, p. 113, and Pingree, in Gibson, p. 157, this is not a reference to Symmachus as 'patricius', but to Patrick, the recipient of Boethius's *in Topica Ciceronis* (no. 16 of the *Trivium*).
[9] The text of the *Ordo,* also known as the *Anecdoton Holderi,* is now conveniently available in the Corpus Christianorum edition of Cassiodorus's *Variae* (n. 7 above), pp. v–vi.
[10] R. Peiper, ed., *Boetii Philosophiae consolationis libri quinque,* Leipzig, 1871.

Commentaries on the *Opuscula Sacra*

1. s. ix^{mid}. *The Auxerre commentary on Op. Sac. I–V*

Carolingian manuscripts of the *Opuscula Sacra* usually have marginal glosses, and such annotation can also be found *seriatim,* as a continuous commentary with lemmata. One such commentary was published by E. K. Rand in 1906, with an over-confident attribution to John Scottus Eriugena.[11] Maieul Cappuyns, in a classic article, showed that this commentary, found in twenty Carolingian manuscripts (some marginal in format, some continuous) extended to all five treatises, that it existed in two recensions and that its likely author was Remigius of Auxerre.[12] Cappuyns also found an internal date of 867/91.[13] See most recently C. Jeudy, 'L'Oeuvre de Remi d'Auxerre: état de la question', in *L'Ecole carolingienne d'Auxerre: de Muretach à Remi 830–908*, ed. D. Iogna-Prat *et al.*, Paris, 1991, pp. 373–97 (379–80). Whether or not Auxerre was the principal point of dissemination, this type of broadly Carolingian commentary on the *Opuscula Sacra* persisted throughout Europe into the late twelfth century.[14]

inc. Quinti dicebantur vel a kalendario, quo aut nati fuerant aut memorabile aliquid egerant, vel quod quinquies consulatum meruerant. *Aurelius* dicitur ab aura, id est a claritate, quam pro sapientia et nobilitate meruerat. Aura enim dicitur splendor; *expl.* sed illud specialius bonum est, quod per iustitiam boni operis deo placet quodque et a deo bonum est et a se iustum est, deo tamen donante. *Praescribit.* approbat, commendat.

s. xii^{mid}. *The Schools of Northern France* (2–4)

2. 1140. Gilbert of Poitiers (Gilbert de la Porrée), *Commentary on 'Opuscula Sacra' I–III, V*

First prologue *inc.* Libros questionum Anicii quos exhortationibus precibusque multorum suscepimus explanandos; *expl.* incommutabili proposito sue voluntatis perscribit.

[11] E. K. Rand, *Johannes Scottus,* in *Quellen und Untersuchungen zur lateinischen Philologie des Mittelalters,* ed. L. Traube, I.ii, Munich, 1906, pp. 30–80.

[12] M. Cappuyns, 'Le Plus Ancien Commentaire des "Opuscula Sacra" et son origine', *Recherches de théologie ancienne et médiévale,* 3, 1931, pp. 237–72.

[13] Ibid., p. 262.

[14] G. d'Onofrio, 'Giovanni Scoto e Remigio d' Auxerre: a proposito di alcuni commenti altomedievali a Boezio', *Studi medievali,* n.s. 22, 1981, pp. 587–693; F. Troncarelli, 'Aristoteles Piscatorius: note sulle opere teologiche di Boezio e sulla lora fortuna', *Scriptorium,* 42, 1988, pp. 3–19 [= Troncarelli, 'Opuscula'].

Second prologue *inc.* Omnium que rebus percipiendis suppeditant rationum alie communes sunt multorum generum; *expl.* proprias rationes theologicis communicaverunt esse deceptos.
inc. Premittit prologum in quo quamvis illud de quo locuturus est obscurum sit et plurimis ad cognoscendum difficillimis rebus implicitum minime tamen verbis apertis sese locuturum promittit; *expl. causa* incommutabili proposito sue voluntatis *prescribit.*
Edition: N. M. Häring, *The Commentaries on Boethius by Gilbert of Poitiers*, Toronto, 1966. We have included all manuscripts of Gilbert's commentary that contain the complete text of *Opuscula Sacra* I–III, V.

3. 1145. Clarembald of Arras, *Commentary on 'Opuscula Sacra' I–III, V*
Prefatory letter *inc.* Cum regimini scolarum accitus ab episcopo Laudunensi, qui nunc urbi praesidet; *expl.* opus istud supposui.
Introduction *inc.* Tria sunt quae hominum vitam ita vicissim occupant; *expl.* sine divino afflatu fuit.
Op. Sac. I inc. Virgilius in libro Georgicorum res humiles, id est apes, quadam amplificatione conatur extollere; *Op. Sac. V expl.* nullum bonum criminamur.
Edition: N. M. Häring, *Life and Works of Clarembald of Arras: A Twelfth-Century Master of the School of Chartres,* Toronto, 1965.

4. 1148+. Thierry of Chartres, *Commentary on 'Opuscula Sacra' I, III, V*
inc. I Inchoantibus librum hunc de trinitate primo videndum est que sit auctoris intentio; *expl.* I saltem voluntas supplebit.
Thierry's exposition of III is extant only as a fragment and as a late abridgement; his exposition of V is extant as a 'reportatio' (Häring) and as a late abridgement.
Edition: N. M. Häring, *Commentaries on Boethius by Thierry of Chartres and his School,* Studies and Texts 20, Toronto, 1971.

5. 1256. Thomas Aquinas, *Commentary on 'Opuscula Sacra' I i–ii and III*
I. Prologue inc. Naturalis mentis humane intuitus, pondere corruptibilis corporis aggravatus; *expl.* et abscondita produxit in lucem.
Text *inc.* Huic ergo operi prohemium premittit. In quo tria facit; *expl.* 'Omne namque esse ex forma est' (I.ii.21, p.10)...quamvis enim homo naturaliter inclinetur in finem ultimum, non tamen potest naturaliter illum consequi set solum per gratiam; et hoc est propter eminentiam illius finis.
III. inc. Habet hoc privilegium sapiencie studium quod operi suo prosequendo magis ipsa sibi sufficiat; *expl.* et tamen 'omnia' sunt 'bona' in quantum derivantur a primo bono.
Edition: S. *Thomae de Aquino Opera omnia,* Leonine edition, Rome etc., 1992, 50, pp. 75–171, 267–82.

Symbolum Boethii

inc. Credimus sanctam trinitatem id est patrem et filium et spiritum sanctum unum deum omnipotentem et unius substancie unius essencie unius potestatis; *expl.* cuius visio eterna erit omnium sanctorum beatitudo et gloria. Gratia et pax a deo patre et filio Iesu Christo domino nostro sit ista confitenti in omnia secula seculorum. Amen.
Edition: *PL,* 101: 56D–58C.
An early Carolingian creed, perhaps the work of Alcuin, which is attributed to Boethius by the Augustinian friar, John Capgrave (d. 1464).[15] In his *De fidei symbolis* Capgrave gives the text of nineteen creeds from the Apostles' Creed onwards; Boethius succeeds Augustine. See MS Oxford, All Souls College, 17, fols 38^{r}–39^{r} (catalogue: Watson, pp. 43–5), Capgrave's autograph; and MS Oxford, Balliol College, 190, fols 40^{v}–42^{v} (catalogue: Mynors, pp. 190–92). The dedicatory epistle to William Gray, bishop of Ely, is printed by F. C. Hingeston, *Iohannis Capgrave Liber de illustribus Henricis,* London, 1858, pp. 213–17. Compare the collection in MS Karlsruhe, Badische Landesbibliothek, Aug. XVIII (s. ix^{in}), in which *Op. Sac.* I–II do duty as 'the creed of Boethius'.[16]

v. *DE CONSOLATIONE PHILOSOPHIAE*, 5 bks: ***DCPhil.***

Peiper's Teubner edition of 1871 was in principle replaced by Stewart and Rand for Loeb (1918), by Weinberger for CSEL (1934),[17] by the revised Loeb edition of 1973 and by Ludwig Bieler for CCSL (1984).[18] We have again used Loeb, referring to the proses and metres by the continuous line-numbering of the 1973 edition. We have noted the presence of elaborate *tituli* and colophons, as a likely guide to the textual group to which a manuscript may belong.[19] Rhetorical labels, in the margins of some (generally older) manuscripts identify the rhetorical strategy in the text to which they refer: e.g., apostrophe, question, definition.
inc. Carmina qui quondam studio florente peregi; *expl.* ante oculos agitis iudicis cuncta cernentis.

[15] Emden, *BRUC,* pp. 121–2.

[16] Note Capgrave's reference to another creed found 'in quodam antiquo codice' (MS Oxford, Balliol College 190, fol. 52^{r}: Mynors, p. 191). We are indebted here to Fiona Robb for sound advice.

[17] G. Weinberger, *Anicii Manlii Severini Boetii Philosophiae consolationis libri quinque,* CSEL 67, Vienna and Leipzig, 1934.

[18] L. Bieler, ed., *Anicii Manlii Severini Boetii Philosophiae Consolatio,* CCSL 94, Turnhout, 1984.

[19] Details in the editions of Weinberger and Bieler.

Commentaries on the *De consolatione philosophiae*

Pierre Courcelle's remarkable study of the *Consolation* 'dans la tradition littéraire' (1967) includes twenty-six commentaries from the earlier ninth century to the late fifteenth.[20] Most are unpublished, and few have been fully examined. Yet they confirm the essential pattern of commentary on the *De consolatione philosophiae*: Carolingian, scholastic and humanist. In 1977 Diane Bolton published an article on glossed manuscripts of the *Consolation* written in pre-conquest England; in 1981 Fabio Troncarelli brought to general attention several manuscripts with late antique features in their *mise-en-page,* and marginal annotation that was distinctly prior to the 'Remigian' norm; in 1983 Joseph S. Wittig showed that King Alfred's vernacular 'Boethius' had drawn on continental material that was again distinctly earlier than that commonly ascribed to mid-century Auxerre.[21] There is still much to do. We have where possible identified or characterized glosses accompanying the text of the *Consolation.* Continuous commentary with lemmata (i.e., without the full text of the *Consolation)* is noted only where it appears in a manuscript with which we are already concerned.

s. ix–x. *Carolingian commentary* (1–8)

1. s. ix^{mid}. *The basic commentary, current in Laon and Auxerre.*
inc. Carmina qui quondam. Sensus est talis: qui olim carmina iocunda et delectabilia feci *florente,* id est laeto, *studio* sed digno labore *cogor*; *expl.* imperf. (V.m.iv.l) id est circumcalco. inde peripatetici.
Edition: E. T. Silk, *Saeculi noni auctoris in Boetii Consolationem philosophiae commentarius,* Rome, 1935. See also H. F. Stewart, 'A Commentary by Remigius Autissiodorensis on the *De consolatione philosophiae* of Boethius', *Journal of Theological Studies,* 17, 1916, pp. 22–42; Courcelle, pp. 405–6 (Remigius of Auxerre); and C. Jeudy, 'L'Oeuvre de Remi d'Auxerre: état de la question', in *L'Ecole carolingienne d'Auxerre: de Muretach à Remi 830–908*, ed. D. Iogna-Prat *et al.*, Paris, 1991, pp. 373–97 (388). This is the only Carolingian commentary to have been published in full. Several dozen further manuscripts, perhaps more, are witness to the complexity of the tradition.

2. s. ix. *The St Gall commentary*
inc. Studio, id est doctrina; *florente,* laeto, id est dum flore iuventutis gauderem. Ennius et Lucretius flores dicunt omnes quod nitidum est; *expl.* id est vere vel feliciter.

[20] P. Courcelle, *La Consolation de philosophie dans la tradition littéraire,* Paris, 1967.

[21] J. S. Wittig, 'King Alfred's Boethius and Its Latin Sources: A Reconsideration', *Anglo-Saxon England*, 11, 1983, pp. 157–98.

Unpublished; extant in about a dozen manuscripts, wholly or in part. See Courcelle, pp. 403–4.

3. s. ix. *The Vatican commentary*
inc. Carmina, cantus delectabiles; *peregi,* perfecte *feci*; *flebilis,* lacrimabilis; *expl.* indicta instructa.
Unpublished; extant only in MS Vatican City, Biblioteca Apostolica Vaticana, Vat. lat. 3363 (s. ix). See Courcelle, p. 404, and F. Troncarelli, 'Per una ricerca sui commenti altomedievali al *De consolatione* di Boezio', in *Miscellanea in memoria di Giorgio Cencetti,* Turin, 1973, pp. 363–80, giving excerpts, and id., *Tradizioni,* pp. 150–96.

4–8. s. ix–x. *Various commentaries on III.m.ix, 'O qui perpetua'*
Editions: R. B. C. Huygens, 'Mittelalterliche Kommentare zum "0 qui perpetua", *Sacris erudiri,* 6, 1954, pp. 373–427, with further references. See also Courcelle, pp. 406–8.

Pre-scholastic commentary

9. s. xii$^{2/4}$: Paris. *William of Conches*
inc. Boetius tractaturus de philosophica consolatione primitus ostendit se talem qui indigeat consolatione, ostendens se miserum; *expl.* variable. See MS Troyes, Bibliothèque municipale, 1381, and MS London, BL, Harley 2559.
Edition: *Guillelmi de Conchis Glosae super Boetium*, ed. L. Nauta, Corpus Christianorum continuation medievalis 158, Turnhout, 1999. See also Courcelle, pp. 408–10; Minnis, *Chaucer,* pp. 6–11.
William of Conches confirmed the status of the *Consolation* as a classroom text. His commentary was thus still being rewritten and expanded long after his death.

Carolingian and pre-scholastic commentary persists into the later twelfth century, and perhaps beyond. In this category we include the four anonymous commentaries listed by Courcelle, pp. 410–12; cf. also Minnis, *Chaucer,* p. 8, n. 28. Further unexamined examples may be seen in the present volume.

s. xii–xv. *Scholastic and humanist commentary* (10–22)

10. s. xiii$^{1/2}$. *Ps.-William of Conches*
inc. Boecius tractaturus de philosophica consolatione primitus se ostendit talem qui indigeat consolatione. videlicet ostendendo se miserum.

Unpublished: see MS Dijon, Bibliothèque municipale, 254 and MS London, BL, Royal 15 B. III.
Formerly regarded as a 'second recension' by William of Conches himself, this commentary has now been conclusively redated to the early thirteenth century (Minnis, *Chaucer,* Appendix I, by L. Nauta).

11. s.xiii$^{2/2}$. *William of Aragon*
inc. Sicut scribit Philosophus primo Politicorum, omnia appetunt bonum. Quod non tantum auctoritate Philosophi sed ratione; *expl.* tibi laus sit honor et gloria in saecula saeculorum. Amen.
Unpublished. See Courcelle, p. 414; C. I. Terbille, 'William of Aragon's Commentary on Boethius's *De consolatione philosophiae*' (unpublished PhD thesis, University of Michigan, 1972); Minnis, in Gibson, pp. 312–61 (314–33); Minnis, *Chaucer,* p. 33, whose earlier dating (following Crespo) we accept.

12. c. 1300. *Nicholas Trivet O.P.*
inc. pref. Explanationem librorum Boecii de consolatione philosophica aggressurus, votis quorundam fratrum satisfacere cupiens qui me censentes ex ordinis predicatorum professione tam maioribus quam minoribus apostolico debito obligatum; *expl. pref.* dicta sufficiunt.
inc. comm. 'Consolaciones tue letificaverunt animam meam' (Ps. 93.19). Inter letare et letificari interesse videtur quod letari dicimus ... ut patet per Boecium in prologo musice sue. Volens igitur Boecius agere de consolacione philosophica primo indicit; *expl.* iudicio *cernentis cuncta* (V. pr. vi. 176), qui est dominus deus noster Iesus cui est honor et gloria in secula seculorum. Amen.
Unpublished: see C. Jourdain, 'Des commentaires inédits de Guillaume de Conches et de Nicolas Triveth sur la Consolation de la philosophie de Boèce', *Notices et extraits,* 22.2, 1862, pp. 40–82 (extensive excerpts). E. T. Silk's 'complete but unfinalized edition' (Minnis, *Chaucer,* p. 35) has been made available to Minnis and other scholars. See also Courcelle, pp. 412–13.
Trivet's is the classic scholastic commentary. His text remained very widely known, and apparently stable, for two centuries. Curiously, it failed to attract the attention of Renaissance editors and publishers.

13. flor. 1309–16. *William Wheteley*
Introduction: *inc.* Philosophie servias ut tibi contingat vera libertas. Ista propositio scripta est a Seneca in quadam epistola ad Lucillum; *expl.* natura est indestructibile et inauferribile quid.
Text: *inc.* Hic est sciendum quod Boetius hic non ponit prohemium. Cuius causa potest esse quia hoc subito mutatus de magna felicitate; *expl.* excellencie sue deitatis possimus pertingere.

Unpublished: see H. F. Sebastian, 'William of Wheteley's (fl. 1309–16) Commentary on the Pseudo-Boethius's Tractate *De disciplina scolarium* and Medieval Grammar School Education' (unpublished PhD thesis, Columbia University, 1971); Minnis, in Gibson, pp. 312–61 (315, 354). A grammar school adaptation of Trivet, extant in a few fine English manuscripts, but never widely current. Not to be identified with 22 below.

14–21. s. xiv–xv. Nine later-scholastic and humanist commentaries, including those of Pierre d'Ailly and Denis the Carthusian, are discussed by Courcelle, pp. 415–18.

22. s. xv. *Ps.-Aquinas*
inc. Philosophie servias oportet ut tibi contingat vera libertas; *expl.* Sicut enim scribitur ad hebreos, quarto. Omnia nuda et aperta sunt oculis eius qui est deus benedictus in secula seculorum.
Edition: A. Koberger, Nuremberg, 1473 (*GW* 4573, Proctor 1966, Goff B-816). Ps.-Aquinas is a fifteenth-century German tradition of commentary, which achieved considerable circulation as a printed edition. Courcelle, pp. 322–3, 414–15; but see Minnis, in Gibson, pp. 312–61 (354); and Palmer, ibid., pp. 362–409 (363, 399).

vi. *VITAE BOETII*

In some manuscripts a *vita Boetii* either precedes the *Consolation* or is set as a marginal gloss to the *titulus* of Book I. Thus ANICII MANLII SEVERINI BOETII triggers an account of Boethius's family, his literary achievements and/or his role in politics, his imprisonment and martyr's death. In substance the *Vita* is pre-Carolingian, and perhaps sixth-century; but in form it survives as at least seven interrelated *vitae,* each with its merits and none manifestly superior to the rest. To Peiper's six *vitae* we add *Vita VII,* as associated with the commentary of William of Conches (c. 1130). The later history of this material is as an item in the *Accessus ad auctores*[22] and as the introductory chapter in any commentary on the *Consolation,* whether scholastic or humanist.

Vita I: inc. Tempore Theodorici regis insignis auctor Boetius claruit; *expl.* nec Virgilio in metro inferior floruit.
List of twenty-six MSS in Silk, *Commentarius,* pp. lvi–lviii.

Vita II: inc. Iste Boetius consul fuit Romanorum Theodorico duce, eo tempore invaserunt Gothi Romam et abstulerunt libertatem eorum; *expl.* amicis eius circumstantibus gladiis interemptus est.

[22] R. B. C. Huygens, *Accessus ad auctores: Bernard d'Utrecht, Conrad d'Hirsau,* Leiden, 1970, pp. 47–8.

Vita III: inc. Boetius iste de familia fuit Manlii Torquati nobilissimi viri; *expl.* de instabilitate et mutabilitate fortunae.

Vita IV: inc. Queritur a nonnullis quo tempore fuit iste Boetius. Dicunt enim quidam quod fuit tempore Marciani imperatoris; *expl.* nec Homero in metro inferior videatur.

Vita V: inc. Hic liber componitur quinque partibus. id est de genere specie differentia de proprio et accidenti; *expl.* habens etiam qua gradatim ad summum gradum perveniebat.

Vita VI: inc. Anno dominicae incarnationis quadringentesimo quinto Odoacer quidam rex barbarus invasit Italiam; *expl.* et vocatur sanctus Severinus a provincialibus quod ei prenomen fuit.

I–VI ed. R. Peiper, *Boetii Philosophiae consolationis libri quinque,* Leipzig, 1871, pp. xxix–xxxv.

Vita VII: inc. Iste Boecius nobilissimus civis Romanus et fide catholicus extitit, qui contra Nestorium et Eutychen duos maximos hereticos comprobavit; *expl.* quia facit in hoc opere de philosophica consolatione dicitur tractare.
Edition: C. Jourdain, *Notices et extraits,* 22.2, 1862, from MS Troyes, Bibliothèque municipale 1101; text here from MS London, BL, Harley 2559, fol. 34^r.

vii. EPITAPHS

I. Boethius:
inc. Hic iacet interpres et alumpnus philosophie; *expl.* nomen per secula vivit.
Edition: R. Peiper, *Boetii Philosophiae consolationis libri quinque,* Teubner, Leipzig, 1871, p. xxxv.

II. Helpis, his reputed first wife:
inc. Helpis dicta fui Siculae regionis alumna; *expl.* nectat uterque cinis.
Edition: Peiper, pp. xxxvi–xxxvii.
Tradition had it that Boethius married first Helpis, daughter of Festus, and by her had two sons, both future consuls: Hypatius and Patricius.[23]

[23] Martindale, *Prosopography* (n. 5 above), ii.537–8; iii.581.

III. Boethius:
inc. Heu mallus ille sapor, quo venit mortis amaror.
Walther 7765: an unpublished epitaph that occurs only in MS Oxford, Balliol College, 141, fol. 50^{r-v} (s. xv).

viii. LUPUS OF FERRIÈRES, *DE METRIS*

Quite a common adjunct to the *Consolation* (and a very helpful one) is Lupus's exposition of the twenty-seven verse-forms that Boethius uses in the *metra.*
inc. Quinque libros philosophicae consolationis insignis auctor Boetius xxvii varietatibius carminum respersit; *expl.* eiusque initium est: 'Quam variis terras animalia permeant figuris'. Several MSS add: 'Observa autem quisque legeris finalem sillabam in omnibus metris indifferenter accipi. Dimetrum vero vel trimetrum vel tetrametrum in metris iambicis trochaicis et anapesticis per duplices. In reliquis vero per simplices computari.'
Edition: R. Peiper, *Boetii Philosophiae consolationis libri quinque*, Teubner, Leipzig, 1871, pp. xxiiii–xxviiii; discussed by V. Brown, 'Lupus of Ferrières on the Metres of Boethius', in *Latin Script and Letters A.D. 400–900: Festschrift presented to Ludwig Bieler on the Occasion of his 70th Birthday,* ed. J. J. O'Meara and B. Naumann, Leiden, 1976, pp. 63–79.

ix. VERNACULAR TRANSLATIONS

The *Census* does not include the multifarious vernacular translations of the *Consolation of Philosophy.* We have even omitted manuscripts containing the complete Latin text as an element in a vernacular 'package': e.g. MS London, BL, Harley 43, Walton's English translation of the *De consolatione philosophiae* with the Latin original in the margin; and MSS Harley 4335–39, the five-volume pocket set of *Le Livre de Boèce de Consolation,* with luxury illumination by the workshop of Jean Colombe.[24]

1. **English** (a–c)

a. c. 890. The earliest vernacular translation by nearly half a millennium is the prose version attributed to King Alfred or to his immediate patronage in the court of

[24] *Renaissance Painting in Manuscripts: Treasures from the British Library,* 1983–4 at J. Paul Getty Museum, Pierpont Morgan Library and the British Library, exhibition catalogue, ed. T. Kren, New York etc., 1983, pp. 157–62.

Wessex. This Anglo-Saxon text remained current and consulted into the fourteenth century.
Edition: *King Alfred's Old English Version of Boethius 'De consolatione philosophiae'*, ed. W. J. Sedgefield, Oxford, 1899.
M. Godden, in Gibson, pp. 419–24, confirming Alfred's authorship; J. S. Wittig, 'King Alfred's Boethius and its Latin Sources', *Anglo-Saxon England*, 11, 1983, pp. 157–98; B. S. Donaghey, in Minnis, *Medieval Boethius*, pp. 1–31.

b. c. 1380. Chaucer's *Boece* is a prose version of Boethius's Latin text, with help from Nicholas Trivet (c. 1300: see above) and from *Li Livres de Confort* of Jean de Meun (c. 1305: see below).
Edition: *The Riverside Chaucer*, ed. L. D. Benson, Oxford, 1988, pp. 395–469.
Minnis, in Gibson, pp. 312–61 (341); id., *Chaucer's 'Boece' and the Medieval Tradition of Boethius*, Cambridge, 1993.

c. 1410. John Walton's verse translation of the *Consolation* is fundamentally dependent on Chaucer's *Boece*. It was quite widely current in the fifteenth century.
First edition: Tavistock, 1525 (Gibson, pl. XIII); *Boethius: De consolatione philosophiae translated by John Walton Canon of Osney (Short Title Catalogue*, no. 3200); critical text by M. Science, Early English Texts Society, Old Series 170, London, 1927; Minnis, in Gibson, pp. 312–61 (343–47).

2. **French** (a–c)

For a succinct overview see R. A. Dwyer, *Boethian Fictions: Narratives in the Medieval French Versions of the 'Consolatio philosophiae'*, Cambridge, Mass., 1976, pp. 129–31.

a. c. 1305. Jean de Meun's prose translation of Boethius's text, *Li Livres de Confort*, was influential throughout the fourteenth and fifteenth centuries, without being the 'standard' edition (b below).
Edition: V.-L. Dedeck-Héry, 'Boethius' *De consolatione* by Jean de Meun', *Mediaeval Studies*, 14, 1952, pp. 165–275. See G. L. Cropp, in Minnis, *Medieval Boethius*, pp. 63–88.

b. c. 1360. The anonymous *Livre de Boece de Consolation* (also known to scholars as 'The Anonymous Verse-Prose Translation') makes use of both *Li Livres de Confort* and the Latin commentary of William of Conches in its revised form (s. xiii$^{1/2}$: see above).
Unpublished edition by J. K. Atkinson and G. M. Cropp: see Cropp, in Minnis, *Medieval Boethius*, p. 64, n. 10.

c. s. xiv. For other French versions see Cropp, as above, and J. K. Atkinson, in Minnis, *Medieval Boethius,* pp. 32–62.

3. **German** (a–f)

a. s. ix–x. Old High German glosses to the *Consolation* and to other works of Boethius testify to his role as a school author in northern Europe.[25]

b. c. 1000. Notker III of St Gall, 'der Deutsche'.
Edition: J. C. King and P. W. Tax, *Boethius, 'De consolatione philosophiae',* Altdeutsche Textbibliothek, 94, 100 and 101, Tübingen, 1986–90. See S. Sonderegger, *Althochdeutsche Sprache und Literatur,* Berlin etc., 1974, pp. 106–11; Palmer in Gibson, pp. 362–409, with references; E. Hellgardt, 'Notker Teutonicus: Uberlegungen zum Stand der Forschung', *Beiträge zur Geschichte der deutschen Sprache und Literatur,* 108, 1986, pp. 190–205 and 109, 1987, pp. 201–21; N. Henkel, *Deutsche Übersetzungen lateinischer Schultexte: ihre Verbreitung und Funktion in Mittelalter und in der frühen Neuzeit, mit einem Verzeichnis der Texte,* Münchener Texte und Untersuchungen 90, Munich, 1988, pp. 223–4. In Codices Boethiani volume I, we presumed that a number of copies of Notker's commentary would be present in volume II, but this has not proved to be the case.

The translation of 1401 by the Benedictine Peter von Kastl has not been identified.[26] This is a very early instance of the German vernacular rendering of a major classical text, second only to the German Valerius Maximus by Heinrich von Mügeln.[27] From the mid-fifteenth century three translations (c, d, e) survive in manuscript and another (f) in the bilingual printed edition of 1473. None had a wide circulation.

c. s. xv^{mid}. Münster fragments (Middle Low German).
Edition: A. Bömer, 'Fragmente einer gereimten deutschen Boetiusübersetzung', *Zeitschrift für deutsches Altertum,* 50, 1908, pp. 149–58. See Palmer, in Gibson, pp. 362–409.

d. 1465. MS Oxford, Bodleian Library, Hamilton 46.
Apparently the translator's original copy, possibly made in the Charterhouse at Erfurt; associated in the manuscript with the name Rotger Scheffer; unedited. See Palmer, in Gibson, pp. 362–409.

[25] F. J. Worstbrock, 'Boethius', in *Verfasserlexikon,* i.919–27.

[26] Ibid., i.921–2.

[27] See K. Stackmann, in *Verfasserlexikon,* iii.815–27.

e. by 1467. Konrad Humery.
Unedited. Proto-humanist translation.[28] See F. J. Worstbrock in *Verfasserlexikon* iv.301–4.

f. 1473. Anton Koberger's edition of the *De consolatione philosophiae* (22 above) includes a complete German translation, anonymous and distinct from c, d, e, in addition to the commentary of Ps.-Aquinas.
GW 4573; Goff B-816.

x. TOWARDS ANALYSIS

Sections i–ix above are largely taken from volume I. The second volume of *Codices Boethiani* is made up of 264 entries from seven countries: Austria, Belgium, Denmark, Luxembourg, The Netherlands, Sweden and Switzerland. The circumstances of the preservation of the codices in each country are very different, and this is reflected in the types and dates of the manuscripts to be found there. Moreover, only two of the countries, Austria and Switzerland, have a sizeable number of Boethius manuscripts. This makes comparisons across the seven countries somewhat difficult, or at least unhelpful—although, of course, interesting as part of the history of manuscript collection and preservation. I shall therefore begin by looking at the contents of the volume as a whole. The 264 codices break down into 274 booklets ('codicological units') containing one or more Boethian texts. Counting each logical work individually, there are some 483 Boethian items, plus 19 *vitae* and 3 epitaphs. Many of the texts of single logical works, however, occur as constituent parts of compendia, the *logica vetus* and *logica nova*; so I have generally counted a collected volume of logic as one text rather than the total number of its constituents. This gives a figure of 310 Boethian texts and it is this number that I have used to calculate the percentages given below.

As with volume I, the figures cannot be precise since some discretion is called for in the grouping of texts; and, as ever, fragmentary or partial texts may skew the figures. Even so, the ratios between the numbers of surviving texts do give an idea of what was popular, and when. Readers comparing the percentages with those of volume I (the United Kingdom and Ireland) and volume IV (Italy and the Vatican) will be struck by the similarity of the figures: in large part, the percentage survivals of *DCPhil.*, *Op. Sac.*, *Arith.*, *Mus.*, and the logical compendia are the same across all three volumes. In what follows I shall assume that readers are familiar with the general remarks made in volume I about the texts, their history and use, and their appearance in the manuscripts

[28] Cf. Niklas van Wyle, d. 1479, a prolific translator of Italian humanist literature, author of another translation of the *DCPhil.,* which has not survived. See Worstbrock, *Verfasserlexikon.* vi.1016–35 (1022).

The most common single text is the *De consolatione philosophiae*: 103 surviving copies make up 37% of the total, vastly more than any other individual work. Next come the *Opuscula sacra* with 44 surviving copies. Of these, 15 contain all five of the *Opuscula*; 17 have only I–III and V, usually because they also contain commentaries on these three texts by Gilbert of Poitiers; 8 (18%) manuscripts have only a single *Opusculum*; and 3 have some other combination. *De arithmetica* is found in 21 manuscripts and *De musica* in 20. They travel together in 7 of these copies, a surprisingly small number, given that they were both texts of the quadrivium and were studied together. Of the 99 copies of logical texts, 39 are sets, either of the *logica vetus*, *logica nova* or both; the rest are copies of individual texts or small groupings different from the usual compendia. As can be seen from the index of Boethian texts at the end of this volume, a much wider variety of logical works is present in this sample of survivors than was the case for the British Isles.

The relatively large number of copies of *DCPhil* stretches from the ninth century to the fifteenth. Almost 50% come from the fifteenth century, but after one allows for the lower number of manuscript survivals in general in the earlier period, it is only during the thirteenth century that there seems to be a relative lack of interest in the text. The results parallel those found in volume I.

The same is true for the *Op. Sac.* As in volume I, although manuscripts survive from the ninth century to the fifteenth, they are concentrated in the twelfth and thirteenth. The majority of copies from these centuries are glossed with, or contain separately, the commentary of Gilbert of Poitiers.

Among the manuscripts of *Arith.* and *Mus.* found in the British Isles, there was a very clear preponderance of copies from the twelfth century. This is not the case, however, for these European libraries. Although numbers are fairly small, there are far more early surviving copies of both texts than in volume I. The reason seems to be the higher rate of survival of early manuscripts in Austria and Switzerland: many have stayed in or close to their original monastic homes or have enjoyed a relatively secure existence in a small number of institutions. These survivals would seem to point to an older tradition of use of these quadrivial texts in cloister schools, an aspect of their transmission which did not emerge from the British figures.

The apparently more stable history of provenance, especially in Austria and Switzerland, leaves its mark on the survival of logical texts as well. A surprising number have come down to us from the ninth, tenth and eleventh centuries. After a dip in the twelfth century, they reach a peak in the thirteenth, with 26 surviving copies, mirroring the similar high point in the British figures. This is the pattern of logic in demand for the new scholastic learning but (unlike the British pattern) here it carries on into the fourteenth and fifteenth centuries, where numbers of extant manuscripts are still relatively high.

Apart from their appearance as sets of *logica vetus*, *logica nova*, or both together, the logical texts tend not to have fellow travellers. Unless they stand alongside other Boethian logical texts, these works are much more likely to appear on their own than with anything else. This is also true of the *Arith.* and *Mus.* Only 7 manuscripts contain both, and elsewhere the *Arith.* in particular is most likely to be found on its own. When the *Mus.* is accompanied, it is by other texts of music theory such as those of Guy of Arezzo or Odo of Cluny.

As in the British context, the brevity of the *Op. Sac.* means that they travel with the largest number of companions. Only about 10% of copies of *Op. Sac.* are not found with other texts, and half of these are early copies (ninth–eleventh centuries). A further 20% are copies from the twelfth or thirteenth century containing only *Op. Sac.* with Gilbert's commentary attached. The remainder come in a variety of contexts, although several are found with *DCPhil.* Other fellow-travellers include various works of Anselm and Augustine, penitential works like those of Raymond of Peñaforte and the treatises of Ps.-Dionysius. Unlike the *Op. Sac.* of volume I, very few of these copies appear in simple trinitarian contexts alongside John Damascene, *De fide orthodoxa*, or Hilary of Poitiers, *De trinitate*.

DCPhil. is found on its own in 29% of its manuscripts. If we include those which also carry a commentary, the number rises to 38%. Adding copies where the only fellow-travellers are other works of Boethius, Ps.-Boethius or the various *vitae* and epitaphs brings the percentage to 57%. In the remaining manuscripts, *DCPhil.* often travels with classical texts such as Sallust, Virgil or Cicero, or their pseudonymous namesakes; it is also found with poetical texts, ranging from Donatus and Priscian to Geoffrey of Vinsauf or Alan of Lille, and even vernacular verses. Unlike the examples in volume I, only occasionally are Augustine or Anselm fellow-travellers.

In a volume containing the extant manuscripts of seven countries, it becomes clear how far, as Neil Ker remarked, manuscript survival is a matter of luck. Especially in Austria and Switzerland, where there has been a great degree of stability in the lives of some of the codices, interesting pictures emerge, as can be glimpsed in the statistics from individual countries:

Austria

In Austrian collections 116 manuscripts survive, and a comparatively large number of them date to before the twelfth century. Although half are now held in the Österreichische Nationalbibliothek, the vast majority come from monastic houses or have been closely associated with such collections for most of their lives; some have stayed in the place they were made to the present day. Perhaps surprisingly, a considerable number of the monastic manuscripts contain logical texts, with a particularly large number of individual works or small collections that do not comprise the standard *logica vetus* and/or *nova*. Again, surprisingly, many of these are rather late.

On the whole, the Austrian manuscripts whose origin or early provenance we can pin down have remarkably stable histories, with most coming from within the modern borders of Austria or from southern Germany. One further manuscript is linked with Prague and another with Budapest. Of the rest, a substantial number

(14) have Italian connections—not very distant, geographically. Very few have travelled from further afield. Taken as whole, the Austrian Boethius seems to present us with a useful sample of monastic interest in the texts over a long period of time.

Belgium

With 28 manuscripts, more than half of which contain *DCPhil.*, Belgium provides a relatively small Boethian sample. The texts follow a chronological pattern, with *Arith.* and *Mus.* in eleventh- and twelfth-century copies, and *DCPhil.* weighted towards the fourteenth and fifteenth centuries. With very few exceptions, the manuscripts come from the area of modern Belgium, and the Boethian texts usually travel alone. Where *DCPhil.* has companions, they tend overwhelmingly to be classical texts.

Denmark

Denmark has 10 manuscripts, split almost entirely between individual logical texts and *DCPhil.* Not indigenous, they come from a range of European countries, reflecting the manner of their acquisition by the Royal Library. There are no home-grown Danish monastic copies.

Luxembourg

Luxembourg has only 2 Boethius manuscripts, but both are interesting. The tenth/eleventh-century *Mus.* travels together with other musical texts. The fifteenth-century *DCPhil.*, however, is unusual in being part of a collection of local material and travel writing.

The Netherlands

The 24 Boethius manuscripts in the Netherlands cover the whole range of texts, and some are unusually early copies. In particular, there are logical texts from the ninth, tenth, eleventh, and twelfth centuries, as well as early *Arith.* and *Mus.* In contrast, the *DCPhil.* and *Op. Sac.* are late, predominantly fifteenth-century.

The texts follow a chronological pattern, with *Arith.*, *Mus.* and logic in early copies, from the ninth century to the twelfth, but nothing beyond that date, and *DCPhil.* weighted towards the fourteenth and fifteenth centuries. While some of the codices come from local religious houses, others have a more exotic provenance, probably reflecting the work of the distinguished collectors whose books came to form these Dutch libraries.

Sweden

Sweden has only 10 manuscripts, with a variety of single books of logic (rather than compendia of *logica vetus* or *logic nova*) as well as 4 copies of *DCPhil.* Most of the texts are late—fourteenth- or fifteenth-century—and many originated in France.

Once again, these books are a small example of the serendipity of manuscript survival. Clearly, if fewer manuscripts from the collection of Queen Christina had found their way to the Vatican Library, the Swedish sample of Boethius would be quite different.

Switzerland

In comparison, the 74 extant Swiss manuscripts contain a disproportionately large number of texts dating from before the twelfth century (40%). The early manuscripts are not concentrated on one particular text; in fact, there is an example of most of the major works in each century, the only anomalies being the large number of eleventh-century logical texts and of fifteenth-century *DCPhil.* The Swiss codices show very clearly the influence of collection history on the statistics of survival. They divide neatly into one group made in or for early monastic houses (or acquired by them at an early date, often remaining there throughout their lives), and a second set which reflects the interests of several important scholar-collectors (sometimes, like Johannes de Lapide in Basel, religious themselves) who acquired books made in study centres in France or Germany. The Swiss figures are also skewed by the presence of 15 manuscripts from the extraordinary library of the abbey of St Gall, much of whose collection of early books remains *in situ.*

* * *

Two interesting points arise from this brief analysis of the collections of Latin Boethius in the individual countries represented in volume II. The first is the obvious impact of the history of collecting in any one country on the number and type of manuscript survivals. In this volume we can see the strong influence of the tradition of monastic scriptoria and of a religious history where those foundations either survive intact or where their book collections enjoyed a relatively smooth transition from religious to secular institutions. A second influence appears in the work of a number of important Continental scholars and bibliophiles, whose libraries, garnered from all over Europe, came to constitute the basis of modern institutional collections. None of the countries in this volume had important early universities, unlike Oxford and Cambridge in volume I. These two separate strands tell us much about the Boethian works that remain.

One might, then, be forgiven for imagining that the pattern of survival of the various Boethian texts might be very different from that found in the first volume of *Codices Boethiani*; and yet this is not the case. The overall picture in both volumes—as well as in volume IV which surveys the almost 600 surviving Italian manuscripts—is very similar. Thus, although we may agree in general with Neil Ker's dictum that the survival of particular medieval manuscripts is largely a matter of chance, from which few conclusions about their comparative medieval importance can be drawn, nevertheless, in a survey such as this, where so many manuscripts are involved, we may begin to be reasonably certain of the relative popularity of the major texts of Boethius in the medieval world and to gain a sense of the way in which they were used.

* * *

The editor of volume II is particularly grateful to her collaborators on the project who have visited libraries and described manuscripts: Richard Gameson (Scandinavia), Fiona Robb and Anke Holdenried (Austria and Switzerland), Teresa Webber (Belgium and The Netherlands). Theodore Christchev not only visited libraries in Austria, but has also, along with Joseph Ziegler, given invaluable assistance with editing of the whole.

Catalogue

AUSTRIA

ADMONT

STIFTSBIBLIOTHEK

The Benedictine monastery of Admont in Styria was founded in 1074 by the Archbishop of Salzburg, Gebhard (1060–88), and the first inhabitants were monks from St Peter's Abbey, Salzburg. The monastic library and scriptorium reached their zenith under Abbot Gottfried I (1138–56). The first lists of MSS date from the first half of the twelfth century and the first systematic catalogue was compiled by Peter of Arbon in 1380.

J. Wichner, *Katalog der Handschriften im Stift Admont*, Admont, 1887, repr. University Microfilms International, Ann Arbor and London, 1981; P. Buberl, *Die illuminierten Handschriften in Steiermark. I. Die Stiftsbibliotheken zu Admont und Vorau*, Beschreibendes Verzeichnis der illumunierten Handschriften in Österreich, IV, Leipzig, 1911; *MBKÖ*, III, pp. 1–65; Unterkircher, Fiedler, Stickler, pp. 15–16; Kristeller, III, pp. 9–11.

1. MS Admont, Stiftsbibliothek, 266
Topica Aris. s. xiv

Parchment; 77 + i fols; page 265x185–95mm.
A (s. xiv): text 2 cols, each 210x65mm; 42–53; several heavily abbreviated hands.
B (s. xiv): text 2 cols, each 190x60mm; 50 lines; one scribe.
C (s. xiv): text 2 cols, each 230x65mm; 60 lines; two heavily abbreviated hands similar to A.
Modern binding.
A rather carelessly executed copy.

CONTENTS A: fols 1ra–24rb Boethius of Dacia, *In Topica Aris.*; 24^{v} notes on logic; 25ra–31vb *Exemplaria syllogismorum*, *inc.* 'illis exemplis fit omne'; 32^{r} blank; 32va unidentified notes; 33ra–36rb *Post. Anal.*, *expl.* imperf. 'quaedam auctoritates libri'; 36rb–44vb ***Topica Aris.***; 45ra–59va Aristotle, *Ethica vetus* (= *Eth. Nic.* II–III).
B: fols 60ra–66ra Cicero, *De amicitia*; 66ra–68vb idem, *Paradoxa*.
C: fols 69ra–74vb Aegydius, *Duae quaestiones*; 75ra–77vb notes on logic.

GLOSS None.

DECORATION None; space left for initials, not supplied. Diagrams, fol. 31^{v}.

PROVENANCE Austria or S. Germany. Listed by Peter of Arbon.

BIBLIOGRAPHY Wichner, p. 139; *MBKÖ*, III, p. 60, l. 35.

2. MS Admont, Stiftsbibliothek, 593
Op. Sac. I s. xiii

Parchment; 132 fols; page 210x145mm.
A (s. xiii): text 180x120mm; 41 lines; one scribe. Greek garbled.
B (s. xiii): text 2 cols, each 170x55mm; 39–40 lines; one scribe.
C (s. xiv): text 160x115mm; 34 lines; one scribe. *Titulus* in red, fol. 67^{r}.
D (s. xiv): text 155x110mm; 31 lines; two scribes.
Modern binding.

CONTENTS A: fol. 1^{r-v} first prologue of Gilbert of Poitiers; 1^{v}–2^{v} second prologue of Gilbert; 3^{r}–8^{v} ***Op. Sac. I***, with commentary of Gilbert of Poitiers, *expl.* imperf. 'sed secundum siccitatem gravitatemque' (10/27).
B: fols 9^{r}–55^{v} Peter of Poitiers, *Sententiae*; 56^{r}–66^{v} Bernard of Clairvaux, *De gratia et libero arbitrio.*
C: fols 67^{r}–97^{v} John Damascene (transl. by Robert Grosseteste), *De fide orthodoxa*, *expl.* imperf. 'non despexit propter plasmatis infirmitatem' (c. 45).
D: fols 98^{r}–132^{r} John Damascene, *De fide orthodoxa*, *inc.* imperf. 'facit vincere tyrannum' (c. 45: text follows on from C after a two-line lacuna).

GLOSS A: see contents. Commentary linked to text by underlining in ink of text.

DECORATION A: none.
C: one major initial in red with penwork flourishing in black, fol. 67^{r}.

PROVENANCE Austria (A, B, C); Italy (D). Listed by Peter of Arbon.

BIBLIOGRAPHY Wichner, pp. 235–6; E. M. Buytaert, '*Damascenus Latinus*. On Item 417 of Stegmueller's *Repertorium Commentariorum*', *Franciscan Studies*, 13, 1953, p. 53; P. Classen, 'Zur Geschichte der Frühscholastik in Österreich and Bayern', *Mitteilungen des Instituts für Österreichische Geschichtsforschung*, 67, 1959, p. 260; *MBKÖ*, III, p. 30, line 28; Häring, 1965, p. 74; id., *Gilbert*, p. 23 ; G. B. Fowler, 'Manuscript Admont 608 and Engelbert of Admont (ca. 1250–1331)', *AHDLMA*, 52, 1977, p. 162, n. 5; Häring, no. 1 Kristeller, III, p. 10.

3. MS Admont, Stiftsbibliothek, 594
Op. Sac. I–III, V s. xii (Häring)

Parchment; 82 fols (fol. 1 is a pastedown; many pages excised); page 220x155mm; text 180x130mm (fols 1^{v}–3^{v} in 2 cols); 32–34 lines, ruled with a stylus; one scribe. Greek in text not very confident. *Tituli* in red, e.g., fols 26^{r}, 30^{r}, 31^{r}. Proverb

'Summum dulce bibit qui cum penna bene scribit' (fol. 82^{v}: ?s. xiv). Modern binding.
A very carefully executed book.

CONTENTS Fols 1vb–2va first prologue of Gilbert; 2va–3va second prologue of Gilbert; 4^{r}–82^{v} ***Op. Sac. I–III, V***, with commentary of Gilbert of Poitiers, many lacunae listed by Häring.

GLOSS See contents. Commentary linked to text by underlining in ink of text.

DECORATION Major and minor initials in red, fols 1^{v}–41^{v}.

PROVENANCE Austria. Listed in the 1380 catalogue by Peter of Arbon.

BIBLIOGRAPHY Wichner, p. 236; *MBKÖ*, III, p. 30, l. 27; Häring, 1965, p. 74; idem, *Gilbert*, p. 33; idem, 'Texts', pp. 192–3; idem, no. 2; Kristeller, III, p. 10.

ALTENBURG

STIFTSBIBLIOTHEK

The Benedictine abbey in lower Austria was founded in 1144 by monks from the monastery St Lambrecht. The oldest library list dates from the beginning of the thirteenth century. There followed several donations in the course of the fourteenth and fifteenth centuries, but the medieval collection has not been preserved in its entirety. The monastery was destroyed several times by the Hussites and the Turks; it also suffered heavy losses in the last years of the Second World War.

G. Schweighofer, 'Die Altenburger Klosterbibliothek', *Biblos*, 7, 1958, pp. 110–23; idem, *Die Handschriften des Stiftes Altenburg* (available on microfilm); Unterkircher, Fiedler, Stickler, pp. 27–8; Kristeller, III, p. 12.

4. MS Altenburg, Stiftsbibliothek, AB 11 (formerly 217)
DCPhil. 1360

Paper; 159 fols; page 280x220mm; text 180x120mm; 19–26 lines; one scribe. Dated colophon, fol. 87^{v}. Binding: s. xvii.

CONTENTS Fols 2^{r}–87^{v} ***DCPhil.***, with commentary, *inc.* 'Vocari philosophiam scientiam veritatis recte se habet'; 88^{r}–89^{v} two s. xv charters; 90^{r}–158^{r} two indices and prologues to Gregory the Great, *Moralia in Iob*.

GLOSS See contents. Interlinear glosses and marginal commentary on a massive scale.

DECORATION Initials in red to begin each book.

PROVENANCE Austria. Belonged to Andreas Chrumicher, rector of the parish church in Zwettl, 1383–1406 (fol. 87^{v}).

BIBLIOGRAPHY Kristeller, III, p. 12.

GÖTTWEIG

STIFTSBIBLIOTHEK

The abbey was founded in 1083 by Bishop Altmann of Passau as an Augustinian house, but in 1094 Bishop Ulrich populated it with Benedictine monks from the abbey of St Blasius in the Black Forest. The first list of MSS was compiled in the first half of the twelfth century.

V. Werl, *Manuscripten-Catalog der Stiftsbibliothek zu Göttweig*, Göttweig, 1844, repr. Ann Arbor and London, 1981; *MBKÖ*, I, pp. 4–14; Kristeller, III, pp. 14–16; W. Telesko, *Göttweiger Buchmalerei des 12. Jahrhunderts*, Studien und Mitteilungen zur Geschichte des Benediktinerordens und seiner Zweige, 37, St Ottilien, 1995; *1000 Jahre Buchmalerei in Göttweig. Sonderausstellung der Bibliothek des Stiftes Göttweig/Niederösterreich anlässlich des Milleniumsjahres 1996*, ed. G. M. Lechner, OSB, Göttweig, 1996.

5. MS Göttweig, Stiftsbibliothek, 59 (formerly 69)

Op. Sac. (2 copies of *III*) s. xiii

Parchment; 275 fols; page 323x225mm; text 2 cols, each 230x70mm; 40–41 lines; several scribes. *Tituli* in red, e.g., fol. 70^{r}. Book numbers as running headers to Augustine. Leather tags at the beginning of each work. Binding for Bessel: s. xviii stamped white leather on wood; two clasps.
A carefully executed book.

CONTENTS Fol. 1^{r} contents list (added later); 2ra–68ra Augustine, *Confessiones*; 68rb–69vb blank; 70ra–103rb idem, *De doctrina christiana*; 103rb–106ra idem, *De disciplina christiana*; 106rb–108vb s. xv index to Augustine; 109ra–126rb Augustine, *Enchiridion*; 126^{v} blank; 127ra–133va idem, *De natura boni*; 133va–134rb Ps.-Augustine, *De generali iusticia*; 134va–144vb Ps.-Augustine (Fulgentius), *De fide ad Petrum*; 144vb–148rb Ps.-Augustine (Gennadius), *De ecclesiasticis dogmatibus*; 148^{v}–150^{v} blank; 151ra–182vb Augustine, *De diversis questionibus lxxxiiii* (*sic*); 182vb–190ra Ps.-Augustine (Quodvultdeus), *Adversus quinque haereses*; 190rb–197va Hugh of St Victor, *De sacramentis*; 197vb–198vb blank; 199ra–222va

Augustine, *Retractationes*; 223^{r-v} blank; 224ra–225ra Gundissalinus, *De unitate et uno*; 225ra–228ra ***Op. Sac. I–III***; 228ra–230rb *Liber de causis*, with intercalated commentary; 230rb–232va *Liber viginti quattuor philosophorum*, with intercalated commentary; 232va–240ra ***Op. Sac. III, V, IV***, glossed; 240ra–275ra John of La Rochelle, *De anima*.

GLOSS Massive marginal and interlinear gloss to *Op. Sac.* fols 232^{v}– 240^{r}. Sparse marginal notes elsewhere.

DECORATION Very finely executed initials in red, blue, green, and gold to begin each of the works of Augustine. Red and blue running headers to Augustine, *Op. Sac.* (fols 236^{r}–40^{r}), John of La Rochelle.

PROVENANCE Germany; Middle Rhine (Lechner). Belonged to the library of the Schottenstift in Vienna (fol. 134^{r}: s. xv). Acquired in 1726 by Abbot Gottfried Bessel.

BIBLIOGRAPHY Werl, I.1, pp. 204–8; *1000 Jahre Buchmalerei in Göttweig*, pp. 64–6 (B 12), pl. (fol. 70^{r}); F. Hudry, ed., *Liber viginti quattuor philosophorum*, CCCM 143A, Turnhout, 1997, pp. lx–lxi.

GRAZ

UNIVERSITÄTSBIBLIOTHEK

The Library began in 1573 as the library of the Jesuits' College in Graz. At that time it accumulated considerable numbers of books (and many MSS) from dissolved monasteries in the area until the Jesuits' College itself was dissolved in 1773, when its library was renamed the Universitätsbibliothek. Its collections were further enhanced in 1782, when another forty Styrian monasteries were ordered to surrender their MSS. The collections suffered heavy losses in the last years of the Second World War.

A. Kern and M. Mairold, *Die Handschriften der Universitätsbibliothek Graz*, 3 vols, Leipzig and Vienna, 1939–67; M. Mairold, *Die datierten Handschriften der Universitätsbibliothek Graz bis zum Jahre 1600*, Katalog der datierten Handschriften in lateinischer Schrift in Österreich, VI, Vienna, 1979; Unterkircher, Fiedler, Stickler, pp. 55–7.

6. MS Graz, Universitätsbibliothek, 1265
Op. Sac. s. xiii 2/2

Parchment; 155 fols (pastedowns from a theological treatise *De natura Dei*); page 210x130mm; text 2 cols, each 180x45mm; 47 lines; one scribe. *Titulus* in red, fol. 6ra. Binding: s. xiv dark brown leather on wood; one central clasp.

CONTENTS Fols 1ra–6ra Nicholas of Amiens, *Ars fidei catholicae*; 6ra–10vb ***Op. Sac. I–IV***; 10vb–93va Raymond of Peñaforte, *Summa de poenitentia*; 93vb–105va Tancred of Bologna, *Summa de matrimonio*; 105vb–106vb notes on baptism; 107ra–147rb *Tractatus de officiis divinis*; 148ra–152ra ***Op. Sac. V***; 152rb–155vb Moysus de Gaecia, *Libellus expositorius grecorum dictionum per prologos S. Jeronimi in libros veteris noveque scripture.*

GLOSS Scattered marginal notes and occasional corrections.

DECORATION Alternating blue and red initials with occasional flourishing.

PROVENANCE Italy (Kern). Belonged to the library of the Carthusian monastery at Seitz (fols 1^{r}, 155^{v}), whence it passed to Graz.

BIBLIOGRAPHY Kern, II, pp. 277–8; M. Mairold, 'Zur Bibliotheksgeschichte der Kartause Seitz', *Die Kartäuser in Österreich*, I, Analecta Cartusiana, 83, Salzburg, 1980, p. 47.

7. MS Graz, Universitätsbibliothek, 1703/122
Cat. s. x

Parchment; 1 bifolium; page 310x195mm; text 115x95mm; 16 lines; one scribe.

CONTENTS ***Cat.***, 'quae ut contraria'–'visus enim non est' (31/15–33/12).

GLOSS None.

DECORATION None.

PROVENANCE Unknown.

BIBLIOGRAPHY Kern, II, p. 395; *AL*, 2016.

HEILIGENKREUZ

STIFTSBIBLIOTHEK

The Cistercian abbey of Heiligenkreuz near Vienna, and its scriptorium, were founded in 1136 by St Leopold. The first list of MSS dates from the time of Abbot Godeschalk (1136–47), but the most important medieval catalogue is from c. 1381, and lists the MSS by author. In 1880 the abbey was united with the Cistercian monastery of Neukloster in Wiener-Neustadt and later received its manuscript collection.

B. Gsell, *Verzeichniss der Handschriften in der Bibliothek des Stiftes Heiligen-*

kreuz, Xenia Bernardina, I, pp. 115–272; E. Bill, *Verzeichniss der Handschriften in der Bibliothek des mit der Abtei Heiligenkreuz vereinigten Stiftes Neukloster zu Wiener-Neustadt*, Xenia Bernardina, I.1, pp. 273–93; *MBKÖ*, I, pp. 15–82; D. Frey and K. Grossmann, *Die Denkmale des Stiftes Heiligenkreuz*, Österreichische Kunsttopographie, 19, Vienna, 1926; F. Walliser, *Cistercienser Buchkunst. Heiligenkreuzer Skriptorium in seinem ersten Jahrhundert 1133–1230*, Heiligenkreuz and Vienna, 1969; Unterkircher, Fiedler and Stickler, p. 24.

8. MS Heiligenkreuz, Stiftsbibliothek, 63
Topica Aris. I–IV, Soph. Elench. s. xv

Paper; 155 fols; page 310x215mm; text 215x105mm; 26 lines; one scribe for text; several hands for gloss. Binding: ?s. xv white leather on wood.

CONTENTS Fols 1^{r}–35^{r} Aristotle, *De anima*; 36^{r}–60^{v} idem, *De generatione et corruptione*; 61^{r}–92^{v} ***Topica Aris. I–IV***; 93^{r}–127^{v} *Post. Anal.*; 128^{r}–155^{r} ***Soph. Elench.***

GLOSS Marginal and interlinear glosses in contemporary hands; text linked to gloss by underlining in red.

DECORATION Initials in red.

PROVENANCE ?Heiligenkreuz.

BIBLIOGRAPHY *Xenia Bernardina* (Gsell), I, pp. 141–2; *AL*, 76.

9. MS Heiligenkreuz, Stiftsbibliothek, 130
DCPhil., Vita I s. xii

Parchment; 121 fols; page 290x210mm; text variable; 23–44 lines; ample space for marginal gloss (fols 5^{v}–76^{r}); two scribes. *Tituli* in red. Greek very confident. Binding: s. xv red leather on wood; one central metal clasp (partially intact).

CONTENTS Fol. 1^{v} Wheel of Fortune; 2^{r}–4^{r} Lupus, *De metris*; 4^{r} *accessus*, *inc.* 'In exponendis auctoribus'; *expl.* 'agnomina solebant habere'; 4^{r-v} *De septem musis*; 4^{v} three poems, the first dedicated to the Muses (*Anthologia latina*, 664), the second to divine Wisdom, the third to the seven arts (ed. K. Strecker, *Die Tegernseer Briefsammlung (Froumund)*, *MGH Epp. selectae*, 3, Berlin, 1925, p. xii); 5^{r} drawing of Boethius and the Muses; 5^{v}–76^{r} ***DCPhil.***; 77^{r} ***Vita I***; 77^{r}–85^{v} anon. commentary on *DCPhil.*; 85^{v}–92^{r} commentary of ?Remigius of Auxerre, *expl.* imperf. II.pr.vii.31 'ad montem Taurum'; 93^{r}–121^{r} William of Conches, commentary on *DCPhil.*; 120^{v} hymn to John the Baptist (s. xv).

GLOSS See contents. Systematic marginal and interlinear glosses to

DCPhil.; interlinear gloss consists of single words rather than whole sentences; marginal gloss is linked to text by reference signs and letters of the alphabet; gloss becomes lemmatized from fol. 28^v onwards.

DECORATION See contents. Two full-page pen-drawings, the first depicting the Wheel of Fortune (fol. 1^v; cf. MS Heiligenkreuz 226 in Walliser, figs 95 and 96); the second representing Boethius with the nine Muses, ?Philosophy and Christ (fol. 5^r). The second drawing is iconographically very similar to a Tree of Jesse. Decorated initials in red and black with penwork flourishing.

PROVENANCE Heiligenkreuz (Häring).

BIBLIOGRAPHY *Xenia Bernardina* (Gsell), I, p. 154; Steinmeyer-Sievers, IV, p. 468, no. 238; *MBKÖ*, I, p. 54; Frey and Grossmann, p. 261, fig. 25 (fol. 5^r); Courcelle, pp. 144, 405, 409, pl. 67 (fol. 1^v); N. Häring, 'Four Commentaries on the *De Consolatione Philosophiae* in MS Heiligenkreuz 130', *Mediaeval studies*, 31, 1969, pp. 287–336; Troncarelli, *Tradizioni*, pp. 3, 36, 66, 74, 77, pl. VI (fol. 5^r); idem, *Boethiana*, pp. 148–9 (no. 2), 276; idem, 'Una nuova editione della *Consolatio Philosophiae* di Boezio nel *Corpus Christianorum*', *Scriptorium*, 41, 1987, p. 143–4; Nauta, pp. lxxxviii–xci (MS H).

10. MS Heiligenkreuz, Stiftsbibliothek, 208
Op. Sac. I–III, V s. xii

Parchment; 125 fols; page 260x190mm. Colophon, fol. 83^v.
A: text 190x93mm; comm. 190x40mm; 25–36 lines; ?several scribes.

CONTENTS A (s. xii): fols 1^r–72^v ***Op. Sac. I–III, V***, with commentary of Gilbert of Poitiers, *expl.* 'hoc est per peccatum concupiscere'.
B (1373): fols 73^r–83^v Johannes de Tambaco, *Tractatus de quantitate indulgentiarum*; 84^r–93^v idem, *Quaestiones septem de indulgentiis*; 93^v–98^r *Abbreviatio vitae S. Thomae de Aquino*; 99^r–125^v sermons.

GLOSS A: see contents. Text linked to commentary by reference signs.

DECORATION A: simple initials beginning each new work.

PROVENANCE Unknown.

BIBLIOGRAPHY *Xenia Bernardina* (Gsell), I, p. 171; Häring, 1965, p. 74 (n. 110); idem, *Gilbert*, p. 20; idem, no. 51; Kaeppelli, nos 2260 and 2262.

11. MS Heiligenkreuz, Stiftsbibliothek, 374
Logica vetus et nova s. xiii

Parchment; 296 fols; page 185x135mm; text 105x60mm; 20 lines; wide margins for gloss; several scribes. Binding: white leather on pasteboard.

CONTENTS Fols 1^{r}–15^{v} ***Isag.***; 16^{r}–42^{v} ***Cat.***; 43^{r}–57^{r} ***De Int.***; 58^{r}–136^{v} ***Topica Aris.***; 137^{r}–146^{r} *Liber sex principiorum*; 147^{r}–174^{r} ***Soph. Elench.***; 177^{r}–237^{r} ***Prior Anal.***; 241^{r}–296^{r} *Post. Anal.*

GLOSS Marginal and interlinear glosses in contemporary and later (s. xv?) hands; text linked to gloss by blue and red paraph signs.

DECORATION ***P****(ropositum)*: bearded Aristotle with cap, holding a book (fol. 58^{r}). Major initials in red, blue, gold, and purple. Drawings of geometrical figures (fol. 244^{r}); diagram of *substantia* and *corpus* in the shape of a tree (fol. 3^{r}); rubrication.

PROVENANCE ?Italy. Probably produced in Bologna (Frey).

BIBLIOGRAPHY *Xenia Bernardina*, I, pp. 208–9; Frey and Grossmann, p. 264; *AL*, 77.

12. MS Heiligenkreuz, Stiftsbibliothek, Neukloster C. 19
DCPhil. s. xiv

Parchment; 61 + i (paper) fols; page 240x175mm; text 160x45–100mm; 27 lines; one excellent scribe. *Tituli* in red, fols 10^{r}, 22^{v}, 39^{v}, 52^{r}. Greek not very confident. Binding: white leather on pasteboard.
A fine copy.

CONTENTS Fols 1^{r}–61^{r} ***DCPhil.***

GLOSS Sporadic marginal and interlinear glosses in a ?s. xv hand to fols 1^{r}–45^{r}. Glosses linked to text by paraph signs, pointing hands, and NOTA signs.

DECORATION Elaborate major initials in red, blue, green, and gold to the beginning of each book. ***C****(armina)* depicting Boethius dressed in a red cloak on a blue background (fol. 1^{r}). Rich border illumination in red, blue, green, and gold to fol. 1^{r}. Finely executed initials in red and blue with exuberant pen work flourishing in the opposite colour to the beginning of each metre and prose. Initial letters touched with ochre; paraph signs in red and blue.

PROVENANCE Italy (script and decoration). Erased older mark of ownership (fol. 1^{r}: lower margin).

BIBLIOGRAPHY Bill, p. 283.

INNSBRUCK

UNIVERSITÄTSBIBLIOTHEK

The library was founded as a public library of the University by a decree of Maria Theresia in 1745. Most of the MSS have come from the Court libraries in the city and from a series of monasteries in the Tyrol which were dissolved in the last quarter of the eighteenth century, the most important being the collections of the Jesuits' Colleges in Innsbruck and Hall, the Dominican convent in Bozen, and the Carthusian monastery of Schnals in Vintschgau.

There is a handwritten catalogue (*Zettelkatalog*), containing only the most basic information; Unterkircher, Fiedler, Stickler, pp. 58–61; Kristeller, III, pp. 19–21; W. Neuhauser, *Katalog der Handschriften der Universitätsbibliothek Innsbruck*, 2 vols in progress (MSS 1–200), Vienna, 1987–.

13. MS Innsbruck, Universitätsbibliothek, 461
Op. Sac. III s. xiv

Parchment; i + 236 + i fols; page 245x160mm.
A (s. xiii): text 2 cols, each 185x60mm; 32 lines; several scribes.
B (s. xiv): text 2 cols, each 165x55mm; 32 lines; several scribes. Colophon, 'Scriptus per manus Hynrici' (fol. 176rb); fols 204–222 dated 1314 (fol. 210^{v}).
Binding: ?s. xv brown leather on wood.

CONTENTS A: fols 1ra–67vb William of Tournai, *Flores beati Bernardi abbatis*; 69ra–91vb Honorius Augustodunensis, *Expositio in Cantica canticorum*; 93ra–94vb *Expositio super 'Nolo mortem'*; 96ra–98vb commentary on *Pater Noster*; 99rb–154ra Life of St Hildegard; 154^{r-v} s. xiii note on a donation of vineyards.
B: fols 155ra–176rb *Post. Anal.*; 177ra–202vb Averroes, *Tractatus de substancia et materia coeli*; 204ra–210vb *Liber de causis*; 211ra–222vb Thomas Aquinas, *De ente et essentia*; 223^{ra-vb} ***Op. Sac. III***; 224ra–236vb Aristotle, *De anima*.

GLOSS A: interlinear and marginal glosses to fols 69ra–98vb; gloss linked to text by red underlining and red paraph signs.
B: sparse interlinear and marginal glosses to *Post. Anal.* None to *Op. Sac. III*.

DECORATION A: elaborate initial in the shape of a female figure, fol. 71vb.
B: crudely executed ***O****(mnis)* in red, fol. 155ra. Minor initials in red, blue and yellow. Red paraph signs to *Post. Anal.*

PROVENANCE Belonged to the Carthusian monastery of Schnals (fol. 1^{r}: s. xvi).

BIBLIOGRAPHY *AL*, 2020; Dondaine-Shooner, no. 1127.

14. MS Innsbruck, Universitätsbibliothek, 655
Logica vetus s. xiii

Parchment with a paper insertion (fols 169–70); 201 fols; page 175x130mm.
A (s. xiii): text 2 cols, each 115x50mm; 34 lines; one scribe.
B (s. xiv): text 2 cols, each 120x40mm; 33 lines; one scribe.
C (s. xiv): text 135x100mm; 34 lines; one scribe.
D (s. xiii): text 100x60mm; 30 lines; one scribe.
E (s. xiv): text 120x80mm; 24 lines; one scribe.
Binding: ?s. xv white leather on wood; one central clasp (lost); parchment label on spine.

CONTENTS A: fols 1ra–30vb Ramon Lull, *Summa pauperum*; 31ra–46rb ?idem, *De virtutibus et vitiis*; 46rb–61vb Alan of Lille, *De arte praedicandi*.
B: fols 62ra–109vb Fr. Heinricus, *Summa casuum*, *expl.* 'et bona fidelibus sunt'; 111ra–225vb *De annunciatione Marie* (fragm.), *inc.* 'Annunciabo tibi gaudia'; *expl.* 'In rorate celi desuper'.
C: fols 127^{r}–239^{r} *Rhetoricale*; 139^{r}–243^{v} John of Aquileia, *Libellus de epyticis*.
D: fols 144^{r}–151^{v} ***Isag.***; 152^{r}–67^{v} ***Cat.***; 168^{r}–177^{r} ***De Int.***
E: fols 178^{r}–186^{v} *Textus algorismi*; 186^{v}–201^{r} *Tractatus de sphera mundi*.

GLOSS D: unsystematic marginal and interlinear glosses in contemporary hands; gloss linked to text by red paraph signs.

DECORATION D: ink drawing of Boethius, sitting on a cloud and pointing to text with his left hand, fol. 160^{r}. Drawing of a leafy plant with CORPUS, ANIMA, PLATO (fol. 146^{v}). Three finely executed gold initials, one to begin each work. Minor initials in red with green penwork flourishing. Two diagrams on fols 172^{r}, 173^{r}. Red paraph signs; explicit in red, fol. 172^{r}.

PROVENANCE Belonged to the Carthusian monastery of Schnals in the Tyrol (fol. 62^{r}: s. xv).

BIBLIOGRAPHY *AL*, 2021; Kristeller, III, p. 20.

KLAGENFURT

UNIVERSITÄTSBIBLIOTHEK (formerly STUDIENBIBLIOTHEK)

The library was founded in 1775 by decree of Maria Theresia. It inherited the MSS of the Jesuits' Colleges in Millstatt and Klagenfurt.

H. Menhardt, *Handschriftenverzeichnis der Kärntner Bibliotheken*, 1, Vienna, 1927; Unterkircher, Fiedler, Stickler, pp. 90–91.

15. MS Klagenfurt, Universitätsbibliothek, Pap. 129
DCPhil. I s. xii

Parchment; 2 fols; page 188x110mm; text 140x40–85mm; 32 lines; one scribe. Greek in text, fol. ii^r.
Front flyleaves of a s. xv paper MS containing sermons of William of Auvergne.

CONTENTS Fols i^r–ii^v ***DCPhil.*** I 'ferrent hanc igitur auctoritatem'–'varia temperat annum' (I.pr.iv.26–I.m.v.18).

GLOSS None.

DECORATION Elaborate major initial in red, fol. ii^v; initial letters touched in red.

PROVENANCE Millstatt (fol. 2^r).

BIBLIOGRAPHY Menhardt, I, pp. 152–3; Kaeppelli and Panella, no. 1623.

KLOSTERNEUBURG

STIFTSBIBLIOTHEK

The Augustinian house (Augustiner Chorherrenstift) of Klosterneuburg near Vienna was founded in 1108 by St Leopold (Duke Leopold III von Babenberg) primarily for lay canons, but after 1133 it was given over to the canons regular. The first liturgical MSS were probably supplied by St Leopold himself. The librarian Albertus Saxo de Hunoldesburch (s. xiii 1/2) gave the books notes of ownership. In c. 1330 the custodian of the library, Magister Martin, compiled the first systematic index. In the course of the fifteenth century, because of the lively contacts of Klosterneuburg with the University of Vienna, the scriptorium became an important centre for book production and exchange.

MBKÖ, I, pp. 83–120; H. Pfeiffer and B. Cernik, *Catalogus codicum manu scriptorum qui in bibliotheca canonicorum regularium S. Augustini Claustroneoburgh asservantur* (MSS 1–452), 2 vols, Vienna and Klosterneuburg, 1922–31; V. O. Ludwig, *Klosterneuburg*, Vienna, 1951, pp. 95–178; H. Pfeiffer and B. Cernik, *Catalog of Manuscripts in Stift Klosterneuburg* (MSS 453–1256, with Incipits and Index), typescript, vols 3–8, Ann Arbor and London, 1980; Unterkircher, Fiedler, Stickler, pp. 20–22; Kristeller, III, pp. 21–2; A. Haidinger, *Katalog der Handschriften des Augustiner Chorherrenstiftes Klosterneuburg* (MSS 1–200), 2 vols in progress, Vienna, 1983–91.

16. MS Klosterneuburg, Stiftsbibliothek, 138
DCPhil. 1372

Parchment; ii + 62 + ii fols; page 360x260mm; text very variable; comm.

275x195–210mm; 4–30 lines for text; up to 59 lines for commentary; scribe Iacomolus de Perego, his dated colophon, fol. 61^{r}. Binding: s. xix.

CONTENTS Fols 2^{r}–61^{r} ***DCPhil.***, with Trivet's commentary; 61^{v}–62^{v} (s. xvi hand) Bartholomaeus de Sancto Concordio, *Tabula in Boetii De consolatione philosophiae*.

GLOSS See contents. A few marginal notes, mostly corrections to commentary.

DECORATION Initials with miniatures depicting the author (fols 2^{r}, 18^{r}), a female figure ?Philosophy (fol. 30^{v}), and Christ (fol. 40^{r}). Finely executed initials in red, blue or burnished gold with respectively, blue, red, and purple flourishing; pen drawings on astronomical and meteorological subjects in brown, red and blue interpolated in the commentary or in the margins (fols 5^{r}, 6^{v}, 12^{v}, 13^{r-v}, 14^{r}, 28^{r}, 51^{r}).

PROVENANCE Lombardy; made for Jacobinus Mondelle of Milan (61^{r}). Klosterneuburg *ex libris* (fol. 61^{r}: s. xv).

BIBLIOGRAPHY Pfeiffer and Cernik, I, pp. 90–91; *Colophons*, no. 8082; Kaeppelli and Panella, no. 3143; Haidinger, II, pp. 58–60, figs 16 and 17 (fols 2^{r}, 18^{r}), pl. 8 (fol. 61^{r}).

17. MS Klosterneuburg, Stiftsbibliothek, 184
DCPhil. s. xiv 1/2

Parchment; 6 fols (two front and two back flyleaves from a s. xv paper MS [Aquinas, *Lectures on John*], and two fragments [numbered 153 and 154] sometime front and back flyleaves to MS 674); page 310x215mm; text 2 cols, each 280x90mm; up to 90 lines; ?one scribe.

CONTENTS Fragm. 154^{r-v} ***DCPhil.*** II.m.vi.1–III.pr.ii.6;
fol. i^{*r-v} III.pr.v.3–III.m.ix;
fol. ii^{*r-v} III.pr.xi.10–III.m.xii;
fragm. 153^{r-v} IV.pr.ii.34–IV.pr.iv.27;
fol. ii^{r-v} IV.pr.vi.27–V.m.i;
fol. i^{*v} William of Conches, *Commentary on 'O qui perpetua'* (III.m.ix.1); part of anon. Erfurt gloss, 'sciendum quod quicumque ... id est exemplarem mundum'; other comments on 'O qui perpetua' including Adelboldus Traiectensis.

GLOSS See contents. Marginal notes and lemmata in larger script.

DECORATION Space left for initials, not executed.

PROVENANCE Klosterneuburg (Haidinger).

BIBLIOGRAPHY Silk, *Commentarius*, pp. 155, l. 16–160, l. 2 (= Erfurt gloss); J. M. Parent, *La Doctrine de la Création dans l'école de Chartres*, Publications de l'Institut d'études médiévales d'Ottawa 8, Paris, 1938, p. 124, ll. 1–18; Haidinger, II, pp. 134–6.

18. MS Klosterneuburg, Stiftsbibliothek, 296
2 in Isag. s. xi

Parchment; 3 fols (flyleaves from a s. xiv paper MS); page 295x215mm; text 230x165mm; 40 lines; one scribe. Modern binding.

CONTENTS Fol. 1$^{r–v}$ ***2 in Isag.***, IV.15 'nunc de propriis'–IV.17 'antiquiora atque maiora' (276/12–281/12); 2^{r}–3^{v} ***2 in Isag.***, V.20 'semper subiectis adest' (340/6)–end.

GLOSS None.

DECORATION Simple initials in ink of text.

PROVENANCE Unknown.

BIBLIOGRAPHY Pfeiffer and Cernik, II, p. 53.

19. MS Klosterneuburg, Stiftsbibliothek, 345
Op. Sac. I–III, V s. xii^{ex}

Parchment; i (paper) + 86 fols; page 315x220mm; text 2 cols, each 240x74mm; 26–27 lines; two scribes, changing at fol. 59^{r}. Modern binding.

CONTENTS Fols 1^{v}–2^{r} Bede, *De schematis et tropis sacrae scripturae* (excerpts); 2$^{r–v}$ *capitula* and profession of faith from the trial of Gilbert of Poitiers (see M. L. Colker, *Mediaeval Studies*, 27, 1965, pp. 152–83); 3^{r}–84^{r} ***Op. Sac. I–III, V***, with commentary of Gilbert of Poitiers; 84^{v}–85^{r} Gerhoch of Reichersberg, *Liber de novitatibus huius temporis*, *inc.* imperf. 'Gislbertus in Boetium de eternitate Dei'; *expl.* imperf. 'vel diversa sentientes approbet vel inprobet' (ed. O. J. Thatcher, 'Studies Concerning Adrian IV', *The Decennial Publications of the University of Chicago*, 4, 1903, pp. 184–238); 85^{v} Definitions, *capitula* and decision of the Council of Rheims on Gilbert of Poitiers (see Colker); 86$^{r–v}$ Hugh Etherian, *De differentia naturae et personae*, *inc.* imperf. 'sancti grecorum doctores'; *expl.* imperf. 'intelliguntur proprietatum'.

GLOSS See contents. Marginal gloss by various hands (cf. MS Zwettl 314). Some of the notes containing critical remarks on Gilbert's teaching (e.g., fols 32^{r}, 35^{r}, 60^{v}, 63^{r}, 80^{r}) might be ascribed to Gerhoch of Reichersberg.

DECORATION Decorated initials in red and gold (fols 3^{r}, 5^{v}).

PROVENANCE 'Liber sancte Marie in Neuenburch. Albertus Saxo de Hunoldesburch (fols 2^{v}, 84^{r}: s. xiii^{ex}); Klosterneuburg *ex libris* (fol. 1^{r}: s. xv).

BIBLIOGRAPHY Pfeiffer and Cernik, II, pp. 105–6; *MBKÖ*, I, p. 116; P. Classen, 'Zur Geschichte der Frühscholastik in Österreich and Bayern', *Mitteilungen des Instituts für Österreichische Geschichtsforschung*, 67, 1959, pp. 265, 273–7; idem, *Gerhoch*, pp. 168, 291, 419–20 and 441–2; Häring, *Gilbert*, pp. 21, 39–40; idem, 'In Search of Adhemar's Patristic Collection', *Mediaeval studies*, 28, 1966, p. 337; Schneyer, III, p. 348; Häring, no. 54; *Die Kuenringer*, no. 246 (Haidinger).

20. MS Klosterneuburg, Stiftsbibliothek, 671
Cat., in Cat., Top. Diff. I–IV, Div. s. xii

Parchment; 117 + i fols; page 288x195mm; text 253x130mm; 33 lines, ruled with a stylus; one scribe. *Titulus* in red, fol. 6^{v}. Binding: s. xix.

CONTENTS Fols 1^{r}–6^{r} ***Cat.***, *inc.* imperf. 'huiusmodi dicuntur qualitates' (27/3); 6^{v}–80^{r} ***in Cat.***; 80^{r}–98^{r} ***Top. Diff. I–III***; 98^{r}–107^{v} ***Div.***, with fragments of *Topica Aris.* on fols 104^{v}–105^{r} and 106^{v}; 107^{v}–109^{v} Ps.-Boethius, *De rhetoricae cognatione*, *inc.* 'Quanta sibimet ars rhetorica'; *expl.* 'erit commodum disserimus'; 109^{v}–110^{v} Ps.-Boethius, *De locorum rhetoricorum distinctione*; 111^{v}–117^{v} ***Top. Diff. IV***.

GLOSS Occasional s. xiii marginal notes; table of *Divisio Themistii* integrated in text, fol. 96^{r}.

DECORATION Major initials in red with occasional flourishing; incipits and explicits in red; sketches for geometrical drawings, fol. 62^{r}.

PROVENANCE Heiligenkreuz. Klosterneuburg *ex libris* (fol. 68^{r}: s. xv).

BIBLIOGRAPHY *MBKÖ*, I, p. 116; Pfeiffer and Cernik, IV, pp. 864–5; *AL*, 43.

21. MS Klosterneuburg, Stiftsbibliothek, 672
1 in Isag., Isag., 2 in Isag. s. xiii

Parchment; ii + 78 + i fols (flyleaves include fragments of a s. xii antiphonary and a s. xiii missal); page 302x195mm; text 230x135mm; 33 lines, ruled with a stylus; several scribes. Binding: ?s. xv wooden covers with leather spine; one central metal clasp; chain mark on back cover.

CONTENTS Fol. 1^{r} table of contents; 1^{v}–31^{v} ***1 in Isag.***; 31^{v}–38^{v} ***Isag.***; 38^{r}–77^{v}

2 in Isag.

GLOSS Scattered marginal notes.

DECORATION Elaborate initials in red; incipits and explicits in red; rubrication; unfinished geometrical drawing, fol. 74^{r}.

PROVENANCE Heiligenkreuz. 'Liber sancte Marie in Neuenburch. Albertus Saxo de Hunoldesburch' (fols 1^{r}, 77^{v}: s. xiii^{ex}); Klosterneuburg *ex libris* (fol. 46^{r}: s. xv).

BIBLIOGRAPHY *MBKÖ*, I, p. 116; Pfeiffer and Cernik, IV, pp. 866–7.

22. MS Klosterneuburg, Stiftsbibliothek, 738

De Int., 1 in Int., 1 in Isag. s. xi

Parchment; 62 fols; page 302x200mm; text 235x145mm; 34 lines; several scribes. *Titulus* in red, fol. 1^{r}. Binding: s. xix.

CONTENTS Fols 1^{r}–6^{r} ***De Int.***; 7^{r}–57^{r} ***1 in Int.***; 57^{v}–62^{v} ***1 in Isag.***, *expl.* imperf. 'quidquid illud vel rerum vel sermonum' (*PL*, 64:14A).

GLOSS Many marginal and interlinear glosses to fols 1^{r}–6^{r}.

DECORATION Decorated major initials in red; rubrication. Circular diagrams of *affirmacio* and *propositiones* (fol. 34^{r}), *homo iustus* (fol. 36^{r}), *possibile* and *non possibile* (fol. 43^{r}).

PROVENANCE Klosterneuburg: *ex libris* (fols 1^{r}, 32^{r}, 62^{v}: s. xv).

BIBLIOGRAPHY *MBKÖ*, I, p. 116; Pfeiffer and Cernik, IV.ii, p. 107; *AL*, 46.

23. MS Klosternburg, Stiftsbibliothek, 1098

Logica vetus et nova s. xii 2/2

Parchment; i + 230 fols; page 230x155mm; text 2 cols, each 160x47mm; 33 lines; two scribes. *Tituli* in red. Binding: s. xix.

CONTENTS Fols 1ra–6va ***Isag.***; 6vb–17ra ***Cat.***, *expl.* imperf. 'vel lagena habens vinum' (79/3); 17rb–23ra ***De Int.***; 23rb–27vb Ps.-Apuleius, *Peri Hermenias*; 28ra–31rb *Liber sex principiorum*; 31va–32vb Aristotle, *Ethica vetus* (beginning only); 33^{r}–35^{v} blank; 36ra–43vb Cicero, *Topica*; 44ra–67rb ***Top. Diff.***; 68ra–75vb ***Div.***; 76ra–92va ***Syll. Cat.***; 92vb–114vb ***Syll. Hyp.***; 116ra–162vb ***Topica Aris.***; 164ra–179ra ***Soph. Elench.***; 180ra–213ra ***Prior Anal.***; 213ra–229rb *Post. Anal.*

GLOSS Contemporary unsystematic marginal glosses; gloss linked to text by reference signs.

DECORATION Multicoloured ornamental and inhabited initials with gold, e.g., fols 1^{r}, 17^{v}, 61^{r}, 116^{v}, 164^{v}, 180^{r}. Incipits in red.

PROVENANCE Klosterneuburg: *ex libris* (fols 1^{r}, 107^{r}, 229^{r}; s. xv).

BIBLIOGRAPHY *MBKÖ*, I, p. 116; Pfeiffer and Cernik, VI, pp. 745–9; *AL*, 51; Munk Olsen, I, pp. 22 (Apul.C.58) and 190 (Cic.C.183); W. Cahn, *Romanesque Manuscripts. The Twelfth Century. A Survey of Manuscripts Illuminated in France*, 2 vols, London, 1996, I, p. 20, fig. 10 (fol. 1^{r}).

KREMSMÜNSTER

STIFTSBIBLIOTHEK

The Benedictine abbey of Kremsmünster and its monastic library were founded in 777. The first list of MSS was compiled in the eleventh century under Abbot Sigmar. The monastery reached its zenith under Abbot Friedrich von Aich (1275–1325), when Bernhardus Noricus was librarian and head of the scriptorium. In the following years, the abbey was an active participant in the inter-monastery book loan system, and in the course of the fifteenth century, because of its contacts with the University of Vienna, the scriptorium became an important centre for book production.

MBKÖ, V, pp. 30–48; Unterkircher, Fiedler and Stickler, pp. 10–12; Kristeller, III, pp. 23–4; H. Fill, *Katalog der Handschriften des Benediktinerstiftes Kremsmünster. I. Von den Anfängen bis in die Zeit des Abtes Friedrich von Aich (ca. 800–1325)*, Vienna, 1984.

24. MS Kremsmünster, Stiftsbibliothek, CC 123
Logica nova s. xiii 2/2

Parchment; 265 fols; page 220x160mm.
A (s. xiii): text 140x90mm; 35 lines; partly ruled for gloss; one scribe.
B (s. xiii 2/2): text 115–27x75mm; 29–34 lines; ruled for gloss; one scribe.
Binding: s. xv^{ex} leather on wood.

CONTENTS A: fols 1^{r}–3^{v} various s. xiii–s. xv notes incl. an introductory poem to Aristotle, *Physica* in a s. xv 1/2 hand; 4^{r}–54^{r} Aristotle, *Physics*; 54^{v}–69^{r} idem, *Metaphysics*; 69^{v}–86^{v} idem, *De anima* (in the margins of fols 77^{v}–80^{v} 57 distichs *De sapientia*, from s. xiii 3/3); 86^{v}–88^{v} Aristotle, *De memoria*; 89^{r}–92^{r} Alkindi, *De somno*, with extensive s. xiii 3/3 gloss; 92^{r}–96^{r} Costa ben Luca, *De differentia spiritus et animae*; 96^{r}–108^{r} Aristotle, *De generatione*; 108^{v}–116^{v}

Aristotle, *Ethica vetus* (= *Eth. Nic.* II–III), with s. xiii 3/3 marginal gloss.
B: fols 117^{r}–119^{v} various notes incl. s. xv table of contents; 120^{r-v} Ovid, *Tristia* (fragm.); 121^{r-v} s. xiii 2/2 notes; 122^{r}–73^{r} ***Topica Aris.***, glossed at the beginning; 174^{r}–206^{v} ***Prior Anal.***, with marginal gloss; 207^{r}–231^{r} *Post. Anal.*; 231^{v}–238^{r} Aristotle, *Ethica nova* (= *Eth. Nic.* I); 238^{r}–249^{r} idem, *Ethica vetus* (= *Eth. Nic.* II–III); 249^{v}–264^{v} ***Soph. Elench.***, with marginal gloss.

GLOSS A: see contents. Later gloss, locally extensive; frequent NOTA signs.
B: see contents. Many marginal and interlinear glosses in contemporary or slightly later hands; frequent NOTA signs.

DECORATION A: historiated ***Q****(uoniam)*, teacher seated with an open book facing a student in a golden frame on blue background (fol. 4^{r}); ***I*** in red and blue decorated with green, purple, brown and yellow (fol. 92^{r}); initials in red and blue with penwork flourishing. Red and blue paraph signs from fol. 36^{r} onwards.
B: initials in red and blue with flourishing; alternating red and blue paraph signs; partial rubrication.

PROVENANCE France; purchased by Johannes Schreiner, Abbot of Kremsmünster 1505–24 (fol. 3^{v}).

BIBLIOGRAPHY *AL*, 52; M. C. Díaz y Díaz, *Index scriptorum Latinorum medii aevi Hispanorum*, Madrid, 1959, no. 928; Fill, pp. 164–8, figs 52 and 53 (fols 4^{r} and 231^{v}).

25. MS Kremsmünster, Stiftsbibliothek, CC 139
Isag. s. xiv

Parchment; 331 fols; page 225x160mm.
A (s. xiv): text 2 cols, each 184x65mm (fols 1^{r}–18^{v} text 150x65–85mm; 28 lines); 51 lines, ruled for gloss; several scribes.
B (s. xiii): text 175x105–15mm; 27–29 lines; several scribes. *Tituli* in red rustic capitals.
C (s. xiv 2/2): text 2 cols, each 185x55mm; 50–55 lines; several scribes. *Tituli* in red.
D (s. xiv 2/2): text 2 cols, each 180x57mm; 43–47 lines; one scribe. *Tituli* in red.
Binding: s. xv (Kremsmünster) brown leather on wood; two clasps (renewed).

CONTENTS A: fols 1^{r}–18^{v} Prudentius, *Psychomachia*, glossed; 18^{v} seven distichs *De tollerandis temptacionibus*, *inc.* 'Carpe libenter iter quod ducit ad etheris aulam'; *expl.* 'Nemo algore perit quisquis amore venit'; 19ra–22va commentary on *Psychomachia*, *inc.* 'Prudentius iste Terraconensis fuisse dicitur'; *expl.* 'pollens sapientia id est ipse Deus'; 22va–23va allegorical interpretation of

twelve precious stones, *inc.* 'Hec scripsit Salomon in Ecclesiasten et eius structura'; *expl.* 'Bartholomeus nomen accepit ex Syriorum lingwa' (*sic*); 23va–31rb commentary on *Psychomachia*, *inc.* 'In principio istius libri'; *expl.* imperf. 'et ubi exerceo potentiam meam'; 31^{v} notes on *passio*, *eductio in actum*, *forma*, *materia*; 32$^{ra–vb}$ ***Isag.***, *inc.* imperf. 'in solis et nudis purisque intellectibus posita sint' (5/11); *expl.* imperf. 'planum autem' (9/15).
B: fols 34^{r}–77^{v} Hugh of Fouilloy, *De claustro animae* (*PL*, 176: 1051–1104); 77^{v}–153^{v} Hugh of St Victor, various short works incl. two copies of *De quinque septenis*; 153^{v}–174^{v} Bernard of Clairvaux, *De XII gradibus humilitatis et superbiae* (ed. J. Leclercq and H. Rochais, *Sancti Bernardi opera*, III, Rome, 1963, pp. 13–59); 174^{v}–193^{r} idem, *De gratia et libero arbitrio* (ed. Leclercq and Rochais, III, pp. 165–203); 194^{r}–206^{v} *De novem beneficiis religionis*, *inc.* 'Habundans est pauperi religio'; *expl.* 'Deo autem vindictam committentes finem ponamus'; 206^{v}–209^{v} sentences from works of Bernard.
C: fols 210ra–295ra Antonius Rampegolus, *Figurae bibliorum* (*RB*, 1420); 295va–297va sermon *In passione Domini*, *inc.* 'Hodie agitur dies in qua Deus'; *expl.* 'ad eterna gaudia perducat'.
D: fols 298ra–329vb Ps.-Albert the Great, *Biblia Mariana*.

GLOSS A: interlinear and marginal glosses to Prudentius; commentary on a massive scale for *Isag.*, *inc.* imperf. 'sint corporales vel incorporales'; *expl.* imperf. 'species est que ponitur sub assignato genere'. Lemmata underlined in red; text linked to commentary by red paraph signs.
B: scattered marginal notes by Bernardus Noricus and NOTA signs in later hands.
C: contemporary and later marginal notes.
D: none.

DECORATION A: initials (to begin each chapter) in alternating red and blue, with occasional pen flourishing.
B: initials in red.
C: initials in red, from fol. 234^{v} onwards in alternating red and blue; red paraph signs.
D: initials in red and blue with self-coloured flourishing; red paraph signs.

PROVENANCE Bavaria or Austria. A was produced in Kremsmünster (script); B belonged to Kremsmünster Abbey library in s. xiv (fol. 209^{v}).

BIBLIOGRAPHY *MBKÖ*, V, p. 36; Goy, pp. 105, 119, 200, 371, 386; Manning and Rochais, no. 3871; Kristeller, III, p. 23; Fill, pp. 227–33, fig. 34 (fol. 19ra).

LAMBACH

STIFTSBIBLIOTHEK

Founded in 1040 as an Augustinian House, in 1056 the abbey was populated with Benedictine monks from Münsterschwarzach. Some of the MSS they brought with them are still preserved. The scriptorium and school of illumination reached their zenith in the second half of the twelfth century. The first list of MSS was compiled at the beginning of the thirteenth century by the monk and scribe Gottschalk. The library collections were further enriched in the course of the fifteenth century under Abbot Thomas Messerer (1436–74), when numerous paper MSS were copied in the monastic scriptorium.

F. Resch, *Katalog der Handschriften im Stift Lambach*, 2 vols, Ann Arbor and London, 1981; K. Holter, 'Die Handschriften und Inkunabeln', *Die Kunstdenkmäler des Gerichtsbezirkes Lambach*, ed. E. Hainisch, Österreichische Kunsttopographie, 34, Vienna, 1959, pp. 213–70; *MBKÖ*, V, pp. 49–58; Unterkircher, Fiedler, Stickler, pp. 12–13; Kristeller, III, pp. 24–5.

26. MS Lambach, Stiftsbibliothek, 319

Logica vetus 1502–3

Paper; i (parchment) + 244 + i (parchment) fols (the flyleaves contain a fragment from a ?s. xiv missal); page 210x160mm; text 150–60x100mm; 10–33 lines. Scribe: presbyter Leonard; his colophons, fols 37^{r}, 51^{r}, 178^{r}, 242^{r}, some dated. *Tituli* in red for Boethius. Binding: s. xvi white leather on wood (the boards are now half cut off on both sides); chain-mark on front cover.
A student copy.

CONTENTS Fols 1^{r}–177^{v} Peter of Spain, *Summulae logicales*; 179^{v}–186^{v} notes on sciences and liberal arts; 187^{r}–212^{r} ***Isag.*** (many blank pages); 213^{v}–232^{r} ***Cat.***; 232^{r}–241^{v} ***De Int.***; 242^{v} prayers; 243^{v} notes on *suppositio* and *acceptio*; 244^{v} Leonard's booklist and explanation of punctuation marks.

GLOSS Marginal and interlinear glosses in scribe's hand to fols 187^{r}–234^{r}; gloss linked to text by underlining in red.

DECORATION Major and minor initials in red with penwork flourishing and animal patterns, fols 187^{r}–244^{v}; paraph signs in red; diagrams, fols 15^{r}, 30^{r}.

PROVENANCE Austria. Lambach Abbey *ex libris* (inside front cover: s. xvi).

BIBLIOGRAPHY Resch (not paginated); Kristeller, III, p. 24.

LILIENFELD

STIFTSBIBLIOTHEK

The Cistercian abbey of Lilienfeld in Lower Austria was founded in 1202 by Duke Leopold the Glorious and in 1206 was populated with monks from Heiligenkreuz, who brought along books and scribes. The first list of MSS dates from the first half of the thirteenth century. The library suffered heavy losses during the dissolution of the monastery in 1789, and after its restoration in 1790, to make up for the losses, it was presented with the library of the dissolved Benedictine monastery Klein Mariazell.

C. Schimek, *Verzeichniss der Handschriften des Stiftes Lilienfeld*, Xenia Bernardina, I, pp. 481–561; *MBKÖ*, I, pp. 121–32; Unterkircher, Fiedler, Stickler, pp. 32–3.

27. MS Lilienfeld, Stiftsbibliothek, 153
Logica vetus et nova s. xiv

Parchment; i (paper) + 277 + i (paper) fols; page 285x200mm; text 2 cols, each 150x45mm; 28 lines, ruled with a stylus; very wide margins; one excellent scribe. *Tituli* in red throughout. Book numbers as running headers. Binding: s. xviii brown leather on wood; two clasps.
An excellent copy, hardly used.

CONTENTS Fols 1ra–9vb ***Isag.***; 9vb–24ra ***Cat.***; 24ra–32vb ***De Int.***; 32vb–40va *Liber sex principiorum*; 40va–53ra ***Div.***; 53ra–88va ***Top. Diff.***; 89ra–143ra ***Prior Anal.***; 143ra–180va *Post. Anal.*; 180va–256rb ***Topica Aris.***; 256rb–277va ***Soph. Elench.***; 277^{v} table of contents.

GLOSS None.

DECORATION Elaborate ***C(um)*** in red, blue, and gold, fol. 1^{r}. Finely executed major and minor initials in red and blue with exuberant penwork flourishing in the opposite colour; red and blue paraph signs.

PROVENANCE Austria. Belonged to Ulrich from Sieghartskirchen (in Lower Austria), a s. xiv monk and scribe in Lilienfeld (fol. i^{v}: s. xviii).

BIBLIOGRAPHY Schimek, pp. 533–4; *AL*, 40; *1000 Jahre Buchmalerei in Göttweig. Sonderausstellung der Bibliothek des Stiftes Göttweig/ Niederösterreich anlässlich des Millenniumsjahres 1996*, ed. G. M. Lechner, OSB, Göttweig, 1996, p. 68; A. Fingernagel and M. Roland, *Mitteleuropaïsche Schulen I*, Die illuminierten Handschriften der Österreichischen Nationalbibliothek, 2 vols, Vienna, 1997, 38–9, 84.

MELK

STIFTSBIBLIOTHEK

In 985, count Leopold of Babenberg founded a house for twelve secular canons, but in 1089 count Leopold III the Handsome populated it with Benedictines from Lambach. The first note of the monastic library is from 1123. In 1297, the monastery and the library were destroyed by fire and only twenty-three MSS from the twelfth and thirteenth centuries have been preserved. As a centre of monastic reform, the abbey reached its zenith in the first decades of the fifteenth century, and the library collections were significantly enriched under Abbots Nikolaus Seyringer (1417–25) and Johannes Hausheimer (1453–74). The first systematic catalogue was compiled in 1483.

Catalogus codicum manu scriptorum qui in bibliotheca monasterii Mellicensis O.S.B. servantur (1–234), Vienna, 1889; *Katalog der Handschriften im Stift Melk (235–1822)*, vols 2–3, Melk, 1889 (repr. Ann Arbor and London, 1980; since 1889, however, the shelfmarks have been changed); *MBKÖ*, I, pp. 137–261; Unterkircher, Fiedler, Stickler, pp. 18–19; Kristeller, III, pp. 29–35; C. Glassner and A. Haidinger, *Die Anfänge der Melker Bibliothek. Neue Erkenntnisse zu Handschriften und Fragmenten aus der Zeit vor 1200*, Melk, 1996.

28. MS Melk, Stiftsbibliothek, 63 (formerly 174/D. 11)
DCPhil. s. xv

Paper; 183 fols; page 213x160mm; text 140x95mm; 15 lines, ruled with a stylus and ink; one scribe. Greek confident. Binding: s. xv wooden boards with leather spine; one central clasp.

CONTENTS Fols 1^r–177^r ***DCPhil.***, with gloss; 177^v–182^v blank.

GLOSS Profuse marginal and interlinear glosses in contemporary hand.

DECORATION Large ***C****(armina)* in blue with red penwork flourishing, fol. 1^r; otherwise no decoration.

PROVENANCE Melk (fol. 1^r: ?s. xvi).

BIBLIOGRAPHY *Catalogus*, p. 253; *MBKÖ*, I, p. 234.

29. MS Melk, Stiftsbibliothek, 621 (formerly 1121)
Cat., De Int. s. xv

Parchment; i + 115 fols (pastedowns are s. xiii fragments); page 215x145mm; text 145x100mm; 17 lines; several scribes. Binding: original wooden boards (in very bad condition) with leather spine.

CONTENTS Fols 1^{r}–50^{v} Peter of Spain, *Dialectica*; 51^{r}–55^{v} blank; 56^{r}–62^{v} Peter of Dresden, *Tractatus de natura*; 63^{r}–102^{v} ***Cat.***; 103^{r}–115^{v} ***De Int.***

GLOSS Sporadic marginal and interlinear glosses or readers' notes to *Cat.* and *De Int.*

DECORATION Small red ***E****(quivoca)* with simple penwork flourishing, fol. 63^{r}.

PROVENANCE Melk.

BIBLIOGRAPHY *Katalog*, III.2, p. 1455; *MBKÖ*, I, pp. 259–60 (F 206); *AL*, 67; Kristeller III, p. 34.

30. MS Melk, Stiftsbibliothek, 839 (formerly 916/Q. 53)
Logica vetus et nova s. xiv

Parchment; 212 fols; page 240x180mm; text 140–75x80–95mm; 19–30 lines; spacious margins for gloss; several scribes. Binding: brown leather on wood.

CONTENTS Fols 2^{r}–10^{v} ***Isag.***; 11^{r}–24^{v} ***Cat.***; 24^{v}–35^{r} ***De Int.***; 35^{v} blank; 36^{r}–56^{r} ***Soph. Elench.***; 56^{v}–120^{v} ***Topica Aris.***; 121^{r}–162^{v} ***Prior Anal.***; 163^{r}–203^{v} *Post. Anal.*; 204^{r}–210^{v} *Liber sex principiorum*; 210^{v}–212^{v} Aristotle, *Ethica vetus* (fragm.).

GLOSS Intercalated commentary in several hands to *Isag.* and *Cat.*; text linked to gloss by reference signs. Marginal gloss in separate blocks to *Soph. Elench.*; text linked to gloss by Greek letters.

DECORATION Major initials in red and green; incipits and explicits in red.

PROVENANCE Melk (fol. 1^{r}: s. xv).

BIBLIOGRAPHY *Katalog*, III.1, p. 1272; *MBKÖ*, I, p. 259 (F 198); *AL*, 2018; Kristeller III, p. 33.

31. MS Melk, Stiftsbibliothek, 847 (formerly 800/O. 38)
DCPhil. 1421

Paper; 309 fols; page 215x140mm; text 145x85mm; 15 lines; scribe Johannes Vichk de Ratispona, i.e. Regensburg (dated colophon, fol. 273^{r}). *Tituli* in red to each book of *DCPhil.* Binding: wooden boards with white leather spine; one central metal clasp.

CONTENTS Fols 1^{r}–141^{v} ***DCPhil.***, with an anonymous commentary; 142^{r}–144^{v} unidentified material; 145^{v} notes; 146^{r}–82^{v} Ps.-Boethius, *De disciplina scolarium*; 183^{r}–273^{r} anonymous commentary on *De disciplina scolarium*, *inc.* 'Ex quo intentio praesentis notitiae de qua praesens nostrum versatur propositum'; *expl.* 'inquiri quod est polluo vel maculo'; 275^r–301^v Prudentius, *Tituli historiarum*; 301^v–305^v text on baptism; 306^r–309^v blank.

GLOSS Interlinear and marginal gloss to *DCPhil.* in two hands; text passages repeated in gloss in larger script.

DECORATION Initials in red to mark the beginning of each prose and metre.

PROVENANCE S. Germany (?Regensburg).

BIBLIOGRAPHY *Katalog*, III.1, pp. 1159–60; Weijers, p. 75 (no. 47); Kristeller III, p. 32.

32. MS Melk, Stiftsbibliothek, 928 (formerly 907/Q. 46)
DCPhil. 1420–24

Paper; 226 fols; page 215x145mm; text 130x75mm; 12 lines; one scribe. Book numbers as running headers for *DCPhil.* Dated colophons, fols 154^r, 225^v. Binding: original parchment chemise cover with leather spine (cf. MS 1712).

CONTENTS Fols 3^r–154^r ***DCPhil.***; 155^v schemata; 157^r–225^v Ps.-Boethius, *De disciplina scolarium.*

GLOSS Contemporary sporadic marginal and interlinear glosses to *DCPhil.*; systematic commentary and interlinear glosses to *De disciplina scolarium.*

DECORATION Badly executed major initials in red and gold; explicits in red.

PROVENANCE ?Melk.

BIBLIOGRAPHY *Katalog*, III.1, p. 1269; Weijers, p. 21, no. 8 (listing only commentary); Kristeller, III, p. 33.

33. MS Melk, Stiftsbibliothek, 1675 (formerly 852/P. 42)
Logica vetus et nova 1361

Parchment; 247 fols; page 185x115mm; text 100x50mm; 28–30 lines; several scribes. Dated colophon, fol. 72^r. Binding: ?s. xv brown leather on wood; one central metal clasp.

CONTENTS Fols 1^r–72^r ***Prior Anal.***; 74^r–117^r *Post. Anal.*; 119^r–128^v ***Isag.***; 128^v–144^r ***Cat.***; 144^v–154^r ***De Int.***; 154^r–176^v ***Top. Diff.***; 176^v–201^r ***Syll. Cat.***; 201^r–235^r ***Syll. Hyp.***; 235^v–246^v ***Div.***

GLOSS Marginal gloss to *Post. Anal.*; gloss linked to text by reference signs. Marginal and interlinear gloss in several cursive hands to *Isag.* and *Cat.*

DECORATION Major initials in red and blue; red, blue and brown paraph signs. Incipits and explicits in red. Tree diagram of philosophical categories, fol. 121^{r}.

PROVENANCE Prague (fol. 72^{r}).

BIBLIOGRAPHY *Katalog*, III.1, p. 1223; *MBKÖ*, I, p. 259 (F 201); *AL*, 64; Kristeller, III, p. 33.

34. MS Melk, Stiftsbibliothek, 1712 (formerly 940/R. 20)
Logica vetus et nova s. xiv

Parchment; 145 fols; page 175x130mm; text 120x85mm; 29 lines; several scribes. *Titulus* in red, fol. 2^{v}. Binding: original parchment chemise cover (cf. MS 928).

CONTENTS Fol. 1^{r-v} s. xv contents list; 2^{r} s. xv notes; 2^{v}–8^{v} ***Isag.***; 8^{v}–19^{r} ***Cat.***; 19^{v}–26^{r} ***De Int.***; 26^{v}–30^{v} *Liber sex principiorum*; 31^{r}–37^{v} ***Div.***; 39^{r}–76^{v} ***Top. Diff.***; 77^{r}–91^{r} ***Soph. Elench.***; 91^{r}–109^{v} *Post. Anal.*; 110^{r}–139^{v} ***Prior Anal.***; 140^{r}–145^{v} blank.

GLOSS Marginal and interlinear gloss to *De Int.*; readers' notes to *Post. Anal.*

DECORATION Major initials in red and blue; red paraph signs. Incipits and explicits in red. Diagrams in red, fols 82^{r}, 125^{v}.

PROVENANCE Melk (fol. 1^{r}: s. xv).

BIBLIOGRAPHY *Katalog*, III.1, p. 1290; *MBKÖ*, I, p. 259 (F 202); *AL*, 66; Kristeller III, p. 33.

35. MS Melk, Stiftsbibliothek, 1847 (formerly 229/G. 31)
Op. Sac. I–III, V s. xiii (Courcelle: s. xii)

Parchment; i + 44 + i fols; page 280x220mm; text 225x175mm; 28–32 lines; one scribe. Greek confident. Modern brown leather binding.

CONTENTS Fols 1^{v}–25^{v} ***Op. Sac. I–III, V***; 26^{r}–38^{v} Gilbert of Poitiers, Commentary on *Op. Sac.*; 38^{v}–44^{v} commentary on bk II of *Arith.*, *inc.* 'Ne subisse possit similitudo falsitatis'; *expl.* 'quod est incomprehensibile omnibus'.

GLOSS Marginal and interlinear glosses to *Op. Sac.*; text linked to gloss by Greek letters.

DECORATION Portrait of Boethius and John the Deacon seated under a double arcade, fol. 1r; large green ***I(nvestigatam)***, fol. 1r.

PROVENANCE Unknown.

BIBLIOGRAPHY *Katalog*, II.1, p. 517; *MBKÖ*, I, p. 234; Courcelle, p. 71, pl. 7 (fol. 1r).

REIN (Reun)

STIFTSBIBLIOTHEK

The abbey of Rein in Styria was founded in 1129, the first Cistercian monastery to be established in Austria. The medieval library has not been preserved and most of the MSS surviving from the thirteenth century are now in the Österreichische Nationalbibliothek in Vienna. In the fifteenth century the monastic library suffered heavy losses from the Turkish invasions.

A. Weis, *Handschriftenverzeichniss der Stiftsbibliothek zu Reun*, Xenia Bernardina, I, pp. 1–114; Unterkircher, Fiedler, Stickler, pp. 23–4.

36. MS Rein, Stiftsbibliothek, 16
DCPhil. s. xii/xiii

Parchment; 138 fols; page 190x105mm; text 140x65mm; 41 lines; one scribe. Binding: s. xv white leather on wood.

CONTENTS Fols 1r–99r *Miracula S. Mariae, inc.* 'Ad omnipotentis dei laudem cum sepe recitantur'; 101r–138r ***DCPhil.***

GLOSS None.

DECORATION Elaborate initials in red and gold with occasional penwork flourishing.

PROVENANCE Rein. '1549. Rabanus. Si quis non vescitur verbo dei, non vivet Fr. pe. kh.' (fol. 138v).

BIBLIOGRAPHY *Xenia Bernardina* (Weis), I, p. 14.

37. MS Rein, Stiftsbibliothek, 19
DCPhil. s. xv

Paper; 229 fols; page 220x145mm; text 150x85mm; 32 lines, frame-ruled; wide margins for gloss; two scribes. Binding: s. xv white leather on wood (Rein).

CONTENTS Fols 1^{r}–4^{v} blank; 5^{r}–169^{v} ***DCPhil.***; 170^{r}–228^{r} Ps.-Boethius, *De disciplina scolarium.*

GLOSS Interlinear and marginal glosses on a massive scale to both works; text linked to gloss by underlining in red.

DECORATION Major initials in red, black, green and gold.

PROVENANCE ?Rein.

BIBLIOGRAPHY *Xenia Bernardina* (Weis), I, p. 15; Weijers, no. 80.

SALZBURG

STIFTSBIBLIOTHEK ST PETER, f. 700

One of the oldest monastic libraries in the world, its manuscript tradition may be traced back to the time of Abbot Arno (785–98), who later became Archbishop of Salzburg. The book collections of the abbey and of the cathedral library were separated in the tenth century. Noteworthy is the almost total absence of medieval catalogues and the fact that the library has not preserved its original collection, parts of which may be found in most major libraries in the world.

H. Tietze, *Die illuminierten Handschriften in Salzburg*, Beschreibendes Verzeichnis der illuminierten Handschriften in Österreich, II, Leipzig, 1905; A. Jungwirth, *Beschreibung der Handschriften des Stiftes St. Peter in Salzburg*, 6 vols, Salzburg, 1910–12, repr. as *Catalog of Manuscripts in Stift St. Peter, Austria*, Ann Arbor and London, 1981; *MBKÖ*, IV, pp. 59–74 (with detailed bibliography); Unterkircher, Fiedler, Stickler, pp. 9–10; Kristeller, III, pp. 37–40.

38. MS Salzburg, Stiftsbibliothek St Peter, a. VI. 54
DCPhil. s. xv

Paper; 170 fols; page 205x145mm; text 160x110mm; 38 lines; several scribes. Binding: s. xix.

CONTENTS Fols 2^{r}–156^{r} ***DCPhil.***, *inc.* imperf. I.m.ii.19 'ut terram roseis floribus ornat', with commentary of Ps.-Aquinas; 159^{r}–165^{v} misc. *questiones* on philosophical and theological topics; 166^{r}–170^{r} sermon *De situ paradisi*.

GLOSS See contents. Commentary written in margins; text linked to commentary by paraph signs, underlining in red until fol. 34^{r}, and pointing hands.

DECORATION Simple red capitals.

PROVENANCE Salzburg.

BIBLIOGRAPHY Jungwirth, vol. I (unpaginated).

ST FLORIAN

STIFTSBIBLIOTHEK

The Augustinian house of St Florian in Upper Austria was founded in the first half of the ninth century for lay canons. In 1071 Bishop Altmann of Passau gave it to the canons regular. No medieval catalogues or indices have been preserved. The scriptorium may be traced back to the first half of the twelfth century and the school of illumination to the second half of the thirteenth century. The MSS were given marks of ownership in the fifteenth century.

A. Czerny, *Die Handschriften der Stiftsbibliothek St. Florian*, Linz, 1871; G. Schmidt, *Die Malerschule von St. Florian. Beiträge zur süddeutschen Malerei des 13. und im 14. Jahrhundert*, Linz, Graz and Cologne, 1962; *MBKÖ*, V, pp. 98–101; Unterkircher, Fiedler, Stickler, pp. 13–14; K. Holter, 'Cimelien aus der Stiftsbibliothek St. Florian', *Oberösterreich Kulturzeitschrift*, 1, 1986, pp. 11–18; K. Holter, 'Bibliothek und Archiv: Handschriften und Inkunabeln', *Die Kunstsammlungen des Augustiner-Chorherrenstiftes St. Florian*, Österreichische Kunsttopographie, 48, Vienna, 1988, pp. 29–91.

39. MS St Florian, Stiftsbibliothek, XI. 14

DCPhil. I, II s. xi; xii

Parchment; first two front flyleaves in the binding of a s. xiii MS of Gregory the Great, *Moralia in Iob*.
i (s. xi): page 205x152mm; text 180x110mm; 41 long lines; one scribe. Greek confident.
ii (s. xii): page 245x180mm; text 180x115mm; 41 lines; one scribe.
Modern binding.

CONTENTS Fol. i^{r-v} ***DCPhil.*** 'Hi semper eius'–'fomenta quaedam sunt' (II.pr.i.29–II.pr.iii.12).
Fol. ii^{r-v} ***DCPhil.*** 'Carmina qui'–'cernere terram' (I.m.i.1–I.m.ii.27).

GLOSS i: sparse interlinear and marginal glosses; text linked to gloss by underlining in red.
ii: marginal and occasional interlinear glosses; linked to text by underlining of text passage in gloss.

DECORATION i: red initials to mark the beginning of metre; large initials in red to mark transition from verse to prose. Initial words of sentences

written in brown capitals touched in red.
ii: plain ***H****(ec)* in red.

PROVENANCE Unknown.

BIBLIOGRAPHY Czerny, pp. 4–5; Holter, *Die Kunstsammlungen*, p. 61.

40. MS St Florian, Stiftsbibliothek, XI. 35
Op. Sac. s. xii

Parchment; 149 fols (flyleaves contain a fragment of s. xiii treatise on the production of the organ, and s. xi fragment of *De re musica*); page 220x155mm; text 150x110mm; 22 lines; several contemporary scribes. *Titulus* in red (s. xiii), fol. 6^{r}. Modern binding.

CONTENTS Fols 2^{r}–74^{r} Bible: Sapiential books, with Jerome's prologue and list of *capitula*; 74^{v} crude pen drawing of a hunter and monstrous beasts; 75^{r}–105^{v} Bernard of Clairvaux, *On the Song of Songs*; 105^{v} notes on the reaction to the fall of Jerusalem in 1187; 106^{r}–129^{v} ***Op. Sac.***; 130^{r}–149^{v} Bible: Revelation.

GLOSS Occasional marginal notes to *Op. Sac.*

DECORATION See contents. Plain red initials.

PROVENANCE St Florian (fols 2^{r}, 82^{r}, 149^{v}).

BIBLIOGRAPHY Czerny, p. 11; Manning and Rochais, no. 4583; Holter, *Die Kunstsammlungen*, p. 62, fig. 67 (fol. 74^{v}).

41. MS St Florian, Stiftsbibliothek, XI. 58
Op. Sac. s. xi

Parchment; i + 159 + i fols; page 175x140mm.
A: text 120x85mm; 23 lines, ruled with a stylus; several scribes. *Titulus* in red rustic capitals, fol. 1^{r}.
Binding: ?s. xv white leather on wood (restored).

CONTENTS A (s. xi): fols 1^{r}–47^{v} ***Op. Sac.*** (fol. 1^{v} *Historia de Arrio*, *inc.* 'Arius fuit doctor Alexandriae'; *expl.* 'sic remansit vacuus'); 47^{v}–48^{a} *Brevissima expositio orationis dominicae*; 48^{v} *Ordo romanae missae et orationum*; 49^{v}–80^{v} Ambrose, *De bono mortis*; 80^{v}–83^{r} Anon., *De brevitate huius vitae et de exitu ejusdem*; 83^{v} poem in a s. xiii hand (Walther, 2372).
B (s. xiii): fols 84^{r}–89^{r} Hugh of St Victor, *De quinque septenariis sacrae scripturae*; 89^{r}–118^{v} idem, *De operibus trium dierum* (= *Didascalicon* IV); 84^{r}–99^{v} in the margins and under main text

Carmina latina (Walther, 4953); 119^{r} miscellaneous s. xiii notes; 120^{r}–139^{v} Statius, *Achilleis*, with notes; 140^{r} fragment of a Latin glossary; 140^{r}–154^{r} fragments of Latin poets especially Ovid; 154^{v} several neumed hymns; 155^{r}–158^{v} *Argumenta sermonum* (s. xv hand); 159^{r} *Expositio fidei catholica*, *inc.* 'Omnes per fidem salvari credimus' (s. xi).

GLOSS — Systematic marginal and interlinear glosses to *Op. Sac.*; text linked to gloss by letters of the alphabet and reference signs.

DECORATION — On the front flyleaf, pen drawing of Boethius writing (in the upper part, an inscription of mixed ?Greek and Latin with Greek letters: see Bischoff). Occasional initials in red; headings and explicits in brown.

PROVENANCE — ?France (Bischoff). Probably belonged to Garsten OSB, 'Curia in Gaualenz' (fol. 119^{r}: s. xiii).

BIBLIOGRAPHY — Czerny, pp. 23–5; Bischoff, II, p. 254; Goy, pp. 103 (no. 36), 370 (no. 16); Holter, 'Cimelien', p. 11, fig. 2 (flyleaf); idem, *Die Kunstsammlungen*, p. 64, fig. 41 (flyleaf).

42. MS St Florian, Stiftsbibliothek, XI. 75

DCPhil. (2 copies) — s. xi; s. xii

Parchment; 133 fols; page 295x220mm.
A (s. xi): text 205x135mm; 27 lines, ruled with a stylus; wide margins for gloss (ruled separately); several scribes.
B (s. xii): text 190x85mm; 38 lines; ?one scribe.
Modern binding.

CONTENTS — A: fols 1^{r}–2^{v} Augustine, sermon (unidentified); 2^{v} *Brevis exhortatio ad dandam eleemosynam*; 3^{r}–17^{r} *Disputatio Luciferiani et Hieronymi orthodoxi*; 18^{r}–44^{v} Jerome, *Epistolae*; 45^{r}–101^{v} ***DCPhil.***; 101^{v} schematic description of the seasons and ages of man; 102^{r-v} *De lectione librorum* (excerpts); 103^{r-v} schemata of heavenly bodies; 104^{r} biographical notes on Boethius.
B: fol. 105^{r} *Carmina in laudem Boethii*; 105^{v} crude drawing of Boethius visited in prison by Philosophy; 106^{r}–132^{v} ***DCPhil.***, *inc.* imperf. II.pr.iv.85 'vel nescit esse mutabilem'; 133^{v} crude drawing of tree of knowledge, with male figure holding a cross and a book.

GLOSS — A: systematic marginal and interlinear glosses to *DCPhil.* in Latin and Old High German.
B: similar to A.

DECORATION — A: red ***C****(armina)* with yellow infill (fol. 45^{r}); ***P****(ost)* in red with the head of a man (?Boethius, fol. 53^{r}); pen drawing of the Wheel of

Fortune (fol. 53^{v}), similar drawings on fols 101^{v}, 103^{r-v}.
B: see contents. Inhabited initials in red; figural initials: snake (fol. 110^{r}) and dragon (fols 119^{r}, 126^{v}).

PROVENANCE ?St Florian. No marks of ownership.

BIBLIOGRAPHY Czerny, pp. 30–31; Steinmeyer and Sievers, iv, p. 433, no. 140; Holter, 'Cimelien', p. 11, fig. 3 (fol. 105^{v}); idem, *Die Kunstsammlungen*, p. 65, figs 50 (fol. 53^{r}) and 56 (fol. 105^{v}).

43. MS St Florian, Stiftsbibliothek, XI. 82
Op. Sac. s. xii

Parchment; 189 fols (pastedowns contain a fragment of s. xii scholastic treatise *De peccato*); page 270x150mm; text 200x115mm; 24 lines. Binding: ?s. xv light brown leather on wood; five metal bosses.

CONTENTS Fols 1^{r}–5^{r} Hincmar of Rheims, Letter to Charles the Bald (s. xii); 5^{r}–54^{r} Gregory the Great, Letter to Reccardus, King of the Visigoths, with other *sententiae* (s. xii); 55^{r}–78^{v} s. xiii patristic excerpts; 79^{r}–85^{v} Henry of Langenstein, *Tractatus contra proprietatem religiosorum* (s. xiv); 85^{v}–101^{v} idem, *Epistola contra proprietatem religiosorum*; 102^{r}–108^{v} Arno of Reichersberg, *Scutum canonicorum regularium* (s. xiv); 109^{r}–110^{v} blank; 111^{r}–145^{v} Ramon Lull, *Summa de matrimonio* (s. xiii); 145^{v} notes on book of Enoch (s. xiii); 146^{r} note on the seven sacraments (s. xiii); 146^{v} short letters and treatise on a mystical stone (s. xiii); 147^{r}–162^{v} s. xiii patristic excerpts; 163^{v}–188^{v} ***Op. Sac.***; 189^{v} s. xv table of contents.

GLOSS Sparse marginal glosses to *Op. Sac.*

DECORATION Space left for initials, not executed; explicit in ink of text, fol. 188^{v}.

PROVENANCE St Florian (fol. 189^{v}).

BIBLIOGRAPHY Czerny, pp. 35–6; Classen, *Gerhoch*, p. 445.

ST PAUL IM LAVANTTAL

STIFTSBIBLIOTHEK

The library of the Benedictine monastery in Carinthia (dissolved in 1787, restored in 1809) now also comprises the collections of the Augustinian house of Spital am Pyhrn in Upper Austria and of the Benedictine monastery of St Blasien in the Black

Forest (dissolved in 1787).

Catalogus codicum manuscriptorum ex monasteriis S. Blasii in Silva Nigra et Hospitalis ad Pyrhum montem in Austria nunc in monasterio S. Pauli in Carinthia, Ann Arbor and London, 1981; A. Trende, 'Die Stiftsbibliothek St. Paul', *Carinthia I*, 142, 1952, pp. 609–68; K. Holter, 'Die Bibliothek. Handschriften und Inkunabeln', *Die Kunstdenkmäler des Benediktinerstiftes St. Paul im Lavanttal und seiner Filialkirchen*, ed. K. Ginhart, Österreichische Kunsttopographie, 37, Vienna, 1969, pp. 340–441; Unterkircher, Fiedler, Stickler, p. 19; Kristeller, III, pp. 44–8.

44. MS St Paul im Lavanttal, Stiftsbibliothek, 4/2
DCPhil. 1481–83

Paper; 110 fols; page 310x220mm; text 198x99mm (fols 1^{r}–8^{v} 2 cols, each 224x70mm); 22–37 lines; several scribes. Dated colophons, fols 104^{r}: 1481, and 107^{v}: 1483. *Tituli* in red and blue. Binding: s. xix.

CONTENTS Fols 1^{r}–104^{r} ***DCPhil.*** (glossed); 105^{r}–107^{v} Lombardello Gregorio, *Elegia Aldae et miserabilium casuum Aldae virginis*; 108^{r}–110^{v} Ps.-Hannibal, *Epistola de amore*.

GLOSS Extensive marginal and interlinear glosses to fols 9^{r}–101^{r}.

DECORATION Elaborate initials in red and blue.

PROVENANCE St Blasien; no marks of ownership.

BIBLIOGRAPHY Kristeller, III, p. 44.

ST PÖLTEN

DIÖZESANBIBLIOTHEK (formerly Bischöfliche Alumnatsbibliothek)

The Diözesanbibliothek is an heir to the library of the Augustinian house in St Pölten in Lower Austria. The Augustinian house was founded in the eighth century, populated with Augustinian canons in 1080 and the abbey library was first mentioned in the thirteenth century. After the dissolution of the House in 1784, the library collections were handed over to the Diözesan-bibliothek for the newly founded archbishopric of St Pölten.

There is a typed inventory of the 197 MSS; G. Winner, 'Zur Bibliotheksgeschichte des ehemaligen Augustiner-Chorherrenstiftes St. Pölten', *Translatio Studii. Manuscript and Library Studies Honoring Oliver L. Kapsner O.S.B.*, ed. J. G. Plante, Collegeville, MN, 1973, pp. 43–74; idem, *Katalog der Handschriften der Diözesanbibliothek Sankt Pölten*, St Pölten, 1978; Kristeller, III, pp. 48–9.

45. MS St. Pölten, Diözesanbibliothek, 84
Op. Sac. I–III, V s. xiii

Parchment; 243 fols; page 195x145mm; text 155x115mm; 31 lines; one scribe for Boethius. *Tituli* in red. Neumes, fol. 106^{r}. Binding: ?s. xv red leather on wood; two clasps (restored); chain-mark on front cover. Related to MSS Vienna, ÖNB, 1618, and Zwettl 248, 253.

CONTENTS Fols 1^{v}–2^{v} first prologue of Gilbert of Poitiers; 2^{v}–3^{v} second prologue of Gibert of Poitiers; 3^{v}–101^{v} ***Op. Sac. I–III, V***, with commentary of Gilbert of Poitiers; 102^{v}–105^{v} Gennadius Massiliensis, *De ecclesiasticis dogmatibus* (*PL*, 58: 979–1000); 106–107^{v} verses (neumed); 108^{r}–164^{v} Siboto, *Sermones super psalmum quinquagesimum*, *inc.* imperf. 'triumphabit et tyranni'; *expl.* 'dilectioni eternitati perseveranciam ad honorem'; 165^{r}–174^{v} ?Siboto, *Super symbolum*, *inc.* 'credo in Deum. Nota si aliquis rex militi suo'; *expl.* imperf. 'nullum medicamentum utilius esse'; 175^{r}–187^{v} *Miracula Beatae Mariae Virginis*, *inc.* 'Accidit in Anglia. Erat quidam monachus'; 188^{r}–190^{v} *Tractatus de decem praeceptis*, *inc.* 'Sapiens est qui sat'; *expl.* imperf. 'vita privatur'; 191^{r}–195^{r} *Miracula Beatae Virginis Mariae* (continued from fol. 187^{v}), *expl.* 'aput Coloniam urbem in monasterio Sancti Petri'; 196^{r}–200^{r} *Miracula*; 200^{v}–201^{v} *Tractatus de Antichristo*, *inc.* 'Incipiunt herrores (*sic*) tractati de evangelio eterno'; *expl.* imperf. 'predicatores ut congregent'; $202^{r–v}$ notes; 202^{v}–203^{v} anon. treatise, *inc.* 'isti sunt denunciandi in cena Domini'; *expl.* 'enormis factus non sudditus (?) aut alienus'; 204^{r}–243^{v} Honorius Augustodunensis, *Expositio in Cantica canticorum*, *expl.* imperf. 'que fulget instancia predicatione' (*PL*, 172: 445).

GLOSS See contents.

DECORATION Simple initials; rubricated.

PROVENANCE Austria. Probably produced in the Augustinian House in St Pölten (G. Winner). Probably belonged to the Cistercian Abbey of Vallis Dei (Säusenstein) near Ybbs in Lower Austria (Häring).

BIBLIOGRAPHY Häring, 'Texts', pp. 188–9; Winner, *Katalog*, pp. 84–6.

SCHLÄGL

STIFTSBIBLIOTHEK

The Premonstratensian monastery of Schlägl in Upper Austria was founded in the first half of the thirteenth century. No medieval lists of MSS or catalogues have been preserved, but a number of thirteenth- and fourteenth-century MSS are intact.

In the fifteenth century the library underwent a new growth from its own scriptorium and from donations.

G. Vielhaber and G. Indra, *Catalogus codicum Plagensium (Cpl.) manuscriptorum*, Linz, 1918; Unterkircher, Fiedler, Stickler, pp. 33–3; Kristeller, III, p. 50.

46. MS Schlägl, Stiftsbibliothek, 7 Cpl. 60
Logica vetus et nova s. xiii

Parchment; i + 259 fols; page 250x180mm; text 140x90mm; 26 lines; one scribe for text. Book titles and numbers as running headers. Binding: s. xv.

CONTENTS Fol. i^r s. xv philosophical notes, *inc.* 'Nota quod genus'; *expl.* 'quomodo se habet'; 1^r–8^v ***Isag.***; 8^v–23^v ***Cat.***; 23^v–33^r ***De Int***; 33^v–41^r *Liber sex principiorum*; 41^v–52^v ***Div.***; 52^v–86^r ***Top. Diff.***; 87^r–138^r ***Prior Anal.***; 139^r–170^v *Post. Anal.*; 171^r–192^r ***Soph. Elench.***; 192^v–259^r ***Topica Aris.***; 259^v s. xv philosophical notes and table of contents.

GLOSS Unsystematic interlinear and marginal glosses in a later hand to each work.

DECORATION Finely executed initials in red, blue, and gold (some of them inhabited, e.g., fols 1^r, 87^r, 139^r) to the beginning of each work. Carelessly executed pen-drawing of a medieval castle (fol. i^r: s. xv); drawing of coats of arms depicting a unicorn lying under a tree (fol. 1^r); an elaborate drawing of a crowned figure holding a sceptre in each hand, and of eighteen explanatory roundels (fol. 8^v). Paraph signs in red and blue.

PROVENANCE Italy. Belonged to Johannes von Rabenstein (1437–73), humanist and diplomat, who purchased the codex in 1461 in Pavia (fols i^r, 259^v: s. xv).

BIBLIOGRAPHY Vielhaber and Indra, pp. 10–13; *AL*, 69.

SEITENSTETTEN

STIFTSBIBLIOTHEK, f. 1112

Two major fires destroyed most of the medieval books from the library of the Benedictine Abbey; only fourteen MSS date from the thirteenth and fourteenth centuries. However, the library acquired additional MSS in the course of the fifteenth century from the collection of Johann Hofmüller, and in the later eighteenth century under abbot Dominikus and from the collections of the dissolved libraries of the University of Vienna and the monastery of Ardagger.

H. Cerny, 'Beiträge zur Geschichte der Wissenschaftspflege des Stiftes Seitenstetten im Mittelalter', *Studien und Mitteilungen zur Geschichte des Benediktiner-Ordens und seiner Zweige*, 78, 1967, pp. 68–143; Unterkircher, Fiedler, Stickler, pp. 22–3; Kristeller, III, pp. 22–3.

47. MS Seitenstetten, Stiftsbibliothek, 61
Vita VII, DCPhil. s. xv

Paper; i (parchment) + 256 + i (parchment) fols (front flyleaf contains a fragment from a s. xiii breviary); page 210x150mm; text 130–50x80mm; 15–16 lines for text, up to 60 lines for commentary; several scribes. Binding: s. xv wooden boards with leather spine; one central clasp (lost).
A rather carelessly executed volume.

CONTENTS Fol. 1^{r} notes on the sacraments, *inc.* 'septem sunt sacramenta nobis a Domino Christo instituta'; 1^{v} contents list for *DCPhil.*; 2^{r-v} ***Vita VII***; 3^{r}–173^{r} ***DCPhil.***, with commentary of Ps.-Aquinas until V.pr.v.12 'sensus enim solus' (fol. 163^{v}); 173^{v}–182^{v} blank; 183^{r}–185^{r} *Carmen de ascensione Domini*, *inc.* 'Salve festa dies toto venerabilis aevo'; *expl.* 'consolidaris nobis sine fine suis amen'; 185^{r-v} verse, *inc.* 'si cupis capiti tibi calvo tibi posse mederi'; *expl.* 'aquilam e nido curvae'; 186^{r}–248^{v} Sallust, *Catiline*; 249^{r}–251^{r} Boccaccio, *Historia Lucretiae*; 252^{r}–255^{v} Ps.-Virgil, *Moretum*; 256^{r-v} patristic *sententiae*.

GLOSS See contents. Intercalated commentary on a massive scale to *DCPhil.*; commentary linked to text by underlining in red and ink of text; interlinear glosses throughout. Interlinear and marginal glosses to Sallust, Boccaccio and Virgil.

DECORATION Clumsily executed ***C****(armina)* in red (fol. 3^{r}); initials in red up to fol. 10^{r}; thereafter none.

PROVENANCE Austria. In Seitenstetten by s. xv.

BIBLIOGRAPHY Cerny, pp. 74, 127; Kristeller III, p. 51.

48. MS Seitenstetten, Stiftsbibliothek, 281
DCPhil. s. xv

Paper; i (parchment) + 330 + i (parchment) fols (flyleaves contain fragments from a theological treatise); page 220x155mm.
A: text 170x100mm; 21 lines; one scribe.
B: text 165x100mm; 42 lines; one scribe.
C: text 120x90mm; 13–20 lines for text, up to 60 lines for commentary; one scribe (same as MS 61). *Titulus* in red, fol. 66^{r}.
D: text 180x120mm; 37 lines; one scribe.

E: text 165x110mm; 43 lines; two scribes. *Tituli* in red.
F: text variable; up to 56 lines; one scribe.
G: text 180x140mm; 36 lines; one scribe.
Binding: identical with MS 61.

CONTENTS A: fol. 1^{r-v} Ovid, *De siculo* (?= Ps.-Ovid, *De cuculo*).
B: fols 2^{r}–63^{r} *Tractatus de philosophia naturali.*
C: fols 66^{r}–172^{v} ***DCPhil.***, with commentary of Ps.-Aquinas.
D: fols 173^{r}–189^{r} *Tractatus de corpore Christi*; 189^{v}–195^{v} Rabbi Samuel, *De Messia.*
E: fols 197^{r}–204^{v} *Collectanea de penitentia*; 205^{r}–209^{v} *De interrogandis penitentibus*; 210^{r}–25^{r} *De necessitate confessionis*; 225^{r}–262^{v} Nicholas of Poland, *Tractatus de sacramentis.*
F: fols 263^{r}–302^{v} ecclesiastical hymns with commentary.
G: fols 307^{r}–326^{v} Andrew of Spain, *Lumen confessorum*; 327^{r}–330^{v} blank.

GLOSS C: see contents. Intercalated commentary on a massive scale; text surrounded by commentary. Commentary linked to text by underlining in red and red paraph signs. Interlinear glosses throughout.

DECORATION C: ***C****(armina)* in red (fol. 66^{r}); initial letters touched with red.

PROVENANCE Austria. In Seitenstetten by s. xv.

BIBLIOGRAPHY Cerny, pp. 74, 113, 127; Kristeller III, p. 51.

WIEN (Vienna)

ÖSTERREICHISCHE NATIONALBIBLIOTHEK (formerly Kaiserlich-Königliche Hofbibliothek)

The library started as a private collection of the Habsburgs in the second half of the fourteenth century. The turning point came in 1575 when Emperor Maximillian II invited the Dutch humanist Hugo Blotius as a court librarian. He reorganized the library and compiled the first systematic catalogues. In the next centuries the library acquired some important collections, among them the library of Philipp Edward Fugger from Augsburg in 1655, the Stadtbibliothek of Vienna in 1780 and, at the end of the eighteenth century, the collections of a number of dissolved monasteries.

Tabulae codicum manu scriptorum praeter graecos et orientales in Bibliotheca Palatina Vindobonensi asservatorum, 10 vols, Vienna, 1864–99; H. J. Hermann, *Die illuminierten Handschriften und Inkunabeln der Nationalbibliothek in Wien*, 7 vols, Leipzig, 1923–38; F. Unterkircher, *Inventar der illuminierten Handschriften, Inkunabeln und Frühdrucke der Österreichischen Nationalbibliothek*, 2 vols, Vienna, 1957–9; O. Mazal and F. Unterkircher, *Katalog der abendländischen*

Handschriften der Österreichischen Nationalbibliothek "Series nova" (Neuerwerbungen), 4 vols, Vienna, 1963–75; F. Unterkircher, *Die datierten Handschriften der Österreichischen Nationalbibliothek bis zum Jahre 1400*, Katalog der datierten Handschriften in lateinischer Schrift in Österreich, 1, Vienna, 1969; O. Mazal, E. Irblich and I. Németh, *Wissenschaft im Mittelalter. Ausstellung von Handschriften und Inkunabeln der Österreichischen Nationalbibliothek*, Vienna, 1975; Unterkircher, Fiedler, Stickler, pp. 42–50; O. Mazal, *Byzanz und das Abendland. Ausstellung der Handschriften- und Inkunabelsammlung der Österreichischen Nationalbibliothek. Handbuch und Katalog*, Graz, 1981; Kristeller, III, pp. 57–70.

49. MS Wien, Österreichische Nationalbibliothek, 50

Arith., Mus. s. x 2/2

Parchment; 135 fols (pastedowns include a s. xiv medical fragment and a 1282 Salzburg diploma); page 322x230–63mm.
A (s. x 2/2): text 2 cols (fols 1^r–46^v), each 240x80mm; 27 lines; one scribe. *Tituli* in red.
B (s. x 2/2): text 245x160mm; 29 lines; one scribe. Greek, fol. 122^r. *Tituli* in red.
Bound together in 1435 in Salzburg by Georg Feychter (Mazal); white leather binding on wood; two clasps (lost); parchment label on front cover.

CONTENTS A: fols 1ra–46vb ***Arith.***; 47^r *De asse et partibus eius* (s. xiii); 47^v–48^v Ps.-Jerome, *De diversis generibus musicorum ad Dardanum* (*PL*, 30:213–15); 49^r–54^v ***Mus.***, *expl.* imperf. I.12 'divisioni vocum earum' (199/1).
B: fols 55^r–135^v ***Mus.***, *inc.* imperf. I.12 'sed de his hactenus nunc vocum differentias' (199/2).

GLOSS A: systematic marginal and interlinear glosses (Bernhard *W*).
B: marginal glosses and tables.

DECORATION A: major and minor initials in red; many schematic pen-drawings, some with infilling. Drawing of genealogical tree of Philosophy, fol. 1^r; diagram of five empty circles within a larger circle, fol. 1^v; nine drawings of musical instruments, fols 48^v–49^r.
B: major and minor initials in red. Numerous pen-drawings, e.g., fols 61^v, 100^r, 122^r.

PROVENANCE A: Upper Italy.
B: written in Salzburg. Belonged to Friedrich von Chiemgau, Archbishop of Salzburg (958–991), from whom it passed to the Chapter library (Domkapitelsbibliothek) in Salzburg, whence to the Nationalbibliothek (then Hofbibliothek) in 1806.

BIBLIOGRAPHY *Tabulae*, I, pp. 6–7; Hermann, I, pp. 208–10, no. 80; Unterkircher, *Inventar*, I, p. 4; *MBKÖ*, IV, p. 41, no. 223; Mazal, Irblich and Németh, pp. 188–9, no. 159; O. Mazal, 'Die Salzburger

Domkapitelbibliothek vom 10. bis zum 12. Jahrhundert', *Paläographie 1981. Colloquium des Comité International de Paléographie. München, 15.-18. September 1981. Referate*, ed. G. Silagi, Münchener Beiträge zur Mediävistik und Renaissance-Forschung, 32, Munich, 1982, pp. 71–91 (73–74); Masi, p. 63; Bernhard, p. 23; Bower, no. 131; A. Fingernagel and M. Roland, *Mitteleuropaïsche Schulen I*, Die illuminierten Handschriften der Österreichischen Nationalbibliothek, 2 vols, Vienna, 1997, S. 360; O. Mazal, *Einbandkunde*, Elemente des Buch- und Bibliotheks-wesens 16, Wiesbaden, 1997, p. 364, no. 3.

50. MS Wien, Österreichische Nationalbibliothek, 51

Mus. s. xii

Parchment; 166 fols; page 340x265mm; text 2 cols, each 270x95mm; 50–51 lines; several scribes. Book numbers in red as running headers. Greek in *Mus. Tituli* in red rustic capitals throughout. Binding: s. xv brown leather on wood; spine renewed; two clasps (lost).
A well-executed functional book.

CONTENTS Fols 1^{r}–2^{r} Odo of Cluny, Guy of Arezzo, William of Hirsau, *Monochordum*; 2^{v} Guy of Arezzo, *Manus symbolica sive figuralis divisio tonorum secundum articulos manus humanae*; 3^{r} blank; 3^{v} portrait of Boethius; 4^{r} *De ephoris Ephororum Spartanorum*; 4rb–34vb ***Mus.***; 35rb Hucbald of Elnon, *De musica* (fragm.); 36rb–41va Guy of Arezzo, *Micrologus*; 41vb–43rb idem, *Regulae musicae rhythmicae*; 43rb–44ra idem, *Regulae de ignoto cantu*; 44rb–45rb idem, *Tractatus de ignoto cantu*; 46ra–48va Ps.-Odo of Cluny, *Dialogus de musica*; 49ra–52va Berno of Reichenau, *Musica*; 52vb–55ra idem, *De monochordo mensurando* and *De mensura fistularum*; 55^{ra-vb} Gerlandus Vesontius, *De fistulis* (fragm.); *De mensura organistri*; *De ponderatione cymbali*; 56rb–62rb Berno of Reichenau, *Tonarius*; 62va–70va Johannes Cotto of Trier, *Musica*; 71ra–72vb idem, *Tonarius*; 73va–81va William of Hirsau, *Musica*; 82ra–90rb Hermannus Contractus, *Musica*; 90rb–91ra Henry of Augsburg, *Institutio catechetica musices*; 92ra–117vb Cicero, *De inventione*; 118ra–135vb Ps.-Cicero, *Ad Herennium*; 136ra–145vb *Ars geometrica* (excerpts from Cassiodorus, M. Capella, Isidore and *Agrimensores*); 146ra–611vb Hyginus, *Astronomicon*; 162ra–166ra Martianus Capella, *De nuptiis*, VII (excerpts).

GLOSS A few marginal glosses to *Mus.*

DECORATION Three full-page portrait miniatures: Boethius (fol. 3^{v}); Guy of Arezzo and Bishop Theobald of Arezzo, each with a monochord (fol. 35^{v}); and Odo of Cluny writing (fol. 45^{v}). One smaller author-portrait (fol. 62^{v}). Historiated ***O****(mnium)*: Music playing harp (green background speckled with red: fol. 4^{v}). Red major initials with yellow infill on blue or green background, e.g., fols 11^r, 22^v, 31^r, 105^v, 146^v. Forty drawings of constellations in red and purple (fols 147^v–155^r). Schematic pen-drawings in red, yellow and green to the musical treatises.

PROVENANCE Produced in Austria or S. Germany. Belonged to the old University Library in Vienna, whence it passed to the Hofbibliothek in 1756.

BIBLIOGRAPHY *Tabulae*, I, p. 7; Hermann, II, pp. 260–70, no. 177, figs 153 (fol. 3^v), 154 (fol. 4^r), 155 (fol. 35^v), 156 (fol. 45^v), 157 (fol. 146^v), 158 (fol. 149^v); Zinner, nos 1948 (M. Capella) and 5219 (Hyginus); Saxl, pp. 69–75; Unterkircher, *Inventar*, I, p. 4; Folkerts, p. 96; Glorieux, *Arts*, pp. 459 (no. 2154), 461 (no. 2204), 463 (no. 2260); W. Fitzgerald, 'Nugae Hyginianae', *Essays in Honour of A. C. Pegis*, ed. J. R. O'Donnell, Toronto, 1974, p. 199; S. Gallick, 'Medieval Rhetorical Arts in England and the Manuscript Traditions', *Manuscripta*, 18, 1974, p. 89; Mazal, Irblich and Németh, pp. 231–32, no. 211; O. Mazal, *Buchkunst der Romanik*, Graz, 1978, figs 34 (fol. 157^r), 62 (fol. 3^v); Bolton, in Gibson, p. 432; Mazal, *Byzanz und das Abendland*, pp. 281–82, no. 210; G. Viré, 'La transmission du *De Astronomia* d'Hygin jusqu'au XIIIe siècle', *Revue d'histoire des textes*, 11, 1981, no. 84, pp. 243–5; V. I. J. Flint, 'Heinricus of Augsburg and Honorius Augustodunensis: Are They the Same Person?', *Revue Bénédictine*, 92, 1982, pp. 150, 156–7; Munk Olsen, I, pp. 98 (Cens.C.9), 309–10 (Cic.C.559), 534–5 (Hyg.C.37); *Musik im mittelalterlichen Wien. Katalog der Ausstellung*, Vienna, 1986, p. 172, no. 2; Bower, no. 132; Toneatto, III, pp. 985–95.

51. MS Wien, Österreichische Nationalbibliothek, 53
DCPhil. 1307

Parchment; 162 fols; page 330x220mm; text 215x122mm; 23 lines for text; 46 lines for commentary; scribe Philippus de Altavilla (dated colophon, fol. 162^v). Book numbers in red as running headers. *Titulus* in red, fol. 161^r. Binding: s. xix white leather on pasteboard.
Beautifully executed.

CONTENTS Fols 1^r–161^v ***DCPhil.***, with commentary of Ptolemaeus de Asinariis (*DCPhil.* text starts fol. 5^v); 161^v–62^v Lupus, *De metris*.

GLOSS See contents. Intercalated commentary on a massive scale.

DECORATION Red and blue initials with penwork flourishing, four with gold background (fols 1^r, 2^r, 5^r, 113^r).

PROVENANCE Italy. Belonged to the humanist Johannes Sambucus (1531–1584), whose library was acquired by the Hofbibliothek in 1578 and 1587.

BIBLIOGRAPHY *Tabulae*, I, p. 8; Hermann, V.1, pp. 21–22, no. 20; Unterkircher, *Inventar*, I, p. 4; Courcelle, pp. 413–14 (Ptolemaeus); Unterkircher, *Die datierten*, I, p. 17, fig. 68 (fol. 162^{v}).

52. MS Wien, Österreichische Nationalbibliothek, 55

Arith., Mus. s. x

Parchment; 208 fols; page 316x234mm; text 250x180mm; 24–26 lines; several scribes. Greek in text, fol. 94^{r-v}. *Tituli* in red rustic capitals, e.g., fol. 92^{v}. Binding: s. xviii white leather on pasteboard.

CONTENTS Fols 1^{r}–23^{r} Ps.-Boethius, *Geometria I*; 23^{v}–92^{v} ***Arith.***; 93^{r}–167^{r} ***Mus.***; 167^{r-v} *Fragmentum de musica*, *inc.* 'Quinque sunt consonantie musice'; *expl.* 'cordarum in quibus constituit'; 168^{r}–82^{r} Hucbald of Elnon, *Musica enchiriadis*; 182^{r}–208^{v} idem, *Scholia enchiriadis de arte musica*; 208^{v} idem, *De musica* (fragm.).

GLOSS Systematic gloss to *Arith.* and *Mus.*; s. xiv readers' notes to fols 206^{v}–7^{r}.

DECORATION Three large decorated initials in red and brown (fols 23^{v}, 25^{r}, 52^{r}). Many schematic drawings and tables throughout; a number of s. xiii^{in} pen-drawings (fols 164^{v}, 166^{r-v}, 167^{v}).

PROVENANCE Produced in Southern Germany. Belonged to the Dominican convent in Buda (fol. 208^{v}: s. xv), whence it passed to the Hofbibliothek in 1755.

BIBLIOGRAPHY *Tabulae*, I, p. 8; Hermann, II, pp. 311–12, no. 205, fig. 189 (fol. 207^{v}); Unterkircher, *Inventar*, I, p. 4; Folkerts, p. 96; Mazal, Irblich and Németh, pp. 230–31, no. 210, fig. 24 (fol. 174^{r}); Cs. Csapodi, 'Codices, die im Jahre 1686 nach Wien geliefert wurden', *Codices Manuscripti*, 7, 1981, p. 123; Mazal, *Byzanz und das Abendland*, pp. 282–83, no. 211; *Musik im mittelalterlichen Wien. Katalog der Ausstellung*, Vienna, 1986, p. 172, no. 3; Bernhard, p. 23; Bower, no. 133; Toneatto, III, pp. 908–12.

53. MS Wien, Österreichische Nationalbibliothek, 74

DCPhil. s. xv

Parchment; i + 64 fols; page 310x210mm; text 200x120mm; 26 lines, ruled with a stylus; one scribe. Greek in text, e.g., fol. 12^{r}. Modern binding.
A carefully written book.

CONTENTS Fols 1^{v}–62^{r} ***DCPhil.***

GLOSS None.

DECORATION Major initials in red and blue with penwork flourishing, one to begin each new book; capital letters touched in red; incipits and explicits in red.

PROVENANCE Unknown.

BIBLIOGRAPHY *Tabulae*, I, p. 11.

54. MS Wien, Österreichische Nationalbibliothek, 80
De Int., 2 in Int. s. x

Parchment; i + 177 fols; page 302x235mm; text 230x160mm; 27 lines; one scribe. *Tituli* in red. Binding: s. xv brown leather on wood; two clasps (lost); parchment label on front cover.

CONTENTS Fols 1^r–8^v ***De Int.***; 9^r–177^v ***2 in Int.***

GLOSS Unsystematic contemporary glosses throughout; frequent NOTA signs with explanatory notes to fols 9^r–30^v.

DECORATION Occasional capital letters in red; schemata, fols 59^v, 172^v, 173^r.

PROVENANCE German (Mazal). Belonged to the Chapter library in Salzburg, whence it passed to the Hofbibliothek in 1806.

BIBLIOGRAPHY *Tabulae*, I, p. 12; *AL*, 86; *MBKÖ*, IV, p. 41, no. 225; Mazal, Irblich, Németh, p. 110, no. 53; Mazal, *Byzanz und das Abendland*, p. 342, no. 266; idem, 'Die Salzburger Domkapitelbibliothek vom 10. bis zum 12. Jahrhundert', *Paläographie 1981. Colloquium des Comité International de paléographie. München, 15.-18. September 1981. Referate*, ed. G. Silagi, Münchener Beiträge zur Mediävistik und Renaissance-Forschung, 32, Munich, 1982, pp. 71–91 (75); Markowski, p. 225; Hoffmann, I, p. 364.

55. MS Wien, Österreichische Nationalbibliothek, 83
Arith. s. xiv

Parchment; i + 65 + i fols; page 297x200mm; text 200x120mm; 36–37 lines (for *Geometria* variable); two scribes (one for *Arith.*). *Tituli* in red to both works. Binding: s. xiv blue leather on wood; one central clasp (lost); paper label on front cover.

CONTENTS Fols 1^r–38^v ***Arith.***; 39^r–65^v Ps.-Boethius, *Geometria* I.

GLOSS Unsystematic marginal notes to *Arith.* Interlinear gloss to *Geometria*.

DECORATION Initials in red. Numerous geometrical drawings in red and black; pen drawings of *Templum Ezechielis* (fols 37^{v}–38^{r}).

PROVENANCE Italy. Belonged to Johannes von Gmunden (d. 1442), university professor and astronomer, who left the book to the faculty of Arts in Vienna; at the Jesuits' College in Vienna in s. xvii (fol. 1^{r}), then back to the University Library, whence it passed to the Hofbibliothek in 1756.

BIBLIOGRAPHY *Tabulae*, I, p. 12; Hermann, V.2, p. 195, no. 99; Unterkircher, *Inventar*, I, p. 5; Folkerts, p. 175.

56. MS Wien, Österreichische Nationalbibliothek, 84
DCPhil. s. xiv

Parchment; i + 95 + i fols; page 290x210mm; text 255x200mm; 22 lines (fols 1^{r}–4^{v} 17–19 lines) for text; 80–93 lines for commentary; one scribe. Binding: s. xviii white leather on pasteboard.
Well made.

CONTENTS Fols 1^{r}–95^{v} ***DCPhil.***, with commentary of William of Conches.

GLOSS See contents. Intercalated commentary on a massive scale; text surrounded by commentary.

DECORATION Seven large historiated initials on a golden background: Boethius holding a book (fol. 1^{r}); portrait of Boethius (fol. 14^{v}); personification of Philosophy (fol. 29^{v}); Boethius kneeling before Christ in Majesty (fol. 41^{v}); figure of Philosophy (fol. 53^{r}); portrait of Boethius (fol. 72^{r}); portrait of Boethius or ?commentator (fol. 86^{r}). 101 multicoloured minor initials on red and blue background with penwork flourishing.

PROVENANCE Italy. Belonged to Johannes Sambucus (fol. 1^{r}; cf. MS 53).

BIBLIOGRAPHY *Tabulae*, I, p. 12; Hermann, V.2, pp. 195–97, no. 100, pl. 81 (fols 1^{r}, 29^{v}, 41^{v}); Unterkircher, *Inventar*, p. 5; Courcelle, pp. 73, 81, 185–186, pl. 101.1 (fol. 41^{v}); Mazal, Irblich, Németh, pp. 73–74, no. 5; A. Pattin, 'Note sur un manuscrit de Guillaume de Conches', *Bulletin de philosophie médiévale*, 20, 1978, p. 65; Mazal, *Byzanz und das Abendland*, pp. 503–4, no. 408, fig. 96 (fol. 41^{v}); Nauta (this MS not used).

57. MS Wien, Österreichische Nationalbibliothek, 157
Top. Diff. IV s. xiii 1/2

Parchment; i + 192 fols; page 255x175mm; text 165x90mm; 27–28 lines; one scribe. *Tituli* in red. Binding: s. xviii white leather on pasteboard.

CONTENTS Fols 1^{r}–78^{r} Cicero, *De inventione*; 78^{v}–156^{v} Ps.-Cicero, *Ad Herennium*; 157^{r}–158^{v} Marbod of Rennes, *De ornamentis verborum* (Walther, 20244); 159^{r}–180^{v} Cicero, *De partitione oratoria*; 180^{v}–191^{r} ***Top. Diff. IV***.

GLOSS Marginal and interlinear glosses to Cicero, systematic in the beginning.

DECORATION Seven finely executed major initials to each book of Cicero with red, blue, and yellow infill and penwork flourishing (fols 1^{r}, 37^{r}, 78^{v}, 88^{r}, 106^{r}, 120^{v}, 159^{r}). Minor initials in red and blue; explicits in red.

PROVENANCE Italy. Philippus Podocatharus of Cyprus purchased it from Thomas de Urbino in 1452 (fol. 191^{r}); belonged to Johannes Sambucus (s. xvi).

BIBLIOGRAPHY *Tabulae*, I, p. 21; Hermann, III, p. 117, no. 78, fig. 126 (fol. 120^{v}); Unterkircher, *Inventar*, I, p. 8; S. Gallick, 'Medieval Rhetorical Arts in England and the Manuscript Traditions', *Manuscripta*, 18, 1974, p. 89; Mazal, Irblich, Németh, pp. 92–3, no. 31; O. Mazal, *Buchkunst der Romanik*, Graz, 1978, fig. 41 (fol. 1^{r}); Bursill-Hall, no. 299.006 (Marbod of Rennes); Munk Olsen, III.2, pp. 45–6 (Cic. C. 560.5).

58. MS Wien, Österreichische Nationalbibliothek, 159
2 in Int. s. xiii

Parchment; 79 fols; page 252x155mm; text 2 cols, each 185x55mm; 38 lines; one scribe. *Titulus* in red, fol. 1^{r}. Binding: s. xix white leather on pasteboard.

CONTENTS Fols 1^{r}–77^{r} ***2 in Int.***; 77^{v}–79^{r} logical figures with explanations.

GLOSS Contemporary marginal annotation to fols 1^{r}–15^{v}.

DECORATION See contents. Large initial in red on blue background, fol. 1^{r}. Other major and minor initials in red; numerous schematic drawings, e.g., fols 27^{v}, 48^{v}, 51^{v}, 54^{r}, 68^{r-v}.

PROVENANCE S. Germany; probably produced in the Benedictine abbey of Ottobeuren. Belonged to the humanist Alexander Brassicanus (d. 1539), from whom it passed to Johannes Faber, Bishop of Vienna (d. 1541). He bequeathed it to the library of St Nicholas' College, whence it passed to the old University Library and, in 1756, to the Hofbibliothek.

BIBLIOGRAPHY *Tabulae*, I, p. 22; Hermann, II, pp. 312–13, no. 206; *AL*, 91; Unterkircher, *Inventar*, I, p. 8; Markowski, p. 227.

59. MS Wien, Österreichische Nationalbibliothek, 166

Logica nova s. xiii

Parchment; ii + 219 fols; page 254x174mm; text 150x55mm; 22–24 lines; wide margins for gloss; several scribes. Binding: s. xv 2/2 white leather on wood; two clasps (lost).
Well written.

CONTENTS Fols 1^{r}–82^{v} ***Topica Aris.***; 83^{r} prayers to the Mother of God (added); 84^{r}–144^{r} ***Prior Anal.***; 144^{r}–81^{v} *Post. Anal.*; 181^{v}–209^{r} ***Soph. Elench.***; 209^{r}–19^{v} *Liber sex principiorum.*

GLOSS Extensive marginal glosses in several contemporary hands; occasional interlinear glosses.

DECORATION Blue initials to begin each treatise on red, white, green, and golden background (fols 1^{r}, 84^{r}, 144^{r}, 181^{v}, 209^{v}). Several ?s. xiv crudely executed pen-drawings of Christ on the cross (fols 31^{r}, 77^{r}, 86^{r}), a seated teacher (fols 39^{r}, 59^{r}), heads (fols 44^{r}–45^{r}), women (fols 49^{r}, 80^{r}, 169^{r}). Schematic drawings in red, green, and black (fols 107^{v}, 118^{r-v}). Red paraph signs; explicit in red (fol. 82^{v}).

PROVENANCE France. Belonged to the library of the Augustinian house of St Dorothea in Vienna (fols 1^{r}, 219^{v}: s. xiv^{in}), whence it passed to the Hofbibliothek in 1786.

BIBLIOGRAPHY *Tabulae*, I, p. 23; Hermann, VII.1, pp. 57–58, no. 16; *AL*, 92; Mazal, Irblich, Németh, p. 114, no. 60; Mazal, *Byzanz und das Abendland*, p. 344, no. 268, fig. 73 (fol. 1^{r}); E. Madas, 'Die in der Österreichischen Nationalbibliothek erhaltenen Handschriften des ehemaligen Augustiner-Chorherrenstiftes St. Dorothea in Wien', *Codices Manuscripti*, 8, 1982, p. 82; Markowski, pp. 35, 41, 44, 48, 227; Burnett, *Glosses*, p. 131.

60. MS Wien, Österreichische Nationalbibliothek, 177

Arith. s. xi 1/2

Parchment; i + 229 fols; page 240x190mm.
A (s. x): text 185x105mm; 26–27 lines; one scribe.
B (s. x): text 175x145mm; 24 lines; one scribe.
C (s. xi): text 2 cols, each 195x75mm; 27 lines; one scribe. *Tituli* in red.
D (s. xi 1/2): text 190x130mm; 26 lines; one scribe.
E (s. xii): text 2 cols, each 185x60mm; 26 lines; one scribe.
Binding: s. xv white leather on wood; one central clasp (lost); s. xv 1/2 parchment

label on front cover COMMENTUM SUPER RETHORICAM TULLI. ITEM QUIDAM SERMONES DOMINICALES IMPERFECTI ET ARITMETICA BOETII QUIA INTERPONITUR.

CONTENTS
A: fols 1^{r}–16^{v} Martianus Capella, *De nuptiis* ^{v}*–VI* (fragm.).
B: fols 17^{r}–22^{v} ?Helferich of Lune, *De ratione temporum* (fragm.).
C: fols 23ra–110vb Cicero, *De inventione I*, with commentary of M. Victorinus.
D: fols 111^{r}–117^{v}, 166^{r}–229^{r} ***Arith.***
E: fols 118^{r}–165^{v} sermons.

GLOSS
A: marginal glosses in scribe's hand.
C: see contents.
D: extensive marginal glosses to *Arith.* (fols 111^{r}–17^{v}) in scribe's hand; gloss linked to text by reference signs. Occasional marginal contemporary glosses to fols 166^{r}–229^{r}.

DECORATION
A: marginal drawing of the zodiac in ink of text, fol. 2^{r}; pen-drawing of Pallas-Athena, fol. 14^{r}.
B: initials in red and black.
C: space left for a large initial, not executed, fol. 23ra.
D: large decorated interlace initial in red, fol. 111^{r}. Numerous explanatory drawings.

PROVENANCE
Germany. A (fols 1^{r}–16^{v}) was probably produced in Reichenau; the other parts were executed in Salzburg. Bound together in s. xv 1/2 in Salzburg. Belonged to the Chapter Library, whence it passed to the Hofbibliothek in 1806.

BIBLIOGRAPHY
Tabulae, I, pp. 24–5; Hermann, I, pp. 183–84, no. 69, fig. 125 (fol. 14^{r}); Zinner, nos 4121, 12219 (Helferich); Unterkircher, *Inventar*, I, p. 9; Leonardi, no. 227; F. Mütherich, '"De Rhetorica". Eine Illustration zu Martianus Capella', *Festschrift B. Bischoff*, ed. J. Autenrieth and F. Brunhölzl, Stuttgart, 1971, pp. 199–200, pl. 14 (fol. 14^{r}); *MBKÖ*, IV, p. 40, no. 214; Mazal, *Byzanz und das Abendland*, p. 489, no. 391; Hoffmann, p. 437, figs 269 (fol. 23^{r}), 270 (fol. 111^{r}); Munk Olsen, III.1, p. 240; III.2, pp. 46 (Cic. C. 562), 179.

61. MS Wien, Österreichische Nationalbibliothek, 190
Op. Sac. s. xii 1/2

Parchment; 54 fols; page 250x173mm; text 190x90mm; 22 lines for text; up to 49 lines for commentary; ?one scribe. *Titulus* in red, fol. 1^{r}. Binding: s. xix white leather on pasteboard.

CONTENTS
Fols 1^{r}–53^{v} ***Op. Sac.***; 54^{v} neumed fragment of Lamentation 1:6.

GLOSS
Extensive contemporary marginal glosses throughout; scattered

interlinear glosses (Cappuyns N).

DECORATION Large interlace ***I(nvestigatam)*** in blue and red (1^{r}); minor initials with yellow and blue infill.

PROVENANCE Italy. In the Hofbibliothek by s. xviii 2/2.

BIBLIOGRAPHY *Tabulae*, I, p. 26; Hermann, III, pp. 80–81, no. 58, fig. 86 (fol. 1^{r}); Cappuyns, 'Opuscula sacra', p. 240; Unterkircher, *Inventar*, I, p. 9; Troncarelli, 'Opuscula', p. 18.

62. MS Wien, Österreichische Nationalbibliothek, 198
DCPhil. s. xv^{in}

Parchment; 69 + ii fols; page 234x177mm; text 150x85mm; 26 lines; one scribe. Greek in text with interlinear Latin translation. Binding: s. xvi white leather on wood; two clasps (lost).

CONTENTS Fols 1^{r}–69^{r} ***DCPhil.***

GLOSS None.

DECORATION Poor quality historiated ***C****(armina)* in gold depicting Boethius (with an open book, dressed in blue gown and cap), Philosophy (in blue with an open book), and the four Muses (in blue and brown dresses), fol. 1^{r}; five animal-pattern initials in blue with penwork flourishing (18^{r}, 22^{r}, 23^{r}, 41^{v}, 57^{v}); pen-drawings of animals (16^{v}, 23^{v}, 31^{v}, 39^{v}, 47^{v}, 55^{v}, 63^{v}). Elaborate initials in red and blue mark the beginning of each prose and metre.

PROVENANCE Italy. Belonged to a Francesco Sango (fol. ii^{v}: s. xv^{ex}); passed to the Hofbibliothek in 1756.

BIBLIOGRAPHY *Tabulae*, I, p. 27; Hermann, VI.1, pp. 2–3, no. 2, pl. I (fol. 1^{r}); Unterkircher, *Inventar*, I, p. 10; Courcelle, p. 91; Bolton, in Gibson, p. 430.

63. MS Wien, Österreichische Nationalbibliothek, 235
Logica vetus s. xiv

Parchment; iii + 64 fols; page 236x160mm; text 150x90mm; 24 lines, ruled in ink; one scribe. Greek in text with Latin interlinear translation. Binding: s. xix white leather on pasteboard.
A standard and heavily used book.

CONTENTS Fols 1^{r}–9^{v} ***Isag.***; 9^{v}–24^{v} ***Cat.***; 25^{r}–32^{v} *Liber sex principiorum*; 32^{v}–41^{r} ***De Int.***; 41^{r}–56^{r} ***Top. Diff.***; 56^{v}–64^{v} *De partibus* *rhetoricae*, *inc.* 'Partes rhetorice sunt sex'; *expl.* imperf. 'racionibus eorum quibus non'.

GLOSS Systematic, often barely legible, interlinear and marginal glosses in contemporary and later hands to fols 1ʳ–41ʳ; no gloss to fols 41ʳ–64ᵛ.

DECORATION Initials in red with yellow and black penwork flourishing; incipits and explicits in red; red paraph signs throughout.

PROVENANCE Belonged to the old University Library in Vienna, whence it passed to the Hofbibliothek in 1756.

BIBLIOGRAPHY *Tabulae*, I, p. 33; *AL*, 97; Markowski, pp. 21, 30, 229.

64. MS Wien, Österreichische Nationalbibliothek, 242
Vita II, DCPhil. s. xii (Hoffmann s. xi)

Parchment; 85 fols; page 220x162mm; text 165x100mm; 22 lines; several scribes. *Tituli* in red rustic capitals. Binding: s. xix white leather on pasteboard.

CONTENTS Fol. 1ʳ ***Vita II***; 1ᵛ–84ᵛ ***DCPhil.***, with commentary of Remigius of Auxerre; 84ᵛ–85ʳ prophecies about the Roman Empire (cf. MS St Gall 844).

GLOSS See contents. Heavily glossed in the beginning; commentary linked to text by letters. The text of Remigius is very incomplete; the glosses to III.m.ix are of different origin (Cf. MS Bern 179).

DECORATION Drawing of Philosophy with nimbus, book in left hand, flowers in right (fol. 3ʳ); six Carolingian-style initials (fols 1ʳ, 2ʳ, 13ʳ, 27ʳ, 50ʳ, 70ʳ). Minor initials in red; first letter of each line of metre touched in red.

PROVENANCE S.W. Germany. Probably produced in Reichenau (Hoffmann: St Gall). Belonged to Alexander Brassicanus (Cf. MS 159).

BIBLIOGRAPHY *Tabulae*, I, p. 34; Hermann, II, pp. 44–5, no. 29, fig. 22 (fol. 13ʳ); Courcelle II, p. 122; Silvestre, p. 51; Unterkircher, *Inventar*, I, p. 11; K. Ostberg, 'The Prologi of Notker's Boethius Reconsidered', *German Life and Letters*, 16, 1963, p. 258; Courcelle, pp. 78, 241, 406, pl. 26.1 (fol. 3ʳ); R. Reiche, 'Unbekannte Boethiusglossen der Wiener Handschrift 271', *Zeitschrift für deutsches Altertum und deutsche Literatur*, 99, 1970, p. 93; Mazal, Irblich, Németh, pp. 110–11, no. 54; O. Mazal, *Buchkunst der Romanik*, Graz, 1978, fig. 33 (fol. 70ʳ); Hoffmann, I, pp. 242, 396; Troncarelli, *Boethiana*, pp. 33, 149–50 (no. 3).

65. MS Wien, Österreichsche Nationalbibliothek, 271 Plate 1
Vita II, DCPhil. s. x

Parchment; 81 fols; page 212x180mm; text 165x100mm; 23–25 lines (fols 76^{v}–77^{v} 26–33 lines, text 2 cols, each 180x70mm); several scribes. *Tituli* in red rustic capitals. Binding: s. xv white leather on wood; one central clasp (lost).

CONTENTS Fol. 1^{r} ***Vita II***; 1^{v}–76^{r} ***DCPhil.***; 76^{v}–77^{v} *Somniale Danielis prophetae*; 78^{r}–80^{v} Lupus, *De metris*; 81^{v} notes on the elements.

GLOSS Contemporary marginal and interlinear glosses in Latin and Old High German throughout; occasional annotation in a ?s. xv hand.

DECORATION Wash-drawing of the Dream of Boethius (1^{v}); genealogical tree of Philosophy (1^{r}). Major initials in red and black.

PROVENANCE S.W. Germany: probably produced in Reichenau. In the Hofbibliothek by 1783.

BIBLIOGRAPHY *Tabulae*, I, p. 37; Steinmeyer-Sievers, IV, p. 633, no. 587; Hermann, I, pp. 184–5, no. 70, fig. 126 (fol. 1^{v}); Unterkircher, *Inventar*, I, p. 12; P. Courcelle, *Histoire littéraire des grandes invasions germaniques*, 3rd edn, Paris, 1964, p. 366, pl. 37b (fol. 1^{v}); R. Reiche, 'Unbekannte Boethiusglossen der Wiener Handschrift 271', *Zeitschrift für deutsches Altertum und deutsche Literatur*, 99, 1970, pp. 90–95; Bergmann, no. 904; Mazal, Irblich, Németh, p. 73, no. 4; L. T. Martin, 'The Earliest Versions of the Latin "Somniale Danielis"', *Manuscripta*, 23, 1979, pp. 133, 135–41; Troncarelli, *Tradizioni*, pp. 4, 28, 46, 64, 69, 77, pl. V (fol. 1^{v}); Hoffmann, I, p. 437; Troncarelli, *Boethiana*, pp. 33, 37, 47, 60, 150–51 (no. 4); N. F. Palmer and K. Speckenbach, *Träume und Kräuter. Studien zur Petroneller 'Circa instans'-Handschrift und zu den deutschen Traumbüchern des Mittelalters*, Pictura et Poesis, 4, Cologne and Vienna, 1990, p. 234.

66. MS Wien, Österreichische Nationalbibliothek, 273
Soph. Elench. s. xiii

Parchment; iii + 290 + i fols; page 200x155mm.
A (s. xiii): text 125x75mm; 22–23 lines; wide margins for commentary; several scribes.
B (s. xiii): text 177x129mm; 58 lines; autograph of Albert the Great.
C (1363): text 168–80x132mm; 47–57 lines; three scribes; fols 169^{r}–81^{r} scribe Jodocus of Görze (dated colophon, fol. 181^{r}).
D (s. xiv): text 132x97mm; 36 lines (fols 221^{v}–22^{v} 47 lines); two scribes, changing at fol. 221^{r}.
E (s. xiv): text 2 cols, each 170x55mm; 40–46 lines; several scribes.
F (s. xi^{ex}): text 154x109mm; 26 lines; one scribe.

Binding: red leather on wood.

CONTENTS

A: fols 1^{r}–36^{r} *Post. Anal.*; 37^{r}–64^{v} ***Soph. Elench.***
B: fols 65^{r}–72^{v} Albert the Great, *Physica* VIII 3.1–4.7; 72^{v}–142^{r} idem, *De caelo et mundo*; 142^{r}–156^{r} idem, *De natura loci*; 156^{r}–168^{r} idem, *De duodecim causis proprietatum elementorum*, *expl.* imperf.
C: fols 169^{r}–181^{r} Dietrich of Freiberg, *De origine rerum praedicamentalium*; 181^{v}–196^{r} Johannes Proclus, *De decem dubitationibus circa providentiam*; 196^{v} arithmetical fragment, *inc.* 'Punctum est unitas habens situm'; *expl.* 'antrorsum in posterius'; 197^{v} excerpts from Cicero, Avicenna, Augustine; 198^{r}–201^{r} blank; 201^{v}–202^{v} Johannes de Mo^{a}?, *Quodlibet*, *inc.* 'Contra primam sequitur'; *expl.* 'Hec Johannes de Mo^{a} Polonus in quodlibeto'.
D: fols 203^{r}–221^{r} Martin of Denmark, *De modis significandi*; 221^{v}–222^{v} *Tractatus de fallaciis*, *inc.* 'Secundum philosophum tertio metaphisice Nesciens solvere'; *expl.* 'duplex est consequentia scilicet in tempore'.
E: fols 223ra–255vb Johannes Dominicus de civitate Missensi (Meissen), *Summa dictandi pro exercendo officio notarum episcoporum et archiepiscoporum*; 255vb–256va *De corpore Christi* (Walther, 1746); 256va–57^{v} notes on the allegorical interpretation of biblical words, *inc.* 'Angelus Christus unde magni consilii angelus Iohannes'; *expl.* 'oculis fui cecus'.
F: fols 258^{r}–290^{v} *Tractatus de ecclesia et personis ecclesiasticis* (fragm.), *inc.* 'Clericus est generale nomen eorum, qui in quocunque gradu deo serviunt'; *expl.* 'stolam collo superpo'.

GLOSS

A: systematic marginal and interlinear commentary.
D: marginal glosses to Martin of Denmark.

DECORATION

A: red and blue initials with penwork flourishing.
B: scattered schematic pen-drawings in ink of text.
F: major initials in red.

PROVENANCE

Germany. Belonged to the library of the Dominican convent in Vienna (fols i^{v}, 2^{r}, 77^{r}: s. xv), whence it passed to the Hofbibliothek in 1576.

BIBLIOGRAPHY

Tabulae, I, p. 38; *MBKÖ*, I, pp. 406–7; *AL*, 98; E. van Balberghe, 'Un album paléographique des manuscrits datés', *Scriptorium*, 25, 1971, p. 316; Mazal, Irblich, Németh, p. 215, no. 193; Unterkircher, *Die datierten*, IV (1976), pp. 173–4, fig. 482 (fol. 181^{r}); Bursill-Hall, no. 299.014; L. Sturlese, *Dokumente und Forschungen zu Leben und Werk Dietrichs von Freiberg*, Corpus Philosophorum Teutonicorum Medii Aevi, 3, Hamburg, 1984, pp. 120–26; Markowski, pp. 42, 49, 51, 146, 229; Kaeppelli and Panella, no. 3687.

67. MS Wien, Österreichishe Nationalbibliothek, 297
Arith. s. xii

Parchment; 59 fols; page 185x130mm; text 130x80mm; 25 lines; several contemporary scribes. Binding: s. xviii white leather on pasteboard.
A carefully written pocket book, little used.

CONTENTS Fols 1^{r}–59^{v} ***Arith.***, *expl.* imperf. II.54 ‘unde notum est quod inter diatessaron’ (172/4).

GLOSS None.

DECORATION Schematic drawings in red and ink of text, fols 10^{v}, 33^{r}, 46^{v}. Initials in red and brown.

PROVENANCE Unknown.

BIBLIOGRAPHY *Tabulae*, I, p. 41; Masi, p. 63.

68. MS Wien, Österreichische Nationalbibliothek, 299
Mus. s. xii

Parchment; 91 fols; page 193x130mm; text 145x90mm (fol. 91^{r-v} text 2 cols, each 140x50mm); 29–30 lines; two scribes, changing at fol. 87^{r}. Greek in red with Latin translation in black, fol. 2^{r}. *Tituli* in red rustic capitals. Binding: s. xix white leather on pasteboard.

CONTENTS Fols 1^{r}–86^{r} ***Mus.***, *inc.* imperf. I.1 ‘musicis adjunguntur’ (180/1); 87^{r}–90^{v} *Apophthegmata veterum sapientium*; 91^{r-v} Publilius Syrus Mimus, *Sententiae*.

GLOSS None.

DECORATION Eight initials in red, yellow, and green (2^{v}, 4^{r}, 5^{r}, 6^{r}, 23^{r}, 43^{r}, 57^{v}, 80^{r}) with dragon patterns and schematic pen-drawings.

PROVENANCE Austria. Belonged to the Chapter Library in Salzburg, whence it passed to the Hofbibliothek in 1806.

BIBLIOGRAPHY *Tabulae*, I, p. 41; Hermann, II, p. 108, no. 55; F. Gianconti, ‘Codici delle sentenze di Publilio Siro’, *Rivista di filologia e di istruzione classica*, 94, 1966, pp. 174–80; O. Mazal, ‘Die Salzburger Domkapitelbibliothek vom 10. bis zum 12. Jahrhundert’, *Paläographie 1981. Colloquium des Comité International de Paléographie. München, 15.-18. September 1981. Referate*, ed. G. Silagi, Münchener Beiträge zur Mediävistik und Renaissance-Forschung, 32, Munich, 1982, pp. 71–91 (78); Munk-Olsen, II, p. 288 (Publil.C.21*); Bower, no. 134.

69. MS Wien, Österreichische Nationalbibliothek, 747

Op. Sac. I, III–V s. xiv

Parchment; 216 fols; page 300x210mm; text 2 cols, each 195x65mm; 30 lines; one scribe. *Tituli* in alternating red and blue rustic capitals. Binding: s. xvii white leather on pasteboard.
Well written.

CONTENTS Fols 1ra–20^{ar} Anselm, *Monologion*; 20rb–25va idem, *Proslogion*; 25vb–46va idem, *Cur deus homo*; 46vb–53va idem, *De incarnatione Verbi*; 53vb–62rb idem, *De peccato originali*; 62va–82va idem, *De concordia praescientiae et praedestinationis*; 82vb–102va idem, *De veritate, De libertate arbitrii, De casu diaboli*; 102vb–107va idem, *De grammatico*; 107vb–134va idem, *De similitudinibus*; 134vb–138va idem, *Disputatio pro insipiente et contra respondentem pro incipiente*; 138vb–145ra idem, seven letters; 145ra–156vb ***Op. Sac. I, III–V***; 156vb–158ra Gundissalinus, *De unitate et uno*; 158rb–204va Isidore, *Sententiae*; 204vb–216vb idem, *Soliloquia*.

GLOSS None.

DECORATION Elaborate major initials in red and blue with penwork flourishing; minor initials in red and blue throughout.

PROVENANCE Unknown.

BIBLIOGRAPHY *Tabulae*, I, p. 125, Bursill-Hall, no. 299.017.

70. MS Wien, Österreichische Nationalbibliothek, 785

Op. Sac. I s. xiii

Parchment; i + 179 fols; page 270x190mm; text 2 cols, each 180x50mm; 63 lines; two scribes writing tiny but legible hands. *Tituli* in rustic capitals in ink of text. Binding: white leather on wood; two clasps (lost); parchment label on front cover, now illegible.
A carefully executed book.

CONTENTS Fol. i^{r} s. xiii table of contents with later additions; 1ra–5ra ***Op. Sac. I***; 5rb–23va Richard of St Victor, *De trinitate*; 23vb–39va Augustine, *De gratia et libero arbitrio*; 39vb–46ra idem, *Soliloquia*; 46rb–56ra idem, *De vera religione*; 56rb–59ra idem, *De agone christiano*; 59rb–65ra idem, *De Genesi contra Manichaeos*; 65rb–73va idem, *Contra Adimantum*; 73vb–82va idem, *De quantitate animae*; 82vb–98ra idem, *De diversis questionibus lxxxiii*; 98rb–108va Anselm, *Cur deus homo*; 108vb–124ra idem, six short treatises; 124rb–130ra Bernard of Clairvaux, three sermons in praise of the Virgin Mary; 130rb–162ra idem, six short treatises and sermons; 162rb–163ra Rule of St Augustine; 163rb–164va Bernard of

Clairvaux, *Epistola ad Robertum nepotem suum*; 164vb–66rb fragmentary commentary on the Song of Songs; 166^{v}–168^{v} blank; 169ra–179rb Augustine, *Enchiridion*.

GLOSS None to *Op. Sac.*

DECORATION Plain initials in red; space left for others not supplied.

PROVENANCE Unknown.

BIBLIOGRAPHY *Tabulae*, I, pp. 130–31; E. Manning and H. Rochais, *Bibliographie générale de l'ordre cistercien. Saint Bernard*, Documentation Cistercienne, 21, 1982, no. 4821.

71. MS Wien, Österreichische Nationalbibliothek, 833 Plate 2
Op. Sac. I–III, V s. xii 2/2

Parchment; i + 55 + i fols; page 210x130mm; text 155x60mm; 22–24 lines; several contemporary scribes. *Tituli* in red rustic capitals. Binding: s. xv stamped brown leather on wood; two clasps (lost). Book numbers in red as running headers. Greek competent.
A practical pocket book.

CONTENTS Fols 1^{r}–55^{r} ***Op. Sac. I–III, V***, with gloss.

GLOSS Extensive contemporary marginal and interlinear glosses linked to text by reference signs (Cappuyns Q).

DECORATION Initials in red or ink of text; touched in red, fols 1^{r}–3^{r}.

PROVENANCE Germany or Austria. Belonged to Johannes Faber, Bishop of Vienna (d. 1541) who left it to St Nicholas' College (fol. i^{v}: Sept. 1540); whence to the old University Library and to the Hofbibliothek in 1756.

BIBLIOGRAPHY *Tabulae*, I, p. 144; Cappuyns, 'Opuscula sacra', p. 240.

72. MS Wien, Österreichische Nationalbibliothek, 836
Op. Sac. s. xii

Parchment; 70 fols; page 210x150mm.
A: text 160x95mm; 19 lines; one scribe. *Tituli* in red. Greek in text with Latin interlinear translation.
B: text 130x35mm; 15 lines for text; 41 lines for commentary; several scribes.
Binding: s. xix white leather on pasteboard.

CONTENTS A: fols 1^{r}–30^{v} ***Op. Sac.***

B: fols 31r–70r Bible: Lamentation, glossed.

GLOSS A: contemporary systematic marginal and occasional interlinear glosses to *Op. Sac.*; gloss linked to text by reference signs (Cappuyns O).
B: systematic commentary on a massive scale; text surrounded by commentary.

DECORATION A: initials in red.

PROVENANCE Belonged to the library of the Augustinian house of St Dorothea in Vienna, whence it passed to the Hofbibliothek.

BIBLIOGRAPHY *Tabulae*, I, p. 144; Cappuyns, 'Opuscula sacra', p. 240; E. Madas, 'Die in der Österreichischen Nationalbibliothek erhaltenen Handschriften des ehemaligen Augustiner-Chorherrenstiftes St. Dorothea in Wien', *Codices manuscripti*, 8, 1982, p. 87; Troncarelli, 'Opuscula', p. 18.

73. MS Wien, Österreichische Nationalbibliothek, 1031
Op. Sac. I–III, V s. xiii

Parchment; 73 fols (pastedown includes text in Hebrew); page 240x175mm; main text 180x25mm; comm. 180x105mm; 38 lines, ruled with a stylus; several scribes. Greek in text. Binding: ?s. xiii stamped red leather (crossed lines and fleur-de-lis) on wood; two clasps (partially preserved).
A carefully executed book.

CONTENTS Fols 1r–73v ***Op. Sac. I–III, V***, with commentary of Gilbert of Poitiers (*Op. Sac.* text begins fol. 3r).

GLOSS See contents. The commentary was probably written before the main text; fols 55v–56v have been ruled for both text and gloss, but contain only gloss.

DECORATION Major initials in red for text and gloss.

PROVENANCE ?France.

BIBLIOGRAPHY *Tabulae*, I, p. 179; Häring, *Gilbert*, p. 30; idem, 'Texts', p. 191; Häring, no. 184.

74. MS Wien, Österreichische Nationalbibliothek, 1082
DCPhil. s. xii

Parchment; i (paper) + 271 + i (paper) fols; page 245x174mm.
A (s. xiv): text 2 cols, each 163x63mm; 34 lines; ?one scribe. *Tituli* in red.

B (s. xiii): text 195x150mm (fols 45^{v}–46^{r} 2 cols, each 205x65mm); 20 lines for text, 30 lines for gloss; several contemporary scribes. *Titulus* in red, fol. 19^{r}.
C (s. xii): text 190x150mm; 20–21 lines; several scribes. *Tituli* in red. Very similar in appearance to B.
D (s. xii): text 190x160mm; 30 lines; ?one scribe.
E (s. xii): text (fols 195^{r}–234^{v}) 2 cols, each 200x60mm, fols 235^{r}–271^{r} 190–205x105–150mm; 30–53 lines; several scribes.
Binding: ?s. xiv blue leather on wood; two later parchment labels on front cover.

CONTENTS A: fols 1^{r}–6^{r} Thomas Aquinas, *De articulis fidei et ecclesiae sacramentis*; 6^{r}–16^{v} idem, *Expositio symboli*.
B: fols 17^{v}–45^{r} Bible: Numbers (glossed); 45^{v}–46^{r} chronological list of popes to Gregory II.
C: fols 47^{r}–105^{v} Gospel of Matthew (glossed); 106^{r} two treatises on the Epiphany; 106^{v} *De sensu biblico vocabuli 'Percussio'*.
D: fols 107^{r}–194^{v} Gregory the Great, *Homilies*.
E: fols 195^{r}–215^{v} Epistle to the Hebrews (glossed); 216^{r}–246^{r} ***DCPhil.***, with commentary of William of Conches; 247^{r}–261^{r} Epistle to the Romans (glossed); 261^{r}–262^{v} commentary on Lamentation; 263^{r}–269^{v} Epistle to the Romans (glossed); 270^{r}–271^{v} commentary on Lamentation (end).

GLOSS E: see contents. Main text and commentary barely discernible; commentary linked to text by underlining in dark ink.

DECORATION C: crudely made initial in red on yellow and brown background (47^{r}).
E: occasional initials in red; marginal annotation touched in red.

PROVENANCE S. Germany or Austria (A, D, E); Italy (?B, C). Belonged to the library of the Jesuits' College in Vienna (s. xviii), whence it passed to the Hofbibliothek in 1773.

BIBLIOGRAPHY *Tabulae*, I, p. 192; Hermann, III, p. 99, no. 69; Unterkircher, *Inventar*, I, p. 34; Courcelle, p. 409; Nauta, pp. cvl–cviii (MS W).

75. MS Wien, Österreichische Nationalbibliothek, 1618
Op. Sac. I–III, V s. xiii

Parchment; 37 + i fols; page 230x147mm; text 180x120mm; 41 lines; two scribes.
Binding: s. xv stamped light brown leather on wood.

CONTENTS Fols 1^{r}–36^{v} ***Op. Sac. I–III, V***, with commentary of Gilbert of Poitiers, *expl.* imperf.

GLOSS See contents. Marginal glosses throughout.

DECORATION Initials in red, fol. 1^{r-v}.

PROVENANCE Austria. Belonged to Alexander Brassicanus, from whom it passed to Johannes Faber, Bishop of Vienna (d. 1541), who left it to the library of St Nicholas' College, Vienna; whence to the old University Library, and to the Hofbibliothek in 1756.

BIBLIOGRAPHY *Tabulae*, I, p. 263 ; P. Classen, 'Zur Geschichte der Frühscholastik in Österreich und Bayern', *Mitteilungen des Instituts für Österreichische Geschichtsforschung*, 67, 1959, p. 260; Häring, *Gilbert*, p. 30; idem, 'Texts', p. 189 ; idem, no. 185.

76. MS Wien, Österreichische Nationalbibliothek, 2269

Logica vetus, Arith., Mus. s. xi (Bischoff)

Parchment; 224 fols (back flyleaf contains a fragment of chronology written in Lombardic script); page 515x330mm; text (fols 1^{r}–107^{v}, 116^{r}–117^{v}, 173^{r}–193^{v}) 3 cols, each 440x65–95mm; text (fols 108^{r}–115^{r}, 118^{r}–172^{r}, 194^{r}–217^{v}) 2 cols, each 425x115mm; 63–93 lines; several scribes. Greek, fol. 152^{v}. *Tituli* in red rustic capitals. Binding: s. xix white leather on pasteboard.
A striking volume.

CONTENTS Fol. 1ra Alcuin, *Carmen* (Walther, 13061a); 1ra–3vb idem, *Dialectica*; 3vb idem, *Carmen* (Walther, 15640); 3vb–6^{vc} idem, *Rhetorica*; 7^{ra-va} Isidore, *Etymologiae* III.1–9; 7vb Alcuin, *Musica*; 8vb idem, *Astrologia*; 9va–24^{vc} ***1 in Isag.***; 25ra–40va ***in Cat.***; 41ra–42va ***De Int.***; 42va–52^{vc} ***1 in Int.***; 53ra–86rb ***2 in Int.***; 86^{rc}–87^{vc} *Sententiae diversorum*; 87^{vc}–90vb ***Top. Diff. III–IV***; 90vb–92ra ***Div.***; 92ra–92^{vc} Ps.-Boethius, *De rhetorice cognatione*; 92^{vc}–96va ***Cat.***; 96va–100^{vc} ***Syll. Cat.***; 100^{vc}–105vb ***Syll. Hyp.***; 105vb–107^{vc} Marius Victorinus, *De definitionibus*; 108ra–133rb ***in Topica Cic.***; 133^{r-v} Easter tables 1206–1324; 134ra–140ra Abbo of Fleury, *In Calculum Victorii Aquitanensis*; 140^{ra-vb} idem, *Regulae de minutiis*; 141ra–152vb ***Arith.***; 153ra–172vb ***Mus.***; 173ra–193vb Calcidius, *In Timaeum Platonis*; 193^{vc}–208ra Macrobius, *In Somnium Scipionis*; 208rb–217va Hyginus, *Astronomicon*; 218^{r}–219^{v} astronomical tables and explanatory notes; 220ra–223ra Euclid, *Geometry*, transl. Boethius; 223rb–224vb three excerpts, including Martianus Capella, *De nuptiis* VIII.860 and VI.595–98.

GLOSS Central tradition for *Mus.* (Bower); gloss linked to text by reference signs.

DECORATION Major initials in brown and red; schematic sketches in brown and red throughout.

PROVENANCE France (Bischoff). Italy (Huglo). Belonged to Pietro Mocenigo, duke of Venice (fol. 1^{r}: s. xv 3/4); in Hofbibliothek by s. xviii^{ex}.

BIBLIOGRAPHY *Tabulae*, II, pp. 44–5; Zinner, nos 5251 (Hyginus), 5612 (fol.

133^{r-v}), 10261; Leonardi, no. 231; *AL*, 2024; Folkerts, p. 71, note 15; Bischoff, *Mittelalterliche Studien*, II, p. 81, n. 26; G. Viré, 'La Transmission du *De Astronomia* d'Hygin jusqu'au XIIIe siècle', *Revue d'histoire des textes*, 11, 1981, no. 85, pp. 210–12; Munk Olsen, I, pp. 313–14 (Cic.C.569) and p. 535 (Hyg.C.38); Bernhard, p. 23; Bower, no. 135; M. Huglo, 'La Réception de Calcidius et des Commentarii de Macrobe à l'époque carolingienne', *Scriptorium*, 44, 1990, p. 18; Toneatto, III, pp. 923–8.

77. MS Wien, Österreichische Nationalbibliothek, 2370

Logica nova s. xiii

Parchment; 160 fols; page 274x190mm.
A (s. xiii): text 133x83mm; 25 lines; one scribe.
B (s. xiii): text 154x90mm; 35 lines; one scribe.
Binding: s. xix thick white leather.

CONTENTS A: fols 1^{r}–41^{r} ***Prior Anal.*** (glossed); 42^{r}–67^{v} *Post. Anal.* (glossed); 70^{r}–123^{v} ***Topica Aris.*** (glossed); 124^{r}–144^{v} ***Soph. Elench.*** (glossed); 145^{r-v} ***Prior Anal.***, *expl.* imperf. I.3 'particularis privativa non convertitur' (8/3–4).
B: fols 146^{r}–155^{v} Aristotle, *Ethica vetus* (= *Eth. Nic.* II–III); 156^{r}–160^{v} idem, *Ethica nova* (= *Eth. Nic.* I).

GLOSS A: see contents. Extensive marginal and interlinear glosses in ?scribe's hand; extensive marginal annotation in several later hands.
B: glossed in tiny minuscule; extensive ?s. xv annotation in several hands.

DECORATION A: initials in red and blue with elaborate penwork flourishing. First line of each work in larger decorated majuscules alternating red and blue; red and blue paraph signs. Large circular schematic drawing (unfinished) filled with s. xv notes.
B: decoration similar in style to A but somewhat inferior in quality.

PROVENANCE France; probably produced in Paris. A belonged to Magister Fridericus de Drosendorf from the Arts Faculty in Vienna (fol. 1^{r}: s. xiv 3/4); B to a Franciscan friar Johannes (fol. 160^{v}: s. xvi). The whole MS belonged to Johannes Faber, Bishop of Vienna (d. 1541), who gave it to St Nicholas' College. Thence to the old University Library in Vienna, and the Hofbibliothek in 1756.

BIBLIOGRAPHY *Tabulae*, II, p. 63 ; Hermann VII.1, pp. 91–2, no. 33; *AL*, 114; Markowski, pp. 42, 44, 129, 239.

78. MS Wien, Österreichische Nationalbibliothek, 2374

Logica vetus et nova s. xiii 4/4

Parchment; i + 241 fols; page 275x187mm; text 135x85mm; 31 lines; spacious margins for gloss; one scribe. Book numbers as running headers. *Tituli* alternating in red and blue. Binding: s. xv white leather on wood; two clasps (lost). An excellent copy.

CONTENTS Fols 1^{r}–8^{v} ***Isag.***; 8^{v}–22^{v} ***Cat.***; 22^{v}–32^{v} ***De Int.***; 32^{v}–43^{r} ***Div.***; 43^{r}–71^{r} ***Top. Diff.***; 71^{v}–78^{r} *Liber sex principiorum*; 79^{r}–126^{v} ***Prior Anal.***; 127^{r}–157^{r} *Post. Anal.*; 158^{r}–221^{r} ***Topica Aris.***; 222^{r}–241^{r} ***Soph. Elench.***

GLOSS Sporadic glosses at the beginning of the MS.

DECORATION Splendidly decorated with initials in red, blue, gold and green with occasional dragon patterns, e.g., fols 22^{v}, 26^{r}, 32^{v}, 43^{r}, 49^{r}, 58^{r}, 64^{r}. Historiated initials, fols 1^{r}, 79^{r}, 127^{r}, 158^{r}, 222^{r} featuring almost identical scenes: a teacher with a raised hand addressing his disciples (monks). Red and blue paraph signs; incipits in white on blue or red background.

PROVENANCE France; probably produced in Paris. Belonged to the old University Library in Vienna, whence it passed to the Hofbibliothek in 1756.

BIBLIOGRAPHY *Tabulae*, II, p. 65; Hermann, VII.1 pp. 88–9, pl. XXV (fols 22^{r}, 79^{r}), no. 30; *AL*, 115; Unterkircher, *Inventar*, I, p. 69; Markowski, p. 239.

79. MS Wien, Österreichische Nationalbibliothek, 2377

Prior Anal., Soph. Elench. s. xiv; xiii

Parchment; 61 fols; page 280x205mm.
A (s. xiv): text 155x100mm; 34 lines; several scribes.
B (s. xiii): text 150x95mm; 36–38 lines; several scribes.
Binding: s. xiv leather on wood (now badly damaged); one central clasp (lost).
A poor quality volume, heavily used.

CONTENTS A: fols 1^{r}–28^{v} ***Prior Anal.***
B: fols 30^{r}–49^{r} *Post. Anal.*; 49^{r}–61^{r} ***Soph. Elench.***

GLOSS A: marginal and interlinear glosses in two contemporary hands.
B: marginal and interlinear glosses in several contemporary hands; plentiful marginal annotations by later users.

DECORATION A: initials in ink of text; poor quality schematic drawings in ink of text, fols 13^{v}, 15^{r}.
B: poorly executed major initials in red, fols 30^{r}, 49^{r}; paraph signs

in red and ink of text.

PROVENANCE Germany. Belonged to the Old University Library in Vienna, whence it passed to the Hofbibliothek in 1756.

BIBLIOGRAPHY *Tabulae*, II, p. 65; *AL*, 116; Markowski, pp. 49, 239.

80. MS Wien, Österreichische Nationalbibliothek, 2407
Logica nova s. xiv

Parchment; i + 133 fols; page 257x186mm; text 2 cols, each 127x47mm; 27 lines; two scribes. Catchwords. *Tituli* in alternating red and blue. Book numbers in alternating red and blue as running headers. Binding: s. xv white leather on wood; two clasps (lost).
A finely executed volume.

CONTENTS Fols 1ra–26vb *Post. Anal.*; 27ra–44vb ***Soph. Elench.***; 45ra–83va ***Prior Anal.***; 83vb–133rb ***Topica Aris.***

GLOSS Scattered glosses in a later hand.

DECORATION Fourteen large initials in red and blue with penwork flourishing; paraph signs in red and blue.

PROVENANCE Italy; probably produced in Bologna. In s. xv belonged to Stift Rein (fol. i^{r}), probably for use by the Cistercian monks of the abbey who studied in Vienna (names scattered throughout). Used in 1455 by Georg Mayr of Amberg (university prof. and rector in 1454); monastic library of Mondsee, OSB. Passed to the Hofbibliothek after the dissolution of the monastery in 1791.

BIBLIOGRAPHY *Tabulae*, II, p. 69; Hermann V.1, pp. 107–8, no. 69; *AL*, 117; Unterkircher, *Inventar*, I, p. 70; Markowski, p. 240.

81. MS Wien, Österreichsche Nationalbibliothek, 2420
Soph. Elench. s. xiv

Parchment; ii + 27 fols; page 243x187mm; text 155x89mm; 28 lines; one scribe. Book numbers as running headers. Binding: ?s. xiv stamped blue leather on wood; two clasps (lost).
A standard, carefully executed book.

CONTENTS Fols 1^{v}–26^{v} ***Soph. Elench.***

GLOSS Scattered marginal notes in several later hands.

DECORATION Initials in red and blue with penwork flourishing, e.g., fols 1^{r}, 14^{r};

paraph signs in red and blue.

PROVENANCE Austria. Belonged to the University Library in Vienna, whence it passed to the Hofbibliothek in 1756.

BIBLIOGRAPHY *Tabulae*, II, p. 70; *AL*, 121; Unterkircher, *Inventar*, I, p. 70; Markowski, p. 241.

82. MS Wien, Österreichische Nationalbibliothek, 2463
Arith. s. xiii

Parchment; i + 42 fols; page 222x138mm; text 170x95mm; 35 lines; ?one scribe. *Tituli* in red. Binding: red leather on thick wooden boards; two clasps (lost); chain-mark on back cover.
A neatly produced pocket book.

CONTENTS Fols 1ʳ–42ʳ ***Arith.***

GLOSS Scattered contemporary marginal notes throughout.

DECORATION Poor quality initials in red and blue; numerous schematic drawings in red and black, some filled with yellow.

PROVENANCE Probably produced in the Dominican convent in Buda. Later it belonged to the library of the Jesuits' College in Vienna, whence it passed to the Hofbibliothek in 1773.

BIBLIOGRAPHY *Tabulae*, II, p. 78; Masi, p. 63; *Kódexek a középkori Magyarországon (Codices in Mediaeval Hungary)*, exhibition catalogue, Budapest, 1985, p. 98, no. 44, pl. (fols 18ᵛ–19ʳ).

83. MS Wien, Österreichische Nationalbibliothek, 2498
Logica vetus s. xiii

Parchment; 85 fols; page 175x125mm.
A (s. xiii): text 145x90mm; 36 lines; one scribe. *Tituli* in red.
B (s. xiii): text 2 cols, each 150x55mm (fol. 49ʳ⁻ᵛ text 147x105); 39–42 lines one scribe.
B inserted between A fols 80 and 81. Binding: s. xix.
An average quality pocket book.

CONTENTS A: fols 1ʳ–7ʳ ***De Int.***; 7ᵛ–20ᵛ ***Top. Diff. I–III***; 20ᵛ–33ᵛ ***Syll. Cat.***; 33ᵛ–48ᵛ ***Syll. Hyp.***, *expl.* imperf. 'homo niger cum sit' (*PL*, 64:873B); 81ʳ–85ᵛ ***Cat.***, *inc.* imperf. 'convertitur si ad aliquem eorum' (cf. 33/16).
B: fols 49ʳ–76ᵛᵃ Peter of Spain, *Summa in Priscianum minorem* (*Absoluta*); 76ᵛᵇ–80ᵛᵇ *Grammatica*, *inc.* 'Boethius dicit vox est aer

tenuissimus'; *expl.* imperf. 'sed et impersonalia sunt verba'.

GLOSS None.

DECORATION A: initials in red; crudely executed schematic drawings in red and ink of text.
B: none.

PROVENANCE ?Austria. Belonged to the Chapter Library in Salzburg, whence it passed to the Hofbibliothek in 1806.

BIBLIOGRAPHY *Tabulae*, II, p. 84; *AL*, 125; Bursill-Hall, no. 299.47; Markowski, p. 243.

84. MS Wien, Österreichsche Nationalbibliothek, 2517
Logica vetus s. xiii 1/2

Parchment; 100 fols; page 162x105mm; text 112x53mm; 29–30 lines; several scribes. *Tituli* in alternating red and green as running headers. Binding: s. xix white leather on pasteboard.

CONTENTS Fols 1^{r}–10^{r} ***Isag.***; 10^{v}–27^{r} ***Cat.***; 27^{v}–38^{v} ***De Int.***; 39^{r}–52^{r} ***Div.***; 52^{v}–85^{v} ***Top. Diff.***; 85^{v}–93^{r} *Liber sex principiorum*; 93^{v}–94^{r} s. xv notes; 94^{r}–95^{r} anonymous verses on grammar, *inc.* 'In his septendecim versibus comprehenduntur'; 95^{v}–100^{v} s. xv notes.

GLOSS Extensive and systematic marginal gloss in scribal hands; gloss linked to text by special reference signs; occasional interlinear glosses and numerous marginal additions by several later hands.

DECORATION Initials in green, blue, red and yellow; minor capitals touched in red.

PROVENANCE France or Low Countries. Belonged to Stephanus de Castello (fol. 95^{v}: s. xv) and many others, including Magister Johannes de Quercu or Quarcu. Later belonged to the old University Library in Vienna, whence it passed to the Hofbibliothek in 1756.

BIBLIOGRAPHY *Tabulae*, II, p. 89; Hermann, III, p. 35, no. 28; *AL*, 126; Unterkircher, *Inventar*, I, p. 72; Bursill-Hall, no. 299.50; Markowski, pp. 21, 30, 243.

85. MS Wien, Österreichische Nationalbibliothek, 3143
DCPhil. s. xiv

Parchment (fols 1^{r}–39^{r}) and paper (fols 40^{r}–208^{r}); i + 208 + i fols; page 290x215mm.

A (s. xiv): text 200x130mm; 33 lines; several scribes. Greek in text.
B (s. xv): text 200x145mm; 32 lines; several scribes. *Tituli* in red.
Binding: white leather with central gold stamp.

CONTENTS A: fols 1r–39r ***DCPhil.***
B: fols 40r–149r Henricus de Isernia, *Liber formularum 249 epistolas praesertim Ottocari II regis Bohemie continens*; 150r–166r John of Limoges, *Somnium Pharaonis moraliter expositum in viginti epistolis*; 166r–167r letters about the plague by the bishop of *Litomislium* (Bohemia) to Petrus Lunensis; 167r hymn on the Nativity; 167v–203v Henricus de Isernia, *Liber formularum* (continued) and letters.

GLOSS A: extensive contemporary marginal gloss to fols 1v–27v only.

DECORATION A: capitals touched in red to the beginning of each metre.
B: major and minor capitals touched in red.

PROVENANCE Unknown. In the Hofbibliothek by the end of the seventeenth century.

BIBLIOGRAPHY *Tabulae*, II, p. 214.

86. MS Wien, Österreichische Nationalbibliothek, 3146
DCPhil. s. xv

Paper; i + 100 fols; page 295x220mm; text 180x95mm; 20 lines for text, up to 56 lines for commentary; several scribes. Book numbers as running headers. Binding: ?s. xv wooden boards half covered with stamped brown leather.

CONTENTS Fols 1r–99r ***DCPhil.***, with commentary of William of Conches (*DCPhil.* text begins fol. 3r).

GLOSS See contents. Commentary added between the lines and in the margins; commentary linked to text by red paraph signs and lemmata.

DECORATION Crudely executed ***C(armina)*** in red and blue (3r); red capitals for each prose and metre.

PROVENANCE Austria; probably produced in Vienna.

BIBLIOGRAPHY *Tabulae*, II, p. 214; Courcelle, p. 410; Nauta (this MS not used).

87. MS Wien, Österreichische Nationalbibliothek, 3150

DCPhil., Op. Sac. V s. xiv

Paper; ii + 308 + ii fols; page 288x200mm; text 197–235x95–180mm (fols 264^{r}–287^{v} text 2 cols, each 205x65mm); 23–25 lines; several scribes. *Tituli* in red for each book of *DCPhil.* Book numbers as running headers. Binding: s. xix.

CONTENTS Fol. i^{r} s. xiv list of contents; 1^{v}–69^{r} ***DCPhil.***; 69^{v}–71^{r} blank; 71^{v} notes and verses on SS Mary and Elisabeth; 72^{r}–122^{v} Alan of Lille, *De planctu naturae* (glossed); 123^{r}–137^{v} Ps.-Boethius, *De disciplina scolarium*; 137^{v}–152^{v} ***Op. Sac. V***; 156^{r}–164^{v} Cicero, *De officiis* (excerpts); 165^{r}–168^{v} idem, *Quaestiones Tusculanae* (excerpts); 168^{v}–171^{v} Macrobius, *In Somnium Scipionis* (excerpts); 171^{v}–716^{r} Valerius Maximus, *Dictorum factorumque libri IX excerpti*; 176^{r}–177^{v} Cicero, *Timaeus* (excerpts); 177^{v}–178^{v} Ausonius Magnus, *Sententiae septem sapientum septenis versibus*; 180^{r}–183^{r} Ps.-Seneca, *Proverbia*; 184^{r}–185^{r} Ps.-Seneca, *Epistolae ad Paulum et Pauli ad Senecam*; 185^{v}–187^{v} Ps.-Seneca, *De remediis fortuitorum*; 192^{r}–203^{r} Cicero, *De senectute*; 203^{v}–215^{v} idem, *De amicitia*; 215^{v}–218^{r} Ps.-Seneca, *De remediis fortuitorum*; 218^{r}–225^{v} Ps.-Seneca, *De morum institutione*; 225^{v}–229^{v} Ps.-Seneca (Martin of Braga), *Formula honestae vitae*; 229^{v}–237^{r} Alan of Lille, *Anticlaudianus* (excerpt); 237^{v}–256^{r} Gaufridus abbas, *Declamationes de colloquio Simonis cum Jesu*; 256^{r}–258^{r} Bernard of Clairvaux, *Epistola de gubernatione rei familiaris*; 264^{r}–287^{v} Robert Holcot, *Moralitates*; 295^{r}–307^{v} Jordan of Quedlinburg, *Sermones de tempore*.

GLOSS Interlinear and marginal glosses in several hands to fols 1^{v}–5^{r}; scattered marginal annotation to Alan of Lille.

DECORATION Red ***C****(armina)* with the two first lines of text in red, fol. 1^{v}; poor quality main capitals in red with ornamentation in blue. First letters of each line of metre touched in red; red paraph signs with blue infill. Well-executed major initials in red for the rest of the volume.

PROVENANCE Austria.

BIBLIOGRAPHY *Tabulae*, II, pp. 215–16; Weijers, p. 86 (no. 98).

88. MS Wien, Österreichische Nationalbibliothek, 3152

DCPhil., Op. Sac. IV 1363

Paper; xii + 109 + xxii fols; page 295x220mm; text 190x110mm; 20 lines; several contemporary scribes, including Petrus de Aquis Grani (dated colophon, fol. 103^{v}). Binding: s. xv stamped brown leather on wood.

CONTENTS Fols 1^{r}–21^{v} Ps.-Boethius, *De disciplina scolarium*; 22^{r}–24^{v} ?Ps.-Boethius, *An omne quod est bonum sit*; 25^{r}–103^{v} ***DCPhil.***; 104^{r}–109^{v} ***Op. Sac. IV***.

GLOSS Extensive marginal and interlinear glosses to *DCPhil.*, *Op. Sac.* and *De disciplina scolarium*; gloss linked to text by underlining in red, catchwords and red paraph signs.

DECORATION Major capitals in red to each prose and metre of *DCPhil.*

PROVENANCE Austria (Vienna). Belonged to the old University Library in Vienna, whence to the Hofbibliothek in 1756.

BIBLIOGRAPHY *Tabulae*, II, p. 216; Unterkircher, *Die datierten*, I, p. 58, fig. 142 (fol. 103^{v}); P. Uiblein, 'Zum Katalog der datierten Handschriften in lateinischer Schrift in Österreich', *Scriptorium*, 25, 1971, p. 87; Weijers, p. 86 (no. 99); K. Holter, 'Verzierte Wiener Bucheinbände der Spätgothik und Frührenaissance. Werkgruppen und Stempeltabellen', *Codices Manuscripti* (Sonderheft), 1977, p. 5 (A.2).

89. MS Wien, Österreichische Nationalbibliothek, 3217
DCPhil. s. xiv

Paper; 129 + ii fols; page 220x150mm; text 150–60x70–85mm; 21–26 lines; eight very different scribes. Binding: ?s. xv leather on wood; chain-mark on back cover.

CONTENTS Fols 1^{r}–13^{v} ***DCPhil.***; 14^{r}–25^{v} *Tractatus de suppositionibus*; 26^{r-v} grammatical verses; 27^{r}–34^{v} Ps.-Boethius, *De disciplina scolarium*; 34^{v}–38^{r} *Poema de liberis educandis*; 38^{v}–39^{r} *Tabulae docentes*; 39^{v}–49^{v} *De complexionibus hominis*; 43^{r}–80^{r} *Synonyma latina cum commentario*; 80^{v} two poems; 81^{r}–118^{v} *Ars medica* (in German), *inc.* 'Edler Kunich Alexander ich han gedacht durch deine lieb'; 119^{r}–125^{v} John of Garland, *Liber de aequivocis*; 126^{r}–128^{v} poems, short treatises in German, *probationes pennae*, pen-drawings.

GLOSS Interlinear and marginal glosses for *DCPhil.* and *De disciplina scolarium.*

DECORATION One diagram (fol. 127^{r}); rubrication.

PROVENANCE Unknown. Belonged to the old University Library.

BIBLIOGRAPHY *Tabulae*, II, pp. 235–6; Weijers, p. 86 (no. 101); Bursill-Hall, no. 299.56.

90. MS Wien, Österreichische Nationalbibliothek, 3219
DCPhil. 1382

Paper; 303 fols; page 250x150mm; text 122x70mm; 14–15 lines; several scribes.

CONTENTS Fols 1^r–48^r ***DCPhil.***, with commentary; 49^r–70^r Geoffrey of Vinsauf, *Carmen de statu curiae romanae*; 70^v–99^r Josephus Brivius Mediolanensis, *Carmina sex: Laudes S. Alexii, De S. Agnete, De S. Maria Magdalena, Laudes S. Barbarae, De S. Caecilia, Laudes S. Jeronimi*; 102^r–118^r Ps.-Ovid (Richard of Furnival), *Vetula*; 118^v–285^r miscellaneous short treatises and poems; 285^r–288^r Hugh of St Victor, *De ratione studiorum*; 289^r–302^r John of Garland, *De mysteriis ecclesiae*, with commentary.

GLOSS Glosses to *DCPhil.* (fols 13^v–45^v), and to fols 179^r–231^v, and 289^r–301^v.

DECORATION Decorated initials in red.

PROVENANCE Unknown. In the Hofbibliothek by 1575.

BIBLIOGRAPHY *Tabulae*, II, pp. 236–7; Unterkircher, *Die datierten*, I, figs 190 and 190a; Glorieux, *Arts*, nos 110c and 235h.

91. MS Wien, Österreichische Nationalbibiothek, 3223
DCPhil. 1488

Paper; iii + 264 fols; page 216x151mm; text 145x73mm; 12 lines; several scribes (dated colophons, fols 1^r, 190^r, 247^r, 262^r). Binding: s. xix.

CONTENTS Fols 1^v–39^v Persius, *Satyrae*, with gloss (1^v–33^r) of Johannes Cuspinianus; 40^r–41^v Alan of Lille, *Anticlaudianus* (excerpt); 44^v–199^r ***DCPhil.***; 199^v–204^v alphabetical table of contents for *DCPhil.*; 208^v–247^r Ps.-Boethius, *De disciplina scolarium*; 248^r–260^r Bernardus Morlanensis, *Carmen de contemptu mundi*; 260^v–262^r *Interrogationes et doctrinae* (for confessors); 262^v–264^v Johannes Faber de Werdea, *Carmen de moribus becanorum et studentium*.

GLOSS Extensive marginal and interlinear glosses in several contemporary hands to *DCPhil.*; gloss linked to text by catchwords and red ink.

DECORATION Crudely executed half-page drawing of ?Boethius (bearded man in a tower giving lessons to a smaller seated figure: fol. 44^r). Inhabited ***C(armina)*** in blue depicting Boethius in green gown seated on a red chair (44^v). Major initials in several styles in red, blue, yellow and green with occasional penwork flourishing; plain red initials to the beginning of each prose and metre.

PROVENANCE Austria (?Vienna). Owned by Johannes Cuspinianus; thence to Johannes Faber, Bishop of Vienna (d. 1541), who left it to the library of St Nicholas' College, Vienna; passed to the old University Library, and Hofbibliothek in 1756.

BIBLIOGRAPHY *Tabulae*, II, p. 238; Unterkircher, *Inventar*, I, p. 92; idem, *Die datierten*, III, p. 69, fig. 557 (fol. 199^r); Weijers, pp. 86–87 (no. 102).

92. MS Wien, Österreichische Nationalbibliothek, 3245
DCPhil. s. xv

Paper; 142 fols; page 217x140mm; text 152x80mm; 16 lines; several scribes. Dated colophon, 'frater Gregorius', 1462, fol. 118^v. Greek in text, e.g., fol. 25^r. *Tituli* in red. Binding: s. xv stamped brown leather on wood; two clasps (lost).

CONTENTS Fols 1^r–119^r ***DCPhil.***, with commentary *inc.* 'Plasmaverat autem Dominus Deus paradisum voluptatis a principio'; 119^v–131^v blank; 132^r–135^r Ps.-Seneca, *De remediis fortuitorum*; 135^v–139^v Ps.-Seneca (Martin of Braga), *Formula honestae vitae*; 139^v–142^r Ps.-Seneca, *Epistolae ad Paulum et Pauli ad Senecam.*

GLOSS See contents. Red-framed marginal gloss to *DCPhil.* on a massive scale; interlinear annotation throughout; gloss linked to text by catchwords.

DECORATION Crudely executed red ***C****(armina)* with green penwork flourishing (1^r); plain red initials mark the beginning of each prose and metre; red paraph signs.

PROVENANCE From the library of the Carthusian abbey of St Mary in Aggsbach (fols 1^r, 118^v). Owned by Master Jacobus de Flanica, who was educated in the theological faculty of the University of Vienna (fol. 119^r: 1469).

BIBLIOGRAPHY *Tabulae*, II, p. 243; Unterkircher, *Die datierten*, III, p. 70, fig. 228 (fol. 118^v).

93. MS Wien, Österreichische Nationalbibliothek, 3251
DCPhil. s. xiv

Paper; i (parchment) + 227 + i (parchment) fols; page 205x137mm; text 170x110mm; 30–35 lines; several scribes. Dated colophons, fols 150^r (1420), 225^r (1313). Greek in text with interlinear translation. Original binding; one central clasp (lost).

CONTENTS Fols 1^{r}–150^{r} Geoffrey of Vinsauf, *Poetria nova*, with commentary; 151^{r}–203^{v} ***DCPhil.***; 203^{v}–227^{v} Ps.-Boethius, *De disciplina scolarium*.

GLOSS Extensive marginal contemporary gloss to fols 151^{r}–157^{v}; extensive interlinear gloss to fols 151^{r}–195^{v}.

DECORATION Plain red initials; minor capitals touched with red.

PROVENANCE ?Austria. Belonged to the Benedictine abbey of Mondsee, whence it passed to the Hofbibliothek after the abbey's dissolution in 1791.

BIBLIOGRAPHY *Tabulae*, II, p. 244; Unterkircher, *Die datierten*, II, p. 53, fig. 158 (fol. 150^{r}); Weijers, p. 87 (no. 103).

94. MS Wien, Österreichische Nationalbibliothek, 3252

DCPhil. s. xiv 3/4

Paper; 106 fols; page 207x148mm; text 132x60mm (fols 101^{r}–106^{v} text 2 cols, each 157x52mm; 25–48 lines; probably one scribe. Binding: beautifully stamped (Madonna and Child) dark leather on wood; restored in 1919.

CONTENTS Fols 1^{r}–100^{r} ***DCPhil.***, with commentary; 101^{r}–106^{r} Ps.-Aristotle, *Secretum secretorum*, with commentary.

GLOSS See contents. Contemporary interlinear gloss throughout *DCPhil.*; at times gloss and commentary merge into one; additional systematic marginal annotation.

DECORATION Poor quality pen-drawing of St George defeating the dragon (106^{v}). Initials in red with penwork flourishing in blue, green and yellow; red paraph signs.

PROVENANCE Probably produced in the Carthusian abbey of Mariengarten (f. 1342) in Prague (fol. 2^{r}). In the wake of the Hussite wars, the MS was taken to safety in the Carthusian abbey of St Mary in Aggsbach, whence to the Hofbibliothek in 1782.

BIBLIOGRAPHY *Tabulae*, II, p. 244; *MBKÖ*, I, p. 538; Unterkircher, *Inventar*, I, p. 92; M. C. Díaz y Díaz, *Index scriptorum latinorum medii aevi hispanorum*, Madrid, 1959, no. 929.

95. MS Wien, Österreichische Nationalbibliothek, 3253

Syll. Hyp., Syll. Cat. s. xv

Paper; ii + 56 + ii fols; page 205x150mm; text 150x100mm; 25 lines; several scribes. Greek in margins. Modern binding.

CONTENTS Fol. i$^{r–v}$ Horace, Poems; ii$^{r–v}$ beginning of gloss on *Syll. Hyp.*; 1^{r}–31^{v} ***Syll. Hyp.***; 33^{r}–44^{v} ***Syll. Cat.***; 45^{r}–54^{v} *Doctrina metrica latina*; 55^{r}–56^{v} anonymous grammatical treatise (fragm.)

GLOSS See contents. Scattered marginal annotation.

DECORATION None.

PROVENANCE Unknown.

BIBLIOGRAPHY *Tabulae*, II, p. 244; Bursill-Hall, no. 299.60.

96. MS Wien, Österreichische Nationalbibliothek, 3693
Op. Sac. III s. xiv

Paper (A: fols 1–181) and parchment (B: fols 182–97); i + 197 + v (paper) fols; page 293x210mm.
A (s. xv): text 2 cols, each 230x70mm; 39–50 lines; several scribes. *Tituli* in red.
B (s. xiv): text 170x140mm; 40 lines; one scribe. *Tituli* in ink of text.
Binding: s. xv brown leather on wood; two clasps (lost).

CONTENTS A: fol. i$^{r–v}$ s. xv list of contents (with mention of B); 1ra–121ra John Buridan, *Quaestiones super quattuor libris ethicorum Aristotelis* (imperf.); 121^{v} *probationes pennae*; 122ra–158vb John of Capistrano, *Sermons*; 159ra–175rb Richard Fitzralph, Anti-mendicant *Propositiones* delivered at the papal court at Avignon, 8 Nov. 1357.
B: fols 182^{r}–194^{v} Aristotle, *De generatione et corruptione*; 195^{r}–196^{r} ***Op. Sac. III***; 196^{r}–197^{v} *De substantia orbis*, *expl.* imperf.

GLOSS Marginal and interlinear glosses for Aristotle; extensive but barely legible marginal glosses to *Op. Sac. III.*

DECORATION Simple initials in red.

PROVENANCE Germany. Belonged to the Benedictine abbey of Mondsee, whence it passed to the Hofbibliothek after the abbey's dissolution in 1791.

BIBLIOGRAPHY *Tabulae*, III, pp. 54–5; *AL*, 129; G. Schrimpf, *Die Axiomenhandschrift des Boethius (De Hebdomadibus) als philosophisches Lehrbuch des Mittelalters*, Leiden, 1966, p. 39, pl. XIII (fol. 195^{r}); Markowski, p. 245.

97. MS Wien, Österreichische Nationalbibliothek, 4776
Isag., Cat. s. xv

Paper (damaged); 114 fols (front flyleaves contain s. xiv biblical fragments and s. xv philosophical treatises); page 150x105mm; text 112x73mm; c. 29 lines; one scribe (except fol. 75^{r-v}).

CONTENTS Fols 1^{r}–30^{r} ***Isag.***, with commentary; 30^{v}–74^{v} ***Cat.***, with commentary of Francis Meyronne; 75^{r-v} added misc. notes, *probationes pennae*, pointing hands, etc.; 76^{r}–114^{v} *Promptuarium axiomaticum* from Aristotle, *Physica*.

GLOSS See contents.

DECORATION Initials in red with penwork flourishing; rubricated.

PROVENANCE ?Italy. 'Iste liber est fratris Zanini de ... ordinis minorum sacre theologiae bachalarii', fol. 75^{v}. In the Hofbibliothek by s. xvii^{ex}.

BIBLIOGRAPHY *Tabulae*, III, p. 384; Markowski, pp. 14, 74, 77, 95, 98, 100, 106, 251.

98. MS Wien, Österreichische Nationalbibliothek, 4778
Logica vetus 1440

Paper; 331 fols (pastedown has fragment of s. xii breviary); page 150x110mm; text 105x70mm; 22–36 lines; several scribes. Dated colophon, fol. 68^{v}.
Binding: s. xv brown stamped leather on wood; one central clasp (lost).

CONTENTS Fols 1^{r}–68^{v} ***Isag.***, with commentary; 69^{r}–164^{v} ***Cat.***, with commentary; 165^{r}–211^{v} ***De Int.***, with commentary; 212^{r}–283^{r} mathematical treatise, reliant on John of Sacrobosco; 284^{r}–330^{r} John of Sacrobosco, *De sphaera*.

GLOSS See contents.

DECORATION Pen-drawings and schemata, partially coloured, fols 53^{v}, 69^{r}, 109^{r}, 164^{v}; occasional initials in red.

PROVENANCE Austria. Belonged to the library of Mondsee abbey, OSB (fol. 1^{r}), whence it passed to the Hofbibliothek after the abbey's dissolution in 1791.

BIBLIOGRAPHY *Tabulae*, III, p. 385; Zinner, nos 4809 and 4864; Unterkircher, Horninger and Lackner, *Die datierten*, IV, p. 202, fig. 554 (fol. 68^{v}); Markowski, pp. 20, 29, 252.

99. MS Wien, Österreichische Nationalbibliothek, 5199
Logica vetus s. xv

Paper; 175 + i fols; page 220x156mm; text 130x80mm; 26–28 lines; one scribe. Original limp leather binding.
A study copy.

CONTENTS Fols 1^{r}–121^{r} *Ars dialectica, inc.* 'Dialectica est ars arcium scientia scientiarum'; 121^{v} *Tabula logicalis*; 122^{r}–133^{v} ***Isag.***; 133^{v}–158^{v} ***Cat.***; 158^{v}–174^{v} ***De Int.***

GLOSS Extensive contemporary marginal annotation to *Ars dialectica*; none to Boethius.

DECORATION Poor quality ***D****(ialectica)* in red with brown and red penwork flourishing, fol. 1^{r}; abstract black and red initial, fol. 16^{v}; space left for initials, not supplied. Crudely executed schematic drawing in ink of text, fol. 16^{r}; schematic black and red drawings elsewhere.

PROVENANCE Austria or Germany. Belonged to the old University Library, whence it passed to the Hofbibliothek in 1756.

BIBLIOGRAPHY *Tabulae*, IV, p. 56; *AL*, 133; Markowski, p. 258.

100. MS Wien, Österreichische Nationalbibliothek, 5201
DCPhil. s. xv

Paper; i (parchment) + 246 fols (flyleaf has s. xiv musical notation); page 205x150mm; text 130x70–120mm; 14–19 lines; several scribes. Book numbers as running headers. Original limp leather binding.

CONTENTS Fols 1^{r}–126^{v} ***DCPhil.***; 126^{v}–128^{r} notes on *DCPhil. I–IV*; 128^{v}–216^{v} Alan of Lille, *De planctu naturae*; 217^{r}–228^{v} Ps.-Seneca (Martin of Braga), *Formula honestae vitae*; 229^{r}–246^{v} Ps.-Aristotle, *De pomo*.

GLOSS All the texts heavily glossed interlinearly and in the margins.

DECORATION Crudely executed red ***C****(armina)*, fol. 1^{r}; initials in red to mark the beginning of each prose and metre; first letter of each line of metre touched in red.

PROVENANCE Dedication in German, back flyleaf. Belonged to the old University Library, whence it passed to the Hofbibliothek in 1756.

BIBLIOGRAPHY *Tabulae*, IV, p. 56.

101. MS Wien, Österreichsche Nationalbibliothek, 5509

DCPhil. IV 1459 / 1464

Paper; i + 258 + i fols; page 218x147mm; text variable, 155x90mm for *DCPhil.*; 34–36 lines; several scribes. Dated colophons, fols 135^v, 140^r, 184^r, 189^v. Binding: s. xviii white leather on pasteboard.

CONTENTS Fols 1^r–4^r contents list; 5^r–8^r ***DCPhil. IV*** 'omnes eo ipso'–'consequens est' (IV.pr.iii.27–IV.pr.iv.88); 8^v–11^r astrological *notabilia* in Latin and German; 11^v–15^r *De quattuor complexionibus*; 15^v–16^v blank; 17^r–257^v 43 mostly short treatises on alchemy and mineralogy.

GLOSS None.

DECORATION None to *DCPhil.*; initials in red and schematic drawings in red and black to fols 8^v–11^r.

PROVENANCE Unclear *ex libris*, fol. 255^v. 'E' on lower edge may indicate provenance of Schloss Ambras (see H. Menhardt, *Verzeichnis der altdeutschen literarischen Handschriften der Österreichischen Nationalbibliothek*, Berlin, 1960–61).

BIBLIOGRAPHY *Tabulae*, IV, pp. 141–2; Zinner, nos 6817, 10060 and 11515; Glorieux, *Arts*, no. 417az; Kaeppelli, no. 3776; Unterkircher, *Die datierten*, III, pp. 166–7, fig. 165 (fol. 140^r).

102. MS Wien, Österreichische Nationalbibliothek, 12754

Topica Aris. s. xiv

Parchment; i + 71 + i fols; page 242x167mm; text 120–30x65–80mm; 27–32 lines; two scribes, changing at fol. 33^r. *Tituli* in red. Book numbers and titles as running headers (bk I only). Binding: s. xv red leather on wood; two clasps (lost).
A carefully made book.

CONTENTS Fols 1^r–71^r ***Topica Aris.***

GLOSS None, but space left for marginal gloss; s. xv notes in several hands on pastedown and front flyleaf.

DECORATION Finely executed major initials in red, gold, black and blue with penwork flourishing to fols 1^r, 10^v, 18^r, 23^r, 31^r, 42^v and 60^v; minor initials in red; red and blue paraph signs.

PROVENANCE N. France. Purchased by the Hofbibliothek in 1847; previously belonged to Franz Goldhan.

BIBLIOGRAPHY *Tabulae*, VII, p. 142; Hermann, VII.1, pp. 99–100, no. 42; *AL*, 139;

Unterkircher, *Inventar*, I, p. 154; Markowski, p. 273.

103. MS Wien, Österreichische Nationalbibliothek, 14356
DCPhil. s. xv

Paper; iii + 179 + i fols; page 210x150mm; text 135x80mm; 13–27 lines; several scribes. Greek in text. Binding: s. xv white leather on wood (restored in 1913). A carefully written copy.

CONTENTS Fols 1^r–4^v and 7^r–8^v parts of an incomplete commentary, *inc.* 'Boecii tractatus de philosophia' (fol. 7^r); 5^r–6^v and 9^r–10^v blank; 12^r–170^v ***DCPhil.***; 170^v–179^v Lupus, *De metris*.

GLOSS See contents. Extensive interlinear gloss and scattered marginal annotation.

DECORATION Red paraph signs.

PROVENANCE Unknown. Purchased in 1861 from *Bibliothek deutscher Orden* together with 339 other MSS.

BIBLIOGRAPHY *Tabulae*, VIII, p. 43.

104. MS Wien, Österreichische Nationalbibliothek, 15470
Mus. s. xiii

Parchment; 10 fols; page 250–60x175–200mm; text 200x140mm; 41 lines; one scribe. *Titulus* in red, fol. 5^r. Greek in text with interlinear Latin translation, fol. 1^v. Modern binding.

CONTENTS Fols 1^r–10^v ***Mus.*** I.1–7 (180/1–194/28); I.19–29 (205/9–220/13); III.2–12 (272/17–291/6).

GLOSS None.

DECORATION One initial in red, fol. 5^r; schematic tables in red and black.

PROVENANCE ?Germany. Belonged to the Cathedral Chapter Library in Salzburg, whence to the Hofbibliothek in 1806.

BIBLIOGRAPHY *Tabulae*, VIII, p. 164; Bower, no. 136.

105. MS Wien, Österreichische Nationalbibliothek, Ser. n. 3635
Cat. s. xiv 2/2

Paper; 15 fols; page 210x145mm; text 155x110mm; 23–24 lines; probably one scribe. Modern binding.

CONTENTS Fols 1^r–15^v ***Cat.***, *expl.* imperf. 'non est facile assignare quid sit contrarium' (40/13).

GLOSS Scattered marginal and interlinear annotations chiefly by one contemporary user.

DECORATION Not executed.

PROVENANCE Unknown.

BIBLIOGRAPHY Mazal and Unterkircher, III, p. 229.

106. MS Wien, Österreichische Nationalbibliothek, Ser. n. 4104
Isag., Cat. I s. xiv

Parchment; 2 fols; page 225x137–67mm; text 180x90mm; 32 lines. *Titulus* in red, fol. 2^r.

CONTENTS Fols 1^r–2^r ***Isag.***, 8.12 'proprie autem differre'–12.15 'medicum vel geometram' (14/21–19/20); 2^r ***Isag.*** 21.2 'in eo quod est praedicatur' (30/11)–end; 2$^{r–v}$ ***Cat.*** I, *expl.* imperf. 'ut album, cum in subiecto sit, de subiecto praedicatur' (8/1).

GLOSS Extensive marginal gloss in several contemporary hands; scattered interlinear annotation.

DECORATION Simple red initials; red and brown paraph signs.

PROVENANCE Unknown.

BIBLIOGRAPHY Mazal and Unterkircher, IV, pp. 36–7.

SCHOTTENSTIFT

The Benedictine monastery was founded in 1155 by Duke Heinrich Jasomirgott of Babenberg and populated with Irish monks from Regensburg. In 1418 it was repopulated with German monks from Melk, but the name 'ad Scotos' was preserved. Almost nothing has been preserved from the old monastic library. The first new abbots, Johann of Ochsenhausen (1428–46) and Martin of Lewbicz (1446–61), established the scriptorium; numerous donations of books by university professors followed in the sixteenth century.

A. Hübl, *Catalogus codicum manu scriptorum, qui in bibliotheca monasterii B. M. V. Ad Scotos Vindobonae servantur*, Vienna and Leipzig, 1899; *MBKÖ*, I, pp.

431–43; Unterkircher, Fiedler, Stickler, pp. 29–31; F. Unterkircher, H. Horninger and F. Lackner, *Die datierten Handschriften in Wien ausserhalb der Österreichischen Nationalbibliothek bis zum Jahre 1600*, Katalog der datierten Handschriften in lateinischer Schrift in Österreich, V, Vienna, 1981; Kristeller, III, pp. 70–73.

107. MS Wien, Schottenstift, Cod. 304 (Hübl 224)
Top. Diff. 1485

Paper; i + 250 + i fols; page 215x147mm; text 130–60x75–100mm; 16–31 lines; one scribe for text. Dated colophons, fols 124^{v}, 185^{r}, 201^{r}, 249^{r}. Book numbers as running headers. Binding: half-leather and speckled pasteboard on wood; one central clasp (partially intact).

CONTENTS Fols 1^{r}–124^{v} Cicero, *De rhetorica*, glossed; 125^{r}–128^{v} blank; 129^{r}–147^{r} idem, *Paradoxa*, glossed; 149^{r}–185^{r} idem, *De amicitia*, glossed; 186^{r}–196^{v} Seneca, *De mundi gubernatione*; 197^{v} excerpt from *DCPhil.*; 198^{r}–201^{r} Ps.-Seneca, *De morum institutione*; 202^{r}–206^{r} Ps.-Seneca, *De remediis fortuitorum*; 206^{v}–207^{v} Ps.-Seneca, *Proverbia secundum ordinem alphabeti*; 210^{r}–249^{r} ***Top. Diff.***

GLOSS Scattered marginal annotation in ?scribe's hand to *Top. Diff. I–III.*

DECORATION Initials in red; minor capitals in text touched with red; red paraph signs.

PROVENANCE ?Schottenstift. No original marks of ownership.

BIBLIOGRAPHY Hübl, pp. 244–5; S. Gallick, 'Medieval Rhetorical Arts in England and the Manuscript Traditions', *Manuscripta*, 18, 1974, p. 90; Unterkircher, Horninger and Lackner, *Die datierten*, V, p. 143, fig. 373 (fol. 249^{r}).

ZWETTL

STIFTSBIBLIOTHEK

The Cistercian abbey was founded in 1138 as a daughter-house of Heiligenkreuz and most of the early MSS were produced in the monastic scriptorium. In the course of s. xiv the abbey acquired additional MSS from donations. The first catalogue was compiled in the first half of the thirteenth century.

S. Rössler, *Verzeichniss der Handschriften der Bibliothek des Stiftes Zwettl*, Xenia Bernardina, I, pp. 293–479; *MBKÖ*, I, pp. 507–20; P. Buberl, H. Göhler and A. Wagner, *Die Kunstdenkmäler des Zisterzienserklosters Zwettl*, Ostmärkische

Kunsttopographie, 29, Vienna, 1940; Unterkircher, Fiedler, Stickler, pp. 24–5; C. Ziegler, *Zisterzienserstift Zwettl. Katalog der Handschriften des Mittelalters*, 4 vols, Vienna and Munich, 1985–97.

108. MS Zwettl, Stiftsbibliothek, 244
Vita, DCPhil. I s. xiii

Parchment; i + 123 fols; text, fols 1ra–24rb, 2 cols, each 225x75mm; fols 24^{r}–122^{v} 192–205x126–42mm; 23–37 lines; several scribes. *Tituli* in red and brown. Greek confident. Binding: ?original damaged light leather on wood; two clasps (lost).

CONTENTS Fol. i^{r-v} s. xv table of contents and s. xiii *probationes pennae*; 1va–2va notes on Boethius and versification, *inc.* 'In exponendis auctoribus hec consideranda sunt'; *expl.* 'in reliquis per simplices computare'; 3^{r} notes on *metra*, with interlinear gloss, *inc.* 'id est grave id est mundi'; *expl.* 'celestem mathesin et astronomia' (*sic*); 3va–4rb ***Vita***, *inc.* 'Tempore illo quo Gottorum rex Theodoricus Romanam'; *expl.* 'cum in commune deducitur'; 4va–23vb ***DCPhil. I***, *expl.* imperf. 'tactu blandiore mollescant' I.pr.v.44; 24ra–103^{v} Bede, *De tabernaculo*; 104^{v}–122^{v} Hugh of St Victor, *De institutione novitiorum*; 122^{v} poem, *inc.* 'Quisque modo esset penset quod nunc bene restat agendum'; *expl.* 'hac fac et vivas', here attrib. to Bernard of Clairvaux; 123^{r-v} *probationes pennae*.

GLOSS Systematic commentary on a massive scale (ed. Silk, 1935); text linked to commentary by underlining in red and paraph signs.

DECORATION Decorated initials in red and brown, e.g. fols 24ra, 24rb, 104^{v}; explicit in red.

PROVENANCE Zwettl.

BIBLIOGRAPHY *Xenia Bernardina*, I, pp. 383–4; *MBKÖ*, I, p. 514 (line 2); Goy, p. 366; Bloomfield, no. 4685; Ziegler, 3, pp. 108–10.

109. MS Zwettl, Stiftsbibliothek, 248
Op. Sac. s. xiii^{in} (Häring s. xii 2/2)

Parchment; 119 fols; page 270x190mm; text 200x130mm; 29–32 lines; one scribe. *Tituli* in red. Binding: s. xiii white leather on wood; parchment label on front cover.

CONTENTS Fol. 1^{r} s. xv contents list by Nikolaus of Dobersberg; 1^{v} *De phlebotomia* (Thorndike/Kibre, 1681); 1^{v}–116^{r} ***Op. Sac. I–III, V***, with commentary of Gilbert of Poitiers; 116^{v}–119^{v} ***Op. Sac. IV***.

GLOSS See contents.

DECORATION ***I****(nvestigatam)* depicting a gryphon on a column (fol. 1^{v}); inhabited ***Q****(uod)* in red with a human face (fol. 45^{r}); minor Lombardic initials in red, beige, and green, some decorated.

PROVENANCE Zwettl; marks of ownership (fols 1^{r}, 118^{v}).

BIBLIOGRAPHY *Xenia Bernardina* (Rössler), I, p. 384; *MBKÖ*, I, p. 514 (line 25); Häring, *Gilbert*, pp. 28–9, 32; idem, 'Texts', p. 189; idem, no. 189; Ziegler, 3, pp. 116–17.

110. MS Zwettl, Stiftsbibliothek, 253.

Op. Sac. I–III, V s. xiii^{in}

Parchment; i + 169 fols; page 244x173mm.
A (s. xiii^{in}): text 194–230x115–30mm; 34–39 lines; one scribe. *Titulus* in red, fol. 1^{r}.
B (s. xiii 2/4): text 190–200x111–38mm; 32–7 lines; one scribe. *Tituli* in red.
C (s. xiii 1/2): text 2 cols, each 200x60–70mm; 40 lines; two scribes. *Tituli* in red.
Modern binding.

CONTENTS A: fol. i^{r-v} *Quaestiones* (fragm.: s. xiii 2/4), *inc.* 'Questio talis est habebat causam'; *expl.* 'in causa conventionis anime procedatur'; 1^{r}–80^{v} ***Op. Sac. I–III, V***, with commentary of Gilbert of Poitiers.
B: fols 81^{r}–132^{v} Cicero, *De officiis*; 133^{r}–144^{r} idem, *De amicitia*.
C: fols 145ra–164vb Hugh of Fouilloy, *De natura avium*, with drawings; 165ra–169vb idem, *De rota verae religionis*, *expl.* imperf. 'De canto inopie et duobus radiis'.

GLOSS A: see contents. Text surrounded by commentary and linked to it by underlining; paraph signs.
B: marginal and interlinear glosses.

DECORATION A: elaborate interlace initials in red, e.g., fol. 3^{r}.
B: initials in red and black; explicits in red; paraph signs.
C: initials in red. Numerous drawings of birds throughout text. Drawing representing *clericus* and *miles* as personifications of *Vita contemplativa* and *Vita activa*, fol. 145^{v} (cf. MS Heiligenkreuz 226, fol. 129^{v}); two drawings of wheels with monastic virtues and vices, fols 165^{v}, 169^{v}.

PROVENANCE Zwettl.

BIBLIOGRAPHY *Xenia Bernardina* (Rössler), I, p. 385; Buberl, Göhler and Wagner, pp. 207–8, fig. 261 (fol. 145^{v}); Häring, *Gilbert*, pp. 19, 30, 32; idem, 'Texts', p. 189; idem, no. 190; *Die Kuenringer*, no. 248c.2; Munk-Olsen, I, p. 320 (Cic.C.591); Ziegler, 3, pp. 123–6, figs 35 (fol. 3^{r}), 40 (fol. 150^{r}), 41 (fol. 169^{v}), pl. IV (fol. 145^{v}).

111. MS Zwettl, Stiftsbibliothek, 257

Logica nova s. xiii 2/2

Parchment; 111 fols; page 240x175mm; text (fols 1ra–39vb and 54ra–109vb) 2 cols, each 174–205x50–75mm, fols 40^{r}–53^{r} 165x109mm; 49–53 lines; three scribes, changing at fols 40^{r}, 54ra, 78ra. Colophon, 'Qui me scribebat Fridericus nomen habebat', fol. 77va. Binding: combined s. xiv light brown and s. xvii white leather on wood.

CONTENTS Fols 1ra–18va ***Topica Aris.***; 18va–24vb ***Soph. Elench.***; 25ra–39vb ***Prior Anal.***, *expl.* imperf. 'aut enim in prima aut medium aut'; 40^{r}–53^{r} *Post. Anal.*; 54ra–77va *Synkategoremata*; 78ra–109vb Simon of Faversham, *Sententiae super flores*, *expl.* imperf. 'scilicet istum et non illi qui ad completum'.

GLOSS Contemporary marginal glosses; text passages repeated in gloss or underlined in red.

DECORATION Decorated initials in red and blue. Scattered geometrical drawings (fols 120^{v}, 34^{v}, 39^{r}) and diagrams (fols 30^{v}–31^{r}); brown and black paraph signs; incipits and explicits in red.

PROVENANCE Zwettl.

BIBLIOGRAPHY *Xenia Bernardina* (Rössler), I, pp. 368–87; *AL*, 141; Glorieux, *Arts*, p. 449 (no. 1953); Ziegler, 3, pp. 147–8.

112. MS Zwettl, Stiftsbibliothek, 314

Op. Sac. I–III, V s. xii 3/4

Parchment; i + 168 fols; page 235x140mm.
C: text variable, 175–215x95–125mm; lines variable, 40–70; several scribes. *Titulus* in red, fol. 103^{v}.
Binding: leather on wooden boards, renewed.

CONTENTS A: fol. 1^{r} contents list by Nikolaus of Dobersberg, c. 1400; 2^{r}–49^{v} Geoffrey Babion, *On Matthew* (*PL*, 162:1228–1500).
B: fols 51^{r}–102^{r} Gloss on the seven canonical Epistles (*PL*, 114: 671–710).
C: fol. 103^{r} *Diffinitiones Petri Lombardi*; 103^{v}–153^{r} Gilbert of Poitiers, Commentary on *Op. Sac.*; 153^{r}–154^{v} definitions, *capitula* and response from the trial of Gilbert of Poitiers (see M. L. Colker, *Mediaeval Studies* 27, 1965, pp. 152–183); 155^{r} poem, *inc.* 'Doder Secenas attavis edite regibus'; 155^{v}–166^{r} ***Op. Sac. I–III, V***; 166^{v} profession of faith from Gilbert's trial (cont. from fol. 154^{v}).

GLOSS See contents; underlining and corrections in red to commentary; otherwise some readers' notes to *Op. Sac.*

DECORATION C: initials in black and red; paraph marks and NOTA signs.

PROVENANCE ?Zwettl.

BIBLIOGRAPHY *Xenia Bernardina* (Rössler), I, pp. 407–8; Classen, *Gerhoch*, p. 442; Häring, 1965, p. 74; idem, *Gilbert*, pp. 31–2; idem, no. 191; *Die Kuenringer*, no. 245; Ziegler, 4, pp. 35–9.

113. MS Zwettl, Stiftsbibliothek, 318
Topica Aris. c. 1300

Parchment; 163 fols; page 240x170mm.
B: text 155–65x105mm; 32 lines; one scribe (hand C of Ziegler's Zwettl scribes).
Binding: s. xv dark brown damaged leather on wooden boards. *Titulus*, fol. 72^r, by Nikolaus von Dobersberg (c. 1400).

CONTENTS A (c. 1300): fols 1^r–56^r Aristotle, *Ethica Nicomachea*.
B: fols 57^r–81^r *Post. Anal.*; 81^v–90^v ***Topica Aris.***, *expl.* imperf. 'quo difficilior assumptio fiat quoniam non est' (*AL*).
C (s. xiv 2/2): fols 91ra–163vb Iohannes de Fayt?, alphabetical vocabulary from *Abraham* to *Zelus* (Bloomfield, 5072).

GLOSS Sparse marginal glosses and line corrections.

DECORATION B: *Post. Anal.* and *Topica Aris.* begin with large red initials touched with white; elsewhere, simple red initials; rubrication.

PROVENANCE Zwettl: two *ex libris* (one s. xiv 1/2; one by Nikolaus von Dobersberg), front pastedown; 'Liber beate virginis in Zwetla et conventus ibidem. Qui ipsum alienaverit anathema sit' (fol. 56^r).

BIBLIOGRAPHY *Xenia Bernardina* (Rössler), I, p. 409; *AL*, 143; Ziegler, 4, pp. 45–7.

114. MS Zwettl, Stiftsbibliothek, 357
in Cat. s. xiii^{ex}

Parchment; 98 fols; page 210x150mm.
B: text 2 cols, variable, 120–30xc. 60mm; 33–67 lines; one scribe for Boethius.
Binding: light brown leather on wooden boards, renewed. Pastedowns from a ?French legal text. *Titulus* by Nikolaus of Dobersberg, c. 1400, fol. 1^r.

CONTENTS A (s. xiv 2/2): fols 1ra–2va Ps.-Augustine, *De honestate mulierum*; 2vb–6va Ps.-Augustine, *De triplici habitacula*; 6va–12vb Ps.-Augustine, *Meditationes*; 12vb–22rb Ps.-Augustine (Ambrosius Aupertus), *De conflictu vitiorum*.
B: fols 27^r–35^r Bernard of Clairvaux, sermon: *'vidi dominum'*;

sermon: *de sancto Martino episcopo*; 35ra–59ra ***in Cat.***, I–III; 60^{r-v} notes, *De loco*; 61ra–62rb *Liber Methodii*; 62ra–63ra Bernard of Clairvaux, sermon: *in cena domini*; 63vb–65vb *Compendium Anticlaudianum*; 65vb–66ra sermon for 1st Sunday in Quadragesima; 67va–80vb Ps.-Aristotle, *Secretum secretorum*; 81^{r}–88^{v} *Questiones de intellectu*, etc.
C (s. xiv 1/2): fols 89ra–98vb Cato, *Dicz ist daz vorgewirbe Kathonis*.

GLOSS B: None.

DECORATION B: A few initials and paraph marks in ink of text.

PROVENANCE Zwettl.

BIBLIOGRAPHY *Xenia Bernardina* (Rössler), I, pp. 425–6; Ziegler, 4, pp. 193–6.

115. MS Zwettl, Stiftsbibliothek, 363
Op. Sac., DCPhil. I, Vita s. xii 2/2

Parchment; 167 fols; page 195x140mm (fols 132^{r}–139^{v} 185x135mm); text 135–55x75–110mm; 19–40 lines; several scribes. *Tituli* in brown and red rustic capitals, fols 70^{r} and 83^{r}. Fols 1, 167 from a Cistercian breviary (office of the dead). Binding: white leather on wood.

CONTENTS Fol. 2^{r} contents list of Nikolaus of Dobersberg, c. 1400; 3^{r}–33^{r} Didymus, *De spiritu sancto*; 33^{r}–66^{v} Alcuin, *De fide sancte et individue trinitatis*; 66^{v}–70^{r} idem, *Questiones ad Fredegisum de sancta trinitate*; 70^{r}–129^{v} ***Op. Sac.***; 130^{r}–131^{r} Innocent III, *De simoniacis*; 132^{r}–135^{r} commentary on Macrobius, *In Somnium Scipionis*; 136^{r}–139^{r} ***DCPhil. I***, *expl.* imperf. 'quae felicitas commendaverit' I.pr.iv.158, with prologue of William of Conches and Lupus, *De metris*; 140^{r-v} ***Vita***, *inc.* 'Vita tempore illo quo gothorum rex Theodericus' (cf. Zwettl 244); 141^{r}–166^{v} commentary on *DCPhil.*, *inc.* 'Sensus ego qui quondam letus esse'; *expl.* 'tu triplicis philosophiae animam' (cf. Zwettl 244).

GLOSS See contents. Frequent use of paraph signs and pointing hands throughout commentary.

DECORATION Major initials in red, e.g., large ***Q****(uaero)* with penwork flourishing (fol. 83^{r}). Explicit in red (fol. 82^{v}).

PROVENANCE Zwettl.

BIBLIOGRAPHY *Xenia Bernardina* (Rössler), I, p. 427; N. M. Häring, 'Four Commentaries on the *De consolatione philosophiae* in Ms. Heiligenkreuz 130', *Mediaeval studies*, 31, 1969, pp. 288 (n. 2),

292 and 294; Lambert, II, p. 427 (no. 258); Ziegler, 4, pp. 215–18.

116. MS Zwettl, Stiftsbibliothek, 377
DCPhil., Op. Sac. I–III, V 1300–1320

Parchment; 86 fols; page 190x150mm; text (framed) 125x85mm; 33 lines; one scribe for *DCPhil.* and *Op. Sac.* Greek in text. *Titulus* in red, fol. 3^{r}. Binding: white leather on wood; one central clasp.

CONTENTS Fol. 1^{v} contents list of Nikolaus of Dobersberg, c. 1400; 2^{r-v} philosophical notes and tables; 3^{r}–37^{v} ***DCPhil.***, with commentary of Gilbert of Poitiers; 37^{v}–49^{r} ***Op. Sac. I–III, V***, with commentary of Gilbert of Poitiers; 49^{r} *dicta* of Jerome and Bernard of Clairvaux; notes on receipt and return of pawn from 1291 and 1295; 49^{v} blank; 50^{r}–82^{r} Anon., *Summa scientiae sophisticae*; 83^{r}–85^{v} sermon on the Assumption.

GLOSS Marginal glosses on a massive scale to *DCPhil.*, at times text entirely surrounded by gloss, e.g., fol. 34^{v}; text linked to gloss by underlining in red. Contemporary marginal and interlinear glosses to *Op. Sac.*; text linked to gloss by Greek letters and occasionally by underlining in red.

DECORATION ***C****(armina)* in red, black and gold, fol. 3^{r}; initials in red with occasional penwork flourishing. Incipits in red to *Op. Sac.*

PROVENANCE Zwettl.

BIBLIOGRAPHY *Xenia Bernardina* (Rössler), I, p. 431; Ziegler, 4, pp. 254–7.

BELGIUM

ANTWERPEN (Antwerp)

MUSEUM PLANTIN-MORETUS

The collection was established by the great sixteenth-century printer, Christopher Plantin, and continued by his son-in-law and grandson, John and Balthasar Moretus. The two manuscripts described here were among those bequeathed to Plantin in 1581 by the humanist Theodore Poelman.

J. Denucé, *Musaeum Plantin-Moretus: Catalogue des manuscrits*, Antwerp, 1927.

1. MS Antwerpen, Museum Plantin-Moretus, M 16. 8 [190 (38)]
DCPhil. s. x^{ex}/xi^{in}

Parchment; 116 + i fols (fols 1–4 badly eaten away); page 290x215mm; text 185x111mm; text and gloss 202x200mm; 18 lines (text), c. 50 lines (gloss); ruled for gloss, but not integrated ruling; written in English Caroline Minuscule. *Tituli* to bks II–IV; space left at bk V but not supplied. Rhetorical labels, e.g., METAPHORA, I.pr.iv.44 (fol. 8^{r}), I.m.v.22 (fol. 12^{v}); METRUM GLICONICUM, I.m.vi (fol. 15^{r}); METRUM SAPHICUM, II.m.iii (fol. 23^{r}), II.m.vi (fol. 32^{v}); METRUM IAMBICUM ANACREONTICUM II.m.iv (fol. 26^{v}); INCIPIT DE DIGNITATIBVS II.pr.vi (fol. 30^{v}); DIFFINITIO FATI AC PROVIDENTIAE IV.pr.vi (fol. 86^{v}).
A fine MS. It probably originally formed part of the same vol. as MS Antwerpen, Museum Plantin-Moretus, M 16. 2 [47 (32)] + MS London, BL, Add. 32246 (extracts from Priscian; Remigius, Commentary on Donatus; etc.) and MS Brussels, Bibl. Roy., 1520 (Aldhelm, *De virginitate*).

CONTENTS Fols 1^{r}–116^{v} ***DCPhil.***; 116^{v} index of incipits (s. xiv).

GLOSS Glosses in two or more contemporary and later hands derive from at least three traditions, that of the Remigius commentary, that found in MS Paris, BnF, lat. 6401A and that found in MS Cambridge, University Library, Kk.iii.2. Letters, weights and measures and other symbols used as sigla.

DECORATION Plain. Initials in one colour only, generally red, except for II.m.ix.1, where the initial ***O*** is red with green and blue infill (fol. 54^{r}). The first line of each metre and prose is in capitals.

PROVENANCE Abingdon, England. Used by Theodore Poelman for his edition: Antwerp, Chr. Plantin, 1562.

BIBLIOGRAPHY Denucé, pp. 147–8; Ker, *MLGB*, p. 2; Bishop, *English Caroline*, pp. 13, 18; Wittig, p. 187; Bolton, pp. 55–7; Troncarelli, *Boethiana*, p. 151.

2. MS Antwerpen, Museum Plantin-Moretus, M 25. 0 [100 (112)]
DCPhil. s. xii 2/2

Parchment; 50 fols; page 134x103mm; text 103x80mm; 24 lines; one principal scribe writing an informal glossing hand, another later s. xii gloss hand fols 49^{v}–50^{r}; metres written as prose. Greek, III.pr.xi.106, IV.pr.v.196, V.m.ii.1 (fols 29^{v}, 38^{v}, 42^{r}). Parchment binding, s. xvii.
A pocket-size book.

CONTENTS Fols 1^{r}–49^{r} ***DCPhil.***; 49^{v}–50^{r} fragment of comm. on III.m.ix, *inc.* 'Invocatio hec philosophie ad integrum ex Platonis dogmate sumpta est. Ipse namque de mundi genitura intime disserens'; *expl.* 'cum igni concordat'.

GLOSS Users' annotations fols 1^{r}–2^{v}, and occasionally thereafter, e.g., noting metre.

DECORATION Roughly produced plain red ink capitals. Initial letters of metres and capitals within text frequently have red infill.

PROVENANCE 'D. Iohannis Coloniensis Hieronymianus/ Theod. Pulmanno DD/ anno MD LXXI', fol. 1^{r}.

BIBLIOGRAPHY Denucé, p. 83.

BRUGGE (Bruges)

GROOTSEMINARIE

The Grootseminarie occupies the site of the Cistercian abbey of Ter Duinen (Les Dunes), suppressed in 1796. Manuscripts from this house form the largest collection within the library of the Grootseminarie. The abbey and its books, augmented by those of its daughter-house, Ter Doest, moved from its original site near Koksijde in Flanders to Bruges in 1627. A stamp with the device of the cross of Burgundy is found in all of the Ter Duinen manuscripts transferred to Bruges at this time. Many of the manuscripts of Ter Duinen and Ter Doest are now in the Stedelijke Openbare Bibliotheek, Bruges.

M. Th. Isaac, *Les Livres de l'abbaye des Dunes d'après le catalogue du XVIIe siècle*, Aubel, 1984; R. Vander Plaetse, 'Index van de handschriften van het Grootseminarie te Brugge', in A. Denaux and E. van den Berghe, *De Duinenabdij (1627–1796) en het Grootseminarie te Brugge*, Tielt, 1984; G. I. Lieftinck, *De librijen en scriptoria der Westvlaamse Cistercienserabdijen Ter Duinen en Ter Doest in de 12e en de 13e eeuw en de betrekkingen tot het atelier van de kapittelschool van Sint-Donatiaan te Brugge*, Mededelingen van de Koninklijke Vlaamse Academie voor Wetenschappen, Letteren en Schone Kunsten van België, Klasse der Letteren, xv/2, Brussels, 1953; *Vlaamse Kunst op Perkament: Handschriften en miniaturen te Brugge van de 12e tot de 16e eeuw*, Bruges, 1981; handwritten list in 3 vols: 1. MSS 1–66; 2. MSS 67–133; 3. MSS 134–196.

3. MS Brugge, Grootseminarie 100/113
Logica vetus et nova s. xiii^{ex}

Parchment; 260 fols (either leaves are now missing from between fols 187 and 188, or fols 188–260 form part of a different book, lacking leaves at the beginning; the two parts were together by at least s. xvi, see contents list, fol. 160^{r}). Page 260x180mm.
A: text 2 cols, each 130x40mm, with wide margins ruled for gloss; 28–30 lines; two or three scribes.
B: text 2 cols, each 134–142x40mm; wide margins ruled for gloss; 30 lines; two scribes.
Binding: brown stamped leather on boards (repaired); bosses (5 on front, 4 on back) and two clasps now missing.

CONTENTS A: fols 1ra–10ra ***Isag.***; 10rb–27va ***Cat.***; 27va–38ra ***De Int.***; 38rb–46vb *Liber sex principiorum*; 47ra–60rb ***Div.***; 61ra–94vb ***Top. Diff.***; 95ra–117vb ***Soph. Elench.***; 118ra–187rb ***Topica Aris.***
B: fols 188ra–230ra ***Prior Anal.***, *inc.* imperf. I.iv; 231ra–260ra *Post. Anal.*; 260^{r} s. xvi contents list to A & B; 260^{v} prayers in Old French.

GLOSS Several glossing hands, s. xiii–xv (none common to the two parts).

DECORATION A: red and blue initials with pen-flourishing.
B: major inhabited initials painted in blue, red and white (fol. 213^{r}) and with gold (fol. 231^{r}); minor initials in red or blue with pen-flourishing.

PROVENANCE B at least sold by Iohannes Thomas to Iohannes Vandeloo and Folquard de Dacia, 1314 (note on fol. 260^{v} in hand of one of the glossators of B); by s. xvi at Ter Duinen (Les Dunes), Cistercian abbey (*ex libris*, fol. 260^{v}; fols 1^{r}, 259^{v}: stamp of cross of Burgundy).

BIBLIOGRAPHY *AL*, 162; Isaac, 10.36 and 10.131 (pp. 377–80, 431); Vander Plaetse, pp.128–9, 133.

4. MS Brugge, Grootseminarie, 101/135
DCPhil. s. xii 2/2

Parchment; i + 144 (numbered 1–44, 44–123, 123–142); page 296x220mm; text 215–238x145–153mm; 21–26 lines (text), 40–44 lines (gloss); fols 126^{v}/10–142^{v} 2 cols; at least three scribes; post-medieval binding, brown leather on boards.

CONTENTS Fols 1^{r}–124ra ***DCPhil.***, glossed; 125^{r}–142rb continuous commentary on *DCPhil. inc.* prol., 'Boethius iste nobilissimus civis romanus'; *inc.* comm., 'Boetius tractaturus de philosophica consolatione primitus ostendit'. For the prologue to the comm., cf. *Vita VII*, and for the comm., cf. William of Conches.

GLOSS See contents. Gloss *inc.* 'Mos auctorum est operi suo prologos prescribere', fol. 1ra. Greek words glossed with Latin translation. s. xv lexical glosses as far as fol. 25^{r}.

DECORATION Arabesque initial in red and green (fol. 1^{r}) and in gold, blue, red and green (fol. 1^{v}) and blue, green and red (fols 24^{v}, 62^{r}, 81^{r}, 106^{v}); minor initials in green or red or a combination of both.

PROVENANCE Ter Duinen (Les Dunes), Cistercian abbey (fols 1^{r}, 142^{v}: stamp of cross of Burgundy).

BIBLIOGRAPHY Isaac, 10.66 (pp. 398–9); Vander Plaetse, p. 129; Kristeller, III, p. 85a.

5. MS Brugge, Grootseminarie, 110/80
Mus. s. xii

Parchment; i + 72; page 240x170mm; text c. 167x c.100mm; 30–33 lines; two scribes writing small hands with numerous abbreviations, N. French, perhaps Norman; blind-tooled brown leather binding on pasteboard; s. xiv/xv label re-affixed to back cover.
A small, scholar's book.

CONTENTS Fols 1^{r}–59^{v} ***Mus.***; 59^{v}–69^{r} 'Musica est divisio vocum varietas et modulatio … vel ad tritedie zeumenon sese tono habeat' (cf. MS Valenciennes, Bibl. Mun., 249, fol. 113^{v}); 69^{r}–70^{r} a monochord division: 'Boetius vir eruditissimus musicam dicit constare tribus generibus diatono cromatico et enarmonio … et sic perfeceris proemium musicam nobis naturaliter esse coniunctam et mores vel honestare vel inevertere' (also found in MS Saumur, Museé des Arts décoratifs, 3, fol. 59^{r}).

GLOSS None.

DECORATION Major arabesque initials in blue, red and yellow (fols 13^{v}, 26^{r}, 37^{r},

54^{v}); major inhabited initial (fol. 1^{r}); minor initials in red or blue.

PROVENANCE Ter Duinen (Les Dunes), Cistercian abbey (fols 1^{r}, 70^{r}: stamp of cross of Burgundy).

BIBLIOGRAPHY Isaac, 10.68 (p. 400); Vander Plaetse, p. 129; idem, 'Index van de handschriften van het Grootseminarie van Brugge', in A. Denaux and E. van den Berghe, *De Duinenabdij (1627–1796) en het Grootseminarie te Brugge*, Tielt, 1984; Bower, 9.

6. MS Brugge, Grootseminarie, 112/111

DCPhil. s. xv 2/2 (before 1488)

Parchment; iii + 207 (one unnumbered leaf between fols 186 and 187) + iii (numbered 207–209); page 205x140mm; text 112x68mm; ruled in red for 25 lines of text (below top line); one scribe, identified as Georgius Hermonymus, writing a humanistic script; marginal headings and glosses in a humanistic cursive; contemporary elaborate stamped brown leather binding on boards, typical of bindings of books owned by Johannes Crabbe; metal corners at fore-edge on front and back covers; five bosses on front and back and two clasps no longer survive, apart from part of one clasp.
A very fine volume.

CONTENTS Fols 1^{r}–116^{v} Cicero, *De officiis*; 116^{v} 'Tullius hesperios cupiens, conponere mores ...' (*Anthologia latina*, 784–5); 119^{r}–206^{v} ***DCPhil.***; back pastedown addition in continental cursive 'Merlinus dixit illo quo tempore vixit/ Quod rex unus erit qui flandros perdere querit/In bulscamp ibit et ibi moriendo peribit/ Bulscamp ecce dies quo tinctus sanguine fies. 1474.'

GLOSS Rhetorical labels and headings refering to content.

DECORATION Three-sided border (fols 1^{r}, 119^{r}); major and minor initials in gold on blue and purple; armorial shield of Johannes Crabbe, fol. 1^{r}.

PROVENANCE Probably produced in Bruges, c. 1474 (Geirnaert). Johannes Crabbe, abbot of Ter Duinen (1457–88), fol. 1^{r}; fol. 119^{r} J.C. monogram; Ter Duinen (Les Dunes), Cistercian abbey (fols 1^{r}, 206^{v}: stamp of cross of Burgundy).

BIBLIOGRAPHY Isaac, 10.66 (pp. 398–99); Vander Plaetse, p. 129; *Treasures of Belgian Libraries*, no. 59, p. 48; *Vlaamse kunst op perkament*, no. 84, pp. 183–4; N. Geirnaert, 'Classical Texts in Bruges around 1473: Cooperation of Italian Scribes, Bruges Parchment Rulers, Illuminators and Bookbinders for Johannes Crabbe, Abbot of Les Dunes abbey', *Transactions of the Cambridge Bibliographical Society* 10, 1992, pp. 173–81.

STEDELIJKE OPENBARE BIBLIOTHEEK

Many of the books are from the Cistercian abbey of Ter Duinen (Les Dunes), which had already (1624) incorporated its daughter-house, Ter Doest, with its own substantial library ('codices Thosani'), and which in 1627 moved to Bruges. The house was suppressed in 1796. The Ter Duinen manuscripts transferred to Bruges in 1627 bear a stamp of the cross of Burgundy.

A. de Poorter, *Catalogue des manuscrits de la Bibliothèque Publique de la ville de Bruges*, Catalogue général des manuscrits des bibliothèques de Belgique 2, Gembloux and Paris, 1934; M.-T. Isaac, *Les Livres manuscrits de l'Abbaye des Dunes d'après le catalogue du xviie siècle*, Aubel, 1984; G. I. Lieftinck, *De librijen en scriptoria der Westvlaamse Cistercienserabdijen: Ter Duinen en Ter Doest in de 12e en de 13e eeuw en de betrekkingen tot het atelier van de kapittelschool van Sint-Donatiaan te Brugge*, Mededelingen van de Koninklijke Vlaamse Academie voor Wetenschappen, Letteren en Schone Kunsten van België, Klasse der Letteren, xv/2, Brussels, 1953; A. Hoste, *De Handschriften van Ter Doest*, Steenbrugge, 1993; *Vlaamse Kunst op Perkament: Handschriften en miniaturen te Brugge van de 12e tot de 16e eeuw*, Bruges, 1981.

7. MS Brugge, Stedelijke Openbare Bibliotheek, 13
Op. Sac. I s. xiv 1/2

Parchment; i + 182 + i fols; page 334x230mm; text 230x165mm, 2 cols; 41 lines. Fols 1^{r}–180^{v} written in a very fine *textura* (below top line) by one named scribe, Henricus Conuersus de Thosan: 'hunc librum scripsit frater henricus conversus de thosan. orate pro eo' (fol. 180vb: s. xiii^{ex}). Fols 181^{r}–82^{v}, which contain *Op. Sac.*, were added a little later by a different scribe. Good s. xv binding (repaired): tooled leather on wood; five studs now missing; chain mark top centre. Parchment label on back cover, recording all items apart from *Op. Sac.*
A large, fine volume, one of a number copied by Henricus for the abbey of Ter Doest, six of which are known to survive (Lieftinck, pp. 46–8; Hoste, pp. 65–6, 88).

CONTENTS Fols 1ra–83vb Augustine, *De Genesi ad litteram* (with *retractatio*); 84ra–111rb idem, *Retractationes*; 111va–130rb idem, *De quantitate animae* (with *retractatio*); 130rb–144va idem, *Soliloquia* (with *retractatio*); 144va–180vb idem, *De gratia et libero arbitrio* (with *retractatio*); 180vb Walther, 14669a, 14585 (Eugenius of Toledo); 181ra–182rb ***Op. Sac. I***, with very bad text, *expl.* imperf. 'ac per hoc perpetuum' (22/76).

GLOSS None.

DECORATION Fols 1^{r}–180^{v} fine major pen-work initials in red and blue. ***I****(nvestigatam)* simple blue initial with red pen-work flourish, fol. 181va.

PROVENANCE Ter Doest, Cistercian abbey: 'Liber beate marie de thosan' (fol. 182^{v}: s. xiv 1/2).

BIBLIOGRAPHY De Poorter, pp. 30–31; Isaac, 2. 133 (p. 101); Lieftinck, pp. 46–8; Hoste, pp. 65–6, 88, pls. 13, 17.

8. MS Brugge, Stedelijke Openbare Bibliotheek 133
Op. Sac. s. xii 2/2

Parchment; 92 + ii; page 267x175mm; text 198x c. 130mm; 23–27 lines (text); 37 lines (comm.); fols 1^{r}–87^{v} text written throughout in a text hand by one scribe; comm. in hand of text scribe apart from a few passages in another hand (e.g., fols 8^{v}, 11^{r-v}); fols 88^{r}–92^{v} added by another s. xiv scribe. Binding: white leather on wood; chain (missing) top centre; central clasp (missing). Early format: all text written in narrow column at inner margin; commentary with lemmata written as gloss on outer two-thirds of page. Perhaps produced in or near Clairmarais Cistercian abbey, a daughter-house of Ter Duinen (Stirnemann).

CONTENTS Fols 1^{r}–2^{r} Gilbert of Poitier's second prologue, *inc.* 'Omnium que rebus percipiendis'; *expl.* 'esse deceptos'; 2^{v}–87^{v} ***Op. Sac. I–III, V*** with commentary of Gilbert of Poitiers; 88^{r}–90^{v} ***Op. Sac. IV***; 90^{v}–92^{v} Gundissalinus, *De unitate et uno*.

GLOSS See contents. Sporadic user's notes (perhaps s. xiv) in lower margin.

DECORATION Historiated ***I****(nvestigatam)* running full length of page depicting Boethius with book; mask at foot: blue, green, red, gold (fol. 3^{r}). Arabesque initials in red and green to begin each treatise.

PROVENANCE Partially erased donation inscription inside front cover, s. xiii 'Liber <…>a filio magistri Egidii dicti Corenman pro anima patris sui'; s. xvii Ter Duinen (Les Dunes), Cistercian abbey (fol. 1^{r}: stamp of cross of Burgundy).

BIBLIOGRAPHY De Poorter, pp. 176–7; Häring, no. 26; Isaac, 2. 134–5 (pp. 101–2), 10.67 and 10.70 (pp. 399–401); Lieftinck, p. 81; P. Stirnemann, 'Bijlage Hand-schriftencataloog, november 1994' (unpubl. addition to Catalogue); *Vlaamse kunst op perkament*, no. 20, pp. 94–5.

9. MS Brugge, Stedelijke Openbare Bibliotheek 531
Plate 3

Mus. s. xi

Parchment i + 68 (numbered 1–24; 7 leaves cropped at the upper corner and not part of the sequence of foliation; 25–61) + ii fols; fol. 1 is a s. xvi paper replacement leaf; page 295x225mm; text 215/220x135mm; 33 lines; two scribes.

The handwriting suggests an origin in N.E. France or Lotharingia. Fols 37^{r}–40^{v} supplied by a s. xiii/s. xiv hand contemporary with, or possibly the same as, that which supplied the glosses from Gerbert of Rheims (fols 18^{v}, 23^{v}) and rubrics and diagrams elsewhere in the manuscript; fol. 1 supplied s. xvi. *Tituli*, fols 14^{r}, 24[d]^{v}, 31^{r}. *Decretum Lacedaemoniorum* in Greek, with extra space between lines for Latin translation as interlinear gloss (fol. 2^{r}), added (apart from the opening five words in the original hand) by a s. xiv user.

CONTENTS Fols 1^{r}–51^{v} ***Mus.*** with *lacunae* caused by loss of leaves after fol. 11^{v}: I.20–25 (211/25–218/12); fol. 25^{v}: III.9–11 (280/4–286/8); fol. 40^{v}: IV.11–13 (332/22–336/11); fol. 50^{v}: V.15–17 (364/16–369/16); 52^{r}–61^{v} interpolated version of part of *Musica enchiriadis*, *inc.* '(Ha)rmonia est diversarum vocum apta coadunatio' (the 'elaboratio dicta Parisiensis') together with an anonymous treatise, 'De organo', *inc.* 'Dictis autem prout potuimus' (Schmid, pp. 187– 213). Spaces have been left for diagrams in the final item.

GLOSS Fols 2^{v}–4^{v}, 7^{r}, 12^{r}, 15^{v}, 16^{v}–17^{r}, 18^{r}–19^{v}, in a hand contemporary with or slightly later than that of the text scribes, representing the Rhein-Maas tradition of glosses (Bernhard and Bower, pp. viii–ix). Scattered annotation added s. xiii–s. xv, including annotation (s. xiv) at II.10 (fol. 18^{v}) and II.21 (fol. 23^{v}) comprising Gerbert of Rheims, *Epp. ad Constantinum* (Bubnov, pp. 29–31).

DECORATION Simple acanthus and zoomorphic initials at beginning of each chapter, usually in same red pigment as rubrics, some green. Diagrams, when supplied, in same red and green. Many diagrams towards the end of the text were not supplied.

PROVENANCE Ter Duinen (Les Dunes), Cistercian abbey: *ex libris* inscriptions (fols 1^{r}, 2^{r}: s. xvi); stamp of cross of Burgundy (fols 2^{r}, 60^{v}). Probably at Ter Duinen from early on, as it acted as the exemplar for a s. xi Ter Duinen MS, Paris, BnF, lat. 7202 (Bragard, pp. 138–9).

BIBLIOGRAPHY De Poorter, pp. 630–31; Isaac, 10.68 (p. 400); Bragard, pp. 102–4, 120–23; Bower, 10; White, in Gibson, p. 194; Bernhard and Bower, viii–ix; J. Smits van Waesberghe, *The Theory of Music from the Carolingian Era up to 1400, 1: Descriptive Catalogue of Manuscripts*, Répertoire international des sources musicales, Munich, 1961, p. 52; H. Schmid, ed., *Musica et scolica enchiriadis una cum aliquibus tractatulis adiunctis*, Munich, 1981, p. 52.

10. MS Brugge, Stedelijke Openbare Bibliotheek 532
Op. Sac., DCPhil. s. xii/xiii

Parchment; 80 fols; page 201x145mm; text c. 150x95mm (fols 4^{v}–9^{v} text and gloss c. 155x132mm); 36 lines; one scribe writing a small glossing hand, with glosses by same scribe in a tiny hand. *Op. Sac. I* presented as text in central column and marginal gloss on both sides. *DCPhil.* marked off in portions for study, probably by a s. xiv annotator; metres written in two columns.
A scholar's personal book.

CONTENTS Fol. 1^{r} Gerbert of Rheims, *Epistola de horologiis duorum climatum ad fratrem Adam*, *inc.* 'Martianus in astrologia incrementa horarum ita fieri putat' (Bubnov, pp. 39–41); 1^{r}–4^{r} 'Designatio monocordi', *inc.* 'Dulce ingenium musicae' (M. Bernhard, ed., *Anonymi saeculi decimi vel undecimi tractatus de musica 'Dulce ingenium musicae'*, Munich, 1987); 4^{v}–24^{r} ***Op. Sac.***; 24^{r}–53^{v} ***DCPhil.***; 53^{v}–62^{v} Cicero, *De senectute*; 62^{v}–66^{v} idem, *Paradoxa*; 66^{v}–75^{v} idem, *De amicitia*; 76^{r}–80^{v} Martianus Capella, *De nuptiis*, I.1.5–68.18.

GLOSS Interlinear and marginal gloss on *Op. Sac. I*: perhaps based on the Carolingian commentary, *inc.* 'Unaqueque res secundum materie qualitatem eget'. Users' glosses added s. xiv to *Op. Sac.*, *DCPhil.* and Cicero texts.

DECORATION Simple flourished initials in blue and red.

PROVENANCE Ter Duinen (Les Dunes), Cistercian abbey: stamp of cross of Burgundy, fol. 1^{r}.

BIBLIOGRAPHY De Poorter, p. 631–32; Isaac, 10.66 (pp. 398–9); 10.67 (pp. 399–400), 10.70 (p. 401).

BRUXELLES/BRUSSEL (Brussels)

BIBLIOTHEQUE ROYALE ALBERT I / KONINKLIJKE BIBLIOTHEEK ALBERT I

The library of the dukes of Burgundy. Mary of Burgundy married Archduke Maximilian of Austria, whence the library passed to Philip II of Spain, the founder of the Bibliothèque Royale, formed in 1559 by bringing together the books of the various royal residences in the Low Countries. At the suppression of the Jesuits in 1773, their books too passed to the Bibliothèque Royale. Manuscripts from other suppressed abbeys and convents were added c. 1797, and many acquisitions were made during the late nineteenth and twentieth centuries.
J. van den Gheyn, *et al.*, *Catalogue des manuscrits de la Bibliothèque Royale de Belgique*, 13 vols, Brussels, 1901–48; R. Calcoen, *Inventaire des manuscrits*

scientifiques de la Bibliothèque Royale de Belgique, 3 vols, Brussels, 1965–75; M. Wittek, 'Le Cabinet des Manuscrits', in *Bibliothèque Royale: Mémorial 1559–1969*, Brussels, 1969, pp. 157–201; idem, *Librarium* 12, 1969, 145–84; C. Gaspar and F. Lyna, *et al.*, *Les Principaux Manuscrits à peintures de la Bibliothèque Royale de Belgique*, 4 vols, Paris and Brussels, 1937–89.

Van den Gheyn's catalogue is arranged by subject-area. The manuscripts are however primarily known by their inventory numbers, e.g., 1986–95 [a volume containing 10 items], with the catalogue number following in brackets: thus 'MS 1986–95 (2905)'. Some manuscripts are in subsequent series: e.g., II. 1012 (1219). Van den Gheyn's catalogue does not cover science (for which see Calcoen), music, and material from the latter part of Series II onwards.

11. MS Bruxelles, Bibliothèque Royale, 1986–95 (2905)
Logica vetus et nova s. xiii 2/2

Parchment; iv + 294 (foliated 2–295) + iii fols; page 240x180mm; text 115x75mm; 25 lines, ruled to accommodate an extensive user's gloss; two French scribes (scribe 1: fols 2^{r}–288^{v}; scribe 2: fols 289^{r}–95^{v}). Red and blue running headers throughout. Good s. xvi stamped leather binding, originally with two clasps, now missing. A handsome volume produced in N. France or Belgium.

CONTENTS Fols 2^{r}–11^{v} ***Isag.***; 12^{r}–28^{v} ***Cat.***; 29^{r}–39^{v} ***De Int.***; 40^{r}–49^{r} *Liber sex principiorum*; 49^{v}–61^{v} ***Div.***; 62^{r}–96^{v} ***Top. Diff.***; 97^{r}–99^{v} end of quire blank, apart from notes, mainly in pencil; 100^{r}–153^{v} ***Prior Anal.***; 154^{r}–190^{r} *Post. Anal.*; 191^{r}–262^{r} ***Topica Aris.***; 262^{v}–63^{v} end of quire blank, apart from notes; 264^{r}–88^{v} ***Soph. Elench.***; 289^{r}–295^{v} Aristotle, *Ethica vetus* (= *Eth. Nic.* II–III), *expl.* imperf. 'voluntaria magis autem assimulantur'.

GLOSS Extensive users' annotation to *Liber sex principiorum*, *Top. Diff. I*, *Post. Anal. I*, *Topica Aris. I–III, VIII*, *Soph. Elench.* (fols 264^{r}–66^{r} only). Glosses to *Ethica vetus* erased.

DECORATION Major historiated initials with gold at the beginning of each text, with some preliminary drawings visible in margins: 2^{r} excised; 12^{r} master teaching four boys; 29^{r} master; 40^{r} master writing; 49^{v} master teaching four boys, with book (Vitzthum, pl. XXIII); 62^{r} master teaching five boys; 100^{r} master teaching; 133^{v} man with black dog, with white dog at his feet and a dragon; 154^{r} master reading; 176^{v} two tonsured men disputing; 191^{r} master teaching from a book; 200^{v} two dragons (Gaspar and Lyna, I, pl. XXXVC); 208^{r} master teaching five students from a book; 213^{v} two dragons; 223^{r} two tonsured men disputing; 234^{r} master seated at lectern with one pupil; 247^{v} master with book teaching six pupils; 251^{v} lion mask, one dragon; 264^{r} two tonsured men disputing; 277^{r} master seated, teaching. Minor initials red and blue with pen-work flourishes. Pencil drawings (fols 97^{r}–99^{v}, 262^{v}–263^{v}).

PROVENANCE N. France: Jacobus de Varrouze (fol. 102^{r}); Jesuits of Louvain 1640 (fol. 2^{r}).

BIBLIOGRAPHY *AL*, 168; Van den Gheyn, IV, pp. 336–7; Kristeller, iii, p. 91b; G. Vitzthum, *Die Pariser Miniaturmalerei von der Zeit des hl. Ludwigs bis zu Philipp von Valois*, Leipzig, 1907, pp. 102–3 and pl. XXIII; Gaspar and Lyna, I. 75, pl. XXXVc.

12. MS Bruxelles, Bibliothèque Royale, 2135 (2940)
DCPhil. 1399

Paper; vi + 108 (foliated 2–109) + vi fols; page 217x143mm; text 165x100mm; 18 lines; Scribal colophon, fol. 109^{v}: Nicholas de Nievre, 1399.

CONTENTS Fols 2^{r}–109^{v} ***DCPhil.***

GLOSS Some interlinear notes, fol. 25^{v}.

DECORATION Large initials (perhaps by the scribe) in red, with puzzle design, at beginning of each book.

PROVENANCE Stavelot (fol. 2^{r}).

BIBLIOGRAPHY Van den Gheyn, IV, p. 352; *MSS datés Belgique*, I, no. 95, p. 51; pl. 216.

13. MS Bruxelles, Bibliothèque Royale, 2695–719 (3156)
DCPhil. 1388

Paper (fols 95, 105–6, 189 parchment; fol. 33 modern paper); ii + 245 (foliated 2–246; foliation in MS is at variance with that in Van den Gheyn) + i fols; page 208x141mm; text 154x105mm; 24–27 lines; second front endleaf s. xi antiphoner (fol. 1ra). Three booklets bound together, all with similar dimensions. Binding of stamped leather on wood; clasps lost (s. xv).
A (fols 2–94, 190–213): several hands writing variously continental *cursiva* or *hybrida*, s. xv.
B (fols 95–189): one or perhaps two scribes, writing continental *hybrida* (text) and *cursiva* (gloss); scribal colophon, fol. 189^{r}, dated 1388; the name of the scribe is no longer visible. The handwriting of the text on the parchment leaves (see *MSS datés Belgique*, I, pl. 203) is more formal and mannered than that on the paper leaves.
C (fols 214–246): one s. xv scribe.

CONTENTS A: fols 2^{r}–17^{v} *Vitae sanctorum* (Maurus, Augustine of Canterbury, John Chrysostom, Basil of Caesarea); 17^{v}–22^{v} letter of Godfrey of Bouillon, exempla and anecdotes; 23^{r}–27^{v} Geoffrey of Monmouth, *Vita et prophetia Merlini*; 28^{r-v} blank; 29^{r}–31^{r} *Prophetia Sibyllae*;

31^{r}–32^{v} 'De origine et geneologia francorum'; 33^{r-v} blank; 34^{r}–93^{v} Nigel Wireker, *Speculum stultorum*; 94^{r-v} blank; 190^{r}–197^{v} Godfrey of Viterbo, *Pantheon* (excerpts); 197^{v}–199^{r} Ovid, *Metamorphoses*, iv (excerpt); 199^{r}–201^{r} verses, *inc.* 'Qui legis hoc quod vivat enoch' (Walther, 1552); 201^{r-v} verses, *inc.* 'Finibus Yndorum species fuit una virorum' (Walther, 6548); 202^{r}–203^{r} Walter of Châtillon, *Alexandreis* (excerpt); 203^{v}–205^{r} 'De Bragmannis'; 205^{v}–211^{v} verses (Walther, 3665, 19453, 10768, 7450, 16118); 212^{r-v} blank; 213^{r-v} (perhaps an independent leaf) Theophilus, *inc.* 'Virgo parens huius solis qui nescit' (Walther, 20525).
B: fols 95^{r}–189^{r} ***DCPhil.*** with extensive, unidentified marginal gloss.
C: fols 214^{r}–242^{r} Ps.-Homer, *Ilias latina*; 242^{v}–246^{r} Rener of Brussels, *Tragedia*.

GLOSS B: see contents; extensive interlinear annotation.

DECORATION C: simple red scribal initials.

PROVENANCE Stavelot (fol. 1^{r}: 'Liber monasterii stabulen').

BIBLIOGRAPHY Van den Gheyn, V, pp. 111–12; *MSS datés Belgique*, I, no. 85, p. 48, pl. 203.

14. MS Bruxelles, Bibliothèque Royale, 5083–91 (2906)
Logica vetus et nova s. xiii 2/2

Parchment; iv + 224 (foliated 2–225) + ii fols. Fols iii^{r}–1^{v} (endleaves) s. xii liturgical fragment on St John the Baptist, with two kinds of neumes; fols 226–7 (endleaves) s. x fragment of Exodus, 2 cols.
A (s. xiii 2/2): page 235x155mm; text 130x70mm; 30 lines; one scribe, ?French.
B (1274): page 233x161mm; text 130x70mm; 31 lines; one scribe, dated colophon, fol. 225^{v}.
Binding: s. xvi stamped leather, heavily restored.

CONTENTS A: fols 2^{r}–10^{r} ***Isag.***; 10^{r}–24^{v} ***Cat.***; 24^{v}–33^{v} ***De Int.***; 34^{r}–53^{v} ***Soph. Elench.***; 53^{v}–115^{r} ***Topica Aris.***; 115^{r}–158^{v} ***Prior Anal.***; 159^{r}–189^{r} *Post. Anal.* (transl. Iacobi), *expl.* imperf. II.19 'quousque in principium veniet. Anima autem' (106/7); 189^{v} blank.
B: fol. 190^{r} *Post. Anal.* (transl. Iacobi), *inc.* imperf. II.19 'huiusmodi cum sit qualis possit pati' (106/7) to end; 190^{r}–225^{v} Aristotle, *De anima*.

GLOSS Very substantial users' glosses throughout, except *Topica Aris.* VIII and *De anima*.

DECORATION A: blue and red initials with pen-work flourishing.
B: one fine initial, with gold, depicting a small animal (fol. 190^{r}).

PROVENANCE Jesuits of Louvain, 1640 (fol. ii^{v}).

BIBLIOGRAPHY Van den Gheyn, IV, p. 337; *AL*, 170; Calcoen, II, no. 149; Kristeller, iii, p. 95a; *MSS datés Belgique*, I, no. 16, p. 23, pl. 58–9.

15. MS Bruxelles, Bibliothèque Royale, 5439–43 (2939)
Logica vetus s. xi

Parchment; ii + 94 (foliated 1–20, 20*bis*, 21–93) + i fols; page 325x260mm; text 2 cols, c. 290x230mm; between 37 and 46 unevenly ruled lines, sometimes ignored by scribes; several scribes writing more or less uncalligraphic hands; heavily corrected during s. xi over extensive erasures and on replacement leaves; subsequently another s. xi scribe or scribes added variant readings.
Antique colophon, 'Marcus Novatus Renatus v[ir] c[larissimus] et sp[ectabilis] relegi meum', fol. 57ra; 'relectum', fols 57vb, 58ra, 58rb.

CONTENTS Fols 1ra–8rb ***Cat.***; 8va–46ra ***in Cat.***; text missing between fols 16^{v}–17^{r} (*PL*, 64:181/31–181/50 'fiunt ut' to 'Substancia autem'); 46rb list of Boethius' ten works on logic; 46va–57ra ***Top. Diff.***; 57ra–57vb Ps.-Boethius, *De rhetorice cognatione*; 57vb–58ra Ps.-Boethius, *De locorum rhetoricorum distinctione*; 58ra–58rb *De multifaria predicatione potestatis et passibilitatis*; 58rb–58va *Quomodo vel unde argumentorum colligantur loci*; 58va–67ra ***intr. Syll. Cat.***; 67ra–77rb ***Syll. Cat.*** with additional matter before the *expl.*: 77rb–77va 'Prime quintus in primum eiusdem sextum in secundum … Primus in secundum. Aliter id. in eundem resolvitur'; 77vb 'Omnis homo animal rationale mortale … Omne igitur risibile homo'; 77vb (s. xi 2/2/xii addition) Fulbert of Chartres, *De luscinia* (*WIC*, 18030; 78ra (s. xi 2/2 addition) 'Ad occasum cuncta ruunt sed et ipsa studia' (*WIC*, 409); 78va–92^{r} ***Syll. Hyp.***; 92va–93rb Adalbero, bishop of Laon, letter on logic to Fulco, bishop of Amiens (see M. Manitius, *Geschichte der lateinischen Literatur des Mittelalters*, 2, Munich, 1923, pp. 529–31).

GLOSS Very spasmodic contemporary or near contemporary annotation.

DECORATION Some red initials, now oxidized to black.

PROVENANCE ? Gembloux (Van den Gheyn).

BIBLIOGRAPHY Van den Gheyn, IV, pp. 351–2; A. van de Vyver, 'Les Étapes du développement philosophique du haut Moyen-Age', *Revue belge de philologie et d'histoire*, 8, 1929, pp. 446–7; *AL*, 171, *Suppl. Alt.*, pp. 65–6; Kristeller, iii, 95a.

16. MS Bruxelles, Bibliothèque Royale, 5444–46 (163)

Arith., Mus. s. xi 1/2

Parchment; i + 98 + iii fols; page 300x230mm; text 240x170mm; 34 lines; one main scribe and at least two others writing very similar, excellent bookhands and drawing very fine diagrams; *capitula* to *Arith.* I, II and to *Mus.* II, IV, V; *titulus* to *Arith.* only (fol. 2^{r}); *Decretum Lacedaemoniorum* in Greek with Latin translation as interlinear gloss, fol. 42^{r-v}. Fols 99ra–100vb are endleaves from a s. xi 2/2 homiliary, in 2 cols.

A very expertly produced book, very similar in script to those associated with Saint-Pierre, Gembloux during the abbacy of Olbert (1012–48), and probably produced there.

CONTENTS Fol. 1^{r} schema of latitude and longitude; 1^{v} notes on the *artes*, *inc.* 'In vii liberalibus artibus tres docent. id est grammatica rethorica dialectica'; *expl.* 'permutarique videatur'; 2^{r}–37^{r} ***Arith.***, with *lacuna* after fol. 8 caused by loss of leaves I.11–28, 'procreabuntur'–'due enim' (27/10–58/8); 37^{v}–39^{r} mathematical tables and their explanation; 39^{v}–40^{r} (s. xi^{ex} or xii^{in} addition, in 2 cols) scholarly accessus to *Arith.* and *Mus.*, *inc.* 'In omni libro divine scientie quatuor inquiruntur scilicet intentio materia cui parti philosophie supponatur et finalis causa'; *expl.* 'Phisice liber iste supponitur'; 40^{r-v} mathematical table and explanation, continuing notes begun on 1^{v}; 41^{r} blank; 41^{v}–98^{r} ***Mus.***, *expl.* 'ut in diatonicis generibus nusquam una proportio vincat duas', with *lacunae* (caused by missing leaves) IV.6–8, 'sumo'–'cc litteris' (321/21–325/16) and IV.15–17 'dispectio'–'tonus' (343/5–344/5). Fols 58 and 63 are intercalated slips of parchment, on the rectos of which the scribe of fols 67^{v}/8–98^{r} has copied Gerbert, *Epp. ad Constantinum* (Bubnov, pp. 29–31); 98^{r} musical scale 1–9; 98^{v} 'Regula semitonii inveniendi' (Bernhard and Bower, pp. 398–9).

GLOSS See contents. Scattered notes; main annotation is at fols 37^{v}–40^{v}.

DECORATION Excellent diagrams to *Mus.*, with arcs and lettering in red. Initials very plain; some embellishment at fols 2^{r}, 3^{r}, 41^{v}, 92^{v}.

PROVENANCE Gembloux, Benedictine abbey: *ex libris*, fol. 1^{r}.

BIBLIOGRAPHY Bubnov, pp. 29–35, with this manuscript; Bragard, pp. 105–7, 123–7; H. Silvestre, *Scriptorium*, 3, 1949, pp. 133–4; J. Smits van Waesberghe, *The Theory of Music from the Carolingian Era up to 1400,* Munich, 1961, p. 55; Calcoen II, no. 163; Bower 11; M. Bernhard and C. M. Bower, *Glossa maior in institutionem musicam Boethii*, Bayerische Akademie der Wissenschaften, Veröffentlichungen der Müsikhistorischen Kommission, 11, Munich, 1996, pp. 376–82, 398–9.

17. MS Bruxelles, Bibliothèque Royale, 10114–16
Mus. s. xi 2/2

Parchment; ii + 102 (foliated 2–108, including inserted paper leaves at 4, 12, 16, 60) + iv fols; page 201x160mm; text 155x120mm; 28 lines (fols 70^{r}–75^{r} 26 lines); several scribes. *Capitula* to *Mus.* II.
A well-produced little book; its decoration suggests an origin in or near Liège.

CONTENTS Fol. 2^{r} blank apart from the addition of the melody (without text) of the hymn 'Ut queant laxis' in solmization and neumes; 2^{v}–75^{r} ***Mus.***; 75^{v} blank; 76^{r}–108^{v} *Musica et scolica enchiriadis* (attrib. here to 'Obdo abbas'); *expl.* imperf., 'Nec enim consonantiam prestaret si vel tonum in semitonum vel semitonum e regione offenderet' (Schmid, p. 155, l. 639).

GLOSS Glosses on *Mus.* II.20–29 (fols 30^{v}–36^{r}) from the Rhein-Maas tradition (Bernhard and Bower, pp. viii–ix).

DECORATION Orange initials and rubrics; fol. 2^{v} ornamented ***O*** in a style distinctive of manuscripts from Liège and surrounding region (cf. M. R. Lapière, *La Lettre ornée dans les manuscrits mosans d'origine bénédictine (xie–xiie siècles)*, Paris, 1981, pp. 55–167).

PROVENANCE Liège area, from evidence of neumes added on fol. 2^{r}; crude s. xvi armorial design of jester with attributes and other symbols, including two hands (palms outwards, one with heart), a lily, a bee, and a die, and the legends 'Ingenium superat vires' and 'Oderunt hilarem tristes tristemque jocosi', fol. 1^{v}; similar image, fol. 109^{r}, with legend 'media media me'; Charles de Langhe (1521–73, canon of St-Lambert, Liège), André de Pape (d. 1581) (donation inscription: fol. 110^{r}); Jesuits, perhaps of Antwerp (mark of cross: fol. 2^{r}; Bragard, pp. 110–11).

BIBLIOGRAPHY Bower, 12; Bragard, pp. 107–11, 127–32; Bernhard and Bower, pp. viii–ix; Smits van Waesberghe, p. 59.

18. MS Bruxelles, Bibliothèque Royale, 18397
Arith., Mus. s. xii

Parchment; i + 59 + i fols; page 186x110mm; text 146x75mm; 50 lines; two scribes writing tiny informal glossing hands. *Capitula* to *Arith.* I and II. Representation of string length in diagrams in *Mus.* I.20 typical of manuscripts from Flanders (Bower, 13).

CONTENTS Fols 1^{v}–45^{v} ***Arith.***, incorporating the schema of longitude and latitude found in Brussels, Bibliothèque Royale, 5444–46 (**16**) (fol. 8^{v}); 46 an inserted slip of parchment with a diagram on the recto relating to *Mus.* I, 'Tractaturus auctor de musicis proportionibus premittit prohemium quasi ... non sine industria obtinetur'; 47^{r}–58^{v} ***Mus.*** I–I.30 'ait consonantiam miscet'; 58^{v}–59^{v} ?s. xiv addition, ***Mus.*** I.31–II, *capitula*, *capitulum* xxiv.

GLOSS Some marginal annotation in a later hand.

DECORATION Diagrams in *Mus.* I.16 and I.21 again like those in MS Brussels, Bibliothèque Royale, 5444–46. Simple red initials.

PROVENANCE Cornelius Duyn, Amsterdam (fol. 1^{r}).

BIBLIOGRAPHY Bower, 13, Bragard, pp. 111–14, 133–4; Smits van Waesberghe, pp. 62–3.

19. MS Bruxelles, Bibliothèque Royale, 20760–82 (1120)

Vita VII **(2 copies),** ***DCPhil.*** s. xiii/xiv

Parchment; iii + 313 + 1 fols; page 247x185mm; text 177x130mm, 2 cols; 60 lines; one scribe writing a tiny hand on very thin parchment.

CONTENTS Fol. ii^{r-v} contents list arranged by author; 1ra–12vb Bernard of Clairvaux, *De consideratione*; 13ra–17vb idem, *De praecepto et dispensatione*; 17vb–22ra Hugh of St Victor, *Didascalicon* (excerpts); 22ra–27va Augustine, *De musica*; 27vb–35rb idem, *De gratia et libero arbitrio*; 35rb–36vb idem, *De praesentia Dei* (*ep.* 187); 36vb–38ra Cassiodorus, *De anima*; 38ra–38va Anselm, *Epistola ad Waleramnum de sacramentorum diversitate*; 38va–39rb idem, *De sacrificio azymi et fermentati*; 39rb–40ra idem, *Meditatio 3 de redemptione humana*; 40ra–52vb Anselm, *De similitudinibus*; 52vb–54vb Hugh of St Victor, *De virtute orandi*; 54vb–59vb idem, *Soliloquium de arra animae*; 60^{r-v} blank; 61ra–64rb Anselm, *De incarnatione Verbi*; 64rb–68vb idem, *De concordia praescientiae et praedestinationis*; 68vb–76vb Anselm, *Monologion*; 76vb–79ra idem, *Proslogion*; 79rb–80vb idem, *Responsio Anselmi contra Gaunilonem*; 80vb–83rb Anselm, *Epistolae*: *Ep. de sacrificio azymi et fermentati*; *Ep. de sacramentis ecclesiae*; *Epp. 65, 2, 37, 187, 337*; 83rb–87va Anselm, *De casu diaboli*; 87va–89vb idem, *De veritate*; 89vb–93rb idem, *De conceptu virginali et de originali peccato*; 93rb–96va Augustine, *De perfectione iustitiae hominis*; idem, *De natura et gratia*; 102va–106ra idem, *De gratia et libero arbitrio*; 106ra–111va idem, *De correptione et gratia*; 111va–116rb idem, *De praedestinatione sanctorum*; 116rb–121vb idem, *De dono perseverantiae*; 121vb–125vb idem, *De agone christiano*; 125vb–129ra idem, *De natura boni*; 129ra–131va idem, *Sermo 351 de utilitate paenitentiae agendae*; 131va–133ra idem, *De disciplina christiana*; 133ra–157va Isidore, *Sententiae*; 158ra–164vb Ps.-Augustine, *De spiritu et anima*; 164vb–166va Ps.-Augustine (Fulgentius), *De fide ad Petrum*; 166va–168ra Ps.-Augustine,

Dialogus quaestionum LXV; 168^{ra-vb} Ps.-Seneca (Martin of Braga), *Formula vitae honestae*, *expl.* imperf.; 168vb–173vb Bernard of Clairvaux, *De XII gradibus humilitatis*; 173vb–175ra Augustine, *De disciplina christiana*; 175ra–178vb Ps.-Bernard, *Meditationes piissimae de cognitione humanae conditionis*; 178vb–183ra Bernard of Clairvaux, *De gratia et libero arbitrio*; 183^{ra-va} *Vita Secundi philosophi*; 183va–191vb Anselm, *Cur Deus homo*; 191vb–199rb Augustine, *Enchiridion*; 199rb–206vb Ps.-Seneca, *Epistolae ad Paulum et Pauli ad Senecam* and other letters; 206ra–208ra Seneca, *De beneficiis* (excerpts); 208^{ra-vb} idem, *De clementia* (excerpts); 208vb–241ra Augustine, *Confessiones*; 241va–247vb ?Ps.-Bernard, *De domo conscientiae* (excerpts); 247vb–248va Alfarabi, *De ortu scientiarum* (Thorndike/Kibre, 1387); 248va–249rb Ps.-Aristotle, *Secretum secretorum* (excerpt); 249rb–51vb Aristotle, *Ethica Nicomachea*, IV (transl. Grosseteste); 252ra–254rb ?Henry of Southwark, *De visu et speculis* (Thorndike/Kibre, 392, 911); 254rb–254va idem, letter on optical problems, *inc.* 'Solucionem de topazio' (Thorndike/Kibre, 1518, 1618); 254va–255vb Alfarabi, *De intellectu* (Thorndike/ Kibre, 448, 915); 255vb–2261ra Bernard of Clairvaux, Four sermons on *Missus est*; 261ra–294vb ***Vita VII*** and *accessus* followed by ***DCPhil.***, accompanied by intercalated commentary of Ps.-William of Conches; 294vb–299ra Plato, tr. Calcidius, *Timaeus*; 299ra–313^{v} ***Vita VII***, with *accessus* and commentary closely based on those at 261^{r}–294^{v}, comm. *expl.* imperf. at IV.m.iii.

GLOSS See contents.

DECORATION Extensively decorated with fine initials; running titles in red and blue.

PROVENANCE St Trond (fol. 314: slip of paper containing material relating to St Trond, s. xvii); College de Clermont, S. J., Paris; 'E biblioteca D. Abbatis Fauvel (*ex libris* plate: inside front cover).

BIBLIOGRAPHY Van den Gheyn, II, pp. 151–54; *Handschriften uit de abdij van Sint-Truiden*, Exhibition catalogue, Leuven, 1986, p. 286.

20. MS Bruxelles, Bibliothèque Royale, 21124 (2941)
DCPhil. s. XV

Paper; ii + 84 + i fols; page 215x143mm; text c. 145x70mm; amount of gloss varies considerably, from almost nothing to filling margins on all four sides; 20–22 lines; one probably Netherlandish scribe writing a continental *cursiva*. Binding: s. xv stamped leather on wood, much restored; chain and staple on front cover.

CONTENTS Fols 1^{r}–84^{v} ***DCPhil.***, *inc.* imperf. 'Ut movere loco quid hominem possint', I.pr.vi.31.

GLOSS Extensive marginal and interlinear gloss.

DECORATION Initials roughly executed by the scribe.

PROVENANCE Unknown.

BIBLIOGRAPHY Van den Gheyn, IV, p. 352.

21. MS Bruxelles, Bibliothèque Royale, II. 1012 (1219)
DCPhil., Vita VII s. xiii 2/2

Parchment; i + 191 + i fols; page 330x225mm; text c. 245x163mm; fols 1^{r-v}, 164^{r}–91^{r} 2 cols; *DCPhil.* 35 lines of text (written below top line), gloss written on alternate lines; *Vita Boethii* 39 lines; one scribe writing a good *textura* for both text and (to a smaller module) gloss. Restored s. xiv stamped leather binding on wood with hunting scenes; horn-covered label 'Boecius glosatus'.
A large formal glossed book.

CONTENTS Fols 1^{r}–163^{r} ***DCPhil.***, glossed; 164^{r}–191^{r} ***Vita VII***, with *accessus* and commentary on some of the metres.

GLOSS *Inc.* 'Mos auctorum est operi suos prologos praescribere' (cf. MS Brugge, Grootseminarie, 101/135). Some annotation in French.

DECORATION Red and blue initials, some with elaborate pen flourishing; Portrait of Boethius, fol. 1^{v}, stylistically linked to a group of manuscripts associated with St Martin, Tournai.

PROVENANCE St Martin, Tournai (*ex libris*, fol. 1^{r}); Phillipps 2113; acquired by the Bibliothèque Royale in 1888.

BIBLIOGRAPHY Van den Gheyn, II, p. 223; Kristeller, iii, p. 108a; Gaspar and Lyna, I, no. 58, pl. XXXC (fol. 1^{v}); Courcelle, pl. 9 (fol. 1^{v}).

22. MS Bruxelles, Bibliothèque Royale, II, 6188
Mus. s. xv

Paper; i + 86 + iii fols; page 209 x 138mm; text 145–153x107mm; 26–30 lines; one scribe writing *cursiva*. The manuscript probably once formed a pair with Brussels, Bibliothèque Royale, II. 4141, written on the same paper by the same scribe (Bragard, pp. 134–35, n. 2).

CONTENTS Fols 1^{r}–86^{v} ***Mus.***, *expl.* imperf. V.18 'ad acutissimum 1412' (370/2–3).

GLOSS Some marginal notes from the French and German traditions (Bernhard and Bower, viii–ix) in a contemporary *cursiva* (fols

11^{v}, 13^{v}, 14^{r}, 33^{v}–35^{r}, 41^{v}–44^{r}, etc.).

DECORATION Simple single colour initials in red, purple, green or yellow.

PROVENANCE Vienna, Dominican friary (*ex libris*, fol. 84^{r}).

BIBLIOGRAPHY Bragard, pp. 134–37; Bower, 14; M. Huglo, 'Les Anciens Manuscrits du fonds Fétis', *Revue belge de musicologie*, 32–3, 1978–79, pp. 35–9 (38).

23. MS Bruxelles, Bibliothèque Royal IV. 129
DCPhil. s. xiv^{in}

Parchment; i + 56 (foliated 1–29, 29a, 30–55) + 1 fols; fols 1 and 8 are s. xiv replacement leaves by a later scribe; page 143x122mm; text 152x96mm; some metres written in two columns; 28 lines; one Italian scribe writing an elegant *littera textualis rotunda*.

CONTENTS Fols 1^{r}–55^{v} ***DCPhil.***

GLOSS Some s. xiv and s. xv users' glosses (mostly brief interlinear glosses).

DECORATION Large pen-flourished initial in blue and red, fol. 20^{r}; minor initials in blue and red with pen-flourishing.

PROVENANCE Unknown until acquired by the Bibliothèque Royale in 1961.

BIBLIOGRAPHY *Fine Books, Manuscripts, Incunabula, Autographs and Other Subjects to be sold by Auction on March 22, 1961*, Amsterdam Internationaal Antiquariaat Menno Hertzberger, Amsterdam, 1961, no. 910.

24. MS Bruxelles, Bibliothèque Royale IV. 1097
DCPhil. s. xv

Parchment; i + 44 + i fols; page 278x192mm; text 177x97mm (some metres in 2 cols); 32 lines; one Italian scribe writing *textura* influenced by humanistic script.

CONTENTS Fols 1^{r}–43^{v} ***DCPhil.***; 43^{v}–44^{v} Jerome, *Adversus Iovinianum*, bk 1 (excerpt); 44^{v} two excerpts from *Flos medicinae scolae Salernitanae* (Walther, 10131, 18083).

GLOSS None.

DECORATION Major and minor initials in blue and red with pen-flourishing.

PROVENANCE Medieval provenance unknown, but probably Italian; purchased by Thomas Webb (1807–85) from the collection of Gian Vincenzo Pinelli (1535–1601) (fol. i^r); acquired by the Bibliothèque Royale in 1977.

BIBLIOGRAPHY [M. Wittek], *Vijf Jaar Aanwinsten 1974–1978: Tentoonstelling georganiseered in de Koninklijke Bibliotheek Albert I van 22 september tot 31 october 1979*, Brussels, 1979, p. 71, no. 31; *Bibliothèque royale Albert Ier Bulletin 21e année, 5, 10 Sept. 1977*, pp. 78–80.

LIÈGE

BIBLIOTHÈQUE DU GRAND SÉMINAIRE

There is no printed catalogue of the large collection of manuscripts which include many from the libraries of the Crutched Friars of Huy and Liège, only a s. xix handwritten catalogue. Many manuscripts are described by J.-P. Depaire, 'La Bibliothèque des Croisiers de Huy, de Liège et de Namur', 2 vols, unpublished thesis, Institut d'histoire, Université de Liège, 1969–70. The exhibition catalogue, *Les Manuscrits des Croisiers de Huy, Liège et Cuyk au xve siècle*, Bibliotheca Universitatis Leodiensis 5, Liège, 1951, describes none of the manuscripts catalogued below.

25. MS Liège, Bibliothèque du Grand Séminaire 6 F 3
DCPhil. 24 November 1477

Paper; ii + 196 + i fols; page 210x146mm; text (without gloss) 122 x c. 50–70mm; (with gloss) up to 192x120mm; 11 lines of text; written throughout by Laurencius Itter: scribal dated colophon, fol. 196^r.

CONTENTS Fols 1^r–196^r ***DCPhil.***

GLOSS Added only as far as fol. 18^v.

DECORATION Major initial in blue with red pen-flourishes, fol. 1^r; minor initials in red.

PROVENANCE Huy (dioc. Liège), Crutched Friars (*ex libris*: fol. i^r).

BIBLIOGRAPHY Depaire, vol. 2, p. 99.

26. MS Liège, Bibliothèque du Grand Séminaire 6 H 15
DCPhil. s. xv^{ex}

Paper; ii + 413 (foliated as 2–413) + i fols; page 211x150mm; text (of *DCPhil.*) c. 130x80mm; 10–13 lines; the dimensions of the accompanying gloss vary very considerably, maximum dimensions c. 175x135mm; *DCPhil.* and gloss written in perhaps one cursive hand (German or Netherlandish).
A scruffy, presumably owner-produced copy, bound together with a large collection of very similar, roughly contemporary booklets, written in a number of different hands. The date 1487 is written at the end of the text on fol. 387^v, but its status is unclear.

CONTENTS Fols 2^r–170^v ***DCPhil.***, with gloss which begins in a similar fashion to the commentary of Master Rener of St Trond: 'Carmina qui quondam. Hunc librum de consolacione philosophie in quo Boetius ymitando Platonem per dialogum procedit'; 171^v–176^v misc. notes on ***DCPhil.***; 177^r–413^r numerous excerpts from primarily classical texts including Lactantius, *Institutiones* (177^r–209^v); Horace, Virgil, Ovid, Seneca, Prudentius; several letters of Jerome, (245^r–273^v, 389^r–387^v); two verses here attrib. to St Radbod of Utrecht (Schaller, 1013, 15844).

GLOSS Extensive marginal and interlinear gloss (see above).

DECORATION Rough scribal initials, some in red.

PROVENANCE Huy (dioc. Liège), Crutched Friars (*ex libris*: fol. 2^r).

BIBLIOGRAPHY Depaire, vol. 2, pp. 118–9; Kristeller, iii, p. 135.

BIBLIOTHÈQUE DE L'UNIVERSITÉ

The city library (f. 1804) was transferred to the newly founded university in 1817. It received a large part of the libraries of the abbeys of Averbode and St Trond, the Crutched Friars of Liège and Huy, and the Walloon and English Jesuits of Liège. Manuscripts acquired after the publication of the main catalogue (1975) and its supplement are listed by Hoyoux.

M. Grandjean, *Bibliothèque de l'Université de Liège*, Liège, 1875; J. Hoyoux, *Inventaire des manuscrits de la Bibliothèque de l'Université de Liège*, 3 vols, [Liège] 1970–77; C. Opsomer-Halleux, *Trésors manuscrits de l'Université de Liège*, [Liège] 1989.

27. MS Liège, Bibliothèque de l'Université, 3307 C
DCPhil. 1479

Paper, apart from conjoint outer leaves of several quires; ii + 203 + ii fols; page

290x205mm; text *DCPhil.*, fols 1^{r}–44^{v}) 195x135mm, 31 lines; text fols 45^{r}–203^{v} 197x150mm, 2 cols, 41 lines; written throughout by Frater Foillianus de Lintris (dated scribal colophons fols 44^{v}, 48^{r}, 178^{r}).
A large, handsome volume.

CONTENTS Fols 1^{r}–44^{v} ***DCPhil.***; 44^{v}–48^{v} *Tabula* on commentary of Ps.-Aquinas; 49ra–177vb Ps.-Aquinas, *Commentary on DCPhil.*; 178ra–203ra Ménard d'Eisenach, *Tabula omnium divine scripture seu biblie librorum.*

GLOSS None.

DECORATION Well executed major initials with pen-flourishing in varying combinations of red, green and purple (fols 1^{r}, 44^{v}, 49^{r}, 51^{v}, 78^{r}, 103^{v}, 134^{r}, 159^{v}).

PROVENANCE Namur, Crutched Friars (fol. 178^{r}).

BIBLIOGRAPHY Hoyoux, vol. 1, p. 19, no. 134; Depaire, vol. 2, p. 278.

PRIVATE OWNER

*28. MS Liège, private owner (unidentified)
intr. Syll. Cat. s. xi

Parchment; single leaf; page 190x130mm; 30 lines.

CONTENTS Fragment of ***intr. Syll. Cat.***, 'affirmatio negotioque proponant … Si quid de silice vel de huiusmodi ceteris velit intellegi. que cum non sint homi<nes>' (*PL*, 64:779–781).

GLOSS None.

DECORATION None.

PROVENANCE Unknown.

BIBLIOGRAPHY G. Noël, 'Un fragment d'un manuscrit inconnu (xie siècle) de l'"Introductio ad syllogismos categoricos" de Boèce', *Scriptorium*, 40, 1986, pp. 81–2, pl. 2 (which reproduces at reduced scale both sides of the leaf).

DENMARK

KØBENHAVN (Copenhagen)

DET KONGELIGE BIBLIOTEK

The Royal Library was founded c. 1653 by King Frederik III who, between 1661 and 1664, acquired three private libraries, mostly of vernacular literature, which made up the core of the collection. Donations, including more than 200 medieval MSS from the library of Otto Thott (d. 1785), purchases and acquisitions from war, as well as becoming a Depository Library ensured that, by the end of the eighteenth century, the Library had both national and scholarly importance; it was opened to the public in 1793. Shortly after the bequest of medieval MSS by Abraham Kall (d. 1821), the core collection was divided into MSS acquired before the Thott donation, which were named the Old Royal collection (Gammel Kongelig Sammlung) and those acquired after it, the New Royal collection (Ny Kongelig Sammlung). In 1989 the Royal Library and the University Library (f. 1482) were merged, forming one institution on three sites.

E. Jørgensen, *Catalogus codicum Latinorum medii aevi bibliothecae regiae Hafniensis*, Copenhagen, 1923–6.

1. MS København, Det Kongelige Bibliotek, Gl. kgl. S. 421 2°
Top. Diff. IV s. xii 2/2

Parchment; ii (paper) + 82 + ii (paper) fols; page 275x170–80mm; text 180x65mm (fols 54^{v}–59^{r} 195x135mm); 19 lines (fols 54^{v}–59^{r} 35 lines); wide margins for gloss (except Boethius); one scribe for text. Catchwords.
Modern binding.

CONTENTS Fols 1^{r}–54^{r} Martianus Capella, *De nuptiis* I–II; 54^{r} cryptogram relating Greek letters to numbers; 54^{v}–55^{r} notes, *inc.* 'Smaragdus viridissima gemma'; 55^{r}–59^{r} ***Top. Diff. IV***; 59^{v}–81^{v} Martianus Capella, *De nuptiis* VIII.

GLOSS Extensive marginal and interlinear glosses in a contemporary hand, incl. a 'stemma', fol. 56^{r} and diagrams, fols 69^{v}, 77^{v}, 79^{r}; ?s. xiv glosses to fols 1^{v}–2^{r}.

DECORATION None.

PROVENANCE England or France (script).

BIBLIOGRAPHY Jørgensen, p. 333.

2. MS København, Det Kongelige Bibliotek, Gl. kgl. S. 1905 4to

DCPhil., Vita s. xii 1/2

Parchment; 157 fols; page 200x120mm (but parts of C = 175–190x105–115mm). Front and back pastedowns are medieval leaves.
A (s. xii 1/2): text 150x80mm (fols 60^{v}–61^{v} 140x70mm); 27 lines; several scribes.
B (s. xii 2/3): text 150x95mm; 28 lines; one scribe.
C (s. xiii 2/3): text 160x50mm; 43 lines, laid out for gloss; several scribes.
D (s. xii 2/2): text 155x70mm; 29 lines; one scribe.
Binding: s. xv–xvi1/2 white stamped and tooled leather on wood; two clasps; chain marks; produced at the monastery of St Mary, Bordesholm.

CONTENTS A: fol. 1^{r} s. xv–xvi contents list; 2^{r} ***Vita***, added s. xii 2/2, *inc.* 'Ultima semper expectanda dies'; *expl.* 'dum levibus malesi' (*sic*); 2^{v}–59^{v} ***DCPhil.***; 59^{v}–60^{r} misc. notes; 60^{v}–61^{v} Adelman of Liège, *De viris illustribus*.
B: fols 62^{r}–63^{r} blank; 63^{v}–122^{r} Cicero, *De officiis*.
C: fol. 123^{r-v} *De dictionum scientia*; 124^{v}–318^{r} Claudian, *Deraptu Proserpinae*; 138^{v}–139^{v} commentary on Avianus, *Fables*; 139^{v}–141^{r} *De operibus Ovidii*; 141^{v} blank.
D: fols 142^{r}–147^{r} Hildebert of Le Mans, *Passio beate Agnetis*; 147^{r}–157^{v} idem, *Passio beate Katherine*.

GLOSS A: marginal and interlinear glosses throughout; gloss added in a different, slightly later hand.
B: none.
C: contemporary marginal and sporadic interlinear glosses.
D: none.

DECORATION A: plain red initials.
B: plain red initials.
C: crude red initials; one very poor interlace, fol. 124^{v}.

PROVENANCE Germany. Belonged to the Augustinian house of Our Lady in Neumünster, diocese of Oldenburg and, from 1163, Lübeck (fols 1^{v}, 2^{v}, 129^{r}: s. xii–xiii); at Bordesholm by s. xv 2/2.

BIBLIOGRAPHY Jørgensen, pp. 334–5; A. Wetzel, 'Die Reste der Bordesholmer Bibliothek in Kopenhagen', *Zeitschrift der Gesellschaft für Schleswig-Holstein-Lauenburgische Geschichte*, XIV, 80; J. P. Havet, *Oeuvres de Julien Havet*, 2 vols, Paris, 1896, 2, p. 89; Munk Olsen, I, p. 190; III, p. 171; Krämer, 1, p. 100; E. J. Polak, *Medieval and Renaissance Letter Treatises and Form Letters*, Leiden, 1994, pp. 41–2.

3. MS København, Det Kongelige Bibliotek, Gl. kgl. S. 1911 4to
DCPhil. s. xii 2/2

Parchment; ii (paper) + 38 + ii (paper) fols; page 205x140mm; text 160x90mm; 35 lines; one scribe. Modern binding.
A scholar's copy, compact and consciously eschewing all luxury.

CONTENTS Fols 1^{r}–38^{v} ***DCPhil.***

GLOSS None.

DECORATION ***C****(armina)* in red, very modestly decorated (fol. 1^{r}); minor initials in red and one in blue (fol. 19^{v}). Rubrication.

PROVENANCE ?France (script).

BIBLIOGRAPHY Jørgensen, p. 365.

4. MS København, Det Kongelige Bibliotek, Kall 313 4to
DCPhil. s. xv

Paper; 122 fols (two blank leaves after fol. 107, not numbered); page 203x140mm. Modern binding.
A: text 160x80mm; 20 lines, unruled; broad margins for gloss, not used; several scribes.
B: text 150x102mm, 2 cols; 45 lines; one scribe.
C: text 145x90mm; 32 lines; one scribe.
An unpretentious copy.

CONTENTS A: fols 1^{r}–93^{v} ***DCPhil.***; 94^{r}–95^{r} Lupus, *De metris*; 95^{v}–96^{r} blank; 96^{v} Gerbert, epigram on Boethius, *inc.* 'Roma potens dum iura suo declarat in orbe'; expl. 'et bene promeritum meritis exornat honestis' (Peiper, VIIII, pp. xxxx–xxxxi).
B: fols 97^{r}–98^{r} *accessus* to Horace; 98^{r}–107^{r} Ps.-Acron, *accessus* and commentary on Horace, *Odes* I.1–15; 107^{v} and two unnumbered leaves blank.
C: fols 108^{r}–120^{r} commentary on Horace, *Odes* II.1–16, *expl.* imperf.

GLOSS Some contemporary marginal and interlinear glosses up to fol. 87^{r}; no other glosses.

DECORATION A: major initials in red to begin each bk; minor initials to begin each section.
B: space left for initials, not supplied.
C: none.

PROVENANCE Abraham Kall.

BIBLIOGRAPHY Jørgensen, pp. 365–6.

5. MS København, Det Kongelige Bibliotek, Ny kgl. S. 214^{b} 4to

Top. Diff. IV s. xiii 2/2

Parchment; i + 101 + i (paper) fols; page 225x150mm.
A (s. xiii 1/2): text 160x85mm; 36 lines; one scribe for text; glosses added in a contemporary, highly compressed cursive hand. Catchwords.
B (s. xiii 2/2): 140x75mm; 36 lines; one scribe.
Binding: pasteboard covered by part of a leaf from a s. xvi service book.

CONTENTS A: fols 1^{r}–50^{r} Cicero, *De inventione*; 50^{r}–94^{r} Ps.-Cicero, *Ad Herennium*; 94^{v} notes, *inc.* ‘Ars est scientia docendi infinita’.
B: fols 95^{r}–101^{r} ***Top. Diff. IV***.

GLOSS A: intermittent marginal and interlinear glosses.
B: none.

DECORATION A: elaborate major initials.
B: two initials with penwork flourishing, fol. 95^{r}.

PROVENANCE Italy. Belonged to Augusto Barbarico, doge of Venice, d. 1501 (shield: fol. 1^{r}); L. Tross (fol. i^{r}); in the Royal library since 1836.

BIBLIOGRAPHY E. C. Werlauff, *Historiske Efterretninger om det store kongelige Bibliothek i København*, Copenhagen, 1844, p. 357 (A); Jørgensen, p. 296; B. Munk Olsen, *L’Etude des auteurs classiques latins aux xie et xiie siècles*, 3 vols, Paris, 1982–9, 1, p. 192.

6. MS København, Det Kongelige Bibliotek, Ny kgl. S. 2895 4to

Op. Sac. I–III, V s. xiii 2/2

Parchment; i (paper) + 224 + i (paper) fols; page 210x150mm; text 130x70mm; 32 lines; ruled for gloss, added subsequently; possibly two scribes for text, changing at fol. 111^{r}; different, highly compressed cursive hand for glosses. Running headers in red and blue. Binding: leather on pasteboard.

CONTENTS Fols 1^{r}–24^{v} Ps.-Dionysius, *De hierarchia angelica*, transl. John Saracenus; 24^{v}–55^{r} idem, *De hierarchia ecclesiastica*; 55^{r}–95^{v} idem, *De divinis nominibus*; 96^{r}–98^{v} idem, *De mystica theologia*; 98^{v}–110^{v} idem, *Epistolae*; 111^{r}–204^{r} John Damascene, *De fide orthodoxa*; 205^{r}–224^{r} ***Op. Sac. I–III, V***; 224^{v} s. xiv contents list.

GLOSS Intermittent marginal glosses to Ps.-Dionysius and John Damascene; only one gloss for *Op. Sac.* at fol. 207^{r}.

DECORATION Major initials in red and blue with penwork flourishing (fols 1^{r},

111^{r}, 205^{r}); minor initials in red or blue with penwork flourishing; paraph signs in red and blue.

PROVENANCE Italy (script). 'Jurk' (front pastedown: s. xviii–xix); J. A. N. Settegast, d. 1890 (fol. i^{r}). Purchased in 1920.

BIBLIOGRAPHY Jørgensen, pp. 40–41.

7–9. MSS København, Det Kongelige Bibliotek, Thott 166–168

The three volumes were produced as a set in one centre and are now bound separately in matching s. xviii/xix bindings labelled 'Tom. I – Tom. III'.

7. MS København, Det Kongelige Bibliotek, Thott 166 2° Plate 4
Syll. Cat., Syll. Hyp. s. x/xi

Parchment; iv (paper) + 110 + iv (paper) fols (not foliated); page 287x204mm; text 199x146mm; 24 lines, ruled with a hard point; five very different scribes: I (fols 1^{v}–16^{v}), II (fols 17^{r}–48^{v} and 68^{r}–82^{r}), III (fols 49^{r}–68^{r}), IV (fols 83^{v}–104^{v}, main scribe of MS Thott 167), V (fols 105^{r}–110^{r}, scribe II of MS Thott 168).

CONTENTS Fols 1^{r}–35^{v} ***Syll. Cat.***; 36^{r}–82^{r} ***Syll. Hyp.***; 82^{v}–83^{r} blank; 83^{v}–102^{r} Marius Victorinus, *De definitionibus*; 102^{r}–110^{r} Alcuin, *Dialectica* (excerpts); 110^{v} blank.

GLOSS Virtually none for Boethius; light contemporary glosses for Victorinus; sparse glosses to Alcuin.

DECORATION One crudely executed inhabited initial ***C****(onditionalium)* with a bust (labelled PLATO: fol. 65^{r}). Plain orange minor initials; early foliate flourish in margin, fol. 63^{v}; diagrams to *Syll. Cat.*

PROVENANCE N. E. France or the Low Countries (script). 'Liber Ruopperti episcopi/Liber Ruop[er]ti episcopi/Labor carus Waltheri' (fol. 1^{r}). Bequest of Otto Thott.

BIBLIOGRAPHY Jørgensen, pp. 366–7; *Levende Ord & Lysende Billeder. Den middelalderlige Bogkultur i Danmark*, ed. E. Petersen, Copenhagen, 1999, no. 117.

8. MS København, Det Kongelige Bibliotek, Thott 167 2°
Isag., 2 in Isag. s. x/xi

Parchment; iv (paper) + 102 + iv (paper) fols; page 284x201mm; text 202x142mm; 24 lines; several scribes: fols 1^{v}–8^{v}, 16^{r}–95^{v} is scribe IV of MS Thott 166. Chrismons (one labelled 'crismon'), fol. 1^{r}. Several s. xi^{in} definitions, e.g., 'quod est animal: substantia animata sensibilis', fol. 1^{r}.

CONTENTS Fols 1^{r}–16^{r} ***Isag.***; 16^{r}–102^{r} ***2 in Isag.***, *expl.* imperf. 'si subiectum aliquando reliquerit' (*PL*, 64:71A–153A).

GLOSS Very sparse marginal and interlinear glosses.

DECORATION A few plain initials in a later hand (e.g., fols 10^{r}–15^{v}); plain orange capitals to head sections; incipits and explicits in display script (alternating lines of red and brown ink). Diagrams, fol. 98^{r}.

PROVENANCE See MS 166. N. E. France or the Low Countries (script). 'Liber Ruopperti episcopi/Labor carus Waltheri', fol. 1^{r}. Bequest of Otto Thott.

BIBLIOGRAPHY Jørgensen, pp. 366–7; *AL*, 396.

9. MS København, Det Kongelige Bibliotek, Thott 168 2°
in Cat. s. x/xi

Parchment; iv (paper) + 125 + iii (paper) fols; page 285x206mm; text 203x141mm; 24 lines; several scribes: fols 105^{r}–?121^{v} is scribe of Thott 166. *Tituli* planned but not executed.

CONTENTS Fols 1^{v}–125^{v} ***in Cat.***, *lacuna* between 24^{v}–25^{r}: 'post parvissimam in quatuor enumerationem idem in substantiam accidens universalitatem particularitatem'–'Substantiae sunt idcirco quod avis homine' (*PL*, 64:180B–88B); 125^{v} notes, mostly illegible.

GLOSS Intermittent interlinear glosses in contemporary hand to fol. 10^{v}; very rare thereafter.

DECORATION Sections headed by enlarged orange capitals and display script; most capitals touched with orange; diagrams, fols 19^{v}, 64^{r}, 66^{r}, 66^{v}. Foliate sketch in contemporary hand in margin, fol. 115^{v}; series of concentric circles drawn in hard point, fol. 125^{v}.

PROVENANCE See MS 166. N. E. France or the Low Countries (script). 'Liber Ruopperti episcopi/ Labor carus Waltheri' (s. x/xi rustic caps: fol. 1^{r}). 'LIB RUDOLPH' (s. xi/xii: fol. 1^{r}). Bequest of Otto Thott.

BIBLIOGRAPHY Jørgensen, pp. 366–7; *AL*, 397.

10. MS København, Det Kongelige Bibliotek, Thott 303 2°
DCPhil. 1406

Parchment; ii (paper) + 60 + ii (paper) fols; page 275x190mm; 185x110mm; 29

lines; wide margins for gloss, not executed; three scribes. Dated colophon, 25 Jan. 1406, fol. 59^{v}. Greek in text, slightly garbled. Modern binding.
A modest and functional copy.

CONTENTS Fols 1^{r}–59^{v} ***DCPhil.***; 60^{r-v} blank.

GLOSS Profuse interlinear gloss added in a later hand.

DECORATION Decorated initials in pink, green and gold, with penwork flourishing to begin each book (fols 1^{r}, 9^{v}, 20^{v}, 36^{r}, 50^{r}); minor initials in red or blue with alternate-colour flourishing; paraph signs in red and blue.

PROVENANCE Italy. Bequest of Otto Thott.

BIBLIOGRAPHY Jørgensen, p. 365.

GRAND DUCHY OF LUXEMBOURG

BIBLIOTHÈQUE NATIONALE

The library is the successor to the first library instituted in Luxembourg in 1798 by the French authorities. Although joined to the Library of the Athenaeum in 1848, the title of National Library did not begin to be used until 1899.

N. van Werveke, *Catalogue descriptif des manuscrits de la Bibliothèque de Luxembourg*, Luxembourg, 1894.

1. MS Luxembourg, Bibliothèque nationale, 21 (formerly I.21)
Mus. s. x^{ex} / xi^{in}

Parchment; 14 fols; page 180x130mm; text 140x100mm; 33 lines; dry point ruling; one scribe.
Binding: s. xix pasteboard.

CONTENTS Fol. 1^r blank; 1^v–11^v ***Mus.*** IV.5, *inc.* 'De divisione monocordi illud est predicandum'; *expl.* 'triple proportionibus dissonantiam et con-sonantiam reddat' (Friedlein, pp. 314–49); 11^v–12^r *Musica enchiriadis*, excerpt (ed. H. Schmid, *Musica et scolica enchiriadis ...*, Munich, 1981, pp. 4–9); 12^v–13^r *Scolica enchiriadis*, excerpt (ed. Schmid, pp. 84–6); 13^r *Mensura monocordi*, *inc.* 'Monocordum a magada usque ad magadam'; *expl.* 'duplicatis acutis in gravibus'; 13^r–14^r three short extracts on measurement of organ pipes (ed. K. J. Sachs, *Mensura fistularum*, vol. 1, Stuttgart, 1970, pp. 49, 117, 93); 14^v blank.

GLOSS Space left for diagrams in *Mus.*, not supplied.

DECORATION None.

PROVENANCE Echternach: 'M 36. Continet divisionem monocordi', 'Codex sancti willibrordi epternacensis' (s. xv: fol. 1^v).

BIBLIOGRAPHY Van Werveke, pp. 34–5; F. Lochner, 'La Culture musicale de l'abbaye d'Echternach au Moyen Age', unpubl. PhD thesis, Free University of Brussels, Brussels, 1987–8.

2. MS Luxembourg, Bibliothèque nationale, 121 (formerly I.121) Plate 5
DCPhil. 12 March 1449

Paper; 178 fols; page 295x230mm; text 2 cols, each 180–85x90mm; 38 lines;

scribe, Teilmann Pluynsch (or Tilmann Pluntsch) de Euskirchen, canon of the church of SS Chrysanthus and Daria, Munstereifel: signed and dated colophons, fol. 103^{r} (12 March 1449), fol. 175^{v} (1448, 'ipso die Urbani pape').
Binding: s. xix pasteboard.

CONTENTS Fols 1^{r}–103^{v} ***DCPhil.***; 104^{r-v} verses pertaining to Munstereifel; 105^{r}–112^{v} Lives of SS Chrysanthus and Daria; 113^{r}–114^{r} Life of St Longinus; 114^{r}–128^{v} misc. exorcisms, and blessings, with part of a penitential and litany; 129^{r}–155^{v} description of the Holy Land by Ludulphus, parish priest of Suchen; 155^{v}–156^{v} extract of description of the Holy Land by Bartolfus de Nangeio, followed by indulgence for visiting the Holy land; 159^{v}–175^{v} extracts from the works of Marco Polo on Armenia, Persia, Turkey, India; 175^{v}–178^{v} chronical of Munstereifel from 1270 to 1451 (years 1449–51 added later, although still by Teilmann Pluynsch).

GLOSS Extensive marginal and interlinear glosses throughout *DCPhil.*

DECORATION A few rubricated initials.

PROVENANCE Munstereifel. 'Christophorus Ittelius altarista summe aedis Treverice hunc librum iure possidet' (s. xvi^{ex}), 'Franciscus Nicolaus Aegh hunc librum iure possidet anno Domini 1636', fol. 1^{r}; 'Sum Fratrum Praedicatorum Luxemburgensium', fol. 2^{r}.

BIBLIOGRAPHY Van Werveke, pp. 271–7.

THE NETHERLANDS

DEVENTER

STADS- OF ATHENAEUMBIBLIOTHEEK

The majority of the medieval books of the Stads- of Athenaeumbibliotheek come from the lay houses of the Brethren and Sisters of the Common Life in and near Deventer, and from the Augustinian canons of Windesheim and canonesses of Diepenveen.

[J. C. Van Slee], *Catalogus der Handschriften berustende op de Athenaeum-Bibliotheek te Deventer*, Deventer, 1892; J. C. Bedaux, *et al.*, eds, *Stads- of Athenaeumbibliotheek Deventer 1560–1985*, Deventer, 1985.

***1. MS Deventer, Stads- of Athenaeumbibliotheek, I, 88 (101 F 21 Kl.)**
DCPhil. s. xiii^{in}

Description taken from A. S. Korteweg, *Illuminated Manuscripts in Dutch Collections, Preliminary Precursor*, part 2–3, The Hague, 1993, p. 41.

Parchment; 70 fols; page 175x115mm; text 145x73mm. Binding: s. xvii parchment.

CONTENTS Fols 1–70 ***DCPhil.***

GLOSS None.

DECORATION Decorated initials (e.g., fols 1^v, 12^v, 25^v, 44^r, 63^v); pen-work initials (e.g., fols 3^v, 5^v, 10^v, 12^r, 13^r).

PROVENANCE Early history unknown; acquired in 1779 by the Academia Gelro-Zutphanica in Harderwijk, and transferred to the Stads- of Athenaeumbibliotheek in Deventer in 1820.

BIBLIOGRAPHY Van Slee, no. 88, p. 40; Korteweg, p. 41.

DEN HAAG (The Hague)

KONINKLIJKE BIBLIOTHEEK

The oldest and most important of the manuscript collections is that of the Princes of Orange, given to the state after Prince William VI of Orange had become king of the Netherlands (1814). Among other collections acquired subsequently is that of the Chevalier Lupus, compiled during the French Revolution largely from the manuscripts of suppressed religious houses in northern France and Flanders.

Catalogus codicum manuscriptorum Bibliothecae Regiae, 1: Libri theologici, The Hague, 1922; A. S. Korteweg and K. Thomassen, *Inventaris van de handschriften van de Koninklijke Bibliotheek. Voorlopige uitgave*, pt. 1 (classes 66–70), The Hague, 1988–. Card catalogues by author, subject and shelf-mark.

2. MS Den Haag, Koninklijke Bibliotheek, 72 J 51

DCPhil. 1464

Paper; i + 105 + i fols (with slips of paper added for additional notes); page 208x147mm; text 136–148x76mm; text with gloss up to 193x145mm; 18–21 lines; one scribe, writing a French cursive script. Colophon, fol. 98^{v}, 'scriptus anno domini 1464 die sancti Vincentii martyris'.
Omissions signalled by hp ('hic incipit') and hd ('hic dimitte').

CONTENTS Fols 1^{r}–98^{v} ***DCPhil.***, glossed; 99^{r}–105^{v} unidentified text and gloss.

GLOSS See contents.

DECORATION Simple red initials, occasionally with blue or yellow infill.

PROVENANCE Sanctae Crucis, Offémont, Celestine house (*ex libris*: fols 1^{r}, 105^{r}; fol. 1^{r} 'G. 34').

BIBLIOGRAPHY Korteweg and Thomassen, pt. 2 (classes 71–72), p. 135; *CMD-NL*, vol. 2, p. 1, n. 1.

3. MS Den Haag, Koninklijke Bibliotheek, 78 E 59

Arith. s. xi 2/2

Parchment; ii + 48 + ii fols; page 285x212mm; text 202x204–207mm; 32 lines; one scribe, apart from three lines on fols 19^{r} and fol. 1^{r}, rewritten over erasure in s. xii.

CONTENTS Fols 1^{r}–48^{v} ***Arith.*** I–II.54 (169/13) 'Restat ergo de maxima perfectaque armonia disserere quae tribus intervallis constituta magna vim optinet et in musicae modulamini temperamenta' (leaves lost at end).

DECORATION Pen-drawn foliate initial (fol. 21^{v}) characteristic of decoration in manuscripts from the Meuse region (cf. M. R. Lapière, *La Lettre ornée dans les manuscrits mosans d'origine bénédictine (xie–xiie siècles)*, Paris, 1981).

PROVENANCE Medieval provenance unknown; script and decoration suggest an origin in E. France or Lower Lotharingia. Guillaume Pellicier (= Pellissier, c. 1490–1561), bishop of Montpellier (*ex libris* on a loose parchment slip); Jesuits of Paris (fol. 1r).

BIBLIOGRAPHY G. H. Pertz, *Archiv der Gesellschaft für ältere deutsche Geschichtskunde*, 8, 1843, p. 568, which refers to an earlier shelfmark: 559.

4. MS Den Haag, Koninklijke Bibliotheek, 133 M 114
DCPhil. s. xv 2/2

Paper; 71 fols, comprising leaves from three contemporary books or booklets, with several leaves missing from all three.
A: fols 1r–15v page 223x151mm; text and gloss c. 185–90x120mm; text 100x58–65mm; 12 lines of text; one scribe, writing a Netherlandish *hybrida*, with glosses in *cursiva*.
Binding: parchment wrapper. Paper used for A and B has same watermark.

CONTENTS A: fols 1r–15v ***DCPhil.***, glossed; *expl.* imperf. through loss of leaves, ending at I.pr.iv.16 'res pupplicas si eas studio'. Gloss, prol. *inc.* 'Iuxta initium huius libri quedam generali sunt premittenda dubia'; text gloss, written as continuous commentary, *inc.* 'Notandum quod Boecius in istis duobus versibus' (fol. 4r).
B: 15r–45v Eberhard of Béthune, *Laborintus*, lines 23–73, 98–768, with marginal commentary.
C: 46r–71v Ps.-Boethius, *De disciplina scolarium*, with marginal commentary; *expl.* imperf. 'Si autem discipulus magistro suo semper ut necessarium est nequeat exhibere prescenciam' (cap. iv).

GLOSS A: see contents.

DECORATION None. Simple rubrics, fols 1r–25r, 46r–71v.
PROVENANCE Doesburg (Weijers).

BIBLIOGRAPHY Weijers, p. 73.

MUSEUM MEERMANNO-WESTREENIANUM – MUSEUM VAN HET BOEK

The Museum Meermanno-Westreenianum was bequeathed to the State in 1848 by its founder, Baron Van Westreenen van Tiellandt (1783–1848). His collection included both the books and antiquities of Gérard Meerman (1722–11), among them the bulk of the manuscripts of the Jesuit College of Clermont at Paris, and those of Gérard's son, Johan (1753–1818).

P. J. H. Vermeeren and A. F. Dekker, *Inventaris van de handschriften van het Museum Meermanno-Westreenianum*, The Hague, 1960; P. C. Boeren, *Catalogus van de handschriften van het Rijkmuseum Meermanno-Westreenianum*, The Hague, 1979.

5. MS Den Haag, Rijksmuseum Meermanno-Westreenianum, 10 D 35
DCPhil. s. xv

Parchment; ii + 158 fols; page 241x170mm; text 159x85mm; frame-ruled in red with 26 ruled lines for text; one ?French scribe, writing a *fere-humanistica* hand. A very high quality book on fine parchment.

CONTENTS Fols 1^{r}–76^{r} ***DCPhil.***; 77^{r}–150^{v} Jean Gerson, *De consolatione theologiae*; 151^{r}–158^{r} idem, *Dialogus apologeticus*.

GLOSS None.

DECORATION Armorial initial (fol. 1^{r}); historiated initials (fols 80^{r} rural scene, city in distance; two men, one older one young, in foreground; and 151^{r} rural scene, same two men reversed positions); major and minor decorated initials gold on blue or purple with purple or blue infill.

PROVENANCE Armorial shield supported by two angels, with crosier behind, of unidentified bishop or abbot (fol. 1^{r}). The device of the shield is a chevron composed of interlocking crenellations, accompanied by three flagons or jars in gold on an azure ground.

BIBLIOGRAPHY Vermeeren and Dekker no. 22, pp. 8–9; Boeren, pp. 122–3.

’S HEERENBERG

HUIS BERGH

The manuscripts are from the collection of J. H. van Heek, who acquired the castle and its contents in 1912, and subsequently presented it to the state.

Typed catalogue, ‘Lijst van de verzameling handschriften op het Huis Bergh’; exhibition catalogue, *Wat het Huis Bergh in zich houdt*, Nijmegen 1960/61; J. H. van Heek, *Huis Bergh: kasteel en collectie*, Nijmegen, 1987.

6. MS ’S Heerenberg, Huis Bergh, 54 (192)
DCPhil. s. xii

Description taken from the catalogues, above, and information supplied by Dr A. S. Korteweg from records created from the *Illuminated Manuscripts in Dutch Collections* project.

Parchment; 56 fols; page 270x165mm; text 195x80mm; 28 lines (text), 60 lines (glosses); Italian scribe or scribes.

CONTENTS ***DCPhil.*** (incomplete) with marginal gloss.

GLOSS See contents.

DECORATION One schematic drawing; decorated initials, fols 8r, 26r, 41v.

PROVENANCE Unknown.

BIBLIOGRAPHY Kristeller IV, p. 349; *Wat het Huis Bergh in zich houdt*, pl. 10, p. 26 (beginning of bk IV); Van Heek, pl. 54; typed catalogue.

7. MS 'S Heerenberg, Huis Bergh, 69 (248)
DCPhil. s. xiv 1/2

Description taken from the catalogues, above, and information supplied by Dr A. S. Korteweg from records created from the *Illuminated Manuscripts in Dutch Collections* project.

Parchment; 64 fols; page 251x180mm; text 175x105mm; 25 lines; Northern Italian scribe or scribes.

CONTENTS ***DCPhil.***

GLOSS None.

DECORATION One historiated initial with border decoration, penwork initials with pen flourishes, fols 10r, 22r, 39r, 53v.

PROVENANCE Unknown.

BIBLIOGRAPHY Typed catalogue.

LEIDEN

UNIVERSITEITSBIBLIOTHEEK

The library, founded in 1575, contains the manuscript collections of a number of important sixteenth- and seventeenth-century scholars, whose names are now preserved in the classification of the Leiden manuscripts: the Codices Vossiani, Scaligerani, Vulcaniani, Hugeniani, Perizoniani, Lipsiani, etc. The largest of these is the collection of Isaac Vossius (1618–89), which included manuscripts formerly owned by Queen Christina of Sweden, which in turn included manuscripts belonging to Paul and Alexandre Petau. The other main class of Latin manuscripts is the Codices Bibliothecae Publicae Latini (BPL).

P. C. Molhuysen, *Geschiedenis der Universiteitsbibliotheek te Leiden*, Leiden, 1905; Bibliotheca Universitatis Leydensis, *Codices manuscripti*, 27 vols, Leiden 1910–; E. Hulshoff Pol, 'The Library', in Th. H. Lunsingh Scheurleer and G. H. M. Posthumus Meyjes, eds, *Leiden University in the Seventeenth Century. An Exchange of Learning*, Leiden, 1975, pp. 395–459.

8. MS Leiden, Universiteitsbibliotheek, BPL 25
1 in Int. s. x/xi

Parchment; i + 43 fols; page 328x230 mm; text 250x c. 180mm; 33 lines; at least three contemporary scribes. Text and commentary throughout *1 in Int.* labelled respectively *Hystoria*, *Boetius* and *Expositio*.

CONTENTS Fols 2^{r}–38^{r} ***1 in Int.***; 38^{r}–41^{v} Ps.-Apuleius, *Perihermenias*; 1^{r-v} and 42^{r}–43^{v} end-leaves, fragments of a liturgical manuscript (perhaps s. x), some texts notated.

GLOSS A few notes, e.g., fols 7^{r-v}, 8^{v}, 9^{v}; some interlinear glosses in hand of text scribe (e.g., fol. 20^{v}); some s. xiii notes (e.g., fols 4^{v}, 7^{v}, 11^{v}).

DECORATION Diagrams. Plain ink touched with green (fol. 2^{r}). Otherwise plain red capitals (fols 2^{r}, 20^{r}, 38^{r}).

PROVENANCE Medieval provenance unknown; Franciscus Nansius (d. 1595) (Codex Nansianus in 1588 edn of P. Colvius).

BIBLIOGRAPHY *Codices manuscripti*, 3.16–17; *AL*, 144; Goldbacher, *Wiener Studien*, 1885, p. 256.

9. MS Leiden, Universiteitsbibliotheek, BPL 70
DCPhil. s. xv 2/2

Paper; ii + 107 + ii fols; page 286x213mm; text 190x120mm; 16 lines; one scribe writing Netherlandish *hybrida*. Parchment binding, with back cover extending to protect edge of leaves. BOETHIUS MS written bottom to top along this protective extension.

CONTENTS Fols 1^{r}–107^{v} ***DCPhil.***

GLOSS None, other than a few interlinear glosses in hand of scribe (e.g., fol. 48^{r}).

DECORATION Red and blue initials with internal pen-drawn leaf pattern and external flourishing (sometimes extending full length of margin) at beginning of each book; minor initials in red.

PROVENANCE 'Donum Dan. Heremitii' (written on inserted card).

BIBLIOGRAPHY *Codices manuscripti*, 3.39.

10. MS Leiden, Universiteitsbibliotheek, BPL 84
Div., Syll. Hyp., Syll. Cat., Intr. Syll. Cat. s. xi

Parchment; ii + 103 + ii fols; quire signatures indicate that fols 1–16 originally formed the third and fourth quire of a different book, but bound together by s. xiii or s. xiv (contents list fol. 103^{v}); fol. 58 is an inserted leaf (contemporary) to supply text missing from fol. 57^{v}, using 'hic dimitte' and 'hic incipit' as notes of omission; page 265x150mm; text 220x105; several scribes, at least one (fols 67^{v}–89^{v}) from N.E. France or Lotharingia, the others writing less localisable small scholars' hands. *Tituli*, fols 7^{v}, 17^{r}, 24^{r}, 34^{r}, 44^{v}.
A tall, narrow book.

CONTENTS A: fols 1^{r}–7^{v} ***Div.***; 8^{r}–16^{v} Marius Victorinus, *De definitionibus*. B: fols 17^{r}–44^{v} ***Syll. Hyp.***; 44^{v}–67^{r} ***Syll. Cat.***; 67^{v}–89^{v} ***Intr. Syll. Cat.***; 89^{v} types of proposition set out as a descending tree; 90^{r}–103^{v} Alcuin, *Dialectica*; 103^{v} s. xiii or xiv contents list.

GLOSS A: annotation on both *Div.* and *De definitionibus*. Occasional subject headings and simple schemata, e.g., 5^{v}, 10^{v}; cross-references to *in Topica Cic.*, e.g., 14^{r}.

DECORATION Major initials red or blue with brown ink; simple interlace (fols 1^{r}, 8^{r}). Minor initials in plain red with brown ink, e.g., fol. 6^{v}, or brown touched with red. Other initials with thick foliage (fols 86^{r}, 88^{v}); line-drawings (fol. 83^{r-v}), one obscene (fol. 84^{r}).

PROVENANCE Franciscus Nansius.

BIBLIOGRAPHY *Codices manuscripti*, 3.45; A. van de Vyver, 'Les Étapes du développement philosophique du haut Moyen-Age', *Revue belge de philologie et d'histoire*, 8, 1929, pp. 446–7; *AL*, 2026.

11. MS Leiden, Universiteitsbibliotheek, BPL 90
in Topica Cic. s. x ?

Parchment; iv + 81 + i fols (parchment often very poor quality, some leaves ruled several times); page 235–245xc. 190mm; text 188–195x145mm; 30–31 lines; at least three contemporary scribes, writing rather irregular, informal hands; some passages of very poor writing.
A very informal book.

CONTENTS Fols iii^{r}–iv^{v} (endleaves) fragment of a theological work, written in a s. xv cursive hand; 1^{r}–12^{r} Cicero, *Topica*; 12^{r}–81^{v} ***in Topica Cic.*** (fol. 57^{v} lower margin 'Emendata perfecta'; fol. 62^{r} same hand as text 'Conditor operis emendavi': cf. Leiden, MS Voss. lat. F.70.1); 81^{v} *De multiplicatione*, *inc.* 'Si multiplicaveris singularem' (perhaps Gerbert, *Regulae multiplicationis*, from his *Regulae de numerorum abaci rationibus*, ed. Bubnov, pp. 8–11).

GLOSS Almost none.

DECORATION Simple red initials, fols 1^{r} and 12^{r}.

PROVENANCE Although this manuscript shares endleaves from the same s. xv volume as three other BPL manuscripts certainly owned by Franciscus Nansius (MSS 48, 88, 94), it is not known to have been owned by him; see E. Hulshoff Pol, 'Franciscus Nansius und seine Handschriften', *Litterae textuales 4. Miniatures, Scripts, Collections: Essays Presented to G. I. Leiftinck*, ed. J. P. Gumbert and M. J. M. de Haan, Amsterdam, 1976, p. 96.

BIBLIOGRAPHY *Codices manuscripti*, 3.47.

12. MS Leiden, Universiteitsbibliotheek, BPL 133
DCPhil. 1466

Paper; iii + 260 + v fols; page 218x140mm; text (ruled space) 180x105mm; 23 lines for text, 42–44 lines for commentary; one named scribe, Nicolaus Troger, dean of Alt-Wiesloch, Baden (fol. 260^{v} *expl.* and colophon, 'Finita sunt illa propria die Basilii Confessoris et pontificis Anno Domini Millesimo quadringentesimo sexagesimo sexto per me Nicholaum troger prepositum (?)/ plebanum (*or* presbyterum) in Altwisseloch Arcium liberalium Baccalarium hora quarta inorta circa Alvearia deo gracias'); text written in *hybrida* and commentary in *cursiva*.

CONTENTS Fols 1^{r}–6^{v} Prologue to commentary of Pierre d'Ailly, *inc.* 'Reverendi patres magistri ac domini karissimi mihi ardua scandere volenti opusque ultra vires meas agere presumenti'; 4^{r}–5^{v} 'Sequitur historia de venerabili Boecio et rege Theodorica'; 6^{v}–260^{v} ***DCPhil.***, with intercalated commentary of Pierre d'Ailly (Courcelle, pp. 324–5, 415).

GLOSS See contents. Some user's annotations, e.g., fol. 59^{r}.

DECORATION Plain blue initial, fol. 1^{r}; other major initials red with reserve internal foliate design, fols 59^{v}, 171^{r}, 224^{r}. Minor initials, paraphs and rubrics in red.

PROVENANCE Perhaps made by the scribe, Nicholaus Troger, for his own use. Subsequent history unknown.

BIBLIOGRAPHY *Codices manuscripti*, 3.7; *Manuscrits datés Pays-Bas*, I, no. 179, p. 78, pl. 320 (fol. 224^r).

13. MS Leiden, Universiteitsbibliotheek, BPL 139B

Isag. s. x/xi

Parchment; i + 46 + i fols; page c. 223x173mm. All three parts produced at Fleury.
A: text c. 163x122–130mm; 25 lines; one scribe.
B: text 164x125mm; one scribe, whose hand is similar to that of the scribe of A.
C: text 189x129mm; 38 lines; two small informal hands, perhaps later than those of A and B.

CONTENTS A: fol. 1^r verses on Boethius and *Syll. Hyp.*; 1^v dedicatory verses by Abbo; 1^v–16^v Abbo of Fleury, treatise on the propositions and categorical syllogisms; 17^r–30^r idem, treatise on the hypothetical syllogisms; 30^v the parts of philosophy, from the beginning of Ps.-Apuleius, *Perihermenias* (added in another hand).
B: fols 32^r–38^r Ps.-Apuleius, *Perihermenias*; 39^r *probationes pennae*; 39^v schema of syllogisms (in a wheel).
C: fols 40^r–45^v ***Isag.*** (lacks heading or other opening rubric); 46^{r-v} misc. notes on grammar; 46^v acrostic verse, *inc.* 'Sacra tua gratia', with neumes, giving the words SANCTE. BENEDICTE.

DECORATION B: line drawings, fols 32^r (man attacked by two lions) and 36^r (warrior with shield and lion; perhaps added later), touched with yellow.

PROVENANCE Fleury; Alexandre Petau bookplate inside front cover.

BIBLIOGRAPHY *Codices manuscripti*, 3.77–78; M. Mostert, *The Library of Fleury: Provisional List of Manuscripts*, Hilversum, 1989, pp. 89–90; Pellegrin, 'Membra disiecta Floriacensia', p. 14, n. 2; A. van de Vyver, 'Les Oeuvres inédites d'Abbon de Fleury', *Revue bénédictine*, 47, 1935, pp. 133–7.

14. MS Leiden, Universiteitsbibliotheek, BPL 144

DCPhil. s. xii 2/2

Parchment; iii + 94 + i fols; page 228x176mm; text (varies) 138–155x75–85mm (with marginal gloss at either side, 160mm); 25–32 lines of text; same or similar scribes throughout except fols 85^v–86^r which are in another contemporary hand. Text marked B(oethius) amd P(hilosophia).

CONTENTS Fol. 1^r misc. s. xiii or xiv notes; 1^v *accessus*; 2^r–52^r ***DCPhil.***; 52^v–82^v Martianus Capella, *De nuptiis*, I–II; 85^r s. xiv pencil notes; 85^v–93^r Martianus Capella, *De nuptiis*, VIII; 93^v s. xiii or xiv notes; 94^{r-v} s. xi endleaf: Macrobius, *In Somnium Scipionis*, II.3.12–4.4.

GLOSS Contemporary extensive and systematic gloss on *DCPhil.*, in two columns ruled for the purpose on either side of text. In places the gloss surrounds the text on all four sides, e.g., fol. 53^{r}; some leaves (e.g., fols 57, 66, 67) ruled with alternate-line ruling for the gloss, other leaves lack horizontal ruling for the gloss.

DECORATION Arabesque initials in green, ochre, red (fol. 2^{r}) and blue (fol. 9^{v}). Other simpler major initials fols 18^{v}, 32^{v}, 43^{v}. Red and green minor initials throughout.

PROVENANCE France: 'Iste liber est de cardinali monacho teste meo signo' (fol. 93^{r}: s. xv, written in a French *hybrida*).

BIBLIOGRAPHY *Codices manuscripti*, 3.79–80; Leonardi, pp. 64–5.

15. MS Leiden, Universiteitsbibliotheek, BPL 1925

Logica vetus s. xii

Parchment; ii + 175 fols; page 135x88mm. Binding: white tawed skin over boards. Two unrelated elements, probably bound together by Alexandre Petau, whose contents' list on the front pastedown corresponds with current contents of the manuscript. Colophon (in different hand from that of preceding text), fol. 120^{v}, 'anno ab incarnatione domini mclxxviii .iii. kal' octobris Guillelmus philosophus fuit annorum xxxii dierum xi dclxxxviii. 11688 festo sancti michaelis archangeli'.
A: 120 fols comprising several booklets with numerous leaves now missing, fols 1^{r}–104^{v} written in small s. xii scholars' hands; fols 105^{r}–110^{v} perhaps s. xiii with s. xiv additions; fols 111^{r}–120^{v} late s. xii (of which another fragment survives as MS Bern, Burgerbibliothek, 404).
B: text 110x66mm; 30–35 lines; one tiny informal hand, s. xii. Fols 121–175 from a tiny scholar's book.

CONTENTS A: fragments of texts incl. Persius, *Satyrae* and Aulus Gellius, *Noctes atticae*.
B: fols 121^{r}–128^{v} ***Isag.***, ii.9–end; 128^{v}–138^{v} ***De Int.***; 139^{r}–153^{r} ***Cat.***; 153^{v}–174^{v} ***Top. Diff.***, I–III; 175^{r-v} ***Div.***, *expl.* imperf. 'prima sit divisione' (*PL*, 64:877).

DECORATION Red lines scored through incipits and explicits.

PROVENANCE Alexandre Petau; Peter Burman; formerly MS Utrecht, Universiteitsbibliotheek, 816.

BIBLIOGRAPHY *Codices manuscripti*, 3.187; *AL*, 147; 2028.

16. MS Leiden, Universiteitsbibliotheek, BPL 2391A
Arith. II s. ix 2/2

Parchment; page 284x205mm (heavily trimmed); 2 cols of variable width, up to 75–80mm; height 278mm (text lost through trimming); 32 lines; one scribe. A single leaf from a large two-column MS.

CONTENTS Fol. 1^{ra-vb} ***Arith.***, II.46–47: 'habebunt medietates'–'descriptione monstratur' (150/4–152/22).

GLOSS Interlinear notes in Irish, in a tiny glossing hand.

DECORATION Ink-drawn insular initial with bird-heads and dotting: ***A****(rmonica)*, II.47.

PROVENANCE Acquired November 1940 in a portfolio of fragments.

BIBLIOGRAPHY M. Draak, 'A Leiden Boethius-fragment with Old Irish Glosses', *Mededelingen der Koninklijke Nederlandsche Akademie van Wetensch. afd. Letterkunde*, 11/3, 1948, pp. 115–27; idem, 'Construe Marks in Hiberno-Latin Manuscripts', ibid. 20/10, 1957, pp. 261–82; White, in Gibson, pp. 164, 190n.

17. MS Leiden, Universiteitsbibliotheek, BPL 2717
DCPhil. s. xv mid

Paper; iii + 187 fols; page 221x142mm; text 118–130x80mm (with gloss, up to 197x128mm); 10–15 lines (text); 53–58 lines (gloss); two contemporary scribes; that of fol. 1^{v}–139^{v} named on 139^{r}: 'par me Io. De Eschwylre'. Binding: tooled leather on wooden boards with two clasps fastening on front cover.

CONTENTS Fol. 1^{*} (first front end-leaf) s. xv contents list; 1^{r} misc. notes; 1^{v}–2^{v} Prologue to commentary; 2^{v}–139^{v} ***DCPhil.*** with intercalated commentary, partly arranged as gloss; 143^{r}–184^{r} Ps.-Boethius, *De disciplina scolarium*, glossed.

GLOSS See contents.

DECORATION Major initials plain, some with internal reserve decoration; blue initials and rubrication, fols 126^{v}, 130^{v}–31^{r}. Otherwise minor initials, rubrication and paraph signs in red.

PROVENANCE Aachen, Community of Regular Canons (*ex libris* fols 1^{*}, now obliterated, and 142^{r}).

BIBLIOGRAPHY Weijers, p. 74; P. F. J. Obbema, 'Writing on Uncut Sheets', *Quaerendo*, 1978, p. 348, pl. 4; idem, 'Een bijzondere manier van schrijven: werken op onopengesneden vellen', in idem, *De*

Middeleeuwen in handen. Over de boekcultuur in de late middeleeuwen, Hilversum, 1996, p. 63, 57, pl. 27.

18. MS Leiden, Universiteitsbibliotheek, Voss. lat. F. 70 I Plate 6
De Int., in Topica Cic., I in Int. s. x/xi

Parchment; v + 73 + iv fols; now mounted with plain paper intercalated between each leaf; page 285x215mm.
A: text c. 230x160–165; 2 cols; 42–43 lines; several contemporary hands. Colophons, 'Conditor operis emendavi', fols 22vb, 29va, 41ra. Originally part of the same vol. as MS Orléans, Bibl. Mun., 277 (233) and MS Paris, BnF, Nouv. acq., 1630; probably produced at Fleury (Pellegrin).
B (s. x): once part of the same vol. as MS Oxford, Bodl. Libr., Canon. Class. Lat. 279, fols 63–86.
There is no evidence of shared provenance until both parts came into the hands of Pierre Daniel.

CONTENTS A: fols 1ra–5vb Cicero, *Topica*; 5vb–9ra ***De Int.***; 9$^{ra–va}$ *De locis dialecticis* (= excerpts from *Top. Diff* I, IV); 9va–10ra notes on rhetorical texts incl. an excerpt from Grillius, *Commentum in Ciceronis rhetorica*; 10ra–44ra ***in Topica Cic.***; 44ra–50rb Ps.-Augustine, *Categoriae decem*; 50$^{rb–vb}$ ***I in Int.***, I.I.1 'nunc ergo hoc dicit quoniam voces' (38/8); 51$^{ra–b}$ Macrobius, *In Somnium Scipionis* (excerpts); 51rb–66va Cicero, *De inventione*, with *lacunae*; 66$^{va–b}$ Macrobius, *Saturnalia* (excerpts).
B: fols 67ra–69vb continuous glosses on Apocalypse; *Nomina lapidum*; continuous glosses on Pauline Epistles; 69vb glosses on Jerome's letters; 70ra glossary, partly etymological; 70rb–71va Alcuin, *Ep. 136* (*MGH*, *Ep.* IV, pp. 205–10); 71$^{va–b}$ Alcuin (attrib.), poems 'O vos est aetas' and 'Est mihi servili' (*MGH*, *Poet. lat.* I, pp. 299–300, 228); 71vb–73vb Seneca, *Ad Lucilium*, *expl.* imperf. 'vitia subrepunt' (*Ep.* 7.2, ed. Reynolds, p. 12/7).

GLOSS *De Int.*: long formal annotation fols 5^{v}–6^{r}, 7^{r}; otherwise subject titles in rustic capitals in margins in *Topica* and *in Topica Cic.*

DECORATION Decorated initials, fols 1ra, 1rb, 5^{v}, 41rb. Rubrication in two hands (fols 1^{r}–44ra, 44ra–66va). Elaborate schema in margin, fol. 51^{r}.

PROVENANCE A: Fleury; Pierre Daniel.
B: Pierre Daniel.

BIBLIOGRAPHY *Codices manuscripti*, 13.139–44; 16, pl. 28c (fol. 5^{v}), 28d (fol. 44^{r}); *AL*, 148; *Suppl. Alt.*, pp. 62–3; M. Mostert, *The Library of Fleury: Provisional List of Manuscripts*, Hilversum, 1989, p. 93; Pellegrin, 'Membra disiecta Floriacensia', pp. 9–16.

19. MS Leiden, Universiteitsbibliotheek, Voss. lat. Q. 2, part IX

Isag. s. ix/x

Parchment; single leaf; page 268x205mm; text 240x165mm (on recto only; pen trials on verso); two cols, 35 and 38 lines; perhaps two Welsh scribes, the first writing *Isag.* fol. 60ra, lines 1–22.

CONTENTS Fol. 60ra Fragment of end of ***Isag.***, *inc.* ‘Restat ergo de proprio’ (31/5); *expl.* ‘communitasque traditionem. Explicit liber ysagogarum phophirii’ (*sic*); fol. $60^{\mathrm{ra–b}}$ Lorica of Leiden, *inc.* ‘Domine exaudi usque in finem’.

GLOSS A few interlinear glosses in hand of scribe.

DECORATION Insular initial in ink of text.

PROVENANCE Acquired by Paul Petau from Pierre Daniel.

BIBLIOGRAPHY *Codices manuscripti*, 14.2; 16, p. 18a (fol. 60^{r}); W. M. Lindsay, *Early Welsh Script*, p. 23; M. Lapidge and R. Sharpe, *A Bibliography of Celtic-Latin Literature 400–1200*, Dublin, 1985, no. 1239; M. W. Herren, *The Hisperica famina II. Related Poems*, Toronto, 1987, p. 14; M. Mostert, *The Library of Fleury: Provisional List of Manuscripts*, Hilversum, 1989, p. 97.

20. MS Leiden, Universiteitsbibliotheek, Voss. lat. Q. 103

Top. Diff. IV s. xii mid

Parchment; iii + 102 + ii fols; page: 235x150mm; text 178x95mm; 31 lines; one scribe, writing a small calligraphic ‘academic’ hand, apart from fol. 66^{v} lines 1–12, which are in a different hand.

CONTENTS Fols 1^{r}–46^{r} Cicero, *De inventione*; 46^{r}–52^{v} ***Top. Diff.*** IV; 52^{v}–102^{r} Ps.-Cicero, *Ad Herennium.*

GLOSS Later medieval annotation throughout; s. xii notes and schemata in *De inv.*; several s. xii schemata in *Ad Herennium.*

DECORATION Unusual decorated initials in blue and gold with red pen-flourishing fols 1^{r}, 21^{r}, 46^{r}, 52^{v}, 70^{v}, 79^{v}; several minor initials in red, blue and green; *litterae notabiliores* touched with green.

PROVENANCE Richard de Fournival (*Biblionomia*, 27); bequeathed by Gerard of Abbeville to the Sorbonne upon his death in 1271 (fol. 102^{v}, ‘Iste liber est collegii pauperum magistrorum Par. in theologica facultate studencium ex legato magistri <Gerardi> de abbatis villa <…>’; Sorbonne 1338 cat. Ll:11).

BIBLIOGRAPHY *Codices manuscripti*, 14.231–3; 16, pl. 48c (fol. 59^{r}); L. Delisle, 3.61; R. H. and M. A. Rouse, 'Florilegia and Latin Classical Authors in Twelfth- and Thirteenth-Century Orléans', in idem, *Authentic Witnesses: Approaches to Medieval Texts and Manuscripts*, Notre Dame, IN, 1991, p. 162, n. 31.

21. MS Leiden, Universiteitsbibliotheek, Voss. lat. O. 61
Arith. s. xi/xii

Parchment; ii + 64 (fol. 1 is a parchment end-leaf) + i fols; page 196x122mm; text 141x77mm; 29 lines; one text scribe (perhaps Netherlandish), writing a tiny hand of a kind that is difficult to date with precision; diagrams and text on fols 57^{r} and 63^{v}–64^{r} perhaps in another hand; glosses perhaps in hand of text scribe (fols 2^{r}–16^{r}) and in another hand (fol. 16^{v}–63^{r}), perhaps that of the rubricator.
A small, well-made book.

CONTENTS Fols 2^{r}–64^{r} ***Arith.***

GLOSS Interlinear and marginal glosses; diagrams fols 57^{r}, 63^{r}–64^{r}.

DECORATION Initials in red at start of each section.

PROVENANCE St Adalbert, Egmond, s. xii/xiii *ex libris* and anathema fol. 63^{v} 'Liber sancti adalberti in egmont …'.

BIBLIOGRAPHY *Codices manuscripti*, 15.111–12; P. Gumbert, *The Dutch and their Books in the Manuscript Age*, London, 1990, pp. 15, 82, n. 22.

22. MS Leiden, Universiteitsbibliotheek, Voss misc. 38
Mus. s. x

Parchment; single leaf; page 234x196–200mm; text 172x112mm; 19 lines; one scribe. Interlinear translation of Greek.
A detached leaf of MS Vatican, BAV, Reg. lat. 1638, a s. ix^{ex} or s. x^{in} manuscript, parts of which (including this leaf) were recopied in s. x.

CONTENTS ***Mus.***, 'pueros ad omnes modos erudiri'–'quos acceperat erudos (*sic*) officeret et a virtutis' 181/14–184/3 (in i–1, the *Decretum Lacedaemoniorum*).

GLOSS Glosses in s. x recopied portions belong to Bernhard and Bower's French tradition.

PROVENANCE Perhaps Fleury, but not noted by Pellegrin or Mostert; Isaac Vossius.

BIBLIOGRAPHY *Codices manuscripti*, 6.276; Bower, 37, 120; Bernhard and Bower, pp. viii–x.

UTRECHT

UNIVERSITEITSBIBLIOTHEEK

The Universiteitsbibliotheek includes the books of the former City library founded in 1581 from the surviving books of religious houses within the diocese of Utrecht, in particular those of the Carthusians and the Regular canons. The library was supplemented during the first half of the nineteenth century by books from the five chapter houses of the bishopric of Utrecht, dissolved in 1811.

Catalogus codicum manuscriptorum bibliothecae universitatis Rheno-Trajectinae, 2 vols, Utrecht 1887–1909; K. van der Horst, *Illuminated and Decorated Medieval Manuscripts in the University Library, Utrecht*, The Hague and Cambridge, 1989.

23. MS Utrecht, Universiteitsbibliotheek, 78 (3 J 4)
Op. Sac. I–III, V s. xv mid

Parchment; 90 fols (fols 1–6 have been re-numbered fols i, 1–5, but the re-foliation was abandoned; references here are to the earlier foliation); page 311x224mm; text 207–215x150mm; 2 cols; 35 lines; one scribe, writing small *textura*. *Tituli*, fols 1^{v}, 39va, 46vb, 62va. Space left in *Op. Sac.* I, V for Greek, not supplied.
Binding: contemporary brown calf over wooden boards, blind tooled; remnants of clasps; rebacked.
A fine MS with four good initials, produced in the northern Netherlands, and probably copied from MS Vatican, BAV, Reg. lat. 420.

CONTENTS Front pastedown and fol. 1 (end-leaf) fragment from an unfinished s. xv service book; fols 2ra–6ra ***Op. Sac. I***; 6ra–39va Gilbert of Poitiers, *Commentary on Op. Sac. I*; 39vb–40va ***Op. Sac. II***; 40va–46vb Gilbert of Poitiers, *Commentary on Op. Sac. II*; 46vb–48rb ***Op. Sac. III***; 48va–62va Gilbert of Poitiers, *Commentary on Op. Sac. III*; 62va–70vb ***Op. Sac. V***; 70vb–89rb Gilbert of Poitiers, *Commentary on Op. Sac. V*, *expl.* imperf. 'commixtione confundi' IV.34.

GLOSS See contents.

DECORATION Major initials, fols 2ra, 6ra, 39vb, 62vb only. Initials in gold leaf with blue and white decorated surround. Minor initials red or blue; internal paraph signs, often red.

PROVENANCE Regular canons, Utrecht. Verso of front endleaf, two pressmarks, 259t and 294t.

BIBLIOGRAPHY Cat. 1.22; van der Horst, no. 50, pp. 14–15, figs 226–7 (fols 2^{r}, 62^{v}); Häring, *Gilbert*, pp. 29, 36; A. Hulshof and M. J. Schretlen, *De kunst der oude boekbinders. xvde en xvide eeuwsche boekbanden in de Utrechtsche Universiteits-bibliotheek*, Utrecht, 1921, p. 5.

24. MS Utrecht, Universiteitsbibliotheek, 117 (4 B 11)

Op. Sac. II 1489, 1490

Parchment; iii + 159 + ii fols; page 294x215mm; text c. 196x c. 140–150mm; two cols; 32–37 lines; one scribe or two very similar scribes. Plain-tooled leather binding with clasps fastening on front, fol. 99^{v} 'Explicit liber iohannis damasceni … In profesto (*sic*) omnium sanctorum Anno salutis millesimo quadringentesimo octogesimo nono Deo gracias. fol. 128rb 'Explicit liber sancti laurencii de duobus temporibus 1490 In crastino beati gregorii pape'. fol. 159ra 'Explicit liber apologeticus sancti gregorii nazanzeni episcopi ipso festo sancti stephani prothomartiris anno 1490'.

CONTENTS Fol. iii^{v} (original front end-leaf) contents list, as present contents; 1ra–2vb prayers; 3ra–99vb John Damascene, *De trinitate*; 99vb–109ra Gregory of Nazianzus, *De vastatione grandinis* (*oratio* 8); 109ra–114va idem, *In Heremiam*; 114vb–115va ***Op. Sac. II***; 115vb–128rb Laurentius, *De duobus temporibus*; 128va–219ra Martin of Tours, *Sermo de trinitate*; 129ra–130ra Rufinus, *Prefatio ad Apronianum* (the preface to his transl. of the *Liber Apologeticus*); 130ra–159ra Gregory of Nazianzus, *Liber apologeticus* (*oratio* 1).

GLOSS None.

DECORATION Major flourished initials in red and blue with floral infill (fols 3^{r}, 74^{v}, 109^{r}, 115^{v}, 130^{r}). Minor initials plain red or blue; *litterae notabiliores* often touched in red.

PROVENANCE Utrecht Carthusians (*ex libris* front pastedown, 'Liber fratrum carthusiensium domus nove lucis saluatoris prope traiectum inferius').

BIBLIOGRAPHY Cat. 1.34; *CMD-NL*, vol 2, pp. 183–4, no. 637.

SWEDEN

LUND

UNIVERSITETSBIBLIOTEKET

The Library was founded in 1666 and acquired its first important book and manuscript collection in 1670, when it was given the library of the Cathedral Chapter. This collection is now known as the Bibliotheca antiqua. Further acquisitions came from the libraries of former monasteries. Since 1698, the library has been a copyright library for Sweden.

1. MS Lund, Universitetsbiblioteket, 1 Plate 7
Arith. s. x 1/3

Parchment; i (modern paper) + 23 + xxiv (modern paper) fols (*Arith.* text disordered; according to Paulson, the codex was intact when it was bound in s. xv); page 215x210mm; fols 22–23 s. xi–xii: page 210x210mm; text 2 cols, each 170–80x65–70mm; 10–26 lines, varying to incorporate numerous schemata in text; several similar scribes. Greek, fol. 3vb, very confident. *Tituli* in red throughout. Binding: stamped black leather on wooden boards; one central clasp (restored). MS and binding restored in Stuttgart, 1964.
A beautiful copy, although heavily damaged.

CONTENTS Fols 1^{r}–23^{r} *Arith.*:
1ra–8vb I.32 'si vero sesquitertium' (70/15)–end of bk I; capitula list to bk II; II.1–8 'procreabuntur' (93/4);
9^{ra-vb} II.27–28 'ab his, inter quos'–'procreatos videbit' (117/14–120/1);
10ra–11vb II.34–39 'tetragoni'–'xxi' (132/1–136/26);
12ra–22vb II.45 'Quae medietates' (149/5)–end; fol 17 is a single figure pasted onto restorer's paper.

GLOSS Marginal and interlinear glosses in contemporary hands throughout.

DECORATION One major initial *S(uperioris)* in ink of text to begin bk II (fol. 1vb); smaller initials in ink of text to begin each chapter. Drawings and schemata very competently executed in red or ink of text.

PROVENANCE E. France. Andreas Riddermarck, professor of mathematics at Lund (d. 1707).

BIBLIOGRAPHY J. Paulson, *De fragmento Lundensi Boetii de institutione arithmetica librorum*, Acta Uniuersitatis Lundensis, xxi, Lund,

1884–5, pp. 1–30; P. Lehmann, 1937, p. 106; Pellegrin, 1954, pp. 28–9.

STOCKHOLM

KUNGLIGA BIBLIOTEKET (ROYAL LIBRARY)

The collection of medieval MSS is, for the most part, miscellaneous, built up from the spoils of war, purchases, and gifts dating from the sixteenth century onwards. The foundation collection, which dates back to the time of King Gustavus I (1535–60) and his sons Eric XIV and John II, included volumes taken from Swedish monasteries. Further enriched by Gustavus Adolphus (1595–1632) and his daughter Christina, the library lost books when Christina abdicated in 1654, taking her finest MSS with her to Italy; more dramatically, books were lost in the palace fire of 1697. The collection moved to its present premises in the late eighteenth century, since when it has been augmented by purchase and donation, the gifts of Gustavus III (king from 1771–92) and Sven Hedin being particularly important.

2. MS Stockholm, Kungliga Biblioteket, Va. 5
DCPhil., Vitae III, IV, I s. xi 2/3

Parchment; i + 57 fols (not foliated); page 284x190mm; text 182x101mm; 30 lines; two scribes, changing at fol. 57^{v}. *Titulus* (?s. xii), fol. i^{r}. Greek in text not very confident. Binding: badly damaged and partially restored medieval white leather on wood and pasteboard.
A clear s. xi library copy, which enjoyed a new lease of life at the end of the Middle Ages.

CONTENTS Fol. i^{v} s. xvi *probationes pennae*; 1^{r}–56^{r} ***DCPhil.***, *inc.* to bk IV imperf. 'sed summum bonum quod aeque bonis', IV.pr.ii.62; *lacunae*, IV.pr.iv.69–134 'ulterius mali ipsa impunitas' to 'iudicium excitare conantur' and IV.pr.vi.183–pr.vii.38 'faciantque saepe quae cum' to 'confiteri quare inquit'; 56^{r-v}, 57^{v} ***Vitae III, IV, I*** (Peiper, xxx, xxxii–iii); 57^{v} *sententiae*.

GLOSS Marginal glosses in scribe's hand in a series of triangle and lozenge shapes; gloss linked to text by letters; a series of contemporary glosses in another hand. Interlinear and marginal glosses in later ?s. xiv hands; gloss linked to text by pointing hands and NOTA signs.

DECORATION One diagram of concentric circles, illustrating *Providentia et punctum* (fol. 40^{v}); otherwise none.

PROVENANCE France. Probably in the collection of Paul Petau (d. 1614), fol. 1^{r}; whence to Queen Christina of Sweden.

BIBLIOGRAPHY Lehmann, 1938, pp. 162–3; Pellegrin, 1954, p. 11.

3. MS Stockholm, Kungliga Biblioteket, Va. 10
Top. Diff. IV 1465–68, 1485

Parchment; 245 + i (paper) fols; page 255x176mm; text 168x92mm (when only gloss, text is 2 cols, each 205x68mm); 24 lines (text); 58 lines (gloss); one scribe, Jean Poulain (M.A., Paris), writing in Laon between 1465 and 1468 (fols 98^{v}, 236^{v}) and in Paris, 1485 (fol. 236^{v}). Dated colophons, fols 52^{v}, 98^{v}, 157^{r}, 186^{v}, 236^{v}. Catchwords. Binding: s. xvi white leather on wood; two clasps (partially preserved).
A worthy, carefully executed volume.

CONTENTS Fols 2^{r}–99^{r} Cicero, *De inventione*, with marginal commentary by Marius Victorinus, Grillius and others; 96^{v}–98^{v} marginal gloss *De adtributis personae et negotio*; 99^{v}–236^{v} Ps.-Cicero, *Ad Herennium*, glossed; 236^{v}–245^{v} ***Top. Diff. IV.***

GLOSS See contents. Gloss linked to text by red paraph signs and underlining in red for fols 2^{r}–236^{v}. Broad margins left for gloss to Boethius, but not used. Scattered interlinear glosses and marginal rubrication.

DECORATION Plain red initials with occasional penwork flourishing.

PROVENANCE Laon and Paris. Belonged to Paul Petau (d. 1614): T. 35, fol. 2^{r}. Table of contents (fol. 1^{v}) by his son Alexander (d. 1672).

BIBLIOGRAPHY Halm, *Rhet. Lat. Min.* (1863), pp. 305–10; M. Wisén, *De scholiis rethoricis ad Herennium codice Holmiensi traditis*, Diss. Acad. Upsal, 1905, pp. 1–95; J. Martin, *Grillius. Ein Beitrag zur Geschichte der Rhetorik*, Paderborn, 1927, pp. xiii–xix; Pellegrin, 1954, pp. 12–13; Hedlund ii.33; Kristeller V.7b.

STRÄNGNÄS

DOMKYRKOBIBLIOTEKET

A small collection of MSS, mostly from the collection of Bishop Conrad Rogge (1480–1501), kept partly in a side chapel in the cathedral, partly in the museum in the Roggeborg.

H. Aminson, *Bibliotheca Templi Cathedralis Strengnesensis*, Stockholm, 1863.

4. MS Strängnäs, Domkyrkobiblioteket, F 309 (12)

DCPhil. s. xv

Paper; 470 fols; page 290x215mm; text (Boethius) 225x130mm; lines variable, c. 22.
A: dated 1353 'in die Agnetis virginis', fol. 9^v.
B: written by Birger Hamor, canon of Strängnäs, in Rostock and Leipzig, apparently over a period from 1436–1481 (colophons for each text).

CONTENTS A: fols 1^r–5^v *Expositio orationes dominicae*, *inc.* 'Sciendum quod hec oracio dominica super omnes oraciones factas'; 6^r–9^v *Salutatio angelica*, *inc.* 'Quoniam oracioni dominice communiter secundum ritum ecclesie'.
B: fols 10^r–78^v *Articulorum fidei expositio*, *inc.* 'Divino primitus invocato auxilio'; 79^r–84^v *Treatise on the Beatitudes*, *inc.* 'Beatitudines sunt habitus virtutum'; 85^{r-v} *De decimis*; 86^{r-v} biblical exempla; 87^r–171^v Conrad de Soltau, *Commentary on the Sentences*; 172^r–208^r *Expositio Decalogi*; 208^{r-v} Jerome, *Epistola ad Oceanum*; 209^r–214^v Ps.-Seneca (Martin of Braga), *Formula honestae vitae*; 214^v–20^v Jerome, *Epistolae ad Rusticum*, *ad nepociarum*; 221^r–90^r Johannes Calderinus, *Concordantia biblie ad decretum et ad decretales*; 291^r–306^v misc. notes on Boethius; 306^v–310^v Conrad Rogge, *Argumenta*; 311^r–370^v ***DCPhil.***, with gloss of Thomas Aquinas; 371^r–390^v Jacobus de Cessolis, *Tractatus de ludo scacorum*; 390^v–394^v Jerome, *Epistolae ad Eliodorum*, *ad Paulinum*; 394^v–395^v Seneca, alphabetised excerpts; 396^r–452^v Johannes de Mizna, *Tractatus de bono ordine moriendi*; 453^r–468^v biblical exempla; 469^r–70^v blank.

GLOSS See contents. Annotations by Conrad Rogge.

DECORATION A few simple initials in red; space left for initials not supplied.

PROVENANCE Donated by Birger Hamor in 1484, fol. 1^r. Johannes Matthias, bp of Strängnäs.

BIBLIOGRAPHY Aminson, pp. vi, vii, viii, ix, xi, xvi, xxi, xxvii, xxviii, xxxiii, xxxix, xliii, lii, liii, 106 (MSS F 309 and F min. 12); Kristeller V.16b.

UPPSALA

UNIVERSITETSBIBLIOTEKET

Although the University was founded in 1477, it was not until 1620 that it acquired the main body of the MSS it holds today, when King Gustavus Adolphus (1611–32) had the collections of the abbey of Vadstena (the richest source of medieval books written in Sweden), the Franciscan convent in Stockholm, and the

Dominicans of Sigtuna transferred there. Subsequent major benefactors included Magnus Gabriel De la Gardie, who was both Chancellor of the University and Chancellor of Sweden, and who presented the famous *Codex Argenteus* in 1669; and Ulrik Celsing (d. 1805), who left an important collection of Oriental MSS along with the library's other great treasure, the Goslar Gospels of Henry III. The collection moved to its present home in 1841.

M. Andersson-Schmitt, H. Hallberg and M. Hedlund, *Mittelalterliche Handschriften der Universitätsbibliothek Uppsala: C–Sammlung*, 7 vols, Stockholm, 1988–95 [= Andersson-Schmitt]; P. O. Kristeller, *Iter Italicum*, V.

5. MS Uppsala, Universitetsbiblioteket, C. 599
Div., De Int., Soph. Elench. 1481–6

Paper; i (parchment pastedown) + 304 fols; page 295x215mm; text 216x150mm (fols 2^{r}–25^{v}, 79^{r}–91^{r}, 98^{r}–120^{r}, 135^{r}–142^{v}, 214^{r}–266^{v} text 2 cols, each 254x80mm); 20–62 lines; three scribes: Olavus Johannis Guto, Olavus Thorstani, and an unidentified third. Dated colophons, fols 34^{v}, 36^{v}, 48^{v}, 77^{r}, 142^{v}, 213^{v}. Original binding: white leather on wood, two clasps (lost).

CONTENTS Fols 2ra–25va thirty questions on Thomas Maulevelt, *De suppositionibus*; 25vb–28^{v} three questions on Thomas Maulevelt and Marsilius of Inghen, *De ampliationibus*; 28^{v}–29^{v} two questions on Thomas Maulevelt and Albert the Great, *De restrictione*; 29^{v}–32^{v} four questions on Albert the Great, John Buridan, Marsilius of Inghen, *De appellationibus*; 32^{v}, 35^{v}–36^{v} five questions on Marsilius of Inghen, *De consequentiis*; 37^{v}–48^{v} ***Div.***; 49^{r}–78^{v} ***De Int.***, with marginal and interlinear gloss; 79ra–91ra twenty-one questions on *Prior Anal.* (fragment); 92^{r}–97^{r} Ps.-Aristotle, *Oeconomica*, with occasional interlinear gloss; 98ra–120rb thirty-three questions on *Post. Anal.*; 122^{r}–134^{v} twenty-seven questions on *Soph. Elench.*; 135ra–142vb Andreas Brusen, commentary on *Prior Anal.*; 143^{v} commentary on *Physics* bk I; 146^{r}–195^{r} *Post. Anal.*, with marginal and interlinear gloss; 195^{v}–213^{v} ***Soph. Elench.***, with occasional marginal and interlinear gloss; 214ra–266vb Petrus Olavi, commentary on *Soph. Elench.*; 268^{r}–305^{v} idem, *Exercitium sophistriae*.

GLOSS See contents.

DECORATION Initial in ink of text with penwork flourishing, fol. 2^{r}; ink-drawing of Albert the Great and Aristotle, fol. 143^{v}.

PROVENANCE Brought by Guto to the abbey of Vadstena (fol. 1^{r}: ?s. xvi).

BIBLIOGRAPHY *AL*, 1704; Kristeller V.20a; Andersson-Schmitt, 6, pp. 83–7.

6. MS Uppsala, Universitetsbiblioteket, C. 600

Logica vetus 1482–85

Paper; 222 fols; page 295x215mm; text 2 cols, each 240x75mm (fols 87^{r}–94^{v} text 230x150mm); 16–50 lines; at least four scribes, one of them Olavus Johannis Guto (his dated colophons, fol. 19^{v}). Other dated colophons, fols 68^{r}, 86^{v}, 133^{r}, 149^{v}, 185^{r}, 204^{r}. Original binding: white leather on wood; two clasps.

CONTENTS Fols 1ra–19vb Petrus Johannis Galle, commentary on *Isag.*; 20va–58ra commentary on *Cat.*; 58rb–69rb Petrus Olavi, commentary on *De Int.*; 70ra–86vb Petrus Johannis Galle, commentary on *De Int.*; 87^{r}–94^{v} ***De Int.***; 95^{r}–100vb commentary on *Soph. Elench.* (fragm.); 101ra–133rb Aristotle, *De anima*, with marginal and interlinear gloss; 133va–149vb *Parvulus philosophiae moralis*, with marginal and occasional interlinear gloss; 150ra–161vb ***Isag.***, with marginal and profuse interlinear gloss; 162ra–185ra commentary on *Isag.*, with occasional marginal gloss; 185rb–204ra ***Cat.***, with interlinear gloss and marginal commentary by Galle; 204rb–214rb *Liber sex principiorum*, with marginal gloss; 215ra–218ra commentary on *Cat.*

GLOSS See contents. Space left for gloss which is executed in scribes' or other contemporary hands.

DECORATION Simple initials in ink of text with occasional penwork flourishing; one diagram, fol. 20^{r}.

PROVENANCE Brought by Guto to the abbey of Vadstena (Cf. MS C.599).

BIBLIOGRAPHY *AL*, 1705; Kristeller V.20a–b; Andersson-Schmitt, 6, pp. 88–91.

7. MS Uppsala, Universitetsbiblioteket, C. 638

Prior Anal. s. xiii^{ex}

Parchment; 74 fols (some badly damaged); page 210x160mm; text 112x56mm; 27 lines, ruled with a stylus; ample margins for gloss; several very similar scribes. ?Original half-leather binding: the wooden boards are partially covered with white leather; one central metal clasp (possibly not original) on front cover.
A heavily used MS.

CONTENTS Fols 1^{r}–51^{v} ***Prior Anal.***; 52^{r}–74^{v} *Post. Anal.*

GLOSS Heavily glossed in the margins, particularly at the beginning of each work (*Post. Anal.* has received more glossing). Glosses added in a wide variety of s. xiv/xv 1/2 hands; all glossing hands very cursive and heavily abbreviated.

DECORATION One crudely executed initial (a later addition) in red with black penwork flourishing, fol. 1^{r}; plain initials in red. Superb s. xv calligraphic alphabet added, fol. 51^{v}, with splendidly executed animal and human heads emerging from each letter; red paraph signs.

PROVENANCE ?France (script).

BIBLIOGRAPHY *AL*, 1709; Kristeller V.21a; Andersson-Schmitt, 6, p. 188.

8. MS Uppsala, Universitsbiblioteket, C. 648

Isag., De Int., Cat. s. xiv 1/2

Parchment; 99 fols; page 185x135mm.
A (s. xiv 1/2): text 120x75mm; 22 lines ruled with ink; probably one scribe for text. Catchwords.
B (s. xiv 2/2): text 2 cols, each 147x48mm; 34 lines, ruled in ink; two scribes, changing at fol. 76^{v}.
C (s. xiii 2/2): text 145x110mm; 32 lines, ruled with a stylus; several scribes.

CONTENTS A: fols 1^{r}–12^{v} ***Isag.***; 12^{v}–23^{v} ***De Int.***; 23^{v}–42^{v} ***Cat.***; 43^{r-v} notes in a glossing hand (2 cols); 46^{r}–60^{v} *Liber sex principiorum.*
B: fols 61^{r}–88^{v} sermons.
C: fols 89^{r}–99^{v} sermons.

GLOSS A: systematic marginal and interlinear glosses in several s. xiv/xv hands to *De Int.*, *Cat.* and *Liber sex principiorum*; marginal glosses for *Isag.* on fols 1^{r}–2^{r} only.

DECORATION A: major initials in red and blue with penwork flourishing or line-drawn faces; red and blue paraph signs.

PROVENANCE France (script). A in Sweden by s. xiv 2/2, judging by the ‘gloss’ in Swedish, fol. 50^{v}.

BIBLIOGRAPHY *AL*, 1711; Kristeller V.21a; Andersson-Schmitt, 6, pp. 204–8.

9. MS Uppsala, Universitetsbiblioteket, C. 914

Vitae I–II, DCPhil., Epitaphs I–II 1364

Parchment; i + 71 fols; page 210x145mm; text 160–80x60mm; 30–32 lines; scribe for *DCPhil.*, Henricus Iohannis de Lopic filii (dated colophon, fol. 69^{r}). Modern binding.

CONTENTS fol. i^{r-v} ***Vitae I–II*** and other notes, *inc.* ‘O summum lapsorum solamen animorum Hec sunt verba boecii in principio 3^{i} de consolacione philosophie’; 1^{r}–68^{r} ***DCPhil.***; 69^{r} ***Epitaphs I–II***; 69^{v}–71^{r} verses and notes incl. Walther, 1456.

GLOSS Occasional contemporary marginal and interlinear glosses; systematic s. xv marginal and interlinear glosses to fols 1^{r}–20^{v}, thereafter intermittent.

DECORATION Ornamented initials in red and red-gold.

PROVENANCE Probably France; Johannes Catin (fols 69^{r-v}, 71^{r}: s. xv).

BIBLIOGRAPHY Pellegrin, 1955, p. 16; Hedlund I. 19; Andersson-Schmitt, 6, pp. 343–4.

10. MS Uppsala, Universitetsbiblioteket, C. 924

DCPhil., Epitaphs III, II s. xiv 2/2

Parchment; i (pastedown) + 165 (fol. 115 numbered twice) + i (pastedown) fols; page 210x160mm. Front and back pastedowns from the same handsome, square-notated s. xii^{ex}/xiii^{in} liturgical MS.
A: text 155x105mm; 31–32 lines; metres written in two columns; one scribe.
B: text 2 cols, each 130x50mm; 38 lines; one scribe.
C: text variable; lines variable; several scribes.
D: text 140x90mm; 35 lines; two scribes changing at fol. 133^{r}. Dated colophon in red, 1329, fol. 157^{v}.
Fine s. xv binding of white (now yellow) leather on thick wooden boards; one central metal clasp (partially preserved); parchment label on front cover, now illegible.
A well-worn compendium.

CONTENTS A: fols 1^{r}–40^{r} ***DCPhil.***; 40^{r} ***Epitaphs III, II*** (Peiper, pp. xxxvi, xxxviii); 40^{v} added note and diagram.
B: fols 41^{r}–67^{r} Albertus (?de Orlamünde), *Summa naturalium*, *inc.* 'Philosophia dividitur in tres partes videlicet in loycam ethicam et phisicam'; *expl.* 'et malum gracia dificiente. Explicit summa naturalium' (cf. *Traditio*, 23, 1967, p. 346).
C: fol. 68^{r} notes, *inc.* 'Non sis ore celer (*sic*) bona promittendo patenter ... Desiderium pueri deberet esse'; 68^{v}–73^{v} commentary on Martianus Capella, *De nuptiis* II.119–21; 74^{r-v} *In categorias Aristotelis*, *inc.* 'Non videtur secundum philosophum'; 75^{r}–76^{v} commentary on Aristotle, *De memoria et reminiscentia*, *inc.* 'Reliquorum autem primum considerandum'; 77^{r-v} Peter Helias, *Summa in Priscianum* (*Absoluta*) xvii, *inc.* imperf. 'dicendum ergo melius quod'; 78^{r}–79^{r} commentary on Aristotle, *De longitudine et brevitate vitae*; 79^{v}–80^{v} notes on logic, *inc.* 'queritur utrum ex obliquis posset fieri sillogismus'; 81^{r}–84^{v} *Questiones in Meteora Aristotelis* IV.2–3; 85^{r}–89^{r} *Questiones de anima*; 89^{v}–90^{r} *Sophismata*; 90^{v}–91^{v} misc. notes and verses, including *In librum Aristotelis de sensu et sensato*; 92^{r}–100^{v} excerpts from Isidore and Anselm; 101^{r}–108^{r} commentary on Ps. 17:5–18:1; 108^{v}–109^{r} *probationes pennae*.

D: fols 109^{v}–157^{v} Priscian, *Institutiones*, XVII–XVIII, with intermittent glosses; 158^{r}–164^{v} Ps.-Priscian, *De accentibus*, glossed.

GLOSS A: intermittent but quite heavy marginal and interlinear gloss to *DCPhil.*

DECORATION A: crude red or green initials; red paraph signs.
B: none.
C: one plain green initial, fol. 75^{r}.
D: red paraph signs.

PROVENANCE ?English (script).

BIBLIOGRAPHY Pellegrin, 1955, p. 28; Passalacqua, no. 621; Hedlund I. 17; Kristeller V. 22a; Andersson-Schmitt, 6, pp. 366–8.

SWITZERLAND

BASEL/BASLE

UNIVERSITÄTSBIBLIOTHEK (ÖFFENTLICHE BIBLIOTHEK DER UNIVERSITÄT)

The University itself was founded in 1459. Since the Reformation, the University Library has included the collections of the Basel Dominican convent, Carthusian monastery, Domstift and St Leonard's Abbey. Jakob Louber (1440–1513), M.A. and D.C.L., rector of the University (1476–77) and prior of the Carthusian monastery (1480–1500), compiled the first catalogue of the monastic library (now lost). Johannes Heynlin de (a) Lapide (1428–96), O. Carth., M.A. and D.Th., left to the monastery a number of books mostly purchased in Paris. The first systematic catalogues of the University Library were compiled by the librarians Conrad Pfister (1623–36) and Johann Zwinger (1662–96).

G. Binz, *Die deutschen Handschriften der Oeffentlichen Bibliothek der Universität Basel. Die Handschriften der Abteilung A*, Basel, 1907; K. Escher, *Die Miniaturen in den Basler Bibliotheken, Museen und Archiven*, Basel, 1917; Ph. Schmidt, 'Die Bibliothek des ehemaligen Dominikanerklosters in Basel', *Basler Zeitschrift für Geschichte und Altertumskunde*, 18, 1919, pp. 160–254; G. Morin, 'A travers les manuscripts de Bâle. Notices et extraits des plus anciens manuscripts latins', *Basler Zeitschrift für Geschichte und Altertumkunde*, 26, 1927, pp. 175–249; C. Roth, 'Conrad Pfister, Basilius Iselin und die Amerbachische Bibliothek', *Festschrift Gustav Binz*, Basel, 1935, pp. 179–200; M. Burckhardt, 'Aus dem Umkreis der ersten Basler Universitätsbibliothek', *Basler Zeitschrift für Geschichte und Altertumskunde*, 58–9, 1959, pp. 155–80; A. Walz, 'Dominikaner an der jungen Universität Basel (1460–1515)', *Basler Zeitschrift für Geschichte und Altertums-kunde*, 58–9, 1959, pp. 139–53; Bruckner, X, pp. 81–94; G. Meyer, M. Burckhardt and M. Steinmann (vol. III), *Die mittelalterlichen Handschriften der Universitäts-bibliothek Basel. Abteilung B. Theologische Pergamenthandschriften*, 3 vols, Basel, 1960–75; B. Hughes, OFM, *Medieval Mathematical Writings in the University Library Basel, a Provisional Catalogue* (39 MSS), typescript, Northridge, CA, 1972; Scarpatetti, vol. I; M. Steinmann, *Die Handschriften der Universitäts-bibliothek Basel. Register zu den Abteilungen A.I–A.X und O*, Basle, 1982; idem, *Die Handschriften der Universitätsbibliothek Basel. Uebersicht über die Bestände und deren Erschliessung*, 2nd edn, Basel, 1987; Kristeller, V, pp. 40–87; Senser, pp. 53–8. The historic divisions of the collection are: A theology (paper), B theology (parchment), C jurisprudence, D medicine, E history, F liberal arts and philosophy, O includes the Faesch collection, AN masterpieces.

1. MS Basel, Universitätsbibliothek, A. VI. 24
Op. Sac. I–III, V s. xv 2/4

Paper; 270 fols; page 290x202mm; text 190–200x123mm; 26–32 lines; several scribes. Greek very clear. Leather tags to mark new texts. Original stamped brown leather binding with two clasps (lost); chain-mark on front cover.
Planned as a single volume, or at least bound immediately as such.

CONTENTS Fols 1ʳ–21ʳ ***Op. Sac. III, I, II, V***; fol. 21ʳ (added) definitions of Greek terms: *hypostasis, prosopon, ousia*; 22ʳ–113ʳ Gilbert of Poitiers, commentary on *Op. Sac.*; 114ʳ–125ʳ Thomas Aquinas, *De rationibus fidei*; 126ʳ–136ʳ Nicholas of Amiens, *Ars fidei catholicae* (*PL*, 210: 595–618), here attributed to Alan of Lille; 138ʳ–160ʳ Alan of Lille, *Regulae celestis iuris* (*PL*, 210: 621–80); 160ʳ Ps.-Aristotle, *De pomo*; 160ʳ Walther, 7015; 162ʳ–270ʳ Peter John Olivi, *Expositio super Dionysii 'De angelica hierarchia'*, *expl.* imperf. 'immo fere totaliter tollunt penarum dampnacionis eorum. Et certe diabolus in predictis satis' (this MS not listed in Glorieux, *Théologie*).

GLOSS See contents.

DECORATION ***P(ostulans)***, with portrait of king, fols. 1ʳ, 22ʳ. Very crude red initials.

PROVENANCE Basel Dominican convent (Schmidt, no. 74).

BIBLIOGRAPHY O. Holder-Egger, 'Italienische Prophetien des 13. Jahrhunderts', *Neues Archiv der Gesellschaft für ältere deutsche Geschichtskunde*, 33, 1908, pp. 118–29 (on Walther, 7015; this MS not listed); P. C. Balic, OFM, 'De auctore operis quod "Ars fidei catholicae" inscribitur', *Mélanges J. de Ghellinck*, Gembloux, 1951, II, pp. 793–814 (Nicholas of Amiens); Dondaine and Shooner, I, p. 67, no. 177; N. Häring, 'Texts Concerning Gilbert of Poitiers', *Archives d'histoire doctrinale et littéraire du Moyen Age*, 37, 1970, pp. 193–4; Häring, no. 15; N. Häring, 'Magister Alanus de Insulis, Regulae caelestis iuris', *Archives d'histoire doctrinale et littéraire du Moyen Age*, 48, 1981, p. 105, no. 4; Steinmann, *Register*, pp. 21, 337, 382–3.

2. MS Basel, Universitätsbibliothek, F. I. 1
Logica vetus et nova s. xiv^{in}

Parchment; ii + 281 fols; page 346x222mm; text 2 cols, each 153x42mm; 31 lines; very wide margin for gloss; one good scribe. Catchwords. White leather binding on wood with two clasps (lost). Parchment label on spine OMNES LIBRI LOGICE ARISTOTELIS.
A spectacular MS of its kind.

CONTENTS Fols 1ra–10rb ***Isag.***; 10va–27vb ***Cat.,*** with gloss of Albert the Great; 28ra–38va ***De Int.*** (in two sections: fol. 32rb II begins at 'Quoniam autem est de aliquo' [9/11]); 39ra–47vb *Liber sex principiorum*; 48ra–59rb ***Div.***; 59va–89rb ***Top. Diff.***; 90ra–167^{v} ***Topica Aris.***; 168ra–192va ***Soph. Elench.***; 193va–246^{r} ***Prior Anal.***; 247ra–279^{v} *Post. Anal.* with Aquinas's commentary.

GLOSS See contents. A few users' notes throughout.

DECORATION High quality French initial, with half border in blue, red, white, gold, fol. 1^{r}. Minor initials in red or blue with contrasting penwork flourishing to begin each book and chapter; blue and red paraph signs. Splendid personified schema of INCONSTANS CONIUGATIO IN SECUNDA FIGURA (fol. 217^{r}).

PROVENANCE Basel Carthusian house (fol. 1^{r}: s. xvi). Erased older note 'solui parisius tres florenos auri', fol. 279^{v}.

BIBLIOGRAPHY Escher, no. 75, pp. 66–7, pl. XVIII.3; *AL*, 1122; Dondaine and Shooner, I, p. 75, no. 198; W. Fauser, S.J., 'Albertus Magnus-Handschriften. 2 Fortsetzung', *Bullétin de Philosophie Médiévale*, 25, 1983, p. 100; Kristeller, V, p. 65; Lohr, *AH*, pp. 30–31.

3. MS Basel, Universitätsbibliothek, F. I. 5

Logica vetus et nova 1463

Parchment and paper; 487 fols (fols 4^{r}–88^{v}, 99^{r}–147^{v} and 257^{r}–348^{v} parchment); page 290x205mm; text 157x94mm; 21–22 lines; wide margins for gloss; two scribes, changing at fol. 433^{r}. Dated colophon, fol. 482^{r}. Binding of modern wood with original dark leather spine, two clasps (lost).
A spectacular MS of its kind.

CONTENTS Fols 4^{r}–27^{v} ***Isag.***; 27^{v}–69^{v} ***Cat.***; 69^{v}–95^{v} ***De Int.***; 95^{v}–117^{r} *Liber sex principiorum*; 117^{r}–146^{v} ***Div.***; 148^{r}–247^{v} ***Prior Anal.***; 257^{r}–344^{r} *Post. Anal.*, with commentary of Albert the Great; 349^{r}–432^{v} ***Topica Aris.***; 433^{r}–482^{r} ***Soph. Elench.***

GLOSS A few sporadic glosses.

DECORATION Red initials to *Isag.* and *Post. Anal.*

PROVENANCE Basel Carthusian house: fol. 1^{r}.

BIBLIOGRAPHY *AL*, 1125; Scarpatetti, I, p. 171, no. 476, figs 434 and 435 (fols 366^{r}, 482^{r}); Kristeller, V, p. 65; Lohr, *AH*, pp. 33–4.

4. MS Basel, Universitätsbibliothek, F. I. 25
Logica nova s. xiii 1/4

Parchment; i + 120 fols; page 282x200mm; text 2 cols, each 174x58mm; 32 lines; one scribe. Book numbers as running headers. Leather tags mark each new text. Binding: white leather on wood, two clasps (lost). Label upper centre back TEXTUS TOPICORUM ELENCHORUM PRIORUM ET POSTERIORUM ARISTOTELIS.
A rather luxurious manuscript, with good miniatures; illumination as for glossed Bibles.

CONTENTS Fols 1ra–45vb ***Topica Aris.***; 46ra–61vb ***Soph. Elench.***; 62ra–97rb ***Prior Anal.***; 97^{v} commentary on *Post. Anal.*; 98ra–120rb *Post. Anal.*

GLOSS Quite extensive s. xv cursive gloss to *Topica Aris. I–IV*, and to *Soph. Elench.*, mainly bk 1. Scattered glosses to *Prior Anal. I* and the beginning of *Post. Anal.* in another hand.

DECORATION ***P****(ropositum)* excised (fol. 1^{r}); minor initials with gold, e.g., rabbit (fol. 46ra), bird (fol. 62ra). Initials excised, fols 38va, 46ra and 62ra. Red or blue minor initials with contrasting penwork flourishing.

PROVENANCE France. Belonged to Basel Dominican convent (Schmidt, no. 428).

BIBLIOGRAPHY Escher, p. 64, no. 69; *AL*, 1128; Kristeller, V, p. 65; Lohr, *AH*, p. 42.

5. MS Basel, Universitätsbibliothek, F. III. 5
DCPhil. s. xv

Paper; i + 111 + i fols; page 285x207mm; text 155x87–106mm; 14–19 lines; fols 1^{r}–2^{r} two cols, thereafter long lines; ruled for gloss; one scribe for text. Binding: s. xix.

CONTENTS Fols 1ra–2rb ***DCPhil.*** with commentary *inc.* ‘Scribitur per philosophum primo de anima quod intellectus in prima sui creacione est tanquam tabula rasa’ (*DCPhil.* begins fol. 2va); 111^{v} brief subject index.

GLOSS Intercalated commentary on a massive scale; running interlinear gloss throughout.

DECORATION Crude grotesque ***C****(armina)*, fol. 2^{v}. Similar initial at ***H****(aec)*: one-legged man fighting a dragon, fol. 65^{v}. Simple red initials crudely executed, fols 1^{r}, 35^{v}. Red strokes as paraph signs within gloss and at beginning of each line of verse.

PROVENANCE Unknown. At the University Library by s. xvii (fol. 1^{r}: title in the hand of Conrad Pfister).

BIBLIOGRAPHY None.

6. MS Basel, Universitätsbibliothek, F. III. 14
DCPhil. 1473/77

Paper; v + 284 fols; fol. 141 missing; page 285x215mm.
A: text 180–95x110mm; 17 lines; wide right-hand margin; scribe Jakob Louber. Dated colophons, fols 123^{v}, 124^{r}. Book numbers (1–4) as running headers. Paper tags mark each new text.
Smart stamped binding, with roses, now in very poor condition; two clasps (lost).

CONTENTS A: fols 1^{v}–124^{r} ***DCPhil.*** with commentary, *inc.* 'Notandum Philosophie oportet servire Seneca epistola viii ad Lucillum quia philosophia trahit hominem ab obscuritate ignorancie a tenebris stulticie ad lucem sapientie et ad claritatem' (*DCPhil.* begins fol. 2^{r}).
B: fols 130^{r}–240^{v} Roderick of Zamora, *Speculum humane vite*, incunable: Beromünster, 1472 (Hain, 13941).
C: fols 241^{r}–260^{v} *Ars metrica, inc.* 'Tota ars metrica plenissime adquiritur si hec duo dumtaxat noverimus, metrum et eius principia'; 261^{r}–262^{r} Petrarch, *Letter to Guibert of Parma* (ed. V. Rossi, *Opere*, Florence, 1934, pp. 133–6); 262^{r-v} *Quantitates vocabulorum quibus fit saepe abusio, inc.* 'Nota quantitates cunctorum vocabulorum'; 264^{r}–277^{v} Horace, *Ars poetica* vv. 1–204, with gloss.

GLOSS A: see contents. Extensive marginal and interlinear gloss throughout.
B: marginal glosses by Jakob Louber (fol. 222^{r}).

DECORATION Basic red initials. Red paraph signs and underlining to lemmata.

PROVENANCE Basel Carthusian house (fol. 1^{r}). Belonged to Jakob Louber (fols 1^{r}, 123^{v}).

BIBLIOGRAPHY Bruckner, X, p. 90 (Louber); Burckhardt, p. 177; Scarpatetti, I, p. 181, no. 503 (Louber MSS, pp. 261–2, figs 505, 506); Kristeller, V, p. 50.

7. MS Basel, Universitätsbibliothek, F. IV. 16
Logica vetus s. xiii 1/2

Parchment; i + 107 + i fols; page 155x104mm; text 110x62mm; 27–37 lines; a great variety of broadly similar hands, some very small. Later additions fols 74–83 and 100–107. Binding: s. xv white leather on wood, painted diamond criss-cross; formerly a large rectangular label upper front cover exterior; single clasp (lost). Several little octavo booklets, with common rubrication. Pocket-sized collection of poor quality.

CONTENTS Fol. i^{r} contents list; 1^{v}–4^{r} ***Isag.***; 5^{r}–24^{r} ***Cat.***; 24^{r}–33^{v} ***De Int.***; 34^{r}–41^{r} ***Div.***; 41^{v}–58^{v} ***Syll. Cat.***; 58^{v}–80^{r} ***Syll. Hyp.*** (74–83 s. xv^{in} replacement: fols 81–83 blank); 84^{r}–99^{r} ***Top. Diff.***, lacks beginning of bk III; text uncertain, possibly abridged, fols 95^{v}–99^{r}. Bk IV added in s. xv 1/2 cursive (?Johannes de Lapide).

GLOSS Intermittent, not systematic.

DECORATION Reasonable major initials in red acanthus outline, fols 1^{v}, 15^{r}, 22^{r}, 24^{r}, 34^{r}, 41^{v}, 58^{v}, 84^{r}. Odd schemata and doodles in red and black, fol. 2^{v}.

PROVENANCE France. Belonged to Basel Carthusian house. Final assembly by Johannes Heynlin de Lapide, who perhaps wrote the s. xv pages (fols 100^{r}–107^{v}), and from whom it passed to Jakob Louber (fol. i^{r}).

BIBLIOGRAPHY *AL*, 1147; Bruckner, X, pp. 89–90, and Scarpatetti, I, pp. 264–5 (Johannes de Lapide); Kristeller, V, p. 68; Lohr, *AH*, pp. 68–9.

8. MS Basel, Universitätsbibliothek, F. VI. 13
Logica vetus s. xv

Paper; 237 fols; page 219x149mm.
B: text 150x74mm; 25 lines, ruled for gloss; same text hand throughout B. Paper tags mark each new text; blank folio left between texts.
Binding: bevelled wooden boards with central clasp (lost); spine roughly covered in thick white leather; label along spine s. xv TEXTUS UETERIS ARTIS CUM QUESTIONIBUS.

CONTENTS A: fols 3^{r}–169^{r} Master John Rucherat of Wesel, commentary on *Logica vetus* (1466); 169^{v}–171^{v} note on logic, *inc.* 'Utrum loyca que est pars philosophie consideret de vocibus'; *expl.* 'sciencia specialis et ab alijs distincta'; 172^{r} schema of *vox*, *scriptum*, *res*; 172^{v} schema of art and its parts.
B: fols 174^{r}–186^{r} ***Isag.***; 187^{r}–208^{v} ***Cat.***; 210^{r}–224^{r} ***De Int.***; 225^{r}–234^{v} *Liber sex principiorum*, *expl.* imperf. vi.71 'armatus et calciatus est' (52/3); 234^{v} erased date.

GLOSS Added in another hand very extensively to *Isag.* and *Cat.* until fol. 197^{r}; thereafter none.

DECORATION Basic red initials, and rubrication. Text occasionally touched in red.

PROVENANCE Basel Carthusian house. Belonged to Jakob Louber (fol. 1^{r}).

BIBLIOGRAPHY Burckhardt, p. 172; Lohr, IV, p. 276, no. 1; von Scarpatetti, I, p. 196, no. 549; Kristeller, V, p. 70; Lohr, *AH*, 97–8.

9. MS Basel, Universitätsbibliothek, F. VI. 59

DCPhil., Op. Sac. 1476, 1478

Paper; 243 fols; fols 36–51 are a separate MS, after which the original MS resumes; page 212x144mm; text 155x75–95mm; 20–32 lines; scribe Heinrich Karst of Bacharach. Dated colophons, fols 217^{r} and 223^{v}; colophons, fols 40^{v}, 222^{v}. Paper tags mark each new text. Binding: stamped leather on boards; one central clasp (lost); label along spine.
Rather carelessly executed.

CONTENTS Fols 1^{r}–4^{r} *Expositio de canone missae*; 4^{v}–10^{v} Ps.-Seneca (Martin of Braga), *Formula honestae vitae*, *inc.* 'Quatuor virtutum species'; *expl.* 'deficientem puniat ignaviam' with gloss; 11^{r}–13^{v} Ps.-Seneca, *De remediis fortuitorum*; 14^{r}–35^{v} Augustine of Dacia, *Elegantiolae* (*GW*, 8032); 36^{r}–40^{v} *De nominibus latinis*, *inc.* 'Notandum primo circa nomen proprium', referring to Peter Helias, Everard of Bethune and *moriste*; 40^{v}–41^{v} Oration in praise of four Basel masters, 1474; 42^{r}–51^{v} treatise on verbs, *inc.* 'Queritur utrum quilibet infinitivus verbi personalis sit verbum personale vel inpersonale'; 52^{r}–54^{r} Albertus Nichtman, *Tractatus metricus de prosodia* (Walther, 430); 54^{v}–57^{v} Bede, *De die iudicii* (*CCSL*, 122: 439–44); 60^{r}–62^{v} Donatus, *Ars grammatica* I, *expl.* imperf. I.4 'cola et comma' (*GL*, 4, p. 372, line 23); 62^{v}–66^{v} idem, *Ars grammatica* III (*GL*, 4, pp. 392–402); 66^{v} *De vitiis in metrificando occurrentibus*; 67^{r}–71^{v} missing; 72^{r}–76^{v} Ps.-Priscian, *De accentibus* (*GL*, 3, pp. 519–28); 77^{r-v} Isidore, *Etymologiae* i.27, *expl.* imperf. (*PL*, 82: 101–4A); 97^{r}–124^{r} Ps.-Boethius, *De disciplina scolarium* (not listed in Weijers); 124^{v} *Rota ventorum*; 125^{r}–217^{r} ***DCPhil.***, with commentary (*DCPhil.* begins fol. 126^{r}); 218^{r}–226^{v} ***Op. Sac. I–III***; 226^{v}–28^{r} Gundissalinus, *De unitate et uno*; 228^{v}–242^{r} ***Op. Sac. IV–V***, run together, with lacuna at fol. 232^{r}: 'subsistit nunc et regitur'–'ceteris amplius afferebam' (IV.266–V.27).

GLOSS Extensive intercalated and interlinear gloss to *DCPhil.* in contemporary hand. Use of red to link gloss with text.

DECORATION Simple red initials with occasional infill for *DCPhil.* bks I–IV only (fols 126^{r}, 139^{v}, 156^{v}, 180^{r}).

PROVENANCE Basel Carthusian house (front flyleaf).

BIBLIOGRAPHY Scarpatetti, I, p. 201, no. 560, fig. 563, and p. 259 (scribe);

Bursill-Hall, pp. 3031; G. Ballaira, *Per il catalogo dei codici di Prisciano*, Turin, 1982, pp. 28–33, no. 7; Kristeller, V, p. 51.

10. MS Basel, Universitätsbibliothek, F. VI. 63
Prior Anal., Soph. Elench. 1464

Paper; 106 fols; page 225x155mm; text 150x85mm; 19–23 lines, frame-ruled for gloss; one scribe. *Tituli* in red. Colophon, underlined in red, 'Explicit liber priorum Aristotelis anno mcccc lxiiij^{o}' (fol. 74^{r}). Binding: s. xv stamped white leather on wood; one central clasp.

CONTENTS Fols 1^{r}–74^{r} ***Prior Anal.***; 74^{v}–75^{v} blank; 76^{r}–106^{r} ***Soph. Elench.***

GLOSS Interlinear and marginal gloss to *Prior Anal.*; first words of each gloss underlined to link up gloss with text. *Soph. Elench.* less glossed and this linkage technique not used.

DECORATION Basic red strokes and paraph signs to *Soph. Elench.* only. Diagram: circle divided into four by intersecting lines (fol. 30^{v}).

PROVENANCE Basel University (front cover).

BIBLIOGRAPHY Burckhardt, p. 161, no. 3; Scarpatetti, I, p. 203, no. 564, fig. 443 (fol. 15^{r}); Kristeller, V, p. 51; Lohr, *AH*, p. 114.

11. MS Basel, Universitätsbibliothek, F. IX. 10
Logica vetus et nova 1504

Paper; iii + 251 fols; page 195x135mm; text 135x85mm; 27–34 lines; scribe Basilius Amerbach. Dated colophons, fols 191^{v}, 201^{r}. Binding: s. xvi stamped brown leather on pasteboard, with figures of SS Peter and Paul under a double arcade; spine defective; four pairs of leather tags (the lower ones lost).

CONTENTS Fols 1^{r}–7^{v} *Commentum in veterem et novam logicam*, *inc.* 'Antiquorum vestigia imitantes ad illuminandas quodammodo acies intellectus'; *expl.* 'ut est subiectum sciencie topicalis et ut est subiectum totius Logices'; 8^{r-v} blank; 9^{r}–35^{r} ***Isag.***; 36^{r}–56^{v} ***Cat.***; 57^{r}–64^{v} blank; 65^{r}–118^{r} ***De Int.***; 118^{v}–119^{v} blank; 120^{r}–191^{v} *Post. Anal.*; 192^{r}–201^{r} ***Soph. Elench.***; 201^{v}–219^{v} blank; 220^{r}–246^{r} note on Aristotle, *Physica*, *inc.* 'Circa librum phisicorum Aristotelis Ut dicit commentator Averrois In suo prologo more glossatorum antiquorum'; *expl.* 'Contra opinionem Platonis que est extranea in philosophia naturali'; 247^{r}–251^{v} blank.

GLOSS Blank folios left for commentary between each work.

DECORATION Major initials in red and blue, fols 1^{r}, 9^{r}; thereafter occasional initial letters decorated in red. Initial words in capitals in ink of text. Text framed in red and purple.

PROVENANCE Belonged to Basilius Amerbach (front flyleaf and fol. 1^r^); written in 1504 in Paris, where he attended Jean Raulin's lectures on Aristotle's logic.

BIBLIOGRAPHY *Amerbachkorrespondenz*, ed. A. Hartmann, Basel, 1942, vol. 1, p. 206, no. 217; Scarpatetti, I, p. 215, no. 593, fig. 622 (fol. 199^v^); Lohr, *AH*, 145–6.

12. MS Basel, Universitätsbibliothek, O. II. 24
Op. Sac. I–III, V s. xii 3/4

Parchment; 164 fols; page 258x166mm; text 155x115mm; 14 lines for text, 27 for commentary; one scribe throughout. Modern binding.

CONTENTS Fols 1^r^–12^v^ Hilary of Poitiers, *De trinitate*; 13^r^ Hugh Etherian, *De differentia naturae et personae*, prologue (ed. N. Häring, 'The "Liber de Differentia Nature and Personae" by Hugh Etherian and the Letters Addressed to Him by Peter of Vienna and Hugh of Honau', *Mediaeval Studies*, 24, 1962, pp. 1–34 [16]); 13^v^–157^v^ ***Op. Sac. I–III, V***, with commentary of Gilbert of Poitiers; 158^r^–160^r^ John Damascene, *De trinitate* (excerpts); 160^v^–161^v^ Jerome, *De fide* (excerpts); 161^v^–164^r^ Ambrose, *De fide* (excerpts), with some glosses.

GLOSS See contents. Lemmata underlined in red (commentary); red subject markers in text.

DECORATION Lavish illumination with gold and red border, remarkably at fols 20^v^–21^r^, where illumination in text is repeated in commentary. Six figural compositions, one to begin each book: ***L****(ibros)*, Gilbert with gold halo teaching two supplicants (fol. 14^r^); ***O****(mnium)*, Christ sitting on a silver moon surrounded by stars (fol. 15^v^); ***I****(nvestigatam)*, saintly figure (?Boethius) holding book pointing upwards with right hand (fol. 17^v^); ***Q****(uod)*, seated figure of Philosophia and long bird/dragon forming letter stem (fol. 70^v^); miniature of Gilbert writing (fol. 92^v^); ***A****(nxie)*, ?Gilbert in thinking posture (fol. 93^v^). Other minor decoration.

PROVENANCE Probably produced in the scriptorium of the Marbach monastery (Reinhardt) and belonged to the Canons Regular from the region (Häring). Since the 1660s in the collection of Remigius Faesch (1595–1667), a jurist with a Raritätenkabinett.

BIBLIOGRAPHY Escher, pp. 46–7, no. 39, pl. XIII; N. Häring, 'Texts Concerning Gilbert of Poitiers', *Archives d'histoire doctrinale et littéraire du*

Moyen Age, 37, 1970, pp. 183–4, 193; H. Reinhardt, 'Eine Handschrift des 12. Jahrhunderts in der Basler Universitätsbibliothek, die Buchmalerei des elsässischen Klosters Marbach und eine Scheibe aus dem Strassburger Münster', *Basler Zeitschrift für Geschichte und Altertumskunde*, 77, 1977, pp. 5–21; Häring, no. 16; Bolton, in Gibson, p. 433; Steinmann, *Register*, pp. 30, 382–3.

13. MS Basel, Universitätsbibliothek, A. N. III. 18
Arith. s. xii 1/2

Parchment; ii + 52 + ii fols (damaged beginning and end); page 236x166mm; text 190x115mm; 31 lines; ?several scribes. Binding: s. xviii leather.

CONTENTS Fols 1r–51r ***Arith.***, missing I.32 'ita ut'–II.1 'anima' (68/24–77/13: fols 19v–20r); 51v–52v *Saltus Gerberti*, *expl.* imperf. 'sicut ordinata fuerit a principio' (Bubnov, p. 35, lines 15–16; MS not listed in Bubnov).

GLOSS Clear, extensive, contemporary and systematic for fols 1v–2r; otherwise none.

DECORATION ***I****(n)*, red and green with lion mask and foliage twisting round ladder, damaged (fol. 1r); ***I****(nter)* (dragons and acrobat) in red, green and buff (fol. 2r). Minor initials in red, green or buff. Some leaf decoration in contrasting colour, plentiful and competently executed, as are the diagrams. Incipits, explicits and subheadings in red.

PROVENANCE S. Germany (script) or England (initials: Escher). Marcus Meibomius of Tonning, N. Schleswig (fol. 1r). From the library of John Wernher Huber (1700–1755), sold in Basel, 1 November 1789, sale catalogue, no. 26, p. 26 (fol. iiv).

BIBLIOGRAPHY Escher, p. 47, no. 40, pl. X.2; Masi, p. 58.

14. MS Basel, Universitätsbibliothek, A. N. III. 19
Arith. s. x

Parchment; ii + 65 + ii fols; fols 19r–v, 63r–v are single-leaf inserts; page 220x178mm; text 2 cols, each 175–85x70mm; 29 lines; perhaps the same scribe writing a clear, serviceable, not very elegant, script throughout. *Capitula* for both books. Binding: s. xviii leather.

CONTENTS Fols 1ra–65rb ***Arith.***; fol. 19v *Saltus Gerberti*, *expl.* imperf. 'unde venerunt' (Bubnov, p. 33, line 10; MS not listed in Bubnov).

GLOSS Some formal annotation, s. x^{ex}.

DECORATION Minor initials in orange-red or ink of text. Orange-red rubrication; some touching in green; chapter headings in orange-red.

PROVENANCE John Wernher Huber: sale catalogue, Basel, 1 November 1789, p. 18, no. 25.

BIBLIOGRAPHY Masi, p. 58.

BERN/BERNE

BURGERBIBLIOTHEK

The largest number of MSS comes from the collection of the French diplomat and scholar, Jacques Bongars (1554–1612), whose heir, Jakob Graviseth, presented his library of about five hundred manuscripts to the city of Bern in 1632.

H. Hagen, *Catalogus Codicum Bernensium (Bibliotheca Bongarsiana)*, Bern, 1875, repr. Hildesheim, 1974; *Bibliotheca Bernensis-Bongarsiana 1632–1932*, ed. H. Bloesch, Bern, 1932; *Schätze der Burgerbibliothek Bern*, ed. by the Burgerbibliothek, Bern, 1953; O. Homburger, *Die illustrierten Handschriften der Burgerbibliothek Bern. Die vorkarolingischen und karolingischen Handschriften*, Bern, 1962; Scarpatetti, II, pp. 5–33; Kristeller, V, pp. 87–94; Senser, pp. 66–71.

15. MS Bern, Burgerbibliothek, A. 91. 14
Arith. II s. xii

Parchment; 4 fols (now out of order 1, 3, 4, 2); page 222x150mm; 31 lines; one scribe. Discarded leaves re-used as end leaves c. 1200 and now detached.

CONTENTS Fol. 1^{r-v} ***Arith.*** II.31 'variabilis motus'–II.32 'permanere putat individuum inconiunctumque' (123/4–126/4–5);
2^{r-v} ***Arith.*** II.34 'ad eundem ordinem'–II.37 'ad primas secundasque proporciones' (131/21–134/17);
3^{r-v} ***Arith.*** II.27 'Ergo si ab unitate'–II.28 'senarius scilicet fit ex tribus' (116/18–119/24);
4^{r-v} ***Arith.*** II.40 'modo continentiam'–II.41 'nunc vero' (137/15–139/24).

GLOSS None.

DECORATION None.

PROVENANCE St Martin, Sées, S.E. Normandy (fol. 4^{v}: s. xii–xiii).

BIBLIOGRAPHY Hagen, pp. 120–21.

16. MS Bern, Burgerbibliothek, A. 94. 11
Mus. I s. xiii

Parchment; the central bifolium of a quire; page 234x168mm; text 2 cols, each 160x48mm; 39 lines, frame-ruled for gloss; one scribe. *Titulus*, fol. 2rb. Unbound.

CONTENTS Fols 1ra–2rb ***Mus.*** I.23 'generibus proportiones' (178/9)–end; 2^{rb-vb} ***Mus.*** I.1, *expl.* imperf. 'mediocribus quamquam' (180/1–181/7).

GLOSS None.

DECORATION Red and blue initial with penwork flourishing (fol. 2rb). Extensive red and blue rubrication; incipits and explicits in red.

PROVENANCE Unknown; ?Normandy (Bower). Formerly part of MS Paris, BnF, lat. 16652 (= Sorbonne 909).

BIBLIOGRAPHY Hagen, p. 140; Bower, no. 7.

17. MS Bern, Burgerbibliothek, 179
Vitae I, III–IV, DCPhil. s. ix 2/2

Parchment; i + 64 + i fols; page 310x227mm; text 232x125mm; 23 lines; one scribe for *DCPhil. Tituli* in rustic caps throughout. Greek letters identify speakers. Neumes for I.m.ii.2–8 (fol. 3^{r}). Binding: white parchment on wood.

CONTENTS Fol. 1^{r} ***Vitae I, III–IV*** (as gloss to the *titulus*); 1^{v}–63^{v} ***DCPhil.***; 64^{r-v} Priscian, *Partitiones* (*GL*, 3, pp. 459–61), glossed.

GLOSS Exuberant gloss to fols 1^{r}–33^{r}, abridged commentary of Remigius of Auxerre (Courcelle); several layers, with elaborate reference signs. Very little for rest of text except at the beginning of bk V (fols 52^{v}–55^{r}). Notes within text in scribe's hand: III.pr.i (fol. 22^{v}).

DECORATION Quite elaborate ink-drawn initial, with orange-red infill ***C****(armina)*, fol. 1^{v}. Poor s. ix drawing of a scribe writing (fol. 33^{r}). Black initial with upright and leaf terminals filled in partly with red and yellow (fol. 52^{v}). Minor initials plain orange-red (if coloured at all), used erratically, sometimes to start a prose or metre, sometimes at the beginning of each line of a metrum; but almost as often the text runs straight on, some metres being written as prose. Occasional pale yellow infill (fol. 16^{r}).

PROVENANCE ?Brittany. At Fleury by s. xi (s. xi note mentions 'Isemberdis,

Frater Hisembertis', monks from Fleury: fol. 1r). German names in margin of fol. 61v: Rascho Trudo Indeo. In s. xvi belonged to Pierre Daniel, scholar and humanist from Orleans, whence to Jacques Bongars.

BIBLIOGRAPHY Hagen, p. 239; Manitius, I, p. 34; Naumann, pp. X and 9; Karl and Faber, auction catalogue, XI, 7th May 1935, pl. IV, pp. 6–7; Courcelle II, pp. 12 and 122; C. Jeudy, 'L'Enseignement grammatical de Rémi d'Auxerre', *Ecole des Chartes: Positions des thèses*, 1961, p. 51; Homburger, pp. 130–32, fig. 137 (fol. 33r); Courcelle, p. 406; Bischoff, 'Caritas-Lieder', *Mittelalterliche Studien*, II, p. 71; Passalacqua, no. 42; Troncarelli, *Tradizioni*, pp. 28, 110; idem, *Boethiana*, pp. 64, 70–71, 112, 245–6 (no. 111), pl. X.f (fol. 2r); M. Mostert, *The Library of Fleury: a Provisional list of Manuscripts*, Hilversum, 1989, pp. 61–2.

18. MS Bern, Burgerbibliothek, 181
DCPhil. s. xi

Parchment; ii + 83 + ii fols; last few folios damaged; page 308x222mm; text 195–210x120mm; 22 lines, ruled for gloss; several scribes. Space left for *tituli*, not executed. Rhetorical labels, e.g., METAPHORA (fols 25v, 26r), LITOTES (fol. 52r). Binding: s. xix white parchment on pasteboard.

CONTENTS Fols 1r–83v ***DCPhil.***, *expl.* imperf. V.pr.vi.160 'prestare dicantur'.

GLOSS Lupus, *De metris* as gloss (fols 1r–18v). Little contemporary annotation after fol. 18v, but quite extensive s. xiv annotation throughout. Commentary on III.m.ix, fols 43r–45r *inc.* 'Tu triplicis mediam naturae'; *expl.* 'tranquilla piis te cernere finis principium vector dux semita terminus idem'.

DECORATION Good outline initial ***C****(armina)* with acanthus (fol. 1r). Red s. xii ***P****(ost)* with floral terminals and white snake on the stem (fol. 15r), and ***I****(am)* (fol. 31v). Minor initials usually in red. Green, red, and purple rubrication planned throughout but executed only at the beginning. No incipits; each bk begins on a new page (fols 15r, 31r, 53v, 71r).

PROVENANCE France. Belonged to the Celestines in Metz, then to the University of Paris (fol. 1r), whence to Jacques Bongars.

BIBLIOGRAPHY Hagen, p. 239; Delisle, II, p. 201; Troncarelli, *Boethiana*, pp. 36, 246–7 (no. 112).

19. MS Bern, Burgerbibliothek, F 219. 1
Arith. s. ix

Parchment; iii + 14 + iii fols; page 245x182mm; text 175–85x120mm; 27 lines; one scribe, with high ‘r’. Colophon, fol. 1^{r}.

CONTENTS Fol. 1^{r-v} ***Arith.*** I.32, ‘Atque haec quidem’–‘moraremur’ (71/18–72/19); 1^{v}–2^{v} 54 *capitula* to bk II; 2^{v}–14^{v} ***Arith.*** II.1–25, *expl.* imperf. ‘latitudinibus continetur’ (115/4).

GLOSS A few contemporary glosses, e.g., fols 6^{v}–7^{r}.

DECORATION Rubrication and colophon in orange-red; diagrams orange-red and yellow.

PROVENANCE Unknown.

BIBLIOGRAPHY Hagen, p. 271 (dates MS as s. xi).

20. MS Bern, Burgerbibliothek, 265
in Cat. s. x/xi

Parchment; i + 86 + i fols (fol. 62 doubled); page 275x225mm; text 220x160mm; 45–47 lines, ruled for gloss; several scribes. *Tituli* in caps throughout *in Cat.* and commentary to *Op. Sac. V.* Colophon, ‘De cassimo gaudeat et qua scripsit Olibrius’ (fol. 36^{r}: see Scarpatetti). Binding: s. xviii white parchment on pasteboard.

CONTENTS Fol. 1^{r} Persius, *Satyrae* I.1–2, 4–7; 2^{r}–36^{r} ***in Cat.*** (bks III–IV run together; text divided by numbers and Greek letters); 36^{r}–37^{r} Cassiodorus, *Institutiones* ii.11 (ed. Mynors, p. 114, lines 19–22) with other unidentified material; 37^{r}–40^{r} Apuleius, *Peri hermenias*; 40^{v}–47^{v} Martianus Capella, *De nuptiis*; 48^{r}–58^{v} Macrobius, *In Somnium Scipionis* (excerpts); 59^{r} Pliny, *Historia naturalis II* (excerpts); 59^{v}–67^{v} Commentary on Persius, *inc.* ‘Satyre proprium est ut vera humiliter dicat et omnia fama faciat’; 68^{r}–71^{v}, 73^{r}–76^{v} Remigius of Auxerre, commentary on *Op. Sac. I–III, V* and on opening of *DCPhil.*; 72^{r-v}, 77^{r}–84^{v} idem, commentary on *De nuptiis* III, IV; 85^{r} seven lines of Latin glossary.

GLOSS *In Cat.* Otherwise some notes and running titles throughout.

DECORATION Space left for initials, not executed. Diagrams to *in Cat.* (fols 15^{r}, 22^{r}, 35^{v}) and to Macrobius and Pliny (fols 51^{v}–59^{r}).

PROVENANCE St Arnulf Benedictine abbey, Metz: (fol. 1^{r}: s. xii/xiii). Cf. MS Bern 347 (s. x), which contains the same extracts of Macrobius and Pliny. Passed to Jacques Bongars in s. xvi, like other Metz manuscripts: see fol. 1^{r} where, perhaps, his hand appears.

BIBLIOGRAPHY Delisle, II, p. 401; Hagen, pp. 298–9; Usener, p. 57; K. Rück, *Auszüge aus der Naturgeschichte des C. Plinius Secundus in einem astronomisch-komputistischen Sammelwerke des achten Jahrhunderts*, Munich, 1888, pp. 19–20, 29; Rand, pp. 4, 28; Cappuyns, 'Opuscula sacra', p. 240; *AL*, 1153; Leonardi, no. 18; V. Ferraro, 'Semipaganus, Semivillanus, Semipoeta', *Maia*, 22, 1970, pp. 139 and 141 (on Persius); P. S. Piacentini, *Saggio di un censimento dei manoscritti contenenti il testo di Persio e gli scoli e i commenti al testo*, Rome, 1973, p. 14, no. 41; J. Préaux, 'Propositions sur l'histoire des texts des *Satires* de Perse et du *Commentum Cornuti*', *Hommages à André Boutemy*, ed. G. Gambier, Paris, 1976, p. 312, pl. XXIV (fol. 59^{v}); Scarpatetti, II, p. 193, no. 536, fig. 684 (fol. 36^{r}); Munk Olsen, I, p. 21 (B.52), II, pp. 190 (B.5) and 251 (B.6); Hoffmann, I, pp. 358–9; Troncarelli, 'Opuscula', p. 17; Lohr, *AH*, pp. 158–9.

21. MS Bern, Burgerbibliothek, 300

Logica vetus s. xi

Parchment; iii + 64 + ii fols; correct order of quires is 1, 3, 5, 2, 6, 4; page 258x169mm; text 200x110mm; 40–42 lines; several similar hands. *Tituli* in capitals throughout, those of *Top. Diff.*, *intr. Syll. Cat.*, *Syll. Cat.*, and *Syll. Hyp.* showing that they belong together. Binding: s. xvii white parchment on pasteboard.

CONTENTS Fols 1^{r}–3^{r} ***Top. Diff. IV***, *inc.* imperf. 7.41 'ut species constitutiones causae generalis' (p. 82, l. 16); 3^{r}–8^{v}, 17^{r} ***Div.***; 17^{r}–24^{v} ***intr. Syll. Cat.***, *expl.* imperf.; 25^{r}–32^{v}, 49^{r}–50^{v} ***Syll. Cat.***; 50^{v}–56^{v}, 9^{r}–16^{v}, 57^{r}–60^{r} ***Syll. Hyp.***; 60^{r}–64^{v} Apuleius, *Peri hermenias*; 64^{v}, 33^{r}–41^{r} Ps.-Augustine, *Categoriae decem*; 41^{r}–48^{v} Marius Victorinus, *De definitionibus*.

GLOSS *Top. Diff.* none; *Div.* systematic marginalia in a very small hand, with reference signs, not by the scribe but contemporary; *Syll. Cat.* similar marginalia in another hand, with (bk II) different reference signs; *Syll. Hyp.* plentiful notes, as to *Syll. Cat.* No annotation to Apuleius and *Categoriae decem*; a few s. xiii notes to Victorinus. Parisian annotation s. xiv, checking and adjusting the text, e.g., fols 7$^{r–v}$, 16^{v}, 40^{r}, 45^{v}, 46^{v}. In the margin of fol. 40^{r}, 'Hec est quedam prophetia visa a quodam monacho Cicertiensi qui vidit manum scribentem super corporale suum dum celebraret' (s. xiv).

DECORATION None.

PROVENANCE France. 'Liber pauperum magistrorum de Sorbona ex legato magistri Laurentii des Quesnes pretii .x. 1' (fol. 48^{v}: s. xiv). Jacques Bongars, fol. 17^{r} (script).

BIBLIOGRAPHY Hagen, pp. 318–19; Usener, p. 64; Delisle, II, pp. 162, 201 and IV, p. 57; *AL*, 2120; G. F. Pagallo, 'Per una edizione critica del "De Hypotheticis Syllogismis" di Boezio', *Italia medioevale e umanistica*, 1, 1958, pp. 71, 73; Munk Olsen, I, p. 21 (C.53: dates MS s. xi 2/2); Nikitas, p. liii; Lohr, *AH*, p. 159.

22. MS Bern, Burgerbibliothek, 332

2 in Int. s. xii

Parchment; i + 86 fols (some mouse damage); page 249x172mm; text 180x115mm; 35 lines; several scribes, copying simultaneously.
Probably a workshop production.

CONTENTS Fols 1^r–86^r ***2 in Int.***.

GLOSS Very little.

DECORATION A few, finely executed red and blue major initials with penwork flourishing; red and blue paraph signs.

PROVENANCE Paris, theology faculty: 'magistrorum paris. studentium in theologica facultate de Abbatis Villa' (fol. 86^v: s. xiii–xiv).

BIBLIOGRAPHY Hagen, p. 331; Lohr, *AH*, p. 160.

23. MS Bern, Burgerbibliothek, 368

Soph. Elench., DCPhil. II–V s. xiii/xiv; s. xi

Parchment; iv + 57 + iv fols; page 235x164mm.
A (s. xiii/xiv): text 125x63mm; 28 lines; wide margin for gloss; one scribe.
B (s. xi): text 180x100mm; 31 lines; several scribes.
Binding: ?s. xviii.

CONTENTS A: fols 1^r–25^v ***Soph. Elench.***
B: fols 26^r–57^v ***DCPhil.***, *inc.* imperf. II.pr.ii.12 'indulgentius educavi'; *expl.* imperf. V.m.v.2 'pulveremque verrunt'.

GLOSS A: underlining of key words, often in red.
B: sparse interlinear and marginal gloss.

DECORATION A: good initial at fol. 1^r. Alternate red and blue rubrication.
B: red minor initials; running bk nos.

PROVENANCE ?France (Troncarelli). 'Iste liber est Honorati de porta de sancto Justo. Qui inveniet reddeat ei' (fol. 25^v: s. xv).

BIBLIOGRAPHY Hagen, pp. 351–2; Troncarelli, *Boethiana*, pp. 34, 38, 103, 247–8 (no. 113).

24. MS Bern, Burgerbibliothek, 413
DCPhil. s. xii 2/2

Parchment; iv + 46 + iv fols; fols 43–46 badly damaged by mice; page 230x140mm; text 165x85mm; 31 lines; one rather clumsy scribe. *Titulus*, fol. 1^{r}. Binding: s. xviii.

CONTENTS Fols 1^{r}–46^{r} ***DCPhil.***, *expl.* imperf. V.pr.vi.115 'habeat necessitatem'.

GLOSS Quite extensive annotation in another s. xii 2/2 hand to fols 1^{r}–31^{v} (IV.pr.i), thereafter virtually none. Reference symbols connect gloss to text.

DECORATION Acanthus initial with red and green infill (fol. 1^{r}). Thereafter plain red major initials with simple flourishing in red.

PROVENANCE Unknown. 'xxxiiij. 34' (fol. 1^{r}, top margin in centre).

BIBLIOGRAPHY Hagen, p. 370; Troncarelli, *Boethiana*, pp. 34, 38, 248 (no. 114).

25. MS Bern, Burgerbibliothek, 421
Vitae I, V, III, IV, Epitaphs I–II, DCPhil. s. xii 1/2; s. xiii

Parchment; iv + 70 + iv fols; page 221x141mm; text 160x73mm; 26 lines, ruled with a stylus; same or similar hand throughout. No *tituli* or colophons. Bks II–V begin (e.g., fol. 16^{v}) 'Explicit distractio prima incipit secunda.' Binding: s. xviii white parchment on pasteboard.

CONTENTS Fols 1^{r}–3^{v} Lupus, *De metris*; 3^{v}–4^{r} ***Vita I***; 4^{r} ***Vita V*** omitting 'Anic. M. Multi dicunt ista … defendit libertatem' (lines 2–10); 4^{r-v} ***Vita IV*** omitting 'adeoque … videatur' (lines 10–12); 4^{v}–5^{r} ***Vita III***; 5^{r} (added s. xiii) ***Vita VI***, ***Epitaphs I–II***; 5^{v}–6^{r} schema of elements; 6^{v} schema of seasons and elements; 7^{r}–70^{v} ***DCPhil.***

GLOSS Fairly plentiful s. xii–xiii gloss, fols 7^{r}–17^{r}, thereafter very little.

DECORATION ***Q****(uinque)*: outline red acanthus initial (fol. 1^{r}). Thereafter generally good plain red major initials. At *DCPhil.* I, II, III.m.xi, IV, V multicoloured initials in red, blue, green and gold. Concentric circle diagrams of *ignis, aer, aqua* and *terra* (fols 5^{v}–6^{v}).

PROVENANCE Metz: Celestines (fol. 9^{r}: s. xiv). Belonged to Jacques Bongars.

BIBLIOGRAPHY Hagen, p. 374; Peiper, p. viiii; Troncarelli, *Boethiana*, pp. 33, 248–9 (no. 115).

26. MS Bern, Burgerbibliothek, 435
DCPhil. s. xii

Parchment; 68 fols; page 220x135mm; text 160x70mm; 28 lines, ruled with a stylus; two scribes, changing at fol. 33^{r}. Binding: s. xviii white leather on pasteboard.

CONTENTS Fols 1^{r}–68^{v} ***DCPhil.***, *expl.* imperf. V.pr.vi.46 'plenitudinem nequeat possidere'.

GLOSS Systematic marginal gloss in contemporary hands; speakers identified by Greek letters.

DECORATION Initials in brown, green and red, some excised.

PROVENANCE ?Northern France (script). Belonged to Jacques Bongars.

BIBLIOGRAPHY Hagen, p. 383; Troncarelli, *Boethiana*, pp. 33, 249 (no. 116).

27. MS Bern, Burgerbibliothek, 510 Plate 9
Op. Sac. I–IV s. ix^{ex}

Parchment; vi + 17 + vi fols; fol. 12 is a later insertion; page 210x159mm; text 150–75x85mm; 23 lines, ruled with a stylus; one scribe for text and gloss until fol. 10^{v} (end of bk II); gloss hand changes from bk III. *Tituli* in caps, fols 1^{r}, 10^{v}. Binding: white parchment on pasteboard.
MS A 517 is the second part of the same manuscript.

CONTENTS Fols 1^{r}–17^{v} ***Op. Sac. I–IV***, *expl.* imperf. 'iordanis' (IV.174).

GLOSS Tironian notes plentifully throughout gloss (Cappuyns B).

DECORATION Plain red ***I****(nvestigatam)* and red *titulus* (fol. 1^{r}); otherwise none.

PROVENANCE ?Fleury.

BIBLIOGRAPHY Hagen, p. 431; Usener, pp. 55 and 57; Wilmart, Reg. lat. 208; E. Chatelain, *Introduction à la lecture des notes tironiennes*, Paris, 1900, p. 128; Rand, pp. 4, 28, 95, 98; Manitius, I, pp. 337, 518; M. Esposito, 'Hiberno-Latin MSS in the Libraries of Switzerland', *Proceedings of the Royal Irish Academy*, 30, 1912–13, p. 7; Cappuyns, 'Opuscula sacra', pp. 239, 242; Troncarelli, 'Opuscula', p. 16; M. Moster, *The Library of Fleury: a Provisional List of Manuscripts*, Hilversum, 1989, p. 79.

28. MS Bern, Burgerbibliothek, A 517
Op. Sac. IV–V s. ix

Parchment; i + 23 + i fols; page 210x162mm, very uneven; text 155x75mm; 23 lines, ruled with a stylus; same scribe as MS 510. *Tituli* at fols 3^r, 22^r.
The final section of MS 510.

CONTENTS Fols 1^r–3^r ***Op. Sac. IV***, *inc.* imperf.'duce iam Iesu Nave' (IV.174); 3^r–22^r ***Op. Sac. V.***

GLOSS Some Tironian notes and reference signs (Cappuyns B).

DECORATION None.

PROVENANCE ?Fleury.

BIBLIOGRAPHY See MS 510. Hagen, p. 433.

29. MS Bern, Burgerbibliothek, 538
Arith. s. xii 2/2

Parchment; i + 161 + iv fols; both manuscripts, but especially B, damaged by humidity and mice; page 210x146mm.
A (s. xii 2/2): text 150x90mm; 36 lines, ruled with a stylus; one small regular hand.
B (s. xii 1/2): text 175x95mm; 28–29 lines.
Binding: s. xv charter written in French.

CONTENTS A: fols 1^r–35^v ***Arith.***, *inc.* imperf. I.14 'denominata' (30/23); 36^r note, *inc.* 'Quodcumque componitur in ea ex quibus compositum est eadem ratione necesse est ut resolvetur'; *expl.* 'differunt xii. xv. xvi. xxxiiii'.
B: fols 37^r–160^v Justin, *Epitome historiarum philippicarum Pompei Trogi.*

GLOSS None.

DECORATION Plain initials, generally red, with simple penwork flourishing. Chapter headings in red, but no colophons or *titulus* for bk II. Red and blue diagrams.

PROVENANCE ?Fleury. May have belonged to Pierre Daniel (see marginal note, fol. 113^r, which seems to be in his hand); perhaps part of the collection of Jacques Bongars, who used B for his edition of Justin, 1581.

BIBLIOGRAPHY F. Rühl, 'Die Textquellen des Justinus', *Jahrbücher für classische Philologie*, Suppl. VI, Leipzig, 1872–3, p. 19; Hagen, p. 449; *Dictionnaire de biographie française*, X, Paris, 1965, p. 115 (P.

Daniel); Munk Olsen, I, pp. 539–40 (C.2); M. Mostert, *The Library of Fleury: a Provisional List of Manuscripts*, Hilversum, 1989, p. 80.

30. MS Bern, Burgerbibliothek, 618
Op. Sac. s. xii

Parchment; i + 73 + ii fols; page 187x122mm.
A (s. xii): text 130x65mm; 24 lines, ruled with a stylus; one scribe. Quire numbers and catchwords. *Tituli* in red for *Op. Sac. I–III, V*.
B (s. xii): 138x85mm; 25 lines; ruled with a stylus; one scribe.
Binding: white parchment on pasteboard.

CONTENTS A: fols 1^r–36^r ***Op. Sac. I–V***; 36^r–46^v Ps.-Cyprian, *De duodecim abusivis seculi* (*PL*, 4:947–60); 46^v–50^r Gregory the Great, *Responsiones*.
B: fols 51^r–73^v anonymous treatise on logic (incomplete), *inc.* imperf. 'est falsa scilicet non omnis homo animal est'; *expl.* 'per negationem quamvis hoc modo solutio legere non est impossibile'.

GLOSS A: only at fols 9^v, 11^v (s. xii); s. xiii pencil annotation at fol. 17^r.
B: pencil notes at fols 55^v, 56^r, 63^r.

DECORATION A: major and minor initials planned but not executed.
B: initials planned but not executed; paraph signs.

PROVENANCE Chartres, Franciscan convent (fol. 1^r). Belonged to F. Daniel, brother of Pierre Daniel, fol. 1^r.

BIBLIOGRAPHY Hagen, pp. 485–6; Usener, p. 56; S. Hellmann, 'Pseudo-Cyprianus De xii abusivis saeculi', *Texte und Untersuchungen zur Geschichte der altchristlichen Literatur*, 34.1, Leipzig, 1909, p. 30; J. F. Kenney, *The Sources for the Early History of Ireland*, I, New York, 1929, p. 281; Troncarelli, 'Opuscula', p. 16; Lohr, *AH*, p. 164.

31. MS Bern, Burgerbibliothek, 643
Vita I (two copies), ***DCPhil., Op. Sac.*** xiv/xv; s. xii; s. xiii

Parchment; 85 + i fols; page 172x110mm.
A (s. xiv/xv): text 130x74mm; 29 lines; one scribe.
B (s. xii): text 130x76mm; 26 lines, ruled with a stylus; one scribe.
C (s. xiii): text 130x80mm; 26 lines; two scribes, changing at fol. 63^r.
D (s. xiii): text 124x80mm; 26 lines; one scribe.
Binding: suede on pasteboard, parchment spine, two ties (lost).
A scruffy pocket MS.

CONTENTS

A: fol. 1^{r} ***Vita I***; 1^{v} blank; 2^{r} *Septem genera metrorum*; 2^{r-v} *Tabula totius operis valde brevis et utilis*; 2^{v}–3^{r} late ***Vita*** in verse, *inc.* 'Floruit hic doctor clarusque B. auctor plurima romanis qui contulit auribus'; *expl.* 'si celica mente requiris'; 3^{r-v} fragment of commentary; 4^{r-v} ***Vita I*** (as above, but double-spaced to allow interlinear gloss).
B: fols 5^{r}–20^{v} ***DCPhil. I–II***, *expl.* imperf. II.pr.iv.74 'Ostendam'.
C: fols 20^{v}–62^{v} ***DCPhil. II–V***, *inc.* imperf. II.pr.iv.74 'tibi breviter'; 63^{r}–69^{v} ***Op. Sac. I–III***.
D: fols 70^{r}–85^{r} ***Op. Sac. IV–V***.

GLOSS

Much miscellaneous annotation and NOTA signs, but nothing sustained.

DECORATION

A: red and blue penwork initial with grisaille infill (fol. 4^{r}); red and blue rubrication.
B: blue, red and green 'monastic' initials of moderate quality, many plain, some with contrasting leaf terminals (e.g., fol. 5^{r}).
C: single-colour red, blue or green initials. Red initial with blue infill ***O***, *DCPhil.* III.m.ix (fol. 34^{r}). Running book numbers for *DCPhil.*

PROVENANCE

Jacques Bongars (fol. 1^{r}).

BIBLIOGRAPHY

Hagen, p. 491.

COLOGNY–GENÈVE/GENEVA

BIBLIOTHECA BODMERIANA

Martin Bodmer foundation established 1969.

M. Bodmer, *Eine Bibliothek der Weltliteratur*, Zurich, 1947; B. Gagnebin, *La Fondation Martin Bodmer*, exhibition catalogue, Geneva, 1972; E. Pellegrin, *Manuscrits latins de la Bodmeriana*, Cologny–Geneva, 1982; Kristeller, V, pp. 103–4; Senser, pp. 87–9.

32. MS Cologny–Genève, Bibliotheca Bodmeriana, 9

Cat., De Int., in Cat. s. xi/xii

Parchment; ii (modern) + i + 81 + ii (modern) fols; fol. 30 doubled; page 198x123mm.
A (s. xi–xii): text 155x85–90mm; 27 lines; at least two scribes, changing at fol. 19^{r-v}.
B (s. xii): text 165x85–95mm; 42 lines; two scribes. Colophon, fol. 81^{r}.
Modern binding.

CONTENTS A: fol. iii^{r} s. xi–xii table of contents; 1^{r}–19^{r} ***Cat.***; 19^{v}–27^{v} ***De Int.***; 27^{v} ethical schema.
B: fols 28^{r}–81^{r} ***in Cat.***, *inc.* imperf. 'Hec namque etsi qua sunt alia que certe sunt infinita vocabula unius substantie' (*PL*, 64:160C).

GLOSS A: some s. xiv annotation and correction, fol. 15^{r}.
B: a few s. xiv marginal notes to fols 28^{r}, 72^{v}, 73^{r}; s. xvii notes in French, fols 74^{v}–75^{r}.

DECORATION A: ink initials slightly flourished; titles touched with green, fols 1^{r}, 19^{r-v}, 27^{v}; paraph signs.
B: one green initial (fol. 45^{r}); others not filled in. No rubrication.

PROVENANCE France (script). Belonged to Valerien Christofle in 1600 or 1620 (fol. iii^{r}); Sir Thomas Phillipps (fol. i^{v}); acquired by Bodmer in 1948.

BIBLIOGRAPHY *AL*, 267; Pellegrin, pp. 22–4; Lohr, *AH*, p. 173.

33. MS Cologny–Genève, Bibliotheca Bodmeriana, 41
DCPhil. s. xiv 2/2

Parchment; i + 48 + i fols; page 237x175mm; text 185x120mm; 30 lines; one extremely regular hand. *Tituli* in red. Binding: s. xvii–xviii white parchment.

CONTENTS Fols 1^{r}–48^{v} ***DCPhil.***

GLOSS Very few s. xiv–xv marginal and interlinear glosses, fols 1^{r}–2^{v}, 8^{r-v}, 16^{r}–20^{v}.

DECORATION Acanthus border, with half-length figure of Boethius in a red cloak holding a book (fol. 1^{r}). Major initials, fols 8^{r}, 17^{r}, 30^{r}, 41^{r} (beginning bks II–V) in pink and red on a blue background with green and red leaf-work. Minor initials and paraph signs touched with red.

PROVENANCE Italy: ?North. Half-erased s. xvi–xvii Italian inscription (fol. 1^{r}). Acquired by Bodmer in 1958.

BIBLIOGRAPHY Davis and Orioli, *Catalogue 154: Rare Books*, London, 1958, no. 24, with pl. (fol. 17^{r}); Pellegrin, pp. 83–4.

34. MS Cologny–Genève, Bibliotheca Bodmeriana, 175
DCPhil. s. x 2/2

Parchment; iii + 113 + iii fols; page 236x175mm; text 185x120mm; 17–18 lines for text; 42–45 lines for gloss, framed and ruled with a stylus; sometimes 2 cols, e.g., fol. 1^{r-v}; one clear and even hand for *DCPhil.* Greek in text; Greek and Latin letters as reference signs. Neumes (perhaps contemporary), fols 16^{v}–17^{r}, 25^{v}–26^{r}, 41^{v}–42^{r}, 46^{r}, 59^{v}, 63^{r}, 67^{r}, 82^{r}–83^{v}, 94^{v}; neumes without text, fol. 113^{v}. Schemata, fols 55^{v}, 85^{v}. Binding: s. xviii.

CONTENTS Fol. 1^{ra-vb} Lupus, *De metris*; 1^{v}–111^{r} ***DCPhil.***, with commentary of Remigius of Auxerre; 111^{v}–12^{r} Donatus, *Ars maior I* (excerpt: ed. Holtz, pp. 603–4, line 10); 112^{r} *Anthologia latina*, 393; 112^{v} Schaller, 13123; 113^{v} Schaller, 11355.

GLOSS See contents. Some s. xiv interlinear annotation, profuse and systematic (fols 2^{r}–3^{v}, 110^{v}).

DECORATION Interlace ***C(armina)*** with animal heads (fol. 2^{r}). Initials in purple (fols 17^{r}, 38^{r}, 68^{r}) and green (fol. 93^{r}) to each book of *DCPhil.* Elsewhere red or green capitals; metres begin alternately red or green.

PROVENANCE England; ?St Augustine's, Canterbury. Anthony Askew (1722–72), of Emmanuel College, Cambridge. Ultimately bought by Sydney Cockerell in 1909, whence to Bodmer in 1957.

BIBLIOGRAPHY *Catalogue of Nineteen Highly Distinguished Medieval and Renaissance Manuscripts ... The Property of Sir Sydney Cockerell.* Day of sale 3rd of April 1957, Sotheby's, London, 1957, pp. 4–5, no. I and plate (fol. 2^{r}); Courcelle, p. 405; Bolton, pp. 57, 61; H. Gneuss, 'A List of Manuscripts Written or Owned in England up to 1100', *Anglo-Saxon England*, 9, 1981, p. 52; Pellegrin, pp. 411–15 and pl. 27 (fol. 2^{r}); Troncarelli, *Boethiana*, pp. 34, 112, 255–6 (no. 118); Kristeller, V, p. 103.

EINSIEDELN

STIFTSBIBLIOTHEK, f. 934.

The monastic library was founded by Abbot Eberhard (934–58) and St Wolfgang was a leading figure in the scriptorium between 966 and 973. Heinrich von Ligerz, librarian c. 1350, was the first to provide the MSS with marks of ownership. He left numerous notes and grotesque faces in the books he used. Albrecht von Bonstetten, dean c. 1470, a book collector and scholar with broad interests and activities, left his books to the library at his death.

G. Morel, 'Einsiedler Handschriften der Lateinischen Kirchenväter bis zum IX Jahrhundert', *Sitzungsberichte der philosophisch-historischen Classe der Kaiserlichen Akademie der Wissenschaften*, 55, Vienna, 1867, pp. 243–61; G. Meier, 'Heinrich von Ligerz, Bibliothekar von Einsiedeln im 14. Jahrhundert',

Zentralblatt für Bibliothekswesen, 17, 1896, pp. 42–66; idem, *Catalogus codicum manu scriptorum qui in bibliotheca monasterii Einsiedlensis OSB servantur*, Einsiedeln and Leipzig, 1899 (nos 1–500 only); *MBKDS*, I, pp. 25–8; Bruckner, V; *Secundum Regulam S. Benedicti. Ausstellung von Handschriften 8.–17. Jh. zum Gedenkjahr des hl. Benedikt 480–1980. 21 März 1980–21 März 1981*, exhibition catalogue, ed. K. Bugmann, Einsiedeln, 1980; Scarpatetti, II, pp. 52–82; Kristeller, V, pp. 104–7; Senser, pp. 98–9.

35. MS Einsiedeln, Stiftsbibliothek, 149
Vita I, DCPhil. s. x

Parchment; 178 pages; page 238x184mm.
A (s. x): text 190x130mm; text in long lines except at p. 51 which has 2 cols, each 185x65mm; 26 lines, ruled with a stylus; two scribes, changing at pp. 32–3. *Tituli* and subtitles in red.
B (s. x^{ex}): text 182x135mm; 24 lines; several scribes, changing at pp. 72–3, 99–100, 115–16.
Binding: white leather on wood; one central clasp (lost).

CONTENTS A: pp. 1–47 Prosper of Aquitaine, *Epigrammata* (*PL*, 51:497–532); 47–8 Schaller, 10253; 48–51 Prosper of Aquitaine, *Ad coniugem suam* (*PL*, 51:611–16); two schemata of elements. B: p. 52 ***Vita I***; 52–172 ***DCPhil.***, glossed; 172 schema of elements; 173–8 Lupus, *De metris*, *expl.* imperf. 'discors federa rerum' (p. xxviiii, line 145).

GLOSS Extensive gloss to *DCPhil.*, including Old High German. The gloss starts at p. 68 (bk II) and is mainly interlinear until pp. 115–16, where another glossator and another scribe take over.

DECORATION A: beginnings of major initial ***D(um)*** sketched in shaky hand (p. 1). Initial letters alternately in red and ink of text. B: ***C(armina)*** in red with leaf-work (p. 52). Major and minor initials in red against crude blue and yellow. Rubrication; first lines highlighted with yellow ink.

PROVENANCE Einsiedeln (p. 2: s. xiii).

BIBLIOGRAPHY Morel, pp. 243, 249, 258; Steinmeyer-Sievers, IV, p. 423, no. 109; Meier, p. 125; Naumann, pp. IX, 14–15, 17 and 26; Bruckner, V, pp. 22 (n. 38a), 51; Courcelle, p. 404; Bergmann, no. 117; Troncarelli, *Boethiana*, pp. 60, 134, 256–7 (no. 119).

36. MS Einsiedeln, Stiftsbibliothek, 235
Op. Sac. s. xi

Parchment; 165 pages; page 257x202mm.

A (s. x): two scribes.
B(s. xi): text 200x140mm; 25 lines; two scribes. Binding: s. xiv brown leather on wood; spine renewed.

CONTENTS A: pp. 1–41 *De consuetudine in regularibus monasteriis omni tempore observanda*;
B: pp. 42–95 ***Op. Sac. I–III, V, IV***; 96–164 commentary on *Op. Sac.* (Rand E; Cappuyns E).

GLOSS B: see contents. Frequent annotation by Heinrich von Ligerz; a number of NOTA signs.

DECORATION Plain initials in brown with occasional red infill.

PROVENANCE ?Regensburg or Einsiedeln. Listed by Heinrich von Ligerz (Meier, p. 54).

BIBLIOGRAPHY Peiper, pp. xxxxvii–xxxxviiii (E); Usener, p. 57; Meier, 'Heinrich von Ligerz', p. 54; Meier, p. 192; Rand, pp. 4 and 28 (E); Bruckner, V, pp. 33, 47, 88; Cappuyns, 'Opuscula sacra', p. 239; Hoffmann, I, pp. 283–4; Troncarelli, 'Opuscula', p. 17.

37. MS Einsiedeln, Stiftsbibliothek, 282

DCPhil., Vita s. xiii

Parchment; i + 292 pages; page 196x95mm.
A (s. x): text 155x90mm; 22 lines; same or similar scribe.
B (s. xiii): text 160x70mm; 36–8 lines; one hand for *DCPhil.*, changing for *Vita*. *Tituli* in red.
Binding: white leather on wood; one clasp (lost).

CONTENTS A: pp. 1–203 Julianus Pomerius, *De vita contemplativa* I.v to end (*PL*, 59:423–520); 203–16 Gregory the Great, *Epistola ad Secundinum* XI.52 (*PL*, 77:982–91).
B: pp. 217–87 ***DCPhil.***; 288 ***Vita***, *inc.* 'Boetius unus ex nobilissimis Romanis'; *expl.* 'tanto plus commendatur'; 289 schema 'de essentiis et natura'; 289 Greek alphabet.

GLOSS B: sparse marginal glosses in scribe's hand until p. 251, when a much less competent contemporary hand intervenes.

DECORATION B: ***C****(armina)* in red, p. 217. Minor initials in red with flourishing.

PROVENANCE In Einsiedeln by c. 1350: 'Iste liber Johannis Spichwardi de Thurego accomodatus fratri Heinrico de Ligercia Thesaur<ario> Monast<erii> Heremitarum' (p. 289).

BIBLIOGRAPHY Meier, p. 259; Bruckner, V, pp. 87–8.

38. MS Einsiedeln, Stiftsbibliothek, 295
2 in Int. s. xi

Parchment; 200 pages; page 310x260mm.
A (s. xi): text 2 cols, each 267x110mm; 50 lines; one scribe.
B (s. x): text 235x165mm; 35 lines; one scribe.
Binding: white leather on wood; one clasp.

CONTENTS A: pp. 1–97 ***2 in Int.***; 98 *Rhytmus de Maria* (s. xii, 84 verses), *inc.* 'Auctor cunctarum'; *expl.* 'qua non sit visio dura'.
B: 99–199 *Vitae sanctorum*; 200 blank.

GLOSS Very little. Notes by Heinrich von Ligerz.

DECORATION A: initials in black or red; incipits and explicits in red.
B: initials in ink of text.

PROVENANCE Perhaps partly written in Italy (Bruckner). In Einsiedeln c. 1350.

BIBLIOGRAPHY Meier, pp. 268–9; *AL*, 1155; Bruckner, V, pp. 24, 88; Lohr, *AH*, p. 176.

39. MS Einsiedeln, Stiftsbibliothek, 298
Mus. s. x 2/2

Parchment; 146 pages; page 335x260mm; text 220x175mm; 33 lines; several scribes. 'Scribe puer scribe qui nomen habes Herimanne' (p. 143: s. x/xi). Greek in text. *Tituli* in red or ink of text. Binding: white leather on wood; one clasp (lost).

CONTENTS Pp. 1–22 Ps.-Boethius, *Geometria* I and related texts; 23–145 ***Mus.***

GLOSS Cf. Fleury tradition (Bower). In several hands.

DECORATION Major capitals in ink of text; minor capitals alternately in red and black, headings in red. Diagrams in red and ink of text as for *Geometria*. Decoration is variable and changes with each scribe.

PROVENANCE ?Trier. Possibly donated by St Wolfgang, *scholasticus* at Trier before entering Einsiedeln (965).

BIBLIOGRAPHY Meier, p. 272; C. Thulin, 'Zur Überlieferungsgeschichte des Corpus Agrimensorum. Exzerptenhandschriften und Kompendien', *Göteborgs Kungl. Vetenskaps- och Vitterhets-Samhälles Handlingar*, 14, Göteborg, 1911, p. 24; Bruckner, V, p. 23; B. Bischoff, 'Elementarunterricht und *Probationes Pennae* in der ersten Hälfte des Mittelalters', *Mittelalterliche Studien*, I, pp. 74–87 [87]; Folkerts, p. 76; *Secundum Regulam S. Benedicti*, no.

33; Folkerts II, pp. 97, 104; Bower, no. 25; Toneatto, III, pp. 895–8.

40. MS Einsiedeln, Stiftsbibliothek, 301
2 in Int. s. xi

Parchment; i + 240 + i pages; page 275x210mm; text 230x160mm; 27–28 lines; several good but quite different scribes. Binding: s. xiv white leather on wood; one clasp (lost).

CONTENTS Pp. 1–2 and 241–2 flyleaves from a s. xi lectionary; 3–240 ***2 in Int.***, *expl.* imperf. V.13 'de contingenti et possi<bili rationem esse>' (417/18–19); 241–2 (along bottom of page) note concerning a plea of Charles IV in a Nuremberg lawsuit dated 1356.

GLOSS Notes and pointing hands by Heinrich von Ligerz.

DECORATION Initial letters in black. Diagram of *affirmatio-negatio*, p. 98. Other diagrams planned but not executed.

PROVENANCE In Einsiedeln by c. 1350.

BIBLIOGRAPHY Meier, p. 275; *AL*, 1156; Bruckner, V, pp. 88, 183; Parkes, in Gibson, p. 427; Lohr, *AH*, pp. 176–7.

41. MS Einsiedeln, Stiftsbibliothek, 302
Vita I, DCPhil. s. x

Parchment; i + 144 + i pages; page 280x220mm; some pages have been trimmed, losing part of the gloss.
A (s. x): text 235x165mm; 26 lines; one large, regular hand. *Tituli* and rubrication in red.
B (s. x): text 2 cols, each 220x80mm; 33 lines; one scribe. Neumes to *DCPhil.*, p. 94^{b}. *Tituli* to *DCPhil.* in red except bks III–IV.
Binding: white leather on wood; one clasp (lost).

CONTENTS A: pp. 1–16 fragment of a service-book; 17–21 Wandalbert, *Horologium*; 21–26 idem, *De creatione mundi*.
B: pp. 28^{a}–64^{b} Arator, *In actus Apostolorum*; 64^{b}–65^{a} *accessus* to Arator; 65^{a-b} ***Vita I***; 65^{b}–110^{b} ***DCPhil.***; 110^{b}–111^{a} verses (Peiper, p. viii); 111^{a}–112^{b} Lupus, *De metris*; 113^{a}–115^{a} Prosper of Aquitaine, *Epigrammata* and verses (*PL*, 51:527–32); 115^{b}–17^{a} idem, *Ad coniugem suam*; 118^{a}–124^{b} Prudentius, *Psychomachia*, ends v.262 'ut fosse ruentes' (*PL*, 60:43A); 125^{a-b} Aldhelm, *Aenigmata* I.4–18; 126^{a}–131^{b} Boniface, *De virtutibus et vitiis*, *expl.* imperf. 'expellor ab aethere summa' (*PL*, 89:889);

132^{a}–144^{b} Aldhelm, *Aenigmata* I–XIV.

GLOSS Very cramped but extensive marginal and interlinear gloss for *DCPhil.*, with Old High German; fragment of commentary of 'Anonymous of St Gall' (Courcelle). Notes by Heinrich von Ligerz, pp. 7, 9, 13, 113, 118.

DECORATION Systematic initials for every line of Arator in red. *DCPhil.* is much less regular: alternate black and red initials; first lines highlighted in lighter ink.

PROVENANCE In Einsiedeln by c. 1350.

BIBLIOGRAPHY Steinmeyer-Sievers, IV, p. 424, no. 117; Meier, pp. 275–7; Naumann, pp. IX, 14; Silvestre, pp. 98, 111–12; Courcelle, pp. 295–6, 404, 407; Courcelle II, p. 124; Bruckner, V, pp. 23, 88; Bergmann, no. 126; *Secundum regulam S. Benedicti*, no. 34; Troncarelli, *Boethiana*, pp. 35, 38, 114, 133, 257–8 (no. 120).

42. MS Einsiedeln, Stiftsbibliothek, 307
Top. Diff. IV 1442

Paper; 720 pages; page 280x200mm; text 200x115mm; 28–30 lines for Cicero and Boethius; two scribes, changing at p. 345. Dated colophon, p. 525. Binding: s. xv stamped leather on wood; 2 clasps (lost). Many blank pages.

CONTENTS Pp. 1–7 blank; 8–11 contents list in the hand of Michael Datsenbach, OSB, 1794; 12–16 blank; 17–198 Petrarch, *Opera minora*; 207–17 Sallust, *In Ciceronem et invicem invectivae*; 218–22 ***Top. Diff. IV***, *expl.* imperf. IV.7.4 'Scriptum et voluntas' (78/8); 228–73 Petrarch, *Letters*; 274–6 three dictaminal letters; 277–8 Antonius Panormita, *Letter to Franciscus Picinius*; 279–306 Gasparinus of Bergamo, *Praecepta rhetorica*; 307–12 anon. rhetorical treatise, *inc.* 'Tribus ex rebus'; *expl.* 'per occupationem fiat'; 313–22 Pliny, *Letters*; Plutarch, *Ad Trajanum*; 323–427 Cicero, *De inventione*, glossed; 427–525 Ps.-Cicero, *Ad Herennium*; 526, 528, 536 schemata of learning and virtues; 525 Vergerius, *Letter to Ludovicus Alodisius*; 537–602 Cicero, *De oratore*; 607–26 idem, *Paradoxa*; 627–8 Hincmar, *Collecta*; 633–707 Petrarch, *De conflictu curarum suarum*; 708 Albrecht von Bonstetten, *De prepositionibus grecis* (autograph).

GLOSS None.

DECORATION None.

PROVENANCE Belonged to Albrecht von Bonstetten.

BIBLIOGRAPHY Meier, pp. 279–80; Bruckner, V, pp. 110–11; R. Mattmann, *Studien zur handschriftlichen Überlieferung von Ciceros "De Inventione"*, Freiburg i.U., 1975, pp. 42–6; Scarpatetti, II, p. 65, no. 165, fig. 274 (p. 345); Kristeller, V, p. 105.

43. MS Einsiedeln, Stiftsbibliothek, 315
2 in Isag. s. x 2/2

Parchment; i + 170 + ii pages; page 220x165mm; text 180x120mm; 25–26 lines; several scribes. *Titulus* in red, extremely faded, p. 2. Binding: s. xiv white leather on wood; one clasp (lost).

CONTENTS Pp. 2–170 ***2 in Isag.***, *expl.* imperf. V.23 'ut in specie dictum est ra<rissimae>' (345/8).

GLOSS ?Interlinear glosses or corrections to text.

DECORATION Major initials in red, e.g., ***E****(xpeditis)* with leaf-work, p. 114. Subheadings in red. Diagram of *animal rationale*, p. 53.

PROVENANCE Einsiedeln. One of a group of eighteen manuscripts written in-house, s. x 2/2 (Bruckner, V, pp. 34–8). Title in the hand of Heinrich von Ligerz (p. 1).

BIBLIOGRAPHY Meier, p. 286; *AL*, 2124; Bruckner, V, pp. 34–8, 183; Lohr, *AH*, p. 177.

44. MS Einsiedeln, Stiftsbibliothek, 322
Vita I, DCPhil. s. x

Parchment; 310 pages, p. 2 tripled; page 198x142mm.
A: text 150x105mm; 20 lines; three scribes, changing at pp. 123 and 159.
Binding: white leather on wood.

CONTENTS A (s. x): p. 1 ***Vita I***; 2–186 ***DCPhil.***
B (s. xi): pp. 187–308 Otloh, *Life of St Wolfgang*.

GLOSS Notes by Heinrich von Ligerz. Pp. 1–53 heavily glossed, with Old High German; fragment of commentary of 'Anonymous of St Gall'.

DECORATION Initials in red with an occasional touch of purple and green, e.g., pp. 23, 55, 118.

PROVENANCE A was probably produced in St Gall (Hoffmann); B was produced in Einsiedeln, not Bavaria (Hoffmann). The whole in Einsiedeln by c. 1350.

BIBLIOGRAPHY Steinmeyer-Sievers, IV, p. 426, no. 122; Meier, pp. 294–5; Naumann, pp. IX, 14–15, 26; Bruckner, V, pp. 47 (n. 44), 88; Courcelle, p. 404; Bergmann, no. 132; Hoffmann, I, p. 379; Troncarelli, *Boethiana*, pp. 134, 258–9 (no. 121).

45. MS Einsiedeln, Stiftsbibliothek, 324
Logica vetus s. x/xi

Parchment; 242 pages; page 162x158mm; text 110–40x120–35mm; 22–28 lines; several scribes. Binding: white leather on wood; one clasp (lost).

CONTENTS Pp. 3–38 ***Cat.***; 38–53 ***De Int.***; 54–72 Ps.-Augustine, *Dialectica*; 72–92 Cicero, *Topica*; 93–242 ***in Topica Cic.***

GLOSS None to *Cat.* and *De Int.*, otherwise notes by Heinrich von Ligerz *passim*.

DECORATION Initials in black; headings and subheadings in capitals in ink of text; paraph signs, but not systematic.

PROVENANCE ?Italy (Bruckner). In Einsiedeln by c. 1350.

BIBLIOGRAPHY Chatelain, I, p. 6, pl. XXI.2; Meier, pp. 295–6; *AL*, 1157; Bruckner, V, pp. 24, 88; Lewry, in Gibson, p. 91; Munk Olsen, I, p. 168 (B.111); Troncarelli, *Boethiana*, pp. 109, 111; Kristeller, V, p. 105; Lohr, *AH*, p. 177.

46. MS Einsiedeln, Stiftsbibliothek, 325
De Int. s. xi

Parchment; i + 182 pages, pp. 5 and 112 doubled; page 162x130mm.
A (s. xi): text 110x85mm; 17 lines; one scribe. Faded *titulus* in red, p. 3.
B (s. xiii–xiv): text 2 cols, each 130x45mm; c. 17 lines; several scribes.
Binding: white leather on wood; one clasp (lost).

CONTENTS A: pp. 2–55 ***De Int.***, glossed; 56 notes on logic, *inc.* 'Interrogatio genus est cuius species sunt dialectica et non dialectica interrogatio'; *expl.* 'Quale animal est homo rationale'.
B: pp. 58^{a}–128^{b} sermons; 129^{a-b} *Life of Pope Silvester*, *inc.* 'Silvester urbis Rome'; *expl.* 'Constantino apparentes dixerunt'; 129^{b}–135^{b} *De vago scolari*, *inc.* 'Clericus quidem de talibus qualis per diversas'; *expl.* imperf. 'utrum prescius esset vel predestinatus. Si predestinatus'; 136^{a}–80^{b} sermons.

GLOSS Profuse for pp. 3–10; thereafter occasional notes in other hands. Gloss linked to text with Greek letters, p. 3.

DECORATION Simple black initials, some not executed; minor initials on royal blue background; subheadings in red.

PROVENANCE In Einsiedeln c. 1350.

BIBLIOGRAPHY Meier, pp. 296–97; *AL*, 1158; Bruckner, V, p. 22; Kristeller, V, p. 105; Lohr, *AH*, p 178.

47. MS Einsiedeln, Stiftsbibliothek, 338
2 in Isag. s. x

Parchment; 457 + i pages; page 120x105mm; text 90x70mm; 18–20 lines; several scribes. Binding: white leather on wood; one clasp (lost).

CONTENTS P. 1 Greek alphabet and Roman numerals; 1–271 ***2 in Isag.***; 272–301 Priscian, *De figuris numerorum* (*GL*, 3, pp. 405–17); 301–32 idem, *De metris Terentii* (*GL*, 3, pp. 418–29); 332–56 idem, *Praeexercitamina* (*GL*, 3, pp. 430–40); 356–410 Rufinus, *In metra Terentiana* (*GL*, 6, pp. 554–78); 411 sketch for a drawing of a woman's figure; 412 blank; 413–51 Germanicus, *Aratea* (ed. A. Breysig, *Germanici Caesaris Aratea cum scholiis*, Leipzig, 1899); 451–3 Germanicus, *Reliquiae* II–III; 453–55 Avienus, *Aratea* (excerpts).

GLOSS *2 in Isag.*: gloss in several contemporary hands.

DECORATION *2 in Isag.*: incipits and explicits in light red.

PROVENANCE Probably Germany. In Einsiedeln by c. 1350. 'Gehört gan Einsidlen disses büchly in dass gotthuss LXI°' (p. 457: s. xv).

BIBLIOGRAPHY Meier, pp. 311–12; E. Lesne, *Les Livres "Scriptoria" et Bibliothèques du commencement du viii à la fin du xi siècle*, Histoire de la propriété ecclésiastique en France, vol. iv, Lille, 1938, p. 761; *AL*, 2125; Bruckner, V, p. 88; Passalacqua, no. 115; M. D. Reeve, 'Some Astronomical Manuscripts', *Classical Quarterly*, n.s. 30, 1980, pp. 508–22 [518]; Munk Olsen, I, p. 407 (B.9); B. Bischoff, et al., *Aratea. Kommentar zum Aratus des Germanicus MS Voss. Lat. Q. 79*, Lucerne, 1989, pp. 13, 34, 60, 65, 91; Lohr, *AH*, p. 178.

48. MS Einsiedeln, Stiftsbibliothek, 358
Arith., Mus. s. x 4/4

Parchment; i + 274 + i pages (22, 221 both tripled); page 230x173mm; text 185x135mm; 35 lines; one scribe throughout. Greek in text. Chapter numbers in black as running footers. *Tituli* in ochre and red. Binding: white leather on wood;

one clasp (lost).

CONTENTS Pp. 1–39 Ps.-Boethius, *Geometria* I and related texts (as MS 298); 40–137 ***Arith.***; 138–9 *Computus digitorum*, *inc.* 'Si multiplicaveris'; *expl.* 'singularibus subtrahes'; 141–43 Jerome, *De diversis generibus musicorum* (*PL*, 30:213–15); 143–44 Isidore, *Etymologiae* III.18–21; 144 drawings of musical instruments; 145–270 ***Mus.***

GLOSS Sparse interlinear and marginal gloss to *Arith.*, especially at the beginning and pp. 40–48. Moderate gloss in several hands to *Mus.*

DECORATION Elongated ***I****(nter)* with penwork flourishing, p. 44. Minor initials and subheadings in ochre. Drawings in red, green and yellow, p. 144.

PROVENANCE Written in St Gall or Reichenau. Probably belonged to St Wolfgang.

BIBLIOGRAPHY Meier, pp. 322–23; C. Thulin, 'Zur Überlieferungsgeschichte des Corpus Agrimensorum. Exzerptenhandschriften und Kompendien', *Göteborgs Kungl. Vetenkaps- och Vitterhets-Samhälles Handlingar*, 14, Göteborg, 1911, p. 24; Bruckner, V, pp. 22–3, 88; Folkerts, p. 96; idem II, pp. 97, 104; Masi, p. 59; Bower, no. 26; Bernhard, p. 23 (n. 3); Toneatto, III, pp. 913–18.

ENGELBERG

STIFTSBIBLIOTHEK

The monastic library and the scriptorium were founded by Abbot Frowin (1147–1178). The scriptorium and the school of illumination reached their zenith between the twelfth and the fourteenth centuries.

B. Gottwald, *Catalogus codicum manu scriptorum qui asservantur in bibliotheca monasterii OSB Engelbergensis in Helvetia*, Engelberg and Freiburg i. Br., 1891; *MBKDS*, I, pp. 29–33; Bruckner, vol. VIII; S. Beck, 'Die Stiftsbibliothek Engelberg. 800 Jahre nach Abt Frowin, gest. 27. März 1178', *Titlisgrüsse*, 64, 1978, pp. 70–88; Scarpatetti, II, pp. 83–114; Kristeller, V, p. 107; Senser, pp. 99–100.

49. MS Engelberg, Stiftsbibliothek, 94
DCPhil. IV s. xiv

Parchment; 8 fols.
A (s. xiv): page 210x150mm; text 2 cols, each 200x60mm; 36 lines; one scribe.
B (s. xiv): page 205x150mm; text 160x85mm; one scribe. Badly damaged; much

of the text is illegible.
C (s. xiv): page 205x160mm; text 175x105mm; one scribe.

CONTENTS A: fols 1^{r}–2^{v} *Roman de la Rose*: fol. 1^{ra-vb} vv. 10101–10244; 2^{ra-vb} vv. 11115–11267.
B: fols 3^{r}–6^{v} ***DCPhil. IV***: fol. 3^{r-v} IV.pr.i.38 'meis vehiculis revertaris'–IV.pr.ii.48 'minime administrare'; 4^{r-v} IV.pr.iii.28 'beatos liquet'–IV.m.iii.39 'ulcere saeviunt'; 5^{r}–6^{v} IV.pr.vi.125 'geritur quod stupeant'–IV.pr.vii.25 'quae in praemium'.
C: fols 7^{r}–8^{v} Ovid, *Heroides*: fol. 7^{r-v} xviii.144–210; xix.1–6; 8^{r-v} xix.155–228.

GLOSS B: a few contemporary annotations.

DECORATION B: rubrication and minor initials.

PROVENANCE Unknown.

BIBLIOGRAPHY Gottwald, p. 112; Bruckner, VIII, p. 72; M. R. Jung, 'Ein Fragment des Rosenromans in der Stiftsbibliothek Engelberg', *Vox Romana*, 24.2, 1965, pp. 234–7.

FRIBOURG/FREIBURG

BIBLIOTHÈQUE CANTONALE ET UNIVERSITAIRE

Most MSS have come from the Cistercian abbey Altenryf-Hauterive (f. 1138) after its dissolution in 1848.

M. Meyer, J. Gremaud, et al., *Catalogue de la Bibliothèque cantonale de Fribourg*, 4 vols, Fribourg, 1852–86, vol. II (1855), pp. 593–614 (216 MSS); Bruckner, XI; idem, 'Scriptorium Altaripense', *Mediaevalia et humanistica*, 14, 1962, pp. 86–94 (survey); Scarpatetti, II, pp. 125–30; Kristeller, V, p. 108; Senser, pp. 78–9.

50. MS Fribourg, Bibliothèque cantonale et universitaire, L 37 (30)
DCPhil. 1447

Paper; ii + 141 fols; page 220x140mm; text 120x80mm; 15 lines; scribe, Petrus Guilliomennus of Fribourg. Dated colophon, fol. 138^{r}. *Tituli* to bks II–V, fols 21^{v}, 47^{r}, 84^{r}, 115^{v}–16^{r}. Modern binding.

CONTENTS Fols 1^{r}–141^{v} ***DCPhil.*** (64, 67, 117 blank).

GLOSS Interlinear gloss to fols 1^{r}–45^{v} (bks I–II).

DECORATION Ornamental red initials and rubrication for fols 1^{r}–16^{r}; thereafter initials planned but not executed.

PROVENANCE Dijon, 24 Dec. 1447 (fol. 138r).

BIBLIOGRAPHY Bruckner, XI, pp. 19, 48; Scarpatetti, II, p. 126, no. 348, fig. 296 (fol. 138r).

51. MS Fribourg, Bibliothèque cantonale et universitaire, L 162
DCPhil. s. xv

Paper; i + 110 + i (parchment, with s. xv text on verso) fols; page 282x210mm; text 185–200x100mm; 14–15 lines; two scribes. *Tituli* in red to bks I–V, fols 1r, 17v, 40r, 72v, 101v. Binding: stamped white leather on wood; 2 clasps (lost).

CONTENTS Fols 1r–110v ***DCPhil.***

GLOSS Profuse marginal gloss in scribe's hand to fols 1r–7v; thereafter irregular and mainly interlinear contemporary annotation in another hand as well. No gloss to bks IV–V (fols 72v–110v).

DECORATION Crude ***C****(armina)*, fol. 1r, and rubrication.

PROVENANCE 'Au Chan Fontaine 1800' (fol. ir), who presented it to the library of the Jesuits' college in Fribourg in 1824 (fol. 1r).

BIBLIOGRAPHY None.

ST GALLEN/ST GALL

STIFTSBIBLIOTHEK

The monastic library and scriptorium were founded by Abbot Otmar (720–759); they reached their zenith under Abbots Gozbert (816–837) and Grimalt (841–872). The oldest library list was compiled in the middle of the ninth century. Pius Kolb, librarian (1748–1762) and outstanding scholar, compiled the first systematic catalogue.

F. Weidmann, *Geschichte der Bibliothek von St. Gallen seit der Gründung um das Jahr 830 bis auf 1841*, St Gall, 1841; G. Scherrer, *Verzeichniss der Handschriften der Stiftsbibliothek von St. Gallen*, Halle, 1875; *MBKDS*, I, pp. 55–146; Bruckner, vols II–III; J. Duft and P. Meyer, *The Irish Miniatures in the Abbey Library of St Gall*, Olten, Bern and Lausanne, 1954; L. M. de Rijk, 'On the Curriculum of the Arts of the Trivium at St Gall from c. 850–c. 1000', *Vivarium*, 1, 1963, pp. 35–86; B. M. von Scarpatetti and J. Duft, *Die Handschriften der Stiftsbibliothek St. Gallen: Codices 1726–1984 (14.–19. Jahrhundert)*, St Gall, 1983 (with a good account of the catalogues from the ninth to the twentieth centuries); *Die Abtei St. Gallen. Ausgewählte Aufsätze in überarbeiteter Fassung von Johannes Duft*, ed. P. Ochsenbein and E. Ziegler (vols 1 and 2), 3 vols, Sigmaringen, 1990–94; *The Culture of the Abbey of St. Gall. An Overview*, ed. J. C. King and W. Vogler, Stuttgart and Zurich, 1991; Senser, pp. 93–7; *Sangallensia in Washington. The Arts and Letters in Medieval and Baroque St Gall, Viewed from the Late Twentieth Century*, ed. J. C. King, New York, 1993.

52. MS St Gallen, Stiftsbibliothek, 134
Op. Sac. I–III, V s. xi

Parchment; 264 pages; page 205x153mm.
A (s. ix; Lohr s. x): text 155x115mm; 21 lines; one scribe.
B (s. xii; Lohr s. xiii/xiv): text 2 cols, each 175x57mm; 49 lines; one scribe.
C (s. xi): text 160x90mm; 18 lines; one scribe. *Tituli* in ochre to *Op. Sac.* Use of Greek in gloss.
Binding: s. xv tooled white leather on bevelled boards; two clasps (renewed).

CONTENTS A: pp. 1–76 Prudentius, *Cathemerinon* pref. I–X; *Peristephanon* II. 1–42, hymns I and V, with glosses in Latin and Old High German (Bergmann, no. 186).
B: pp. 77–147 commentary on *De Int.*, *inc.* prol. 'Intentio prior est in hoc opere facilem intellectum ad predicamenta Aristotelis preparare'; *expl.* 'unde nobis per opportuna etc'.
C: pp. 148–264 ***Op. Sac. I–III, V*** (glossed: Cappuyns A).

GLOSS C: see contents. Marginal and occasional interlinear gloss in ?scribe's hand. A few reference signs, e.g., p. 166, and letters, but no sustained reference system. Some annotation to III (p. 194), *pace* Rand. Internal headings throughout, e.g., UNDE FIDES DICATUR CATHOLICA (p. 150)—presumably marginal subject headings which have been absorbed into the text.

DECORATION C: abstract ***I****(nvestigatam)*, p. 148; minor initials and rubrication in orange and red.

PROVENANCE St Gall (stamp, pp. 1, 264).

BIBLIOGRAPHY Scherrer, pp. 49–50; Usener, pp. 55, 57; Steinmeyer-Sievers, IV, p. 443, no. 160; Rand, pp. 4, 28; *MBKDS*, I, p. 118, line 30 (no. 23); Cappuyns, 'Opuscula sacra', pp. 239, 242; Bruckner, III, pp. 43, 71 (description); Bergmann, no. 186; Troncarelli, 'Opuscula', p. 17; *Die Abtei St. Gallen*, I, p. 54; Lohr, *AH*, p. 246.

53. MS St Gallen, Stiftsbibliothek, 248
Arith. s. ix

Parchment; 228 pages (pp. 1–2 missing).
A (s. ix): page 292x210mm; text 2 cols, each 260x80mm; 52 lines; many scribes. *Titulus* to bk II (p. 23^{a}).
B (s. ix–x): page 290x216mm; text 2 cols, each 245x75mm; 63 lines; several scribes. *Titulus*, p. 59.
C (s. xi–xii): page 290x216mm; text 2 cols, each 240x75mm; 42 lines; several scribes. *Titulus*, p. 99^{a}.
Binding: s. xv tooled white leather on boards; two clasps (renewed). Parchment label top centre front cover, COMPUTUS BEDE.

CONTENTS A: pp. 3^{a}–56^{b} ***Arith.*** (with *capitula*, pp. 3^{b}–4^{a}, 22^{b}–23^{a}); 57^{a}–58^{b} *probationes pennae*, calendar notes, s. xii verses.
B: pp. 59^{a}–82^{b} Ps.-Bede, *Computus* (*PL*, 90:357–61); 83^{a}–96^{a} Bede, *De natura rerum*; 96^{a}–98^{b} idem, *De sex aetatibus mundi*, *expl.* imperf. 'Iustinus minor anno xi armenii fidem Christi suscipiunt'.
C: pp. 99^{a}–212^{b} Bede, *De natura rerum et ratione temporum*, *expl.* imperf.; 213^{a}–226^{b} *Computistica*.

GLOSS A: rare.

DECORATION Beak-headed ***I(n)***, p. 3. Elsewhere, simple red outline initials; minor initials in ink, or plain red, or ink outline with red infill. Chapter headings as red capitals, but not consistently throughout. Frequent and clear diagrams, with no extra decoration.

PROVENANCE St Gall (stamp, p. 4).

BIBLIOGRAPHY Scherrer, pp. 91–2; *MBKDS*, I, p. 108, line 18 (no. 7); Bruckner, II, pp. 26, 40, 51, 57, 59, 69, 74; K. Ostberg, 'Who Were the Mergothi?', *German Life and Letters*, 33.2, 1980, pp. 98–9; B. Bischoff, 'Irische Schreiber im Karolingerreich', *Mittelalterliche Studien*, III, pp. 39–54 (p. 47, n. 35; p. 50, n. 50); Masi, p. 62; *Die Abtei St. Gallen*, I, p. 44 (n. 42).

54. MS St Gallen, Stiftsbibliothek, 768
Op. Sac. (2 copies of V) s. x/xi; s. xi/xii

Parchment; ii + 113 pages; page 223x182mm.
A (s. x–xi): text 170–80x130mm; 23 lines; good, small Carolingian hand. *Tituli*, pp. 59 (I), 70 (II), and 84 (V).
B (s. xi–xii): text 175x125mm; 23 lines; one scribe for *Op. Sac. V*.

CONTENTS Pp. 4–6 (flyleaves) *Planctus S. Galli* (Schaller, 13647); 6 ***Op. Sac. V****.iv* (41–55) fragment upside down.

A: pp. 7–58 commentary on *Op. Sac. I–III, V*, *inc.* 'Igniculum ingeniolum' (Cappuyns D[1]); *expl.* 'Glose Boetii Sancte Trinitatis perscripte Deo gratias'; 59–95 ***Op. Sac. I–V*** with glosses (Cappuyns D[2]).
B: pp. 96–111 ***Op. Sac. V***; 112 *Septem sunt miracula mundi*, here attributed to Bede.

GLOSS A: plentiful subject headings in capitals in the margin, pp. 59–93, e.g., p. 62 (I) 'sed divina substantia QUID SIT INTER ESSE DEI ET ETERNORUM QUAE NON SUNT DEUS; neque enim subiectum DEUM QUIA FORMA EST NON FIERI SUBIECTUM. ET HANC FORMAM NON INESSE MATERIE: ex his enim formis MATERIALES FORMAS AB AETERNIS FORMIS DESCENDISSE'. Some glosses in various hands, esp. pp. 59–61, 78–9 and 88–93. Reference signs not systematic.

DECORATION A: ***I****(nvestigatam)* in red and buff with internal panels and floral decoration, p. 59. Minor initials and colour spots on capitals within text.
B: rubrication in orange and red.

PROVENANCE St Gall (p. 3: ?s. xiv).

BIBLIOGRAPHY Scherrer, pp. 254–5; Usener, p. 56; Rand, p. 28; *MBKDS*, I, p. 111, line 22 (no. 11); Cappuyns, 'Opuscula sacra', pp. 239, 242; *Die Abtei St. Gallen*, I, p. 54.

55. MS St Gallen, Stiftsbibliothek, 816
Logica vetus et nova s. xiii/xiv

Parchment; 434 pages; page 265x185mm; text 127x82mm; 25–30 lines; wide margins for gloss; several similar scribes. Erased scribal colophon, p. 148. *Tituli* for each new work. Binding: tooled white leather on boards, two clasps (one still present).
A homogeneous book, planned as a whole.

CONTENTS Pp. 1–17 ***Isag.***; 17–46 ***Cat.***; 46–63 ***De Int.***; 63–78 *Liber sex principiorum*; 78–96 ***Div.***; 97–148 ***Top. Diff.***; 149–287 ***Topica Aris.***; 288–322 ***Soph. Elench.***; 323–92 ***Prior Anal.***; 393 blank; 394 misc. notes; 395–434 *Post. Anal.*, *expl.* imperf. 'convertatur conclusione'.

GLOSS Extensive user's gloss almost throughout. Lemmata underlined.

DECORATION Red or blue s. xiv major and minor initials, with highly competent infill in the other colour. Blue and red paraph signs.

PROVENANCE St Gall (front pastedown: s. xv/xvi).

BIBLIOGRAPHY Scherrer, p. 275; *AL*, 1160.

56. MS St Gallen, Stiftsbibliothek, 817 Plate 10
Logica vetus s. xi 1/2

Parchment; 345 pages; page 259x194mm; text 200x115mm; 27–9 lines; several, quite different, hands with Irish elements. Pastedown is offset on front cover. *Tituli* in orange, pp. 6, 44, 203, and in black, pp. 38, 221. Colophons to *Cat.* 'Hic finem tango nec plus sudoris adibo' (p. 38), and to *In Cat.* (p. 202). Riddle: 'Sex mihi litterule sunt et preclara potestas Disrumpis nomen medio de tramite toto Pars colit una deum, hominem pars altera signat' (p. 201).
Binding: standard tooled white leather on wood; two clasps (lost). Parchment label top center front cover ARISTOTELES DE X CHATEGORIIS TRANSLATUS AC COMMENTATUS PER BOECIUM.

CONTENTS P. 2 contents list (s. xviii); 3 animal doodles; 4–5 Schaller, 2452; 6–38 ***Cat.***; 38–43 Remus Flavinus, *De ponderibus* (*Anthologia Latina*, 486), *expl.* imperf. 'Hec quoque dracmarum simili tibi parte notetur' (v. 162); 44–202 ***in Cat.***; 203–20 ***De Int.***; 221–339 ***1 in Int.***; 340–44 *schemata* on the ten categories.

GLOSS *Cat.*: subject headings in margin throughout, some in capitals, by a systematic reader. *In Cat.*: subject headings in margin in scribe's hand, with some additions (p. 72). *De Int.*: subject headings in margin throughout, not by the scribe; tied to text by reference signs (letters of the alphabet and Tironian notes). *1 in Int.*: notes in same style at the beginning; same reference signs. 301–35 headings in capitals as MS 768.

DECORATION Ambitious, varied and ugly initials in black and orange.

PROVENANCE 'Liber S. Galli et Othmari' (p. 4: s. xvii).

BIBLIOGRAPHY Scherrer, pp. 275–6; *MBKDS*, I, p. 118, line 20 (no. 23); *AL*, 1161; Lohr, *AH*, p. 250.

57. MS St Gallen, Stiftsbibliothek, 820
1 in Int. s. ix 4/4

Parchment; 176 pages; page 280x210mm.
A (s. ix 4/4 [pp. 1–30], s. x/xi [pp. 31–62]): text 2 cols, each 206x78mm; 30 lines; hand changes at p. 31. *Titulus* in red capitals, p. 2.
B (s. x/xi): text 220x150mm; 27 lines; several similar scribes.
Binding: white leather on wood; no clasps.

CONTENTS A: p. 1 misc. later librarian's notes, including s. xviii^{mid} contents list; 2–51^{a} ***1 in Int.*** (bk I only), *expl.* imperf. I.9 'Et tamen ita hoc

fieri potest, ut et non fieri impossibile non sit' (121/2–3); 51[b]–62[b] misc. notes on logic and rhetoric, *inc.* 'Dialectica est bene disputandi scientia'; *expl.* 'quod solum sibi assumpserunt magisterium iudicandi'.
B: p. 63 Notker, *De exilio*; 64–71 Cassiodorus, *De rhetorica*; 72–172 Cicero, *De inventione*, *lacuna* at p. 103; 172–6 idem, *De inventione* I.36.62–I.41.76, *inc.* 'Quod enim adiungi et separari ab aliquo potest'; *expl.* 'Nam primum omnium generibus ipsis distinguere convenit. hoc est tum inductione uti tum raciocinatione'.

GLOSS A: orange and red marginal and internal headings in the scribe's hand, pp. 2–30. Frequent subject headings. Later hand has added B and T internally. No gloss, pp. 31–51.
B: Notker: keywords from text repeated in margin; Cicero: subheadings in orange.

DECORATION Plain orange-red capitals and rubrication; some initials in black. Rhetorical *schemata*, pp. 65, 66, 68–70.

PROVENANCE Copied at St Gall (stamps, pp. 1, 176). Glosses in B perhaps by Ekkehard IV (d. 1060).

BIBLIOGRAPHY Scherrer, p. 277; Chatelain, I, p. 5, pl. XVIII.1; Steinmeyer-Sievers, IV, p. 453, no. 209; *MBKDS*, I, p. 118, l. 18 (no. 23); Bruckner, III, pp. 45, 117–18; *AL*, 1163; de Rijk, 'On the Curriculum', p. 55; Bergmann, no. 240; R. Mattmann, *Studien zur handschriftlichen Überlieferung von Ciceros "De inventione"*, Freiburg i.U, 1975, pp. 27–8; S. Sonderegger, 'Notker der Deutsche und Cicero. Aspekte einer mittelalterlichen Rezeption', *Florilegium Sangellense. Festschrift für J. Duft zum 65. Geburtstag*, ed. O. Clavadetscher, H. Maurer and S. Sonderegger, St Gall and Sigmaringen, 1980, pp. 244, 264, 266; Lewry, in Gibson, p. 94; Munk Olsen, I, pp. 285–6 (B. 477); Lohr, *AH*, pp. 251–2.

58. MS St Gallen, Stiftsbibliothek, 821
in Cat. s. xi

Parchment; i + 96 + i pages; page 276x181mm; text 210–20x140mm; 35–8 long lines, except for Ovid (pp. 94–96). One scribe for pp. 2–93, similar scribes thereafter. *Tituli*, pp. 33 (bk II), 57 (bk III). Pages slashed horizontally and stitched with green thread, pp. 67–76. Cheap s. xviii binding.
A functional, undecorated book on rough parchment.

CONTENTS P. 1 s. xviii mid contents list; 2–93 ***in Cat.***; 94–6 Ovid, *Ars amatoria* i.1–230, mutilated at end.

GLOSS A few marginal headings, e.g. pp. 12–13. Miscellaneous notes throughout, but no systematic marginalia.

DECORATION Major initial missing, p. 2; minor initials in plain ink.

PROVENANCE Germany or Switzerland. St Gall (stamp, p. 1).

BIBLIOGRAPHY Scherrer, p. 278; *AL*, 1164; E. J. Kenney, 'The Manuscript Tradition of Ovid's *Amores*, *Ars Amatoria*, and *Remedia Amoris*', *The Classical Quarterly*, n.s. 12, 1962, pp. 1–31 [2]; Munk Olsen, II, pp. 162–3; Lohr, *AH*, p. 252.

59. MS St Gallen, Stiftsbibliothek, 824
DCPhil. 1471

Paper; 530 pages; page 298x199mm; text 174–84x80mm; text and gloss 240–65x150–70mm, generous gaps left between lines; 10 lines for text; single column with ample space for gloss in text and margins, added in small cursive hand by scribe. Book numbers as running headers; prose and metre numbers as running footers. *Titulus* in red, p. 519. Colophon, 'Scriptum per me Iohannem wirt visitantem in sancto gallo sub anno domini Mcccclxxi' (p. 519: Scarpatetti). Binding: s. xv red leather on bevelled boards; two clasps (lost).

CONTENTS Pp. 1–6 blank; 7–519 ***DCPhil.***, with commentary; 520–30 blank.

GLOSS Compilations from the commentaries of Ps.-Aquinas and William of Conches (Courcelle), *inc.* 'Sicut inquit philosophorum princeps Aristoteles eius Eticorum primo quod felicitas est bonum et summum et ultimum atque finale' (p. 7^{a}). Systematic commentary continues throughout. Subject headings in scribe's hand to each prose and metre, e.g., 'Conquestio B. de instabilitate fortune' (I.m.i: p. 9), executed in large letters and red underlining on p. 9, but thereafter only large letters with no colour.

DECORATION Major initials to begin each book planned but not executed. Basic red capitals, e.g., pp. 7 and 9, but very little overall; no paraph signs.

PROVENANCE Dr Caspar Wirt (pp. 1: s. xv). St Gall (stamp, p. 35).

BIBLIOGRAPHY Scherrer, p. 278; Courcelle, pp. 410, 415; Scarpatetti, III, p. 69, no. 189, fig. 376 (p. 519).

60. MS St Gallen, Stiftsbibliothek, 826
DCPhil. I–IV s. xv 2/2

Paper (ox–head watermark); 383 pages; page 303x193mm; text 220–30x

120–30mm; 19–20 lines for text; 53–56 lines for gloss; one scribe. Binding: stamped white leather on wood; two clasps (original and complete).

CONTENTS Pp. 1–2 Lupus, *De metris*; 2–4 fragments of commentary on *DCPhil.*; 6–22 blank; 23–291 ***DCPhil. I–IV***, with commentary, *inc.* 'Philosophie servire oportet Seneca octava epistola ad Lucillum'; *expl.* 'de quo dicit Plato viri speculativi viventis in secula seculorum. Amen Sequitur liber quintus et ultimus Boetii de consolatione' (*DCPhil.* text begins p. 26; pp. 206–21 blank; no commentary to bk V); 292–383 blank.

GLOSS See contents; extensive intercalated commentary, possibly Ps.-Aquinas.

DECORATION Red and blue initials with contrasting infill. Gloss lemmatized; letters touched in red.

PROVENANCE St Gall (stamp: pp. 140, 291). 'Assignatus bibliothecae beati Johannis Baptistae 1620' (p. 23).

BIBLIOGRAPHY Scherrer, p. 279; Manitius, I, p. 34; Courcelle, p. 415.

61. MS St Gallen, Stiftsbibliothek, 830
Logica vetus s. xi 1/3

Parchment; iv + 490 pages; (pp. 1–2 flyleaves, removed); page 229x188mm; text 165x110mm (pp. 3–18), 175x130mm (pp. 19–488); 27–32 lines; several good scribes. *Tituli* in red rustic capitals throughout. 'Marcius Novatus Renatus v. c. et sp. relegit mecum' (p. 353). Colophon, p. 309. Binding: white tooled leather on wood; two clasps (upper one repaired). Parchment label top centre on front cover SEX LIBRI PERIERMENIARUM BOECIUS DE TOPICIS CICERO DE TOPICIS GEOMETRIA.

CONTENTS Pp. 3–264 ***2 in Int.***; 265–82 Cicero, *Topica*; 283–309 Ps.-Boethius, *Geometria* I; 311–53 ***Top. Diff.***, with elegant table in five cols contrasting Themistius and Cicero (p. 340); 353–69 ***Div.***; 369–76 Ps.-Boethius, *De rhetorice cognatione*; 376–408 ***intr. Syll. Cat.***; 408–44 ***Syll. Cat.***; 444–88 ***Syll. Hyp.***; 488 Ekkehart of St Gall, *De Boethio*, *inc.* 'Explicit memorandum dogma sophiae'; *expl.* 'Qui bybliothecas vestisti lumine caecas'; 489 drawings, verses and scribbles; 490 (s. xii addition) *De septem artibus*, *inc.* 'Adstantes avidi vates populusque david'.

GLOSS *2 in Int.* with subject headings, but no extensive annotation; *Topica* with extensive annotation at the beginning; *Top. Diff.* with subject headings and some annotation; *Div.* with a few subject headings, including two passages from *Topica Aris.*; *De rhetorice cognatione* with subject headings and comments; *intr. Syll. Cat.* with subject headings and some notes; *Syll. Cat.* with subject headings and some notes; *Syll. Hyp.* with very little annotation; Ekkehart IV's annotation, p. 488.

DECORATION Consistent throughout volume. Good quality red outline initials at the beginning of each new text. Some internal book-incipits, *2 in Int.* (pp. 3, 46, 101, 136, 186, 226); Cicero, *Topica* (p. 265); *Top. Diff.* (pp. 311, 320, 333, 342); *Syll. Hyp.* (pp. 444, 457, 473).

PROVENANCE Germany. Probably produced in Mainz (Hoffmann). Brought to St Gall by Ekkehart IV.

BIBLIOGRAPHY Scherrer, pp. 281–2; E. Chatelain, *Paléographie des classiques latines*, 2 vols, Paris, 1884–92 and 1894–1900, i, p. 6, pl. XXI.1; C. Thulin, 'Zur Überlieferungsgeschichte des Corpus Agrimensorum. Exzerptenhandschriften und Kompendien', *Göteborgs Kungl. Vetenskaps- och Vitterhets-Samhälles Handlingar*, 14, 1911, p. 25; *MBKDS*, I, p. 118, line 12, no. 23; *AL*, 1165; Bruckner, III, pp. 47, 118; G. F. Pagallo, 'Per una edizione critica del "De Hypotheticis Syllogismis" di Boezio', *Italia medioevale e umanistica*, 1, 1958, p. 73; Folkerts, p. 96; S. Sonderegger, 'Notker der Deutsche und Cicero. Aspekte einer mittelalterlichen Rezeption', *Florilegium Sangallense. Festschrift für J. Duft zum 65. Geburtstag*, ed. O. Clavadetscher, H. Maurer and S. Sonderegger, St Gall and Sigmaringen, 1980, p. 264; Folkerts II, pp. 97, 104; Munk Olsen, I, p. 286 (C. 478); Hoffmann, I, pp. 247, 253, 256–7 (description), 271; Nikitas, p. lvii; *Die Abtei St. Gallen*, II, p. 218, n. 46; Lohr, *AH*, p. 255; Toneatto, I, pp. 348–53; III, p. 922.

62. MS St Gallen, Stiftsbibliothek, 831
in Topica Cic., 1 in Isag., Isag. s. xi/xii; s. xii

Parchment; 364 pages; page 252x175mm.
A (s. xi/xii): text 2 cols, each 185x60mm; 32 lines; several good and compatible scribes. Irish features in script. *Tituli* in orange, pp. 3, 117. Colophon to *in Topica Cic. IV*: 'conditor operis emendavi' (p. 117).
B (s. xii): text 2 cols, each 175–85x60mm; 34 lines; ?scribe. *Tituli* in plain ink, not consistent, e.g. pp. 185^a, 260^a, 266^b.
Pastedowns removed. Binding: tooled white leather on boards; two clasps (lost). Label top centre on front cover EDICIO BOECII IN TOPICA TULII CICERONIS VI LIBRI.

CONTENTS p. 1 doodles; 2 s. xviii contents list.
A: pp. 3^a–168^b ***in Topica Cic.***; 169^a–172^b Walafrid Strabo, *Regulae metricae* (Bischoff); 173^a–175^a *De ceromate*; 175^a–181^a letter of Walafrid Strabo, *inc.* 'Domino meo benedictus salus et vita. Sicut iussisti mi domine flos et paradoxa'; 181^a calendar verses; 182^a book list.
B: p. 183 blank; 184 schema of *substantia*; 185^a–259^b ***1 in Isag.***;

260^{a}–266^{b} Marius Victorinus (Candidus), *De generatione divina*; 266^{b}–280^{b} letter of Marius Victorinus to Candidus; 280^{a}–294^{b} ***Isag.***; 295^{a}–331^{b} commentary on *Isag.*, *inc.* '(C)ur genus speciei differentiae proprio et accidenti disputationis ordine preponatur. Respondendum est iure factum videri'; *expl.* 'sed alius quidem paulo minus niger est alius vero teterimus. explicit'; p. 332 blank; 333^{a}–344^{b} commentary on *Isag.*, *inc.* 'Cum sit necessarium usque coniectans Utilitas huius libri quadrifariam spargitur namque ad illud etiam ad quod eius dirigitur intentio magno legentibus usui est'; *expl.* 'ut tota disputatio ad predicamenta conveniat'; 344^{b}–359^{b} excerpted summary of *1 in Isag.* 1; 359^{b} summary definitions from *Top. Diff.* I–II; 361–364 miscellaneous notes and diagrams.

GLOSS *in Topica Cic.* virtually no annotation; *1 in Isag.* no annotation; *Isag.* no annotation.

DECORATION Competent red, green, purple, and ochre initials with Insular knots begin each book of *in Topica Cic.* Thereafter only a few simple red initials at the beginning of each new text, pp. 185, 260, 280. Much colour in the Strabo section. Quires numbered in colour, contemporaneously until p. 150, thereafter modern numbering.

PROVENANCE Germany or Switzerland (Munk Olsen). 'Liber SS. Galli atque Othmari' (p. 3); stamp, p. 360.

BIBLIOGRAPHY Scherrer, pp. 282–3; *MBKDS*, I, p. 111, line 17 (no. 11); Steinmeyer-Sievers, V, p. 59, no. 698; Bruckner, III, p. 45; *AL*, 2127; Bischoff, 'Eine Sammelhandschrift Walafrid Strabos (Cod. Sangall. 878)', *Mittelalterliche Studien*, II, pp. 34–51 (p. 45, n. 30); Bergmann, no. 241; Munk Olsen, III.1, p. 293 (dates A as s. x); Lohr, *AH*, pp. 255–6.

63. MS St Gallen, Stiftsbibliothek, 844
DCPhil., Vita I s. ix

Parchment; ii + 186 pages (pp. 180–81 missing); page 220x162mm; text 155x103mm; 21 lines; one scribe from p. 6 onwards. *Tituli* (in rustic capitals), pp. 38, 69–70, 116, 157. Binding: plain wood with parchment spine; one clasp (lost).

CONTENTS Pp. 1–3 *accessus*, *inc.* 'Oportet nos memores esse quae de romano imperio Paulus apostolus predixerat quondam'; 3 glosses on *DCPhil.* I.m.i–pr.i.25; 4 later doodles; 5 s. xviii contents list; 6–12 Lupus, *De metris*, with addition; 13–186 ***DCPhil.*** (missing V.m.v.2–V.pr.vi); 186 ***Vita I***, *expl.* imperf. 'conscripserat' (l. 12).

GLOSS Contemporary notes in a very fine, minute hand; fragms of commentary of 'Anonymous of St Gall' (Courcelle). Old High

German glosses, e.g., pp. 133, 134. Annotator has added Greek in capitals in margin as a correction to Greek in the text, e.g., II.pr.ii.40 (p. 43), III.pr.vi.3 (p. 84), IV.pr.vi.145 (p. 147), IV.pr.vi.196 (p. 150). Headings within text, e.g. I.m.v: AD DEUM INVOCATIO (p. 29), III.pr.vi: DE CARNIS VOLUPTATIBUS (p. 86). Metres often identified by glossator at the beginning of each metre.

DECORATION Metres in red rustic capitals, later (from p. 16 on, I.m.ii) in red minuscule. Elaborately drawn, though single colour (orange) initials, pp. 13 (I), 31 (I.pr.v), 39 (II), 70 (III), 116 (IV), 158 (V). Incipits in orange to each bk.

PROVENANCE St Gall (stamp, p. 115).

BIBLIOGRAPHY Scherrer, p. 287; J. Kelle, 'Über die Grundlage, auf der Notkers Erklärung von Boethius De Consolatione philosophiae beruht', *Sitzungsberichte der Bayerischen Akademie der Wissenschaften, philologisch-philosophische und historische Klasse*, 3, Munich, 1896, pp. 349–56; Steinmeyer-Sievers, IV, p. 453, no. 210; Naumann, pp. IX, 14, 17, 20, 72; *MBKDS*, I, p. 111, line 20 (no. 11); Bruckner, III, pp. 25, 37, 45, 118 (description: dates MS s. x); K. Ostberg, 'The "Prologi" of Notker's "Boethius" Reconsidered', *German Life and Letters*, 16, 1963, pp. 256–8, 263; Courcelle, pp. 270, 404; Bergmann, no. 242 K. Ostberg, 'Who Were the Mergothi?', *German Life and Letters*, 33.2, 1980, p. 97; B. Bischoff, 'Bücher am Hofe Ludwigs des Deutschen und die Privatbibliothek des Kanzlers Grimalt', *Mittelalterliche Studien*, iii, pp. 187–212 (193–4, n. 35); Gibson, p. 399; *Notker der Deutsche. Boethius, "De Consolatione Philosophiae" Buch I/II*, ed. P. W. Tax, Tübingen, 1986, pp. xxiv–xxv.

64. MS St Gallen, Stiftsbibliothek, 847
DCPhil. S. XV

Paper; 374 pages.
A (s. xv): page 245x174mm; text extremely variable 130–60x110mm; 10–15 lines, widely spaced with plenty of margin for gloss; one cursive hand.
B (s. xv): page 224x156mm.; text 150–65x97mm; 10–14 lines; wide margin for gloss; one cursive hand.
Tituli, pp. 5, 137. Binding: s. xviii pasteboard with leather spine.

CONTENTS A: pp. 1–2 blank; 3 ?library notes; 5–117 ***DCPhil. I–II***, with commentary beginning on p. 4; 118–29 blank.
B: pp. 130–36 blank; 138–366 ***DCPhil. III–V***, with commentary, continued (pp. 181–84 blank); 367–74 blank.

GLOSS Commentary on *DCPhil.*, possibly Ps.-Aquinas. Added

contemporary gloss, very cramped in B, but subsiding to almost nothing after p. 281.

DECORATION *C(armina)* in green, red and ochre (p. 5); thereafter nothing except slightly elaborated red initials at pp. 214 and 298. Red highlighting of text and gloss until p. 35; boxing of internal divisions (prose and metre) in red.

PROVENANCE 'Frater Ioachim' in large black letters (p. 3). In St Gall library s. xviii: D. n. 267 in Kolb's hand, p. 3.

BIBLIOGRAPHY Scherrer, p. 288.

65. MS St Gallen, Stiftsbibliothek, 854
in Topica Cic. s. xi

Parchment; ii + 216 pages; pastedowns removed; page 200x172mm; text 150x125mm; 21 lines; one scribe. *Tituli* in orange and red capitals to *in Topica Cic.* Signature numbers. Binding: plain white leather on wood; two clasps (lost). Parchment label, top centre front COMMENTARIA ANICII MANLII BOETII IN TOPICA CICERONIS (s. xv).

CONTENTS Pp. 1–21 Cicero, *Topica*, *expl.* imperf. II.18.70 'ab optimo quoque laudata atque ut haec in comparatione' (18/5–6); 21–216 ***in Topica Cic.***

GLOSS A few notes (e.g., p. 23) and marginal subject headings to bk I, but scarce. Notes on law (p. 107).

DECORATION Orange-red outline initials with blue and purple infill, ***M****(aiores)*, p. 1 and ***I****(ncipientes)*, p. 22. ***E****(xhortatione)*: three fishes in rubricator's red and blue, p. 23. Elsewhere, plain orange-red outline initials generally with partial blue infill. No internal rubrication.

PROVENANCE Germany or Switzerland (Munk Olsen). St Gall (stamp, pp. 1, 216); D. 1. 352 in Kolb's hand (p. 1).

BIBLIOGRAPHY Scherrer, p. 289; Sonderegger, 'Notker und Cicero', p. 264; Munk Olsen, I, pp. 286–7 (C. 480).

66. MS St Gallen, Stiftsbibliothek, 859
DCPhil. I–II s. xv^{ex}

Paper; 502 + i pages.
A: page 278x200mm; text 185x125mm; 20 lines for text; wide margins for gloss; one scribe.

B: page 310x220mm; text 190–215x123–32mm; 31–40 lines; two scribes.
C: page 325x215mm; text 235x125mm; 30 lines; two similar scribes.
D: page 325x215mm; text 220x142mm; 32 lines; several scribes.
E: page 315x220mm; text 2 cols, each 231x71mm; 52–55 lines; one scribe.
F: page 320x215mm; text 225x140mm; 32 lines; one scribe.
G: page 315x220mm; text 170–75x110–20mm; 9 lines for text; 35 lines for gloss, with wide margins left for further annotation; one scribe. Very corrupt *titulus*, p. 493.
H: page 295x190mm; text 185x105mm; 22 lines; one scribe.
Binding: pasteboard with leather spine (s. xvii–xix).

CONTENTS Pp. 1–2 flyleaves.
A: p. 3 blank; 4–49 Terence, *Andria*, with gloss; 50 notes and doodles.
B: pp. 51–59 Sylvius, *Epistles II. 51, 61*; 62–70 blank.
C: pp. 71–136 Cicero, *Epistolae ad Familiares*, with commentary; 137–42 blank.
D: pp. 143–62 Aristotle, *Ethica Nicomachaea I–II*, with gloss; 163–6 blank.
E: p. 167^{a} *In Porphyrium*, mutilated at end; 169^{a}–175^{a} *In Porphyrium*, *inc.* 'Cum sit necessarium scire universalis naturam quae fundamentum est omnis scientiae'; *expl.* 'insecutor breviter sufficiant'; 175^{b}–193^{a} *Questiones de ente et essentia*, *inc.* 'circa tractatum nunc de universalibus'; *expl.* 'de ente et essentia secundum dominum Albertum Aristotelis commentatorem determinatarum', with extensive intercalated commentary; 193^{b}–94 blank.
F: pp. 195–203 Aristotle, *Oeconomica*; 204–18 blank.
G: pp. 219–493 ***DCPhil. I–II****.m.ii*, with massive intercalated commentary; 494 blank.
H: pp. 495–6 (a loose folio) Sallust, *Catiline* 57.1 'pistoriensem abduxit eo consilio per tramites oculte' (ed. Kurfess, p. 48, lines 14–15)–58.17 'averteris ea dementiae est semper' (p. 50, line 1).

GLOSS Commentary of Ps.-Aquinas, or a development of same, *inc.* 'Philosophie servire opportet vera ut tibi contingat libertas. Seneca venerabilis octava epistola ad Lucillium. Philosophia dicatur scientia 2o metaphisice' (p. 219).

DECORATION Initials planned, but not executed.

PROVENANCE No St Gall signs at all.

BIBLIOGRAPHY Scherrer, p. 295; *AL*, 1167; Lohr, *AH*, pp. 261–2.

KANTONSBIBLIOTHEK VADIANA (before 1979 STADTBIBLIOTHEK VADIANA)

Most MSS have come from the collections of Joachim von Watt (Vadianus), d. 1551, Mayor of St Gall, rector of the University of Vienna, reformer and historiographer, and of Sebastian and Bartholomäus Schobinger.

G. Scherrer, *Verzeichnis der Manuscripte und Incunabeln der Vadianischen Bibliothek in St. Gallen*, St Gall, 1864; B. Hertenstein, *Joachim von Watt (Vadianus), Bartholomäus Schobinger, Melchior Goldast. Die Beschäftigung mit dem Althochdeutschen von St. Gallen in Humanismus und Frühbarock*, Berlin and New York, 1975; Kristeller, V, pp. 125–7; Senser, p. 104.

67. MS St Gallen, Kantonsbibliothek Vadiana, 296
Arith., Mus. s. xii 1/3

Parchment; i + 108 + i fols; page 252x180mm; text 195x110mm; 34 lines; same or very similar scribe throughout. Greek in red, very clear, fols 47^{v}–48^{r}. *Tituli* in red, fols 2^{v}, 61^{v}, 74^{r}, 83^{v}. *Capitula* for *Mus.* bks II, IV and V, fols 61^{v}, 83^{v} and 101^{v}. Binding: parchment (s. xv sermon) on pasteboard with stamped leather spine; two ties (lost).
Bower notes excellence of execution and text.

CONTENTS Fols 1^{v}–46^{r} ***Arith.*** (1^{v}–2^{r} prologue; 2^{r-v} and 21^{r}–22^{r} *capitula*; 44^{r-v} is a later replacement of 163/17–167/18 in an inexpert humanistic cursive); 47^{r}–108^{r} ***Mus.***

GLOSS None.

DECORATION Simple red, blue or green major and minor initials, with occasional internal floral decoration, or external scroll-work, e.g., fols 1^{v}, 2^{v}, 22^{r}, 47^{r}. Careful diagrams in red, blue, green; paraph signs in plain ink. Rubrication, initials and diagrams all by the same hand.

PROVENANCE ?England (script). Belonged to the Schobinger brothers (fol. 1^{r}); Vadiana stamp (fols 1^{r}, 108^{v}).

BIBLIOGRAPHY Scherrer, pp. 75–6; Bruckner, III, pp. 48–53; Masi, p. 62; Bower, no. 108.

68. MS St Gallen, Kantonsbibliothek Vadiana, 313
Top. Diff. s. x

Parchment; ii + 154 + iii fols; page 216x150mm; text 170x110mm; 29 lines; two similar scribes, changing at fol. 121^{v}. *Tituli* in orange caps, fols 121^{v}–22^{r}, 128^{r}, 137^{r}, 143^{v}. Binding: pasteboard with a s. xv parchment spine (liturgical fragment).

CONTENTS Fols 1^{r}–63^{r} Cicero, *De inventione*; 64^{v}–120^{r} Ps.-Cicero, *Ad Herennium*; 120^{r}–121^{r} Quintilian, *Institutio oratoria*, *inc.* 'Rhetorica est secundum Aristotelem et Patroclem vis inveniendi omnia in oratione persuasibilia'; *expl.* 'que memoria complectitur et pronuntiatione commendamus'; 121^{v}–150^{v} ***Top. Diff.***; 150^{v}–152^{v} Ps.-Boethius, *De rhetoricae cognatione*; 153^{r}–154^{r} Ps.-Boethius, *De locorum rhetoricorum distinctione*.

GLOSS Vertical notes, identifying rhetorical commonplaces, at the outer edges of fols 123^{r}, 125^{r}, 130^{r}, 131^{r}, 133^{r}, 146^{v}; some trimmed by binder.

DECORATION Paraph signs in ink of text.

PROVENANCE Germany or Switzerland (Munk Olsen). Vadiana stamp, fols 1^{r}, 154^{v}. Note in the hand of the librarian Dr Johannes Dieraner, 22 May 1875, fol. iii^{v}.

BIBLIOGRAPHY Scherrer, pp. 82–3; Chatelain, I, p. 5, pl. XVIII.2 (fol. 4^{r}); Bruckner, III, pp. 45, 53, 54; A. Stückelberger, 'Der Kodex Vadianus 313. Eine in der Überlieferungsgeschichte des Herenniustextes vernachlässigte Handschrift', *Museum Helveticum*, 22, 1965, pp. 217–28; idem, 'Anonymus Vadianus De Rhetorica', *Museum Helveticum*, 23, 1966, pp. 197–208; B. Bischoff, 'Das griechische Element in der abendländischen Bildung des Mittelalters', *Mittelalterliche Studien*, ii, pp. 246–75 (257, n. 58); S. Sonderegger, 'Notker und Cicero. Aspekte einer mittelalterlichen Rezeption', *Florilegium Sangallenese. Festschrift für J. Duft zum 65. Geburtstag*, ed. O. Clavadetscher, H. Maurer and S. Sonderegger, St Gall and Sigmaringen, 1980, pp. 264–5; Munk Olsen, I, p. 284 (B. 474); II, p. 304 (B. 41).

SCHAFFHAUSEN

MINISTERIALBIBLIOTHEK, f. 1568 (now in Stadtbibliothek)

The Allerheiligenkloster in Schaffhausen was founded in the second half of the eleventh century and the first catalogue was compiled by Abbot Siegfried (1082–96). After the dissolution of the monastery in 1529, the monastic library was transferred to the St Johann Kirche in Schaffhausen, whence the MSS passed to the Ministerialbibliothek, which was significantly enlarged and revived by Prof. J. Altorfer in 1781. Since 1923 the Ministerialbibliothek and the Stadtbibliothek have shared the same building, but their collections are separate.

H. Boos, *Katalog der Ministerialbibliothek zu Schaffhausen*, Schaffhausen, 1877; Bruckner, vol. VI; *MBKDS*, I, pp. 291–5; Kristeller, V, pp. 129–31; R. Gamper, G. Knoch-Mund and M. Stähli, *Katalog der mittelalterlichen Handschriften der*

Ministerialbibliothek Schaffhausen, Zurich, 1994.

69. MS Schaffhausen, Ministerialbibliothek, Min. 108 (106)
Mus. c. 1100

Parchment; i + 143 + i fols; page 205x145mm; text 135x90mm; 21–22 lines; several similar scribes. Greek clear. Neumes, fols 134^{v}, 140^{v}–41^{r}. *Tituli* and subheadings in ochre (except bk I – black). Binding: white leather on wood; one clasp (lost). Paper label on fol. 1^{r} ITEM LIBER MUSICE BOETII.

CONTENTS Fols 1^{v}–3^{r} Walther, 15898; 4^{r}–131^{v} ***Mus.*** *expl.* imperf. V.18 (371/6); 131^{v}–135^{v} Frutolfus of Bamberg, *Breviarium de musica* (Walther, 15922); 135^{v}–138^{r} Walther, 409; 139^{r}–140^{r} *Versus de alphabetis Graeco et Hebraeo* (Schaller, 13135); 140^{r} map of winds with Old High German wind-names; 140^{v} Schaller, 11080; 140^{v}–141^{r} 'Cambridge song' no. 12 (Walther, 20694); 141^{v}–142^{r} *Laus musicae divinae* 'Proemium et Oratio Gwidonis in musicam', *inc.* 'Rex superne armonie qui contentus angelici vastam gubernas musicam'; *expl.* 'Tu citharista maximus digito sancti spiritus corda reple armonia'.

GLOSS Some interlinear but mainly marginal gloss linked to text by reference signs, diminishing through text.

DECORATION Fine major initials in ochre outline with flourishing (fols 4^{r}, 36^{r}, 65^{v}, 86^{r}, 118^{v}); minor initials in ochre, to begin each chapter. Incipits and explicits in red; diagrams in ochre and black.

PROVENANCE ?Tegernsee (Bower). Belonged to the Allerheiligenkloster in Schaffhausen (fol. 142^{v}: s. xiv), whence to Ministerialbibliothek (fol. 1^{r}: s. xvii).

BIBLIOGRAPHY Boos, p. 12; Bruckner, VI, p. 66, 73, pl. xlvi; Bower, no. 110; Bernhardt and Bower, pp. lxxiii and lxxv; Gamper, Knoch-Mund and Stähli, pp. 246–8.

STADTBIBLIOTHEK, f. 1636.

The first catalogue was compiled in 1753 and the first printed catalogue published in 1824.

H. Boos, *Verzeichnis der Inkunabeln und Handschriften der Schaffhauser Stadtbibliothek*, Schaffhausen, 1903; E. G. Ruesch, *Inhaltsverzeichnis der Handschriften der Ministerial- und Stadtbibliothek nach den fortlaufenden Nummern des Standortes*, Schaffhausen, 1966 (typescript); Kristeller, V, pp. 129–31; Senser, pp. 105–7.

70. MS Schaffhausen, Stadtbibliothek, Gen. 7
DCPhil. s. xiii

Parchment; iii + 74 + iii fols; page 200x140mm; text 130x85mm; 27 lines; several scribes, two scribes for *DCPhil.*, changing at fols 7v–8r. Book numbers as running headers. Binding: brown leather (modern); five metal bosses on front and back.

CONTENTS Fols 1r–50r ***DCPhil.***, glossed; 51r–v faded text; 52r–74r Prosper of Aquitaine, *Epigrammata*, *inc.* imperf. 'hoc pater, hoc verbum patris' (*PL*, 64:499C).

GLOSS Contemporary, mainly marginal gloss, especially to fols 17v–25v (bk III) and 43r–44v (bk V). Pointing hands in margin (s. xiv–xv).

DECORATION Red major and minor initials (minor initials planned, but not executed). Rubrication; incipits in red, fols 17v (bk III), 29v (bk IV), 42r (bk V); paraph signs.

PROVENANCE Unknown.

BIBLIOGRAPHY Boos, p. 68.

SOLOTHURN

STAATSARCHIV

A. Kocher, 'Mittelalterliche Handschriften aus dem Staatsarchiv Solothurn', *Veröffentlichungen des Solothurner Staatsarchivs*, 7, Olten, 1974.

71. MS Solothurn, Staatsarchiv, 8
Mus. s. x 1/4

Parchment; three bifolia, used as binding for building and cellar accounts at Stift Schönenwerd; page 290x210mm; text 210x140mm; 31 lines; ?one scribe.

CONTENTS I: fol. 1r–v ***Mus.*** I.18–20 (204/26–206/29); 2r–v ***Mus.*** I.20 (211/1–20).
II: fol. 1r–v ***Mus.*** I.23–7 (216/25–219/13); 2r–v ***Mus.*** II.8 (234/24–237/4).
III: fol. 1r–v ***Mus.*** IV.18–V *capitula* 1–30 (349/12–351/13); 2r–v ***Mus.*** V.1–2 (351/14–354/4).

GLOSS Some marginal notes to the second bifolium in another hand.

DECORATION None.

PROVENANCE ?East Francia (script).

BIBLIOGRAPHY Kocher, pp. 24–6; Bower, no. 111.

ZÜRICH (Zurich)

ZENTRALBIBLIOTHEK, f. 1897.

The Zentralbibliothek now includes the Stadtbibliothek (f. 1629) and the Stiftsbibliothek of the Carolinum (pressmark Car.) or Grossmünster.

Bruckner, vol. IV; L. C. Mohlberg, *Katalog der Handschriften der Zentralbibliothek Zürich I: Mittelalterliche Handschriften*, Zurich, 1952; A. Cattani and B. Weber, *Zentralbibliothek Zürich: Schatzkammer der Überlieferung*, Zurich, 1989; Kristeller, V, pp. 138–59; Senser, pp. 64–6.

72. MS Zürich, Zentralbibliothek, C. 159
DCPhil. II–III s. xv 1/2

Paper; i + 24 + i fols; page 215x150mm; text: too fragmentary to judge; wide margin for gloss; one cursive hand. Pasteboard binding.
Personal study copy, now in very bad condition, having been retrieved from use in bindings.

CONTENTS Fols 1^r–24^v ***DCPhil. II–III***, fragments:
1^r–10^v II.pr.i.1–II.pr.iv.8 'Nam si te hoc';
11^r–12^v III.pr.ii.54 'num enim'–III.m.ii.11 'Si cruor';
13^r–14^v III.m.ii.35 'reditque suo'–III.pr.iii.35 'quod vel vi';
15^r–18^v III.pr.iii.56 'sufficientiam praestare credatis'–III.pr.v.21 'sed nequeunt';
19^r–22^v III.pr.vi.12 'ipsum propagasse'–III.m.viii.5 'montibus additis';
23^r–24^v III.pr.ix.31 'videatur abiectius'–III.pr.ix.77 'statim videbis'.

GLOSS Extensive gloss, with lemmata generally in capitals.

DECORATION None.

PROVENANCE Unknown.

BIBLIOGRAPHY Mohlberg, p. 71.

73. MS Zürich, Zentralbibliothek, Car. C. 100
Div. 1444

Parchment (section A) and paper (sections B–F); i + 164 fols; page 286x205mm. A: text 205x110mm; 42 lines; two scribes (changing at fol. 18^{r}), writing a good humanistic cursive. Colophon, fol. 26^{v}: 'explicit feliciter xliiij^{o}'.
Binding: s. xvi^{ex} wooden boards with parchment spine; one central clasp (lost).

CONTENTS A: fols 1^{r}–17^{v} treatise on rhetoric attributed to Martianus Capella (ed. Halm, *Rhetores minores*, 1863, 454/5–491/28; 18^{r}–26^{v} ***Div.***, *inc.* imperf. 'Divisio multis modis dicitur. Est enim divisio generis in species' (*PL*, 64:877B); 27^{r}–29^{v} blank.
B–F: fols 30^{r}–164^{r} formularies and letter collections, including much humanistic material.

GLOSS Quite extensive users' annotation to fols 18^{r}, 19^{v}–20^{r} and 22^{v}–23^{r} only.

DECORATION Plain red ***D****(ivisio)*, fol. 18^{r}; thereafter frequent red paraph signs within the text.

PROVENANCE Italy. P. Numagen, notary of Trier, d. 1577.

BIBLIOGRAPHY P. Bänzinger, 'Beiträge zur Geschichte der Spätscholastik und des Frühhumanismus in der Schweiz', *Schweizer Studien zur Geschichtswissenschaft*, NF, 4, 1945, pp. 55–64 (Numagen); Mohlberg, pp. 110–12, 371; Bruckner, IV, pp. 100, 102; Scarpatetti, III, pp. 209–10, no. 603, fig. 192 (fol. 25^{r}).

74. MS Zürich, Zentralbibliothek, Car. C. 170
Logica vetus s. xiii 1/2; s. xiv

Parchment; 86 fols; page 180x115mm.
B (s. xiii 1/2): text 135x60mm; 29 lines. *Tituli* in scribe's hand, fols 11^{r}–72^{v}; s. xiv *titulus* in another hand on fol. 73^{r}.
Parts A & C are s. xiv palimpsests of different MSS.
Binding: white leather on wood, painted in red and grey-blue, with simple leaf-terminals inside a rectangle enclosing a St Andrew's cross; five bosses on front and back and two clasps with foxes' heads. Pastedowns from s. xiii psalter with two good abstract initials: 'Dixi' front, 'Dixit' back. Title on front cover top centre VETUS LOYCA TOTA SIMUL.
A good, clear copy with wide margins, heavily used.

CONTENTS A: fols 1^{r}–10^{v} *Liber sex principiorum*.
B: fols 11^{r}–21^{v} ***Isag.***; 22^{r}–39^{r} ***Cat.***; 39^{v}–49^{r} ***De Int.***; 49^{r}–62^{r} ***Top. Diff. I–II***, *expl.* imperf. II.9.1 'ex divisione nascentes' (p. 41, ll. 10–11), with s. xiv note 'Quere supplementum in ultimo quoterno huius'; 62^{r}–72^{v} ***Div.***; 73^{r}–75^{v} ***Syll. Cat.***, *expl.* imperf. 'sed id quod

diximus demonstremus esse' (*PL*, 64:798–99B); 76^{r-v} blank.
C: fols 77^{r}–80^{r} ***Top. Diff. II–III***, II.9.2 'casus est alicuius nominis'–III.2.7 'alia ex similitudine' (p. 41, l. 11–p. 50, l. 1); 80^{v}–86^{v} blank.

GLOSS Miscellaneous user's gloss throughout.

DECORATION Simple, slightly decorated red initials to *Isag.*, *Cat.*, *De Int.*, *Top. Diff.*, *Div.* Minor initials and paraph signs in red. Competent and quite detailed rubrication at *tituli.*

PROVENANCE Unknown. Press-mark D. 58 (fol. 1^{r}: s. xviii–xix).

BIBLIOGRAPHY Bruckner, IV, p. 92; *AL*, 1168; Mohlberg, p. 141.

Plates

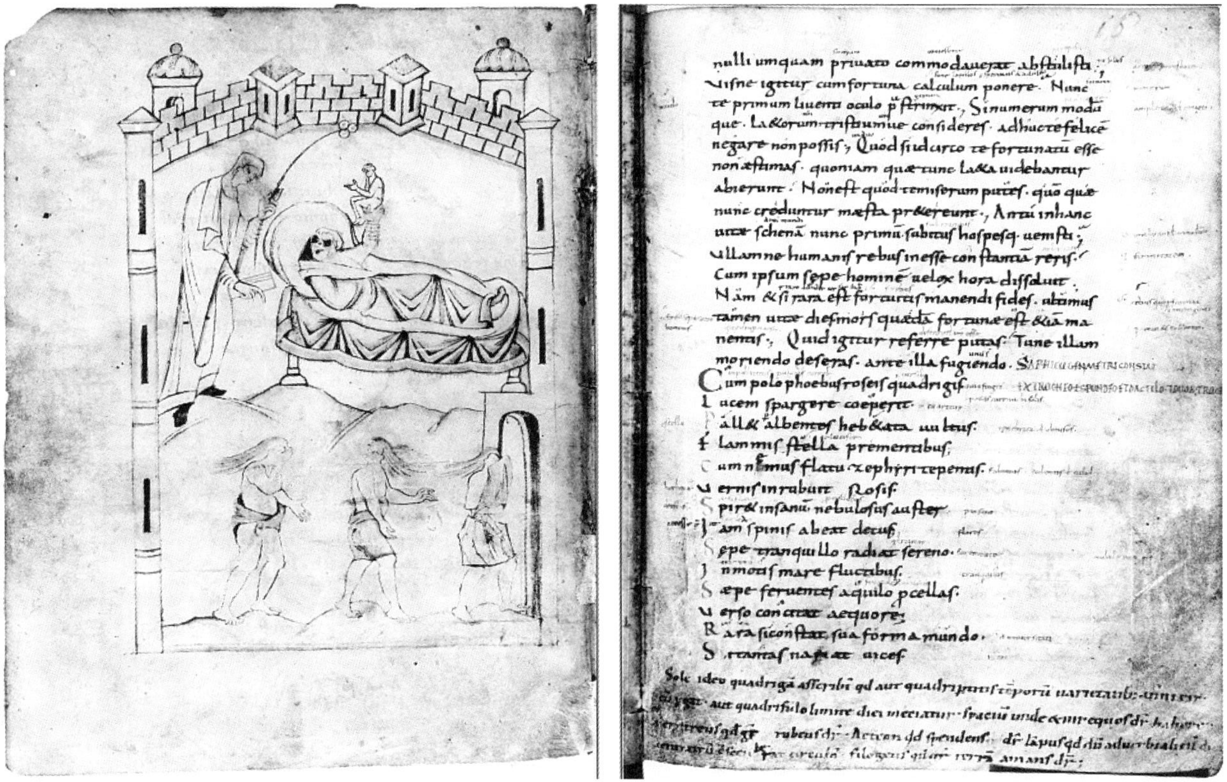

1. MS Wien. Österreichsche Nationalbibliothek 271, fols 1v and 16r.

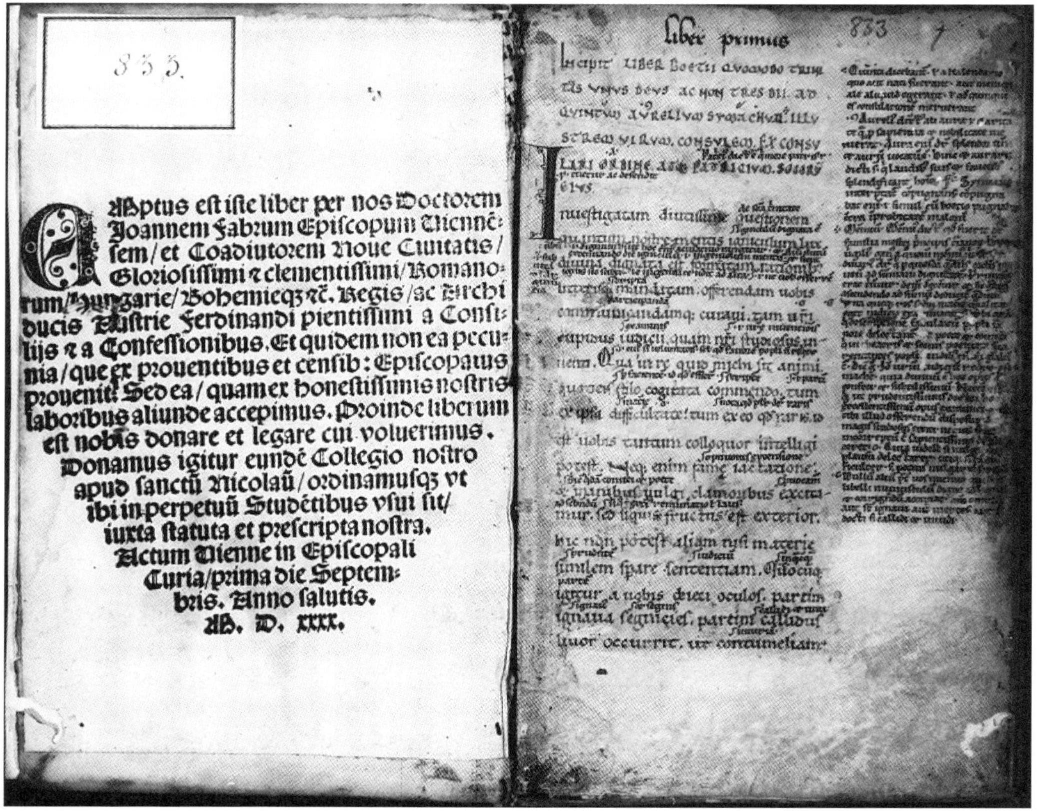

2. MS Wien. Österreichsche Nationalbibliothek, 833, fols i^{v} and 1^{r}.

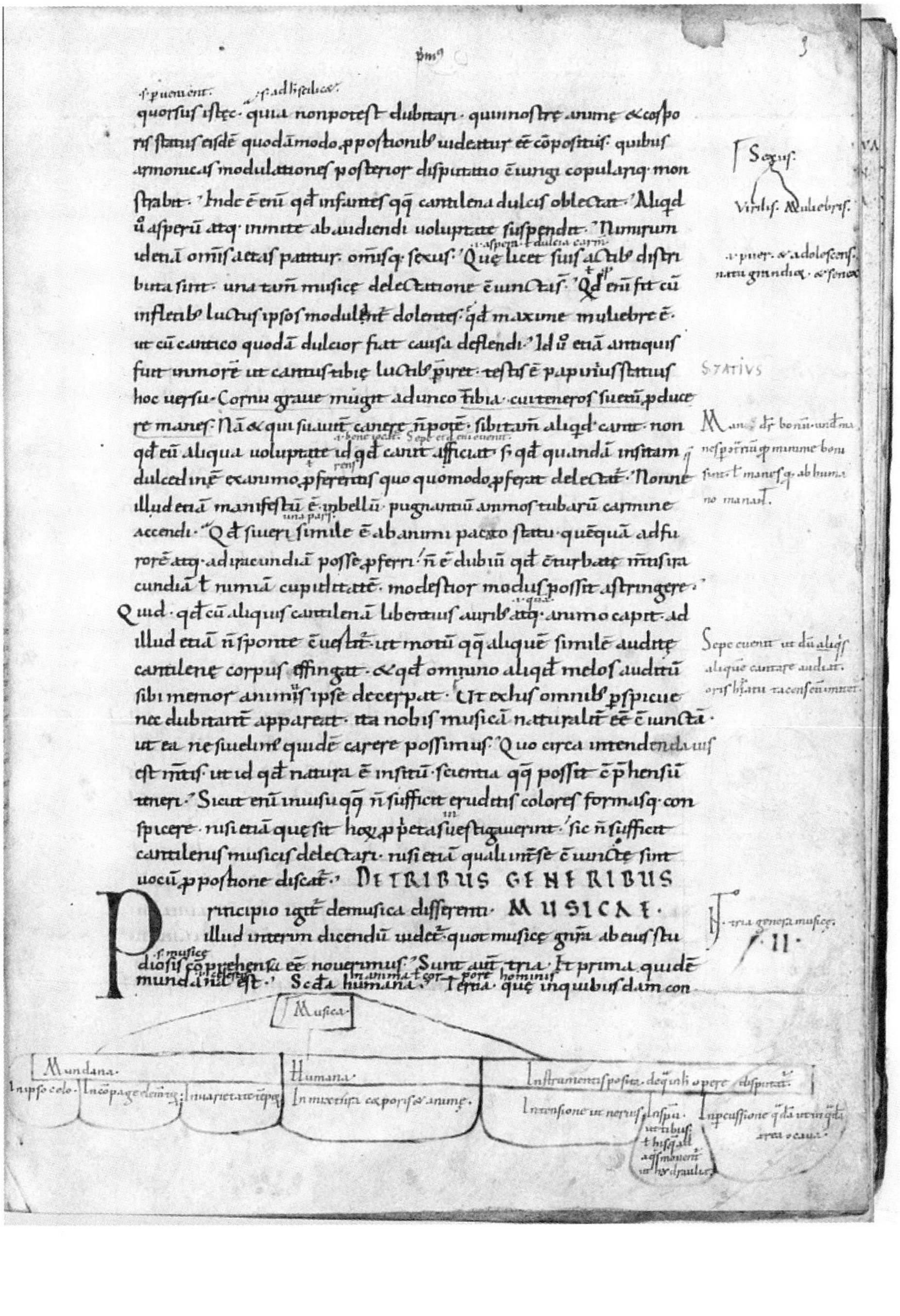

3. MS Brugge, Stedelijke Openbare Bibliotheek, 531, fol. 3r.

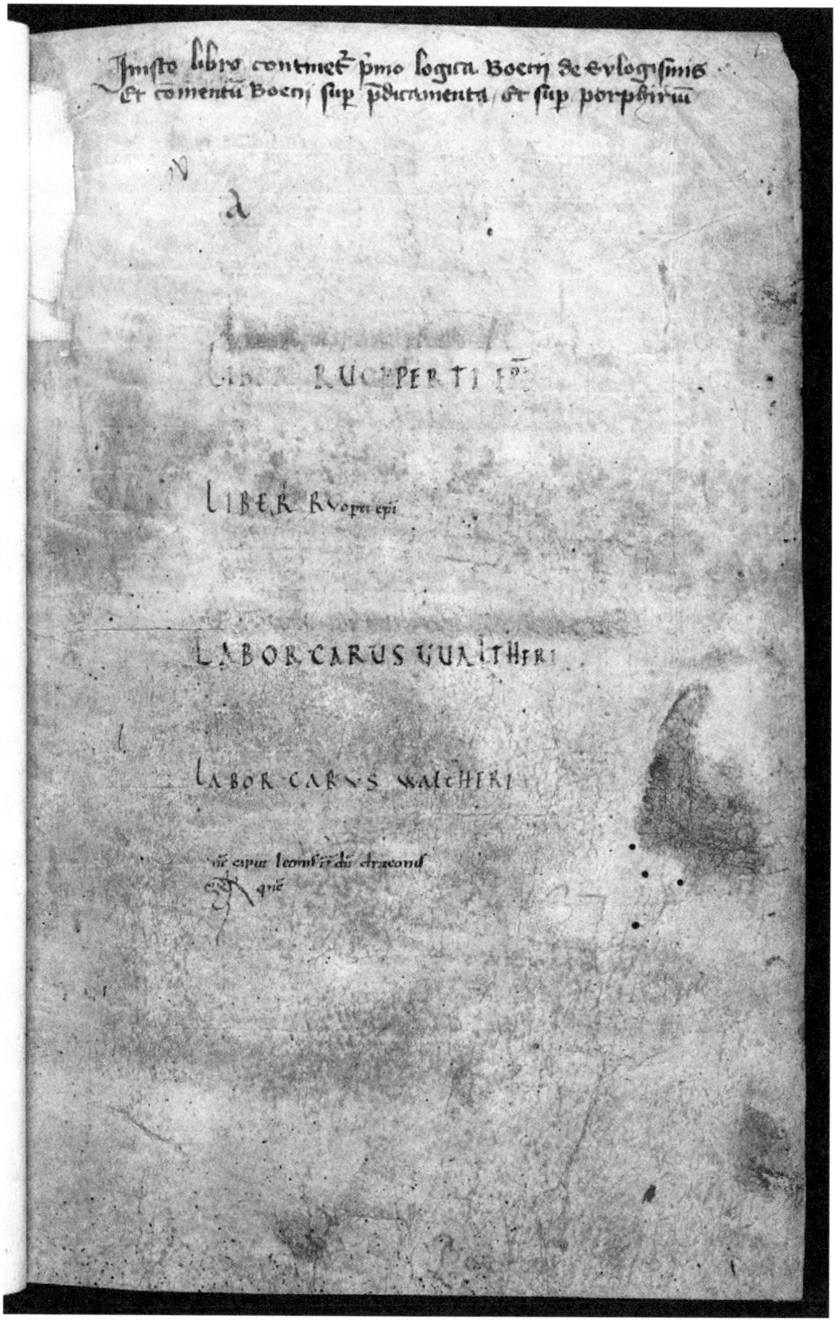

4. København, Det Kongelige Bibliotek, Thott 166 2^{0}, fol. 1^{r}.

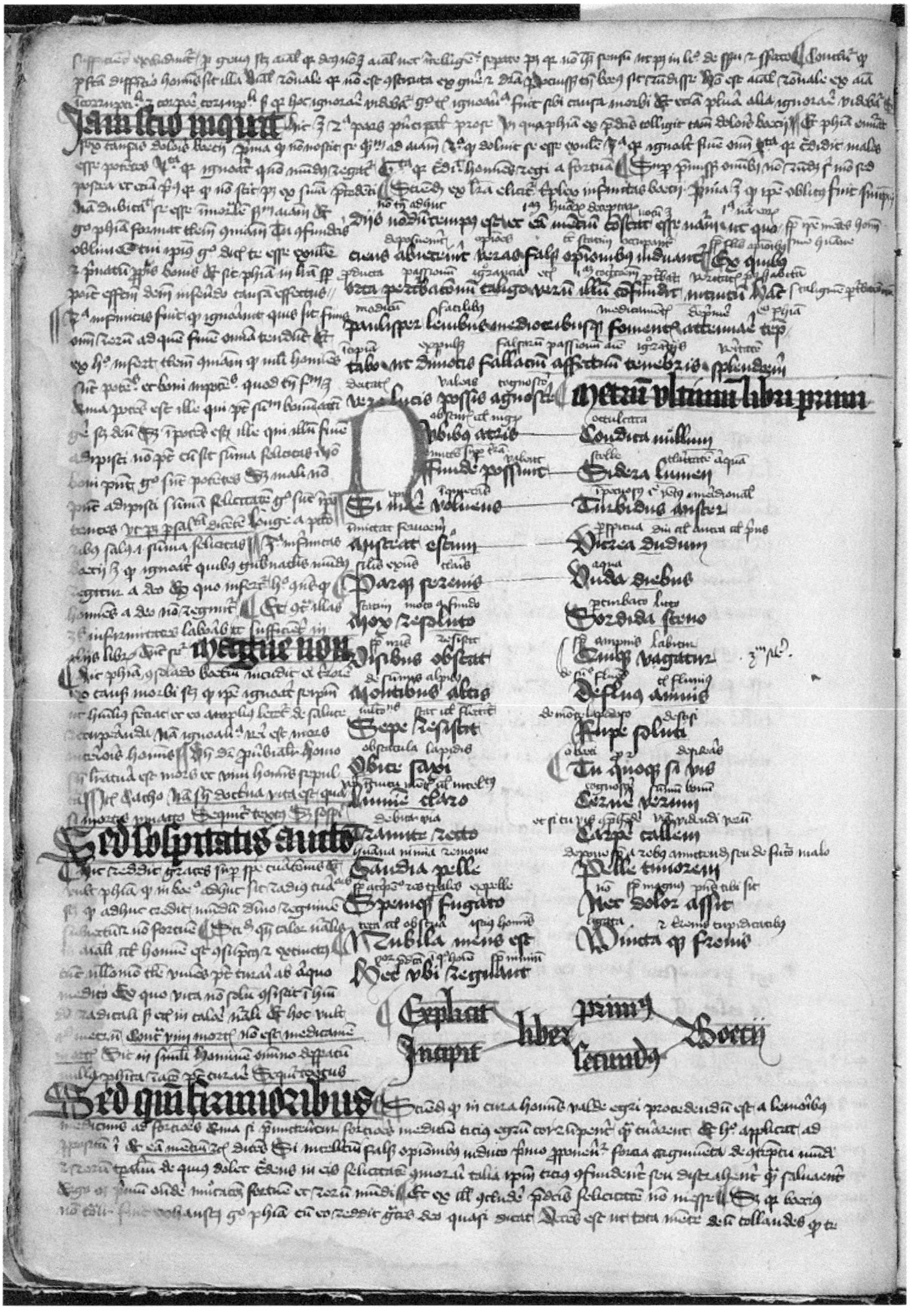

5. MS Luxembourg, Bibliothèque nationale, 121 (formerly I.121), fol. 14v.

6. MS Leiden, Universiteitsbibliotheek, Voss. lat. F. 70 I, fol. 29v.

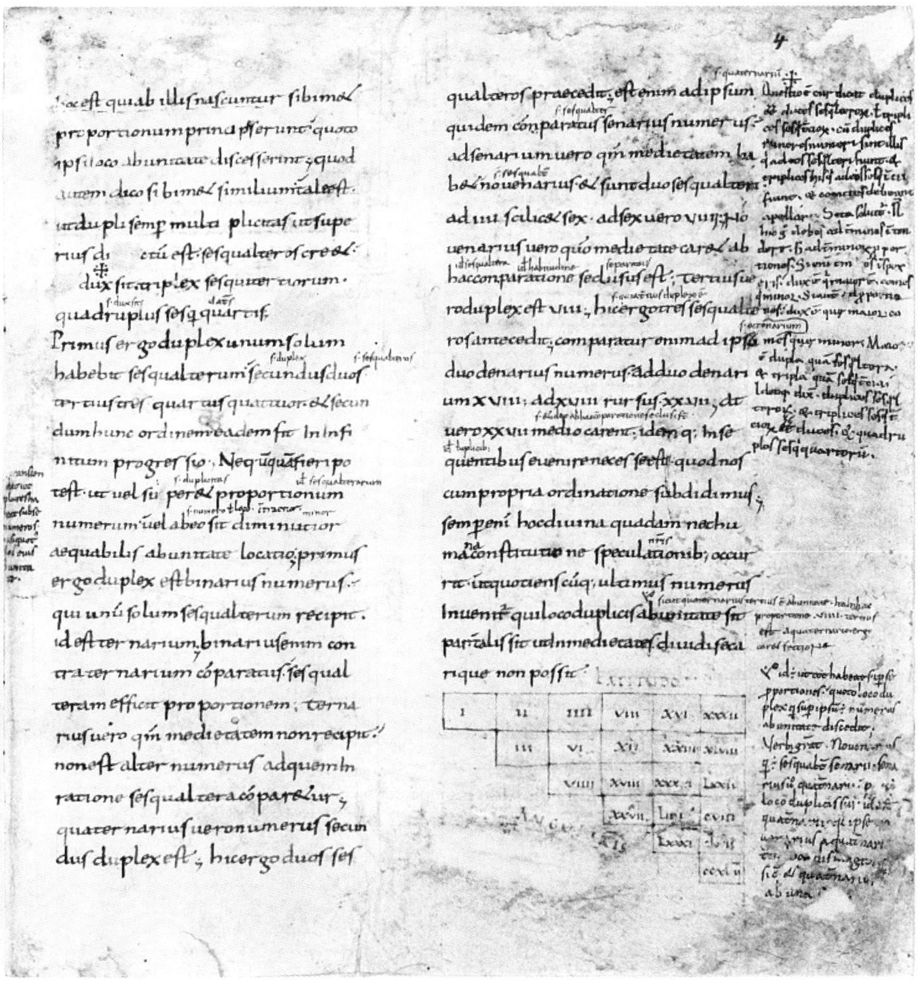

7. MS Lund, Universitetsbiblioteket, 1, fol. 4r.

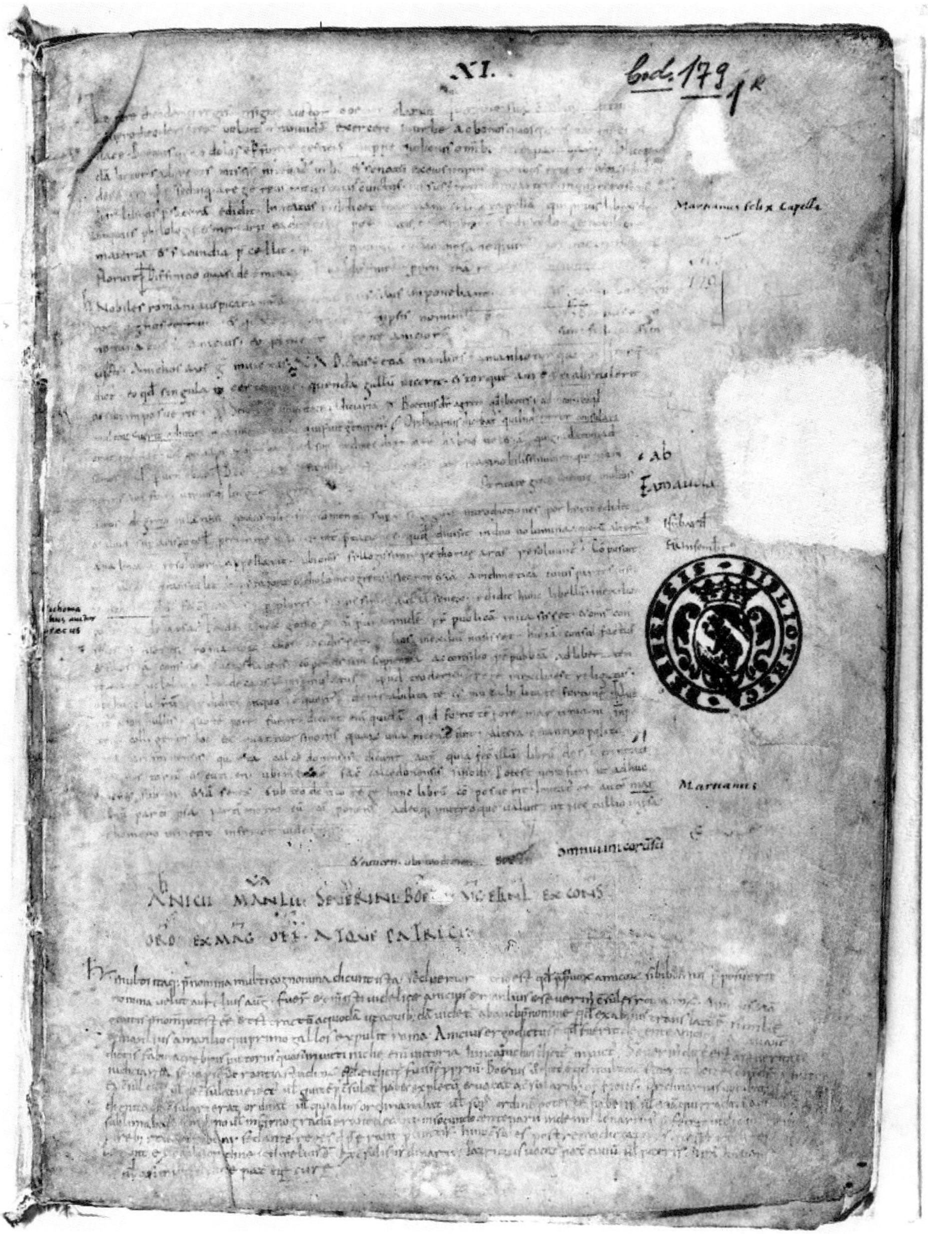

8. MS Bern, Burgerbibliothek, 179, fol. 1r.

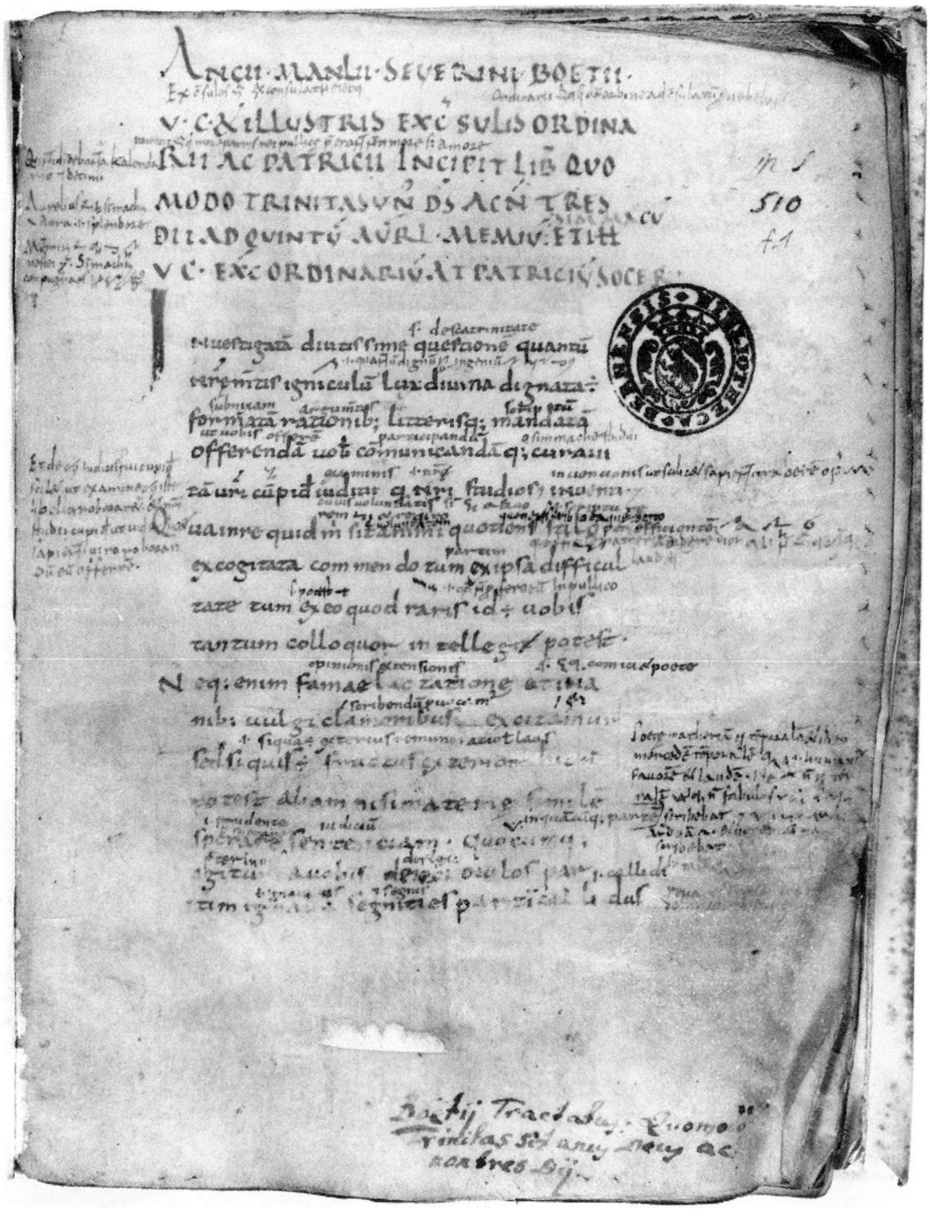

9. MS Bern, Burgerbibliothek, 510. fol. 1v.

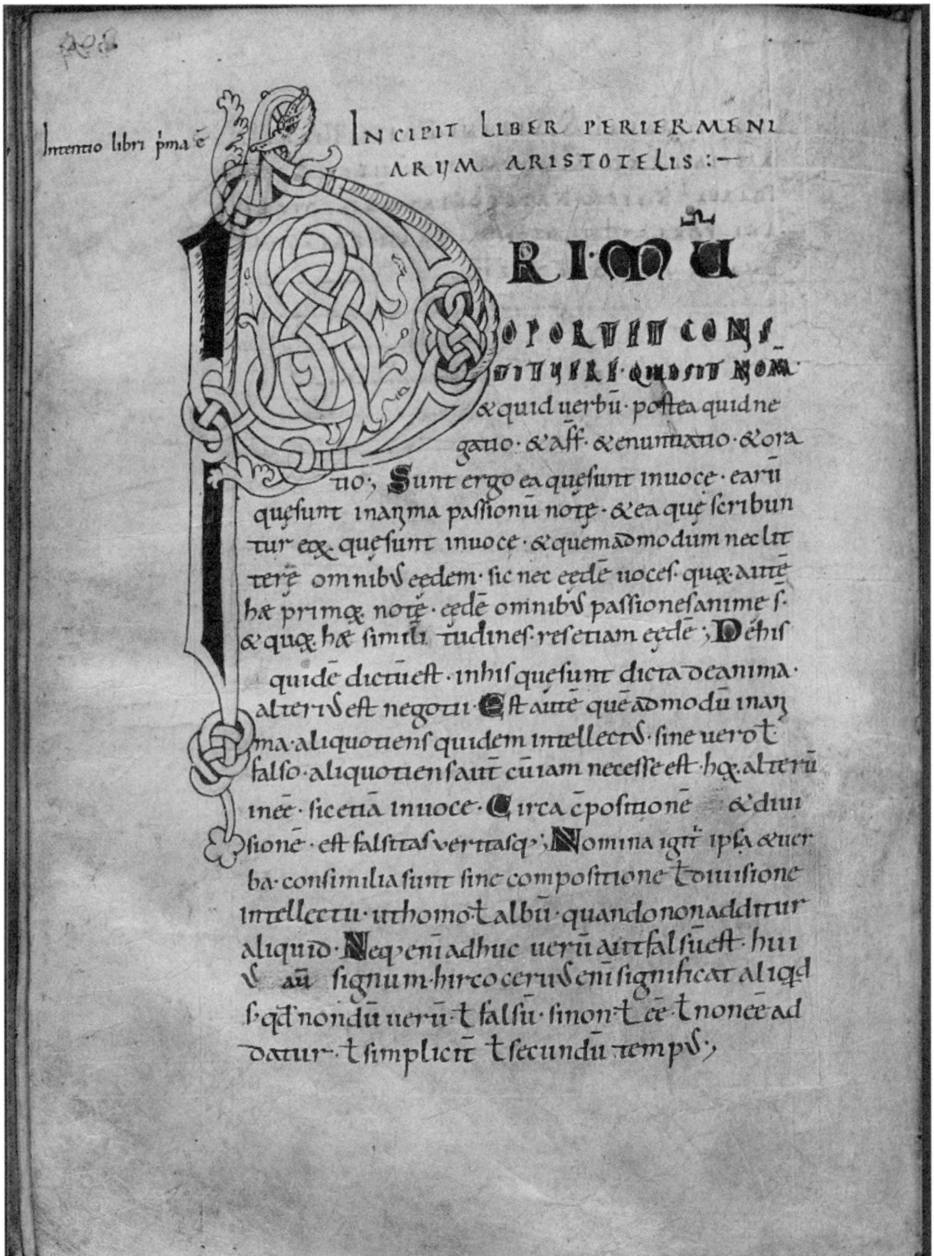

10. MS St Gallen, Stiftsbibliothek, 817, p. 208.

Indexes

INDEXES

NOTE: Numbers in the indexes refer to entries not pages

INDEX OF BOETHIAN TEXTS

INDEX OF DATES

INDEX OF PROVENANCES

GENERAL INDEX

Anonymous texts are listed either by their incipits (in inverted commas) or by their titles (in italics). Before 1450, individuals are listed by forename; after 1450 they are listed by surname.

MANUSCRIPTS

INCUNABULA